## Additional Advance Acclaim for *How to Have a Good Day*

"There's a big difference between having a great, productive day and having a bland, ordinary one. Caroline Webb deftly explains how to squeeze the most out of twenty-four hours to create more of the former. Very useful." —SIR MICHAEL MORITZ, CHAIRMAN OF SEQUOIA CAPITAL

"A powerful toolkit to improve both work and well-being. From email and meetings to making the most out of every day, Webb shows us not just how to be more productive but how to be more fulfilled along the way." —JONAH BERGER, WHARTON PROFESSOR AND BESTSELLING AUTHOR OF *CONTAGIOUS* AND *INVISIBLE INFLUENCE*

"Imagine what your life would be like if you could simply 'choose' to have a good day. Webb makes a powerful case that we can. Best of all, she shows us how. Webb gets her arms around the vast body of information coming at us from behavioral economics, psychology, and neuroscience, and distills the best of it into the kind of practical advice a wise friend might offer. It's the book Daniel Kahneman might write if he'd been working in the business world for twenty years. Masterful." —DOUGLAS STONE AND SHEILA HEEN, COAUTHORS OF THE BESTSELLING *DIFFICULT CONVERSATIONS* AND *THANKS FOR THE FEEDBACK*

"This is a brilliantly useful book. Caroline Webb has a quite exceptional range of organisational experience. She uses it to review a vast span of the latest academic 'thinking about thinking' in the clearest possible way. And then she applies this wisdom to help us all sort out the frazzle of our own working day. Her approach is utterly straightforward but based in deep insights into how human beings really behave." —PETER DAY, BBC BUSINESS CORRESPONDENT AND PRESENTER OF *IN BUSINESS* AND *GLOBAL BUSINESS*

"Years ago I was a rower, and in sports everyone knows you need to pay attention to yourself, your intent, and your mindset to be at your best. This book reminded me of all I learned from those days about the importance of having the right attitude. I found it a great, practical guide to applying these and other helpful psychological insights in business—something we do all too infrequently. Built solidly on the latest research, brought to life with storytelling, it offers many simple ways to boost your performance and give you a better day at work—and if you're a leader, it will show you how to make sure that your colleagues are in top form, too." —MATT BRITTIN, PRESIDENT OF GOOGLE EUROPE, MIDDLE EAST, AND AFRICA; FORMER ROWING WORLD CHAMPIONSHIP MEDALIST AND BRITISH OLYMPIC TEAM MEMBER

"*How to Have a Good Day* speaks to every area of your workday and shows how making a few critical adjustments to your everyday behavior will leave you amazed by the results. By applying the lessons in Webb's book, all based on science, you'll maximize your performance and be more energized than ever." —MARSHALL GOLDSMITH, BESTSELLING AUTHOR OF *TRIGGERS*, *MOJO*, and *WHAT GOT YOU HERE WON'T GET YOU THERE*

"The quest for self-improvement usually takes place on a well-trodden path, with many different gurus offering guidance. But the advice, in addition to being contradictory, often lacks solid foundations. Fortunately, *How to Have a Good Day* is the breakout exception to this category. The evidence and examples packed inside its pages leave the reader in no doubt that Webb's advice will make a real difference. Better days lead to better lives, and this extraordinary book will lead to both." —CHRIS GUILLEBEAU, *NEW YORK TIMES* BESTSELLING AUTHOR OF *THE $100 STARTUP* AND *THE HAPPINESS OF PURSUIT*

Harness the Power

of Behavioral Science

to Transform

Your Working Life

# HOW
## TO HAVE A
# GOOD
# DAY

## Caroline Webb

CROWN
BUSINESS
NEW YORK

Published in the United States by Crown Business, an imprint of the Crown
Publishing Group, a division of Penguin Random House LLC, New York.
www.crownpublishing.com

CROWN BUSINESS is a trademark and CROWN and the Rising Sun colophon are
registered trademarks of Penguin Random House LLC.

Crown Business books are available at special discounts for bulk purchases for
sales promotions or corporate use. Special editions, including personalized covers,
excerpts of existing books, or books with corporate logos, can be created in large
quantities for special needs. For more information, contact Premium Sales at (212)
572-2232 or e-mail specialmarkets@penguinrandomhouse.com.

Library of Congress Cataloging-in-Publication Data
Webb, Caroline, 1971–
How to have a good day : harness the power of behavioral science to transform your
working life / Caroline Webb.—First edition.
pages cm
1. Psychology, Industrial. 2. Neuropsychology. 3. Performance—Psychological
aspects. 4. Job satisfaction—Psychological aspects. I. Title.
HF5548.8.W35 2016
650.101'9—dc23 2015026815

ISBN 978-0-553-41963-4
eBook ISBN 978-0-553-41964-1

Printed in the United States of America

Jacket design by Gabriel Levine

10 9 8 7 6 5 4 3 2 1

First Edition

For my mother and my father,
who gave me both confidence and cause

# CONTENTS

# INTRODUCTION

How we spend our days is, of course, how we spend our lives.
—ANNIE DILLARD

Thirty years ago, I picked up my first paycheck. It wasn't a check, in fact—just a small collection of bills and coins in an envelope, my wages for working as a clerk in a local supermarket. On the face of it, it wasn't a great job. It was poorly paid, and certainly not glamorous. I stacked shelves, mopped floors, and wore a company-issued uniform marked with stains from its previous owner. The manager was gruff and kept an eye on the store from a booth high above the shop floor. And yet, somehow, I liked it. There was camaraderie among the staff, and even the occasional night out together. I took pride in pleasing customers with my speed at the register. I felt useful.

Six years later, I landed a far more upscale role as a researcher at an economics institute. I had my own office and a surprisingly large number of recycling bins all to myself. But I soon felt strangely miserable. I couldn't get anyone to pay attention to my work, and I drifted. I wrote an enormous, earnest report—on economic development in post-Communist Europe—that I'm pretty certain nobody read. I was dealing with what we'd these days call a "first-world problem," and I knew I was lucky to have the job. But it became hard to summon the energy to turn up to work every day. And at that point in my life, I didn't know how to turn it around. I treaded water till my contract was up, then quietly moved on.

Over the course of my life, I've done a lot of different types of work, some of it worse and some of it better than those two early jobs of mine. I've been a hotel maid, receptionist, and waitress. I've had demanding careers as an economist, a management consultant, and an executive coach. I've worked in the private sector and the public sector; I've been part of a huge global company and I've launched my own tiny start-up. And through it all, I noticed the same thing over and again: that the quality of my day-to-day experience wasn't necessarily defined by my title. It was possible to have good days in "bad" jobs, while the more prestigious roles didn't always correlate with great contentment.

That paradox seeded my lifelong curiosity about what it takes to flourish at work, both mentally and emotionally. It became something of a personal cause as I sought to find the right way to handle the increasing intensity of my professional life—and even more so once I noticed how my colleagues and clients often felt frustrated and worn down, making it hard for them to function at their best. In fact, survey after survey suggests that half (or more) of all employees feel disengaged in their work.[1] Add to that the off days experienced by those of us who generally feel motivated and happy, and we're looking at a lot of lost human potential. Yet we often talk about professional dissatisfaction as if it's a casual disappointment, something to be endured until the weekend rolls around, and perhaps joked about with friends. ("What happened to you today?" "Oh, work, you know." "Ha ha. Me too. Have a drink.")

So I've devoted much of my career to figuring out how to improve our chances of saying a cheery "yes, thanks" when we're asked "Did you have a good day?" My twelve years with McKinsey & Company (the management consultancy) helped greatly in my pursuit of that goal, since it gave me the opportunity to find out what everyday life was like inside hundreds of workplaces. I specialized in projects that helped organizations shift their culture in a more positive direction, which meant I spent a lot of time studying behavior, attitudes, and processes. And whenever I could, I'd ask my clients the same three questions: What does a good day look like for you? What about a bad one? What would it take to have more good days? Then, I'd get to work, helping them turn their bad days into better days. Sometimes that would involve coaching individual leaders; other times, I'd convene large groups to help them rethink the way they worked together. Repeatedly, I observed how fairly small changes—for example, finetuning the way people set priorities or handled disagreements—could result in major improvements to performance and job satisfaction. It was uplifting to see.

Throughout those years, my work leaned heavily on the growing body of behavioral science findings on what it takes for human beings to thrive. My first career was in economics, but I became deeply interested in developments in the other behavioral sciences, too, so I did some additional training in psychology and neuroscience. Then I spent countless hours reading academic articles and books (more than six hundred at last count) in the three disciplines, looking for findings that I could translate into actionable advice for my clients. And that abundance of research and practical experience is the bedrock of *How to Have a Good Day.*

## SO WHAT IS A GOOD DAY?

Over the years, I noticed some common answers to my "what is a good day" question—answers that resonated with the small delights of my humble supermarket job. First, people often talked about getting a buzz from feeling productive, and from knowing that their efforts counted toward something worthwhile. The best days also tended to involve people feeling confident that they were doing a fine job, and that they had the support they needed from others. Finally, people talked about good days leaving them feeling more energized than depleted, overall. I don't mean that the work wasn't physically or mentally tiring—just that it gave back enough enjoyment and motivation to make up for whatever it was taking out of them.

Of course, whether we get to have all that agreeable stuff on a given workday is partly the result of luck. If we're handling a cranky colleague or a crisis, it's obvious that we're not entirely in control of the way the day feels. But my experience has led me to a heartening conclusion: we have more room to maneuver than we generally realize. The secret lies in learning some of the science explaining how the brain works, and why people behave the way they do. Less of the day seems driven by chance once we understand some of the forces that shape our choices and our emotions, and once we recognize how our thought patterns can affect everything from our perception of reality to the moods of those around us. Grasp these essentials, and it becomes far clearer how to bring the best out of ourselves and others. And that puts us in a much stronger position to create the kind of day we really want to have.

For example, an executive who shares his story later in the book talks about starting to have "unexpectedly great meetings" after he learned something that behavioral scientists know well: that even small challenges to a person's sense of competence will put their brain on the defensive, making it harder for them to think clearly (in turn creating something of a self-fulfilling prophecy). In his meetings, the executive's take-no-prisoners personal style had inadvertently been triggering this defensive reaction in the people around him, and it was causing a lot of tension. But once he tweaked the way he expressed his views, the quality of his interactions changed within moments.

Elsewhere in the book, another seasoned professional tells us about "suddenly" securing new promotion opportunities after trying out new science-based techniques to sharpen her focus and self-confidence. We hear about a leader who delightedly discovered hidden talents in her team after acting on research showing that people think more creatively when given a particular type of space to think. Once an entrepreneur learns a little about the brain's reward system, he finds he can say no to people while making them feel almost as good as if he'd agreed to their requests. And so on.

*How to Have a Good Day* is all about the ways we can create more of these sorts of lucky breaks once we know more about the science of our magnificent minds.

## ABOUT THIS BOOK

I've arranged the book around seven building blocks that echo the themes in people's answers to my "good day" question. First, there are two sections designed to give you a strong foundation for everything you're doing, by showing you how to set the right kind of priorities and make the best possible use of your time. Next, you'll find three sections that explain how to transform more of your tasks into a pleasure and a triumph, by helping you to ace every interaction, maximize your creativity and wisdom, and boost your personal impact. Finally, I've written two sections on ways to maintain your joie de vivre throughout the workday, by showing you how to boost your resilience in the face of disappointment, and laying out strategies for generating more energy throughout it all.

As a bonus, you'll find advice at the back of the book showing you how to use the book's insights to improve two fixtures of modern working life: meetings and emails. There's also a handy checklist to help you use the book's tips to reinvigorate your morning-to-night routine.

## SCIENCE, STEPS, STORIES

Throughout the book, you'll find a blend of scientific evidence, practical techniques, and real examples from people who've used those techniques in their own lives. Let me say a few words about each of those.

First, every piece of advice in *How to Have a Good Day* is backed up by rigorous scientific evidence from psychology, behavioral economics, or neuroscience. I've taken care to focus only on findings that are widely accepted and have been replicated by multiple research teams, though I've sometimes picked out quirky experiments that manage to illustrate a particular point while raising a smile (or a groan). My aim has been to keep the science as simple as it can be while remaining correct. To help with that, in the "Science Essentials" section which appears right after this introduction, I've written a short guide to three big cross-cutting themes that frame every idea in the book. That's all you'll need to navigate this fascinating evidence with ease.

The central purpose of the book is to translate all that science into step-by-step techniques for improving your day-to-day life. Each chapter is designed to allow you to quickly find the advice you need, because the practical pointers are highlighted with bullet points; each chapter also ends with a box that summarizes its advice for quick reference. I've laid out the chapters in a sequence that I hope is helpful—but if you're wrestling with a specific challenge at work right now, you might choose to flip ahead to material that speaks directly to your current concern. Skipping around should work, especially if you've first read the Science Essentials section.

As I've already hinted, you'll also hear real stories from dozens of successful people who describe how the advice in this book has helped them improve their working lives. Together, they represent most major industries and span every continent of the world (except the coldest one). Some are at the peak of their careers, while others are on their way up. I've used their real names in all but a couple of cases, although I've not included their surnames or organizations to keep them from being deluged with requests for advice once their wise ways are made public. I hope you'll find them as inspiring as I do. And in case you're wondering, I *do* take my own medicine every single day—so I'll also share some examples of times that these techniques helped me flourish in my career.

## SPREADING THE WORD

As well as showing you how to be in top form, *How to Have a Good Day* can be used to help you bring the best out of people you lead, manage, or collaborate with. Most of the techniques here can be used in groups, to improve team interactions, or provide structure for important meetings—whether or not you refer to the science behind the techniques. (If you would like to gather colleagues together to talk about the book's suggestions, you'll find materials to help you facilitate group discussions at www.howtohaveagoodday.com.)

I've also seen the book's advice make a positive difference in settings beyond conventional workplaces. Whether you're a college student or a community volunteer, a retiree or a homemaker, you can use the principles in this book to boost your effectiveness and your enjoyment of the day. Many of my clients have even confided to me over the years that these techniques have improved their marriages and strengthened relationships with children and friends. Some grin when I ask them how it's going, telling me they've surreptitiously used their nearest and dearest as guinea pigs before trying out new approaches at work. So do have some fun experimenting with these suggestions, wherever you are.

◆ ◆ ◆

We all face things we can't change. But behavioral science is sometimes startling in showing us just how much influence we have on the way we experience the world. When we choose to take this evidence on board, the effect can be nothing short of transformational. We can exert more control and start to enjoy more "well-planned luck." And as a result, we can all have many more good days. Now let's get started.

# HOW
## TO HAVE A
# GOOD
# DAY

| FIRST OF ALL... | THEN IN EVERY TASK... | ...AND THROUGHOUT THE DAY |
|---|---|---|
| ↓ | ↓ | ↓ |
| **PRIORITIES** | **RELATIONSHIPS** | **RESILIENCE** |
| Set intentional direction for your day | Make the most of every interaction | Sail through setbacks and annoyances |
|  |  |  |
| **PRODUCTIVITY** | **THINKING** | **ENERGY** |
| Make the hours in the day go further | Be your smartest, wisest, most creative self | Boost your enthusiasm and enjoyment |
| |  |  |
| | **INFLUENCE** | |
| | Maximize the impact of all you say and do | |

# The Science Essentials

I'll believe anything, no matter how wild and ridiculous, if there is evidence for it. The wilder and more ridiculous something is, however, the firmer and more solid the evidence will have to be.
—Isaac Asimov

We're living in a golden age of behavioral science, where every passing week seems to deliver fresh insights into the way we think, feel, and act. Neuroscientists, psychologists, and economists are busy unraveling the important mysteries of our time, questions like: "How can I conquer my inbox?" "Why do perfectly reasonable people get their wires crossed?" "What would it take for me to stop procrastinating right now (or later today, or tomorrow)?" Scientific research has ever more to say in answer to these sorts of pressing questions.

You might reasonably wonder what's changed. Why are so many media articles suddenly illustrated with pictures of brains? The three disciplines that form the backbone of this book—psychology, behavioral economics, and neuroscience—have been around for a century or more, after all. But right now we're sitting at the intersection of some big trends that are making these three behavioral sciences more applicable to our everyday lives. Let me describe some of that backstory, before I lay out the three big cross-cutting science themes that run through the rest of the book.

## PSYCHOLOGY: GREATER FOCUS ON WELL-BEING

For much of its history, psychology was mostly concerned with investigating the causes of negative behavior. Researchers did important work to understand pathologies such as paranoia and depression; they explored the dynamics of fear and aggression. Given this, it's perhaps no surprise that one of psychology's most well-known experiments was Stanley Milgram's controversial exploration of how far people were willing to submit to authority—the one where he tested whether volunteers would be willing to give potentially fatal electrical shocks to strangers when told to do so by someone in a white coat.[1] (A disturbing number of them obeyed.) Obviously, this kind of research did a lot to illuminate the complexities of the human mind, and has laid the foundations of modern behavioral science. But the findings didn't readily translate into uplifting guidance for living a good life.

In recent years, however, the balance has shifted toward exploring the conditions that invite positive behavior. Perhaps the most visible catalyst for the shift came when Martin Seligman, a professor at the University of Pennsylvania, was elected president of the American Psychological Association in 1998. Seligman's own research had previously focused on the study of helplessness. But he announced with some fanfare that the theme for his term of office would be "positive psychology," the serious study of what it takes for us to be the best version of ourselves. And since then, psychologists have directed more energy toward understanding the jollier side of human experience— what helps us thrive, lifts our spirits, and boosts our productivity. These are exactly the sort of things that most of us are hungry to know more about, especially on those days when our workplaces feel like a Milgram experiment.

## ECONOMICS: MORE REALISM IN THEORIES OF BEHAVIOR

At the same time, economics has also moved toward a more rounded view of the human condition. At its heart, economics is the study of the way people make choices: how we weigh the costs and benefits of different options, and what we decide to do as a result. The choices might be mundane, like deciding which snack to buy, or they might be consequential, like deciding which multimillion-dollar project goes forward. Either way, to predict people's choices, economists used to build theoretical models that assumed humans always accurately and independently assessed the benefits of each option open to them. But those models weren't able to explain a lot of real-life behavior: for example, the way we often make snap decisions based on little information; the fact that we sometimes change our minds, based on what others think;

the way we occasionally do nice things for other people without any expectation of payback.

This spurred two psychologists—Daniel Kahneman of Princeton and Amos Tversky of Stanford—to cross enemy lines in 1979 and publish an article in *Econometrica*, an influential economics journal. In the article, they highlighted that people *don't* behave like machines when it comes to the choices they make.[2] Emotional and social considerations drive many of our choices, often for good reason and in quite predictable ways. And with that, they sparked a revolution. Soon there was a new movement called "behavioral economics" that was devoted to applying the powerful analytical tools of economics to the way that real people make decisions in the real world. The result? Well, Kahneman went on to win the Nobel Prize in Economics in 2002. But more important for us is that economists now have a much more nuanced and accurate understanding of the choices we make from day to day, and what it takes for us to nudge our behavior one way or another.

## NEUROSCIENCE: MORE SOPHISTICATED MEASUREMENT OF BRAIN ACTIVITY

Finally, neuroscience has benefitted from dramatic advances in techniques for observing ordinary brains in action. Neuroscientists have long had access to a range of scanning techniques that helped reveal the structures and activities of the brain. Those scanning technologies often came at a cost of exposing the brain's owner to a good deal of radiation—so they weren't ideal for non-medical research. Since the 1990s, though, steady improvements in less risky imaging technologies (including the discovery of functional MRI scanning) have made it easier for neuroscientists to watch what happens to *healthy* people's brains while normal things are happening to them. That means researchers can see which areas of the brain become active when a person is tickled by kindness or energized by accomplishment. They can observe the neural activity associated with someone feeling unhappy or stressed (for reasons beyond the fact that they're lying in a noisy metal tube or have electrodes strapped to their heads).

As a result, neuroscientists are gaining an increasingly refined understanding of the biological mechanisms behind our everyday thoughts, feelings, and actions. And that means they're exploring the kind of behavioral topics that also fascinate psychologists and economists—for example, questions about the way we solve challenging problems and handle complex social interactions. In fact, many of the studies I cite in this book result from collaborations across the three behavioral science disciplines; it feels as if we're living in an era of "neuro-psycho-economics." (Or something like that.) And this multidisciplinary mash-up is great news for us. It means we get to benefit from complementary perspectives (biological, observational, and analytical) on topics that matter to us in the workplace—which in turn results in richer guidance on ways for us to stay in top form.

So all in all, it's an excellent time to be thinking about the way that science can help us flourish.

## THREE BIG THEMES

Now, how do we apply all this evolving, exciting science to the everyday details of our working lives? That's where *How to Have a Good Day* comes in. This book is dedicated to translating the most valuable research into the context of today's working world—the tough assignments, the packed schedules, the complex relationships—to show you how to make every day reliably more enjoyable and productive.

Before we dive into the advice on creating the seven building blocks of a good day, I'm going to highlight three important scientific themes that cut across the boundaries of the disciplines and recur throughout the book, to give you a foundation for the evidence and advice you'll find in each chapter. (If you'd prefer to skip ahead to Part I of the book and get started on the practical applications, that's fine—there's a glossary at the end of the book and you can always come back to this section later.) The three themes, in brief, are:

➡ 1. The two-system brain: The brain's activity is split across two complementary systems—one deliberate and controlled, the other automatic and instinctive. The combination of the two makes us smart and productive. But we can make our cognitive resources go even further if we adjust the way we work to reflect each system's strengths and weaknesses.

➡ 2. The discover-defend axis: Subconsciously, we're constantly on the lookout for threats to defend against and rewards to discover. It takes very little to put our brains into defensive mode, and we're not at our smartest in that mode. However, a dose of self-awareness and the pursuit of certain types of rewards can help us move back into clearer-thinking discovery mode.

➡ 3. The mind-body loop: The state of our bodies and that of our minds are far more deeply entwined than we generally realize. As a result, certain simple physical interventions can immediately boost our intellectual performance, emotional resilience, and personal confidence.

## THEME 1: THE TWO-SYSTEM BRAIN

Our brains are impressive, by any measure. They keep our bodily functions humming while offering us immense storage capacity for complex memories and ideas. They're also capable of remarkable processing and calculating feats, giving us the ability to do things as diverse as mental arithmetic, guessing other people's motivations, keeping our cool in the face of provocation, and telling corny jokes. If brains were smartphones, they'd be flying off the shelves.

To make all of this possible, our brains run two very different systems in parallel. Each has its own strengths, and it's the combination of the two that gives us so much intellectual horsepower. Psychologists had observed for many years that our minds seemed to have two quite different modes—one more analytical, the other more instinctive.[3] But it was Daniel Kahneman who brought the concept into the public spotlight when he accepted his Nobel Prize for Economics in 2002. He centered his acceptance speech on describing the distinction between "effortless intuition" and "deliberate reasoning," concepts central to his bestselling book, *Thinking Fast and Slow*.[4] Let's examine what he meant, and what that means for us in the workplace.

### The Deliberate System

First, let's talk about the system we're more aware of, the one that controls the things we do consciously and carefully. Most of it sits in the part of the brain called the prefrontal cortex, and it goes by a lot of different names. In scientific circles, it's sometimes known as the "controlled," "explicit," or "reflective" system. Daniel Kahneman calls it the "slow" system, because it's indeed the slower of the two systems.[5] I'm going to refer to it as the *deliberate system*.

This deliberate system is broadly responsible for the sort of grown-up behavior that would surprise us in a toddler (or even a teenager): reasoning, self-control, and forward thinking.

By reasoning, I don't just mean logical thinking; I mean any effort to work out the best response to a situation that isn't routine. Whether we're fixing an error-laden document or figuring out how to help a stressed-out colleague, we're leaning on our deliberate system and asking it to do the following: review some information, connect that information to our past experience, make sense of it all, generate options, and evaluate those options wisely. Logic might be involved in that process, but so might empathy and creativity.

Self-control is also a broader concept than you might think. Most obviously, it's involved whenever we resist temptation—for example, when we manage to bite our tongue rather than blurt out the foolish thing that we desperately want to say to our co-worker with the new haircut. But our deliberate system's self-control function is also central to something scientists call "emotional regulation"—that is, not losing our cool when we're upset—and to our ability to concentrate in the face of distractions.

Finally, our hardworking deliberate system is responsible for planning—that is, setting goals and working out how to get there. That requires us to think abstractly: to imagine what the future looks like, to consider the various paths to get there, and to assess the eventual benefits of setting off on any of those paths. We run this sort of complex calculation every day, even when our goal is just to organize ourselves to get to a meeting on time.

In short, the deliberate system is responsible for putting us on our best behavior. When it's in full control, it makes us wise, self-possessed, and reliable. But let's be honest: we're not always like that. That's because our deliberate system has several limitations.

### Smart—but Small, Sequential, and Slow

First, it has limited capacity, because it relies heavily on something called *working memory*. Part notepad for incoming new data, part librarian for accessing stored experience, our working memory is the space where we hold information in our conscious mind as we figure out what to do with it. And our notepad only has so much space on it. For years it was thought we could hold about seven pieces of information in our minds at once, but more recent research suggests it's three or four at most.[6]

Those three or four chunks of information can be big or small. For example, suppose you have an elaborate new idea for a project. Your working memory is full of your thoughts on this new idea. But then the name of a colleague comes to mind—someone you're supposed to call. Then, a message pops up on the screen in front of you. Maybe there's a blinking light on your phone. And all these things demand space in your working memory. Suddenly your deliberate system can't think as clearly about your new project idea, because some of your ideas have been moved off the notepad to make space for the name, the message, and the light. (What *was* that idea again?) So the size of our working memory places a limit on the deliberate system's ability to excel at all the reasoning, self-control, and planning activities I described above.

In fact, while the deliberate system has access to maybe three or four pieces of information at once, research suggests that it's only able to actually *do* one thing at a time. It can give a good impression of multitasking when we're on the phone at the same time as we're checking email. But our deliberate system isn't actually doing anything in parallel at all; it's switching from one task to another and back again.[7] It gets tired pretty easily, too. If we don't regularly rest and refuel our brain, the quality of our reasoning, self-control, and planning declines sharply.[8] And overexertion in one part of the deliberate system can deplete our abilities in other areas. For example, research has found that asking our deliberate system to remember a random seven-digit number makes it harder for it to muster the self-control necessary to resist a calorie-laden piece of cake.[9] No wonder we find it harder to be creative toward the end of an interminable meeting; our deliberate system has spent all its energy on staying focused and polite for hours, leaving little in the tank for brilliant insight.

Those limitations of our deliberate system wouldn't be a problem if we led simple lives. But we don't. We're constantly bombarded with information and possibilities. Even in the briefest of conversations, your brain has to process not only the meaning of the words spoken but also the subtle details of the other person's demeanor: tone of voice, body language, and what the person might be trying to convey with that bold new haircut. There are countless objects in your field of vision, each a potential distraction. Not only that, but your brain has to rapidly calculate the right thing to do, think, or say in response to it all. If you tried to consciously process every single bit of data and assess every possible course of action in depth, your brain would crash like an overloaded computer.

## The Automatic System

So how do we handle that nonstop bombardment? The answer lies in the brain's heroic second system, which I'll call the *automatic system*. Like the deliberate system, it goes by a lot of different names. Some scientists call it the "reflexive system," while others give it animalistic names like the "chimp" or the "elephant." You might know it as the "subconscious." Daniel Kahneman calls it the "fast" system, since it operates so much more quickly than the sophisticated-but-slower conscious mind. By whatever name, the magic of this system is that it has automated the majority of what we do to get from one day to the next, and its quick, automatic processes remove the need for us to think consciously about every single thing we do. That frees up our deliberate system to focus on what it's best at—things like handling unfamiliar situations, resisting temptation, and thinking ahead. It's a beautifully efficient solution, most of the time.

There are a few ways that our automatic system lightens the load on our deliberate system. Perhaps the most obvious is the way it takes care of our more familiar tasks by turning them into autopilot routines. Some routines are quite basic, like locking your front door when you leave home, or knowing how to step on and off an escalator without falling over. But our autopilot function can also handle complex actions as long as they've become very familiar to us, which is how you find yourself able to navigate a complicated route to work without too much conscious thought.

Our automatic system is also capable of doing multiple things in parallel, unlike our "one thing at a time, please" deliberate system. That allows our automatic system to process huge amounts of data—encoding today's experiences and connecting them to our memories of past experiences, for example—while our deliberate system handles the conscious activities of everyday life. We're rarely aware of all that background processing, except when it contributes to a "wisdom of the shower" moment—that is, when a fully formed idea seems to pop into our conscious minds out of nowhere.

That's already quite useful, but there's another way the automatic system saves us mental energy, which is this: it rapidly sifts through information and ideas, prioritizes whatever seems relevant, and filters out the rest. This is all happening below the level of our consciousness, so we're not aware of hearing or seeing anything that our automatic system has filtered out as irrelevant "spam." And this neatly reduces the number of things our deliberate system needs to engage with.

### About That Spam Filter

How does our brain's automatic system sift and filter so quickly? Broadly speaking, it takes shortcuts—rather like your computer's spam filter does when it's assessing incoming email. When your computer flags incoming messages with large numbers of recipients as junk, for example, it hasn't actually read them in depth; it just applies a rule of thumb based on the fact that group emails often *are* junk. Your spam filter doesn't always get it right, but it's faster than you reading every large-group message to see if it's worth your time. Similarly, your brain's automatic system adopts some easy shortcuts to keep your mental inbox a little slimmer—shortcuts that are mostly helpful but occasionally a little off base.

Behavioral scientists have identified hundreds of these shortcuts—which they call *heuristics*—and given them labels you might recognize: confirmation bias, groupthink, priming, and so on. I'll talk about several of them in detail later in the book (and there's a glossary at the back). But what all these shortcuts have in common is this: they direct our deliberate system's conscious attention toward things that feel comparatively easy to wrap our heads around, while deprioritizing anything that feels harder to grasp. They're all versions of the following exchange between the real world and your brain's impatient automatic system:

REAL WORLD: "It's all very complex . . . there's a lot I need to tell you about. There are gray areas . . . everyone's different, and there's no one right way to think about this . . ."

AUTOMATIC SYSTEM: "Look, let's make some simple assumptions about what's important, and focus on that. Okay?"

As a result, the startling truth is that we don't experience the world as it is; we're always experiencing an edited, simplified version. Princeton psychologist Anne Treisman discovered this *selective attention* feature of the automatic system back in 1967.[10] Even so, it's still a little hard for most of us to accept; we rather like the idea that we have a good grip on reality. And since the filtering is automatic—and therefore subconscious—it's often difficult to believe it's really happening.

That's why it was so helpful that psychologists Chris Chabris and Dan Simons, from Union College and Beckman College, respectively, made a video to demonstrate conclusively the existence of selective attention. In this now famous clip, they showed that a person in a gorilla suit could walk through the middle of a basketball game without being noticed by half the people watching the video. That's despite the fact that the "gorilla" stops to face the camera and ostentatiously beats its chest as the players pass the ball around it.[11]

In my consulting practice, I've seen Chabris and Simons's results echoed every time I've shown the clip to groups: without fail, at least half of them miss the gorilla. Why? Because at the beginning of the video, I do what Chabris and Simons did: I ask people to count the passes between the basketball players who are wearing white shirts. At that point, their brain's automatic system applies a simple, powerful rule that looks something like this: "stated task = the thing to focus attention on; everything else = things to ignore."[12]

Our brain's energy-saving automatic system doesn't just filter our perceptions of the world. It also streamlines our decision making by nudging us toward whichever choice requires the smallest amount of conscious effort. If there's a plausible option already on the table, or one that doesn't involve thinking hard about the future, or one that resonates with something we heard recently, our automatic system will say: "Fantastic! Let's apply the 'most obvious option = best option' rule. No need to think further."

Like our perceptual shortcuts, these decision-making shortcuts are mostly helpful in everyday life. If you're trying to pick a restaurant for lunch, your automatic system can relieve you of the need to read a bunch of restaurant reviews; perhaps it subconsciously recalls the Italian co-worker who just said a cheery "*buongiorno*" in the elevator, which spurs you to book a table at Luigi's, that nice new Italian place. Problem solved. But taking shortcuts is less ideal when making our more important decisions. If, instead of finding a place for lunch, you were deciding on the country where your company should expand its business, you wouldn't want your cheery co-worker to be the hidden reason Italy showed up on your short list.

## The Silver Lining

Behavioral scientists often say that the shortcuts taken by our brain's automatic system make us rather irrational, because those shortcuts can lead us to miss important aspects of what's going on around us, or to choose the easy answers rather than the correct ones. But I'd argue that our brain is adopting a highly rational strategy—one that makes the most of our scarce mental energy. We just need to understand the interplay of the brain's deliberate and automatic systems, so we can make best use of their complementary strengths and cover for their weaknesses. And I'll highlight several ways to do this throughout the book.

For one thing, we can be more proactive in telling our brain what's "important" enough to merit our conscious attention, in a bid to get it through the spam filter. Since our reality is subjective, we might as well seize the chance to make that reality more of what we'd like it to be. I'll explain how to do this in the first part of the book, on the value of having clear intentions.

We can also be smart in how we use the limited capacity of our deliberate system, by ensuring we're lightening the load on our precious working memory where possible. I'll show you some techniques for doing this when you're setting goals, managing your workload, and solving problems (in Parts I, II, and IV, respectively). Part IV also contains some simple routines to help us slow down and engage the wisdom of our deliberate system more fully when we're making choices with real consequences.

Understanding that we each see the world in our own incomplete way can also explain a lot of workplace disagreements. Imagine a discussion between the eagle-eyed people who saw the gorilla and the task-focused people who didn't notice it. Both sides will be certain of their view of what happened and think the other group is a little crazy ("There was a gorilla!" "Don't be ridiculous! Also, you can't count!"). These sorts of crossed wires arise every day, since our brains are all making slightly different decisions about what deserves our attention. In Part III I'll look at several ways to resolve these kinds of tensions, and in Part V I'll also cover ways to overcome other people's spam filters when you'd like them to pay attention to your ideas.

And finally, the subjectivity of reality also means that however bad a situation seems, there's always a different way of seeing things. The way we interpret what we've experienced is much more up for grabs than we generally realize. This can be hugely liberating as we ride the ups and downs of working life, as you'll see in Part VI, when I talk about resilience.

---

Things to keep in mind about the two-speed brain:

➡ Your *deliberate* system is responsible for sophisticated functions such as reasoning, self-control, and forward thinking. It excels in handling anything unfamiliar, complex, or abstract. But it has limited capacity and gets tired quickly. When it's overused, overloaded, or distracted, it's harder for you to be wise, balanced, or reliable.

➡ Your *automatic* system lightens the load on your deliberate system by automating most of what you do and taking fast shortcuts that filter out "irrelevant" information and options. That's mostly helpful. But it inevitably leaves you with blind spots. And the fact that nobody ever experiences an entirely objective version of reality can lead to crossed wires and poor choices in the workplace.

➡ You make the most of your brain's talents if you adjust for the limitations of each system. That means creating the conditions for your deliberate system to function at its best, and recognizing when to slow down and come off autopilot.

---

## THEME 2: THE DISCOVER-DEFEND AXIS

Every moment of the day, our brain is busy scanning the environment for unpleasant things we should avoid and pleasant things we should rush toward. "Is this a threat or a reward?" is the first question our brain asks of everything we encounter—each email we read, each conversation we have. Depending on the answer, it triggers the appropriate behavior in us. Either we take steps to defend ourselves from the "threat," or we embrace the "reward" with delight.

This fundamental "threat or reward" question drives much of our day-to-day behavior, and is why we act one way when we're feeling defensive and another way when we're feeling generally charmed by life. Throughout the book, I use the term *defensive mode* to describe the times when we're focused on protecting ourselves, and *discovery mode* to describe those times when it feels as if the world is on our side. And it won't surprise you to hear that we're far more likely to have a good day if we manage to spend as little time as possible in defensive mode. So I'd like to explain these two modes a little more, and start to show how it's possible to spend more of life in the more enjoyable one of the two.

### Defensive Mode: Protecting Ourselves Against Threats

Imagine this: you're heading into work, gearing up for a big meeting on a new project. While you're checking your calendar to confirm exactly where and when it's taking place, you absentmindedly step out between two parked cars to cross the street. Before you know it, a speeding truck whizzes past—but you've somehow already jumped backward, out of harm's way. Your heart is racing, and you notice you've dropped your phone. Luckily, it's still in one piece, and so are you.

When we face this kind of life-threatening experience, we're given a visceral reminder of what NYU neuroscientist Joseph LeDoux calls the "survival circuits" that we all have buried deep in the automatic system of our brain.[13] When those survival circuits pick up any sign of potential danger, they work fast to defend us by launching a *fight, flight, or freeze* response. That means we might hit back (fight), run away (flight), or stand still as we try to work out the nature of the threat (freeze). In the case of the truck, the strategy that saved your life was mostly "flight"—jumping back—perhaps accompanied by a little "freeze," as you try to work out what the heck's going on. If you found yourself shouting something spicy at the truck, you'd be adding a dash of "fight" to the mix, too.

This defensive response is a good example of the brain's powerful automatic system taking control. Here, it's not just affecting our perception or choices, as I described in the last section; it's driving our immediate actions as well. How it does that is actually an extension of something that happens every day. When we're rousing ourselves in any way—getting ourselves ready to start work in the morning, or getting ready to make a comment in a meeting—our nervous system pumps hormones called adrenaline and noradrenaline through our bodies. At moderate levels, these hormones help us feel awake and alive, sharpening our brain's motivation and focusing our attention to enable us to rise to the challenge of the commute or the conference call.

But as soon as a situation feels outside our control, our brain and adrenal glands push much higher levels of adrenaline and noradrenaline into our system, as well as boosting a third hormone called cortisol that's slower-acting but longer-lasting.[14] And this flood of chemicals turns our state of readiness into something edgier. Our breathing accelerates and our heart pounds, to drive maximum amounts of oxygenated blood into our muscles. Our eyesight even becomes more tunnel-visioned, to give us laser-like focus on the threat at hand. "Bring it on," our bodies are saying. "We're ready to fight, flight, or freeze, to defend you against this dastardly threat."

The survival circuits that drive this emergency response include a part of the brain called the *amygdala*. It's constantly on the lookout for things that are uncertain, ambiguous, or novel, including potential threats in our environment, and it's sensitive enough to react to something as mildly worrying as a picture of a frowning stranger.[15] And if our amygdala picks up anything of serious concern, the fight-flight-freeze reaction gets triggered. All this happens more quickly than we can consciously think—which is critical when a split second can save us, like when we're about to be run over by a truck.

This kind of rapid response is impressive. But there are a couple of challenges with the way our survival circuits leap diligently to our defense. First, their speed often comes at the expense of accuracy. It's as if they have a mantra of "better safe than sorry." So if a black shadow in the corner of the room looks like a close enough approximation of an intruder, your defenses will spring into action. It's only *after* this unconscious knee-jerk response that the more sophisticated part of your brain fills in the finer details—at which point it becomes clear that the black blob is the family pet and not a burglar. You feel silly, and you laugh. But you're still breathing hard.

The second challenge is that when you're threatened, your brain powers up for that defensive response by shifting resources away from its sophisticated-but-slower deliberate system. Dialing down the part of your brain responsible for existential reflection is helpful if you're being chased by a tiger on the savannah. But if the "threat" you're facing is one that requires a thoughtful approach rather than a footrace—perhaps it's criticism from a customer or a deadline that's moved unexpectedly—it's not great that you've just taken your strongest cognitive skills offline. In fact, Amy Arnsten, a professor of neurobiology at Yale, recently discovered that falling into defensive mode impacts the intellect more severely than previously suspected. She found that exposure to even fairly mild negative stress can significantly reduce the amount of activity in the brain's prefrontal cortex, where most of the deliberate system's work gets done.[16]

### Are You Threatening Me?

And that brings us to the reason that it's useful to understand how the brain's defensive mode operates: we've escaped the rough-and-tumble of our ancestors' lives on the savannah, but our survival circuits are still working just as hard to protect us in today's polished professional world. Our brain reacts just as quickly to personal affronts and workplace indignities as it does to genuine physical threats. So our fight-flight-freeze defenses can be triggered when someone takes too long to return a text message or when a colleague shows signs of disapproval. We can choke (freeze) when challenged, dissemble or tune out (flight) when we're feeling out of our depth, or snap (fight) at people when we're feeling let down.[17] (I'll talk in more detail later in the book about the types of workplace "threats" that tip most of us into defensive mode; you'll find a handy checklist in Chapter 9.)

And with professional threats, just as with physical threats, our survival circuits can get it wrong. That person near the coffee machine who's frowning in your direction might be annoyed at you because he thinks you cut in line. Or maybe not. Perhaps he just realized he's late to a meeting—but by now you're glowering back at him. Your brain is so busy diverting energy toward "defending" you that you only recognize a few seconds too late that he's the new finance director who could be helpful to a project of yours. What a shame you didn't engage him in friendly conversation. (Survival Circuits 1, Deliberate System 0.)

So that's the conundrum for us in the workplace. Thank goodness we have this defensive system keeping us safe from genuine life-or-death threats—but when it's active, we're not thinking expansively. Just when we want to behave like our most evolved selves, such as in the middle of a delicate or complex situation, our brain can sometimes have us behave more like a cornered animal. We can blame defensive mode for most of our "oh no" (or if you prefer, "oh ****") moments at work, those times when we realize we've done something a little ill-judged. Flaming emails and turf battles would be a lot less common without it.

### Well, That Explains a Lot

But, as ever, there's some good news here. Once you know that the brain's protective instinct is what lies behind a lot of dysfunctional behavior, life can be a lot easier.

For a start, a colleague's inexplicable bad behavior usually makes more sense if we know that we're observing a fight-flight-freeze response. By asking ourselves which "threat" might be causing the reaction, we may be able to improve the situation, rather than making things worse by reacting angrily and amplifying the threat still further. We'll explore this in depth in Part III, on relationships.

And the same goes for ourselves. It's hugely helpful to be able to spot when our own brain is in defensive mode. We can't always stop our instinctive reaction from playing out, but we can notice the signs that it's taking place and try to pinpoint exactly what it is we're reacting to. This self-awareness is the first step toward reengaging our brain's deliberate system and getting back to being at our best. And developing more understanding of the threats we're most sensitive to—our most common "hot buttons"—gives us a much better chance of quickly getting back onto an even keel. I'll explain more about how you can do that later in the book—in Part III, again, but also in Part IV, on handling challenging tasks, and in Part VI, on staying cool in the face of provocations.

### Discovery Mode: Seeking Out Rewarding Experiences

Noticing what's going on is always the first step in extracting yourself from defensive mode. But as well as becoming more adept at recognizing when and why we're triggered, there's one more thing we can do to improve our response to stressful challenges. It involves engaging another network in our brains, one known as the reward system.

While our defensive system looks out for threats to our safety and sanity, our reward system constantly scans the environment for potential treats—including not only primal rewards necessary to survival, like food and sex, but also subtler rewards, like praise and pleasure. Whenever our brain's reward system spots something potentially appealing, it sends us chasing after it like a Labrador retriever after a tennis ball, by releasing neurochemicals (including dopamine and endorphins) that trigger feelings of desire and pleasure in us. Those "I want" and "I like" sensations motivate us to seek out whatever promises to be rewarding, and they put us into an anticipatory, exploratory mental state. This is what I call *discovery mode.*

We can think of discovery mode and defensive mode as being at opposite ends of a spectrum labeled the "discover-defend axis." And when we address workplace challenges from the discovery end of the axis, rather than the defensive end—that is, when we feel rewarded rather than threatened—we handle them better. That's because in discovery mode, our survival circuits aren't freaking out, so they're not launching a fight-flight-freeze response, which means our deliberate system is able to stay fully online. As a result, we have more mental resources to handle whatever the day requires from us. Instead of being simplistic and black-and-white in our thinking, we're able to remain thoughtful and flexible as we roll with the punches. And sure enough, research shows significant correlations between people being in a positive mood and being able to solve tough analytical puzzles.[18] This isn't to suggest that we should ignore any problems that arise, of course— that's not what discovery mode is about. The point is that we're going to be able to think more clearly about those problems if our brains are not on the defensive.

So how can you move away from the defensive end of the axis when you're handling everyday workplace challenges? The answer is to look for potential rewards in the situation you're facing. If you can tempt your brain's reward system with something valuable, you're more likely to be able to respond to a tough situation with the benefit of all your "discovery mode" intelligence.

### These Are a Few of Our Favorite Things

There's an art to finding the right kind of reward at times of stress or tension, of course. Primal rewards like food and sex aren't generally available or appropriate in the middle of our most difficult conversations at work. We know that money excites the brain's reward system, but research suggests that the neurological effects of financial gains are short-lived.[19] Besides, a bonus is hardly likely to drop into your lap every time you're feeling uptight. Luckily, there are more reliable rewards out there for us, if we choose to look for them.

Humor, for example. Suppose you're in a stressful meeting, you can feel the tension rising, and the entire group seems to be in defensive mode. Some people start to make barbed comments (fight), while others keep their heads down (freeze) or step out to take "an urgent call" (flight). But then one of your colleagues makes a witty comment, and everyone laughs. It's a small reward, but it's enough to puncture the tension, which is a sign that everyone has moved back toward discovery mode. As people reengage their brain's deliberate system, progress suddenly feels possible.

One reason that shared humor is powerful is that it tends to make us feel more connected to other people. And social rewards are candy for the human brain. Just think about how good it feels to be respected, appreciated, and treated fairly. We're extraordinarily sensitive to signals that we belong, probably because historically we needed the support of our tribe to survive on the savannah.[20] In fact, social neuroscientists like UCLA's Matt Lieberman have found that our brains respond to signals of belonging in a way that's very similar to more primal rewards.[21] So praise and recognition—even when it's just a simple "job well done" comment—can help to keep us in discovery mode, even when we're in the deep end at work.

Other powerful rewards come from deeper inside ourselves. Extensive research by psychologists Edward Deci and Richard Ryan, at the University of Rochester, has shown that having a sense of autonomy and personal competence is profoundly motivating.[22] It turns out that we perform better, and feel better about ourselves, when we feel in charge of at least some aspects of what we're doing—whether that's in the goals we set for ourselves, the way we work, or the purpose behind our effort.

Finally, our brains also find it rewarding to learn new and interesting things—even if it's just office gossip. George Loewenstein, a neuroeconomist at Carnegie Mellon who has investigated the phenomenon of curiosity, has found that merely getting answers to questions visibly activates the reward system in people who are lying in a brain scanner.[23]

Throughout the book I'll talk more about ways you can summon these social, personal, and informational rewards to keep you out of defensive mode and enable you to stay focused, smart, and adaptable in the face of workplace challenges. As well as using these Jedi mind tricks for yourself, I'll also show you how being generous in doling out brain-friendly rewards to colleagues can improve the quality of all your inter-actions (Part III) and communications (Part V). And in Part VII, we'll see how to weave these rewards into an everyday strategy for boosting your energy at work.

Things to know about the discover-defend axis:

➡ You're constantly moving along a discover-defend axis in your daily life, as your brain scans for threats to defend against and rewards to seek out and discover.

➡ In *defensive mode*, you become less smart and flexible, as your brain devotes some of its scarce mental energy to launching a fight-flight-freeze response to a potential "threat"—leaving less energy to power your brain's deliberate system. Defensive mode can even be triggered by small personal slights.

➡ In *discovery mode*, you're motivating yourself with rewards: a social sense of belonging or recognition; a personal sense of autonomy, competence, or purpose; or informational rewards that come from learning or experiencing new things.

➡ To be at your most resourceful in handling workplace challenges, it helps to become adept at recognizing when you're sliding into defensive mode. Refocusing attention on potential rewards in the situation at hand can also help to reengage your deliberate system and shift you back into discovery mode.

## THEME 3: THE MIND-BODY LOOP

There's one more theme that comes up frequently throughout this book: the constant interplay between our bodies and our minds.

On one level, we know there's a link between our mental and physical state. I've already talked about the way that stress can set our heart pounding. We can admit that it's hard to think clearly in the seconds just after we've painfully stubbed a toe. We're all aware that being sleep-deprived makes it harder to be patient and witty. And so on.

But in practice, we often behave as if there's no link between our physical health and mental functioning—at least, not enough to seriously affect our achievements at work. We catch ourselves saying "I don't have time to take a break right now" or "I'll exercise once I'm through this busy patch," acting as though physical refueling were a luxury rather than a way to boost our performance.

In reality, decades of research suggest that the way we treat our body has a huge effect on the way our brain performs, thanks to the way it affects the brain's blood flow, the balance of its neurochemicals, and the degree of connectivity between different brain regions. As a result, studies have found we can reap immediate intellectual and emotional dividends from investing in exercise and sleep, or even from taking a moment to breathe deeply, smile broadly, and stand a little taller. In just about every section of the book, from Part I through Part VII, I'll show you exactly how these kinds of physical adjustments can support you in achieving your goals. But here's a preview of the main mind-body themes.

### Sleep

Being sleep-deprived makes it difficult for our brain's deliberate system to perform its daily miracles. A tired brain devotes less blood to the prefrontal cortex, where most of the deliberate system lives. That makes it hard for us to respond intelligently to the unexpected, think up new ideas, or stay calm under stress. Skimping on sleep also dents our ability to remember and learn anything new, because sleep is central to the brain's ability to convert the day's experience into long-term memories.[24] (As one CEO I know put it, going short of sleep is like forgetting to save a document that you've worked on all day.)

What's the definition of "sleep-deprived"? It differs from person to person. But the vast majority of us need between seven and nine hours of sleep to function at our best.[25] As Harvard professor of sleep medicine Charles Czeisler says, "We now know that a week of sleeping four or five hours a night induces an impairment equivalent to a blood alcohol level of 0.1 percent."[26] Which is to say, it impairs your cognitive abilities as much as being drunk does. As Czeisler puts it, "We would never say, 'This person is a great worker. He's drunk all the time!' Yet we continue to celebrate people who sacrifice sleep."

So if we're looking for ways to make our brains run more effectively, doing whatever we can to prioritize our sleep has to be high on the list. It's one of the surest ways to increase our control over whether or not we have a good day. So I'll revisit the scientific evidence on the effects of decent sleep on cognitive performance and emotional resilience, in Part IV and Part VI, respectively, along with practical advice on how to get your full quota.

## Exercise

Just as Czeisler is spreading the word about the benefits of sleep, John Ratey is doing the same for exercise. A clinical psychiatrist at Harvard Medical School, Ratey has spent much of the past decade summarizing and publicizing evidence on the link between exercise and mental function.[27]

It's powerful stuff. Research shows that even a single session of aerobic exercise immediately improves our intellectual performance, giving us faster information processing and reaction time, more effective planning, better short-term memory performance, and more self-control.[28] It enhances all the functions of the brain's deliberate system, in other words. Correspondingly, Bristol University researchers found that on days that people exercised before work or did something active during their lunch break, they were far better able to concentrate and handle their workload.[29] Exercise also boosted people's mood and motivation (by 41 percent) and their ability to deal with stress (by 27 percent).

Why is exercise so immediately helpful to us? Partly because it increases blood flow to the brain. But it also stimulates the release of the neurotransmitters dopamine, noradrenaline, and serotonin, which serve to boost our interest, alertness, and enjoyment. That's why Ratey is fond of saying that exercise is "like a little bit of Ritalin and a little bit of Prozac," and why your head feels clearer and your concerns less burdensome after exercise.[30] Furthermore, research suggests that the majority of those cognitive and emotional benefits accrue after as little as twenty minutes of moderate daily activity.[31] So even a fast walk at lunchtime can make a real difference to your mojo.

## Mindfulness

The practice known as mindfulness is another clear bridge between brain and body. For some of you, the word might conjure up an image of meditating monks in colorful robes. But mindfulness is a distinctly mainstream practice these days, used by organizations as diverse as Google and the U.S. Army to improve the performance and resilience of their people. They're responding to scores of studies suggesting that mindfulness enhances our analytical thinking, capacity for insight, ability to focus, self-control, sense of well-being, energy, and emotional resilience.[32] This laundry list covers just about everything that seems useful in an average day, and it sounds almost too good to be true. But it's possible to see tangible changes on brain scans of volunteers before and after learning how to practice mindfulness: improved connectivity between different parts of the brain's deliberate system, and reduced reactivity in the survival circuits when faced with negative stimuli. Which means more time in high-functioning discovery mode, less time in defensive mode. And that's what underpins the impressive laundry list.[33]

But what *is* mindfulness? At its heart, the practice is simply this: you pause, focus your attention on observing one thing, and calmly return your attention to that point of focus if your attention drifts away. *Pause, focus, return*—for anything from a few seconds up to twenty minutes or more. When deciding what to observe, people often focus on their own breathing, since it's always available and doesn't cost a thing. (No robes or mats required.)

Much of the research on the effects of mindfulness has focused on people who have attended multiweek courses in "mindfulness-based stress reduction," "meditation," or "focused attention." But researchers are also finding that people can get results from practicing mindfulness for as little as five minutes a day—something that's easy to fit into our hectic, got-to-get-things-done life.[34] In fact, Ellen Langer, Harvard psychology professor, would argue that it's not even a question of taking minutes out of your day. She says that mindfulness can be simply an attitude, one where you slow down and "notice new things" in whatever you're doing throughout the day.[35] I'll show you ways to exploit the benefits of this kind of bite-sized mindfulness throughout the book, before revisiting the topic in more depth in Part VI.

## Striking a Pose

Finally, perhaps the most surprising way to use our body to improve our mind stems from research showing that there's a two-way feedback loop in the nervous system that connects our brain and body. The mental-to-physical side of this flow is familiar to us; for example, we know that when our minds are relaxed and happy, we tend to breathe and smile more easily. But it also goes the other way. When we slow our breathing and make ourselves smile, our brain appears to interpret that as a signal that we *should* feel relaxed and happy, and it duly creates that state of mind for real. The same thing is true for confidence, too. When we mimic the physical actions we might associate with being an alpha male or female—such as standing up taller, squaring our shoulders, making bold gestures—our brain sees that as a sign that we are genuinely in control, and responds accordingly.

These "fake it till you make it" findings are useful to us, since they suggest it's possible to use our bodies to reverse-engineer the state of mind we want. They're not a replacement for the other advice in the book, but I'll show you how they can make a nice addition to your daily toolbox when you're seeking to boost your confidence and energy (in Parts V and VII, respectively).

Things to remember about the mind-body loop:

➡ The way you treat your body has a direct, immediate impact on your brain's performance, affecting both its cognitive and emotional functions.

➡ Specifically, your brain's deliberate system performs far better when you've had enough sleep, some aerobic exercise, and a few moments of mindfulness.

➡ Mimicking the physical actions associated with feeling happy, confident, and relaxed appears to tell your brain that you *are* in fact happy, confident, and relaxed, creating a self-fulfilling loop.

## SUMMARY

My description of these three themes—the two-system brain, the discover-defend axis, and the mind-body loop—represents a tiny fraction of the knowledge that behavioral scientists have amassed in recent decades. But together, they cover some of the concepts I've found most useful in coaching people to be at their best, because they speak directly to what it takes for us to be smart and effective in handling the challenges of working life. Now let's get into the heart of the book, and see exactly how to apply these big ideas to create the components of a really good day.

# PART I

# Priorities

Setting Intentional Direction for Your Day

> Until you make the unconscious conscious, it will direct your life and you will call it fate.
>
> —CARL JUNG

Let me begin by telling you about a morning some years ago, when I took none of the advice I'm about to lay out.

I was in a bad mood from the moment I woke up. I'd just been asked to join a new project that didn't interest me, and it was my first week on the job. In persuading me to sign up, my boss had suggested I would nicely complement Lucas, another senior colleague on the project. Lucas was a hard-driving operations guy, and I was all about the so-called human side. Lucas would produce reams of analysis and ideas; meanwhile, I'd help our clients create plans that their colleagues could rally around. I understood why our boss thought we'd be a great combination, but I couldn't shake a concern about the mismatch in our working styles.

On this particular morning, our team was about to have its first big meeting with some new clients, and I fell out of bed with barely enough time to get ready. On my way in, my head was a fog of lingering annoyance and tiredness. When I arrived, I discovered the meeting was taking place in one of those dark, cramped, low-ceilinged videoconference rooms that are so common in modern office buildings. Everyone was sitting in a row, as though we were at some kind of judicial hearing, while disembodied faces floated on the video screen in front of us. My heart sank further.

As I thought about how badly I could use another coffee, Lucas plowed into the brick of paper in front of us, without much introduction and with an evidently clear sense of what he wanted to say. I did my best to go with the flow and contribute constructively, but the long discussion felt to me like pushing a boulder uphill—lots of little mis-understandings, people talking over each other, the air thick with un-spoken irritations and concerns. By the end of it, I didn't feel I'd made much of a positive impact. It was just as I'd feared, and it left me with a cloud over my head for the whole day.

Some time later, in a better mood, I felt compelled to talk to Lucas about my concern that we'd started on the wrong foot with the clients. But as I gave him my take on the meeting, he looked incredulous. Lucas hadn't thought the room was particularly unpleasant; he had no recol-lection of the frowns and awkwardness I mentioned. He'd been excited about the new project, happy to have found a time for us all to talk, keen to make progress. He knew what he wanted from the meeting, and he'd achieved it.

Of course, we had different personalities, and that explained some of the variation in our perspectives. But only some of it. Something else was going on: it was truly as if we'd each been in an entirely different meeting. He hadn't seen through his rosier-tinted glasses what I'd seen. From my side, it quickly became obvious that I hadn't paid much atten-tion to his side of the story. He pointed out, convincingly, all the things we'd gotten done; he reminded me of moments of levity, smiles that I barely remembered. It wasn't that either of us was completely wrong, and we avoided outright insults as we traded viewpoints. ("Why are you being so blind? Were we even in the same room? Sheesh. Get real.")

But we'd experienced the same few hours very differently. How could that be? And, of particular interest to me: why had he enjoyed the meeting so much more than I had? The answer, I came to realize, was in the way each of us had approached the day. Lucas had been deliber-ate in deciding what he wanted to see, what he wanted to accomplish, and how he wanted to feel. But I'd let the morning kind of happen to me. I'd been professional, yes, but I'd drifted into the day.

And that lack of direction made me miss what I now know were three big opportunities to influence the quality of my morning. First, our priorities and assumptions determine our perceptions to a sur-prising extent. Second, setting the right kind of goals not only reliably lifts our performance but also makes us feel good. And third, what we imagine in our mind's eye can shape our real-life experience. In the following three chapters, I want to show you how to exploit each of these major behavioral science benefits, to have a much better time than I had with Lucas that day.

# ONE

# Choosing Your Filters

We so often cruise through our busy days on autopilot, rolling from task to task without pausing to stop and think. We work hard and do our best, and we're glad if it all works out to our liking. Sometimes luck is on our side, and sometimes it isn't. "That's just life," we might tell ourselves.

But I'd like to make the case that we can do better than that, thanks to an important aspect of the way our brain makes sense of the world: the fact that we consciously notice only a small selection of what's actually happening around us, and filter out the rest. Because the things that get through the filters are strongly influenced by the priorities and assumptions we take into the day, that gives us a huge opportunity. It means that with a few minutes of mental preparation—involving a quick check and reset of those priorities and assumptions—we can shift the way we experience the day, making it more productive and enjoyable. This mental preparation is a process that I call *setting intentions*, because it's about being more intentional about your approach to the day.

Before I talk about a quick daily intention-setting routine for you to try, let me explain why the reality we experience is so dependent on our filters.

## OUR SUBJECTIVE REALITY

As we learned in The Science Essentials, our brain's deliberate system (responsible for reasoning, self-control, and planning) has only so much attention to give to our complex world. So as we go through the day, our automatic system prioritizes whatever seems most worthy of the deliberate system's attention, while screening out anything that doesn't seem important. This filtering happens without us being aware of it, and it's central to our brain's ability to cope with the complexity of the world. But this selective attention also leaves us experiencing an incomplete, subjective version of reality—one that may or may not serve us well.

Obviously, it's a good thing that our automatic system filters out things that are truly unimportant. Otherwise we'd be obsessively counting carpet fibers or getting mesmerized by the ingredients of our lunch, making it hard to get anything done. The downside, however, is that even potentially useful things can be tagged by our automatic system as "unimportant." For example, if we're intently focused on checking our messages, our automatic system might decide it's not worth diverting some of our attention toward understanding a question we've just been asked by a colleague. When she raises her voice and finally breaks through into our consciousness with a "Hey, did you hear me?" we might apologize and swear we hadn't heard her before. And we'd be technically correct. We *didn't* hear her—not consciously, anyway.

Now, we can't switch off our automatic system's filtering function— by definition, it's automatic. But we *can* adjust the settings, by being more proactive in defining what our brain sees as "important" each day. If we do that, we can affect what our conscious brain gets to see and hear. It's one of the most powerful ways to steer our day toward the reality we'd most like to experience.

### On Autopilot, What Does Our Brain Treat as "Important"?

Our automatic system uses several selective attention rules to decide what's important enough to bring to our conscious attention and what should be filtered out. If we can understand how some of those rules work, we have a better chance of hacking into the system and adjusting its settings.

The first thing to know is that if we've got a task that we're consciously prioritizing, our automatic system will make sure we see anything directly relevant to that specific task, and it will tend to blank out anything that seems off topic. *Anything?* "Surely," you're saying, "if something striking cropped up in front of us, off topic or not, we'd see it, wouldn't we?" Well, an enormous amount of research suggests we might not.[1] Take this recent study, for example. Psychologist Trafton Drew and colleagues at Harvard's Visual Attention Lab asked some experienced radiologists to look closely at a bunch of medical images to spot abnormalities. The radiologists were given a stack of genuine lung scans to work with, some of them with sadly genuine nodules. But the last image was different: it showed a picture of a gorilla inserted inside the lung. (The researchers were paying wry homage to the original gorilla/basketball experiment described in The Science Essentials.) Astonishingly, 83 percent of the radiologists failed to spot the gorilla, although the image was forty-eight times the size of the average lung nodule. Even more remarkable is the fact that the Harvard researchers used an eye-tracking device that showed that most of the radiologists looked directly at the gorilla—and yet they still didn't notice it.[2] It's not that they saw it and discounted or forgot about it. Their brains simply didn't consciously register the ape. In other words: because they weren't actually looking for it, they didn't see it.

This type of selective attention is what scientists call *inattentional blindness*—that is, we see what we've decided merits our attention, and we're remarkably blind to the rest. So the priorities we set for ourselves really matter.

We don't even have to be deeply focused on a task to encounter inattentional blindness. In fact, as soon as we have something on our mind, we become much more attuned to anything related to that concern and less attuned to everything else. In one study that was conducted by psychologist Rémi Radel in France, where mealtimes matter, volunteers who'd been forced to skip their lunch went on to see food-related words more clearly and quickly in a word-recognition test. That is, the hungry people noticed the word "gâteau" more readily than "bateau."[3] (If the researchers had taken their volunteers out on a boat, they might have seen "bateau" even faster than "gâteau.") Our automatic system will generally prioritize information that resonates with anything that's top of mind for us.

Even our attitude can play a part in setting the perceptual filters we apply to the day. Joseph Forgas and Gordon Bower, professors at the University of New South Wales and Stanford, respectively, conducted an experiment designed to put volunteers into a slightly good or bad mood by giving them random positive or negative feedback about their performance on a minor test they'd just taken. After that, the volunteers were given some descriptions of fictional people to read. Those descriptions were carefully calibrated to be neutral: the volunteers could easily interpret the subjects as being either energetic or chaotic, calm or boring, depending on their reading of the text. And what did Forgas and Bower find?[4] That their happier volunteers were significantly more likely to see the people described in a positive light, compared with the volunteers they'd deliberately put into a funk. And it's not just inter-personal judgments that are affected by our mood. Another research team found that sad people perceived a hill as being significantly steeper (and saw scaling it as a less pleasant prospect) than people who were feeling more upbeat.[5]

So it really *is* possible to get up on the wrong side of the bed. Our perceptions of the world can be strongly influenced by our starting point, good or bad, because our brain's automatic system makes sure that we see and hear anything that resonates with our conscious priorities, our top-of-mind concerns, and even our mood. Meanwhile, it downplays everything else.

## What Are Your Filters Doing to Your Reality?

Now let's think about how we can apply this knowledge. Suppose you and I were sitting in the same room, participating in the same conversation. My priorities, concerns, and mood would shape my perceptions of what was going on, while yours would shape yours. As a result, it's entirely possible that I would miss things that matter to you, while getting hung up on things that don't register with you at all. With all this in mind, it's little surprise that my meeting with Lucas didn't seem like the pinnacle of my professional life, given my crankiness when I walked in. Meanwhile, of course, he had a blast. We're each living through our own private reality, a reality shaped by our hardworking automatic system's attempts to allocate our attention to the right things.

So what particular reality would you like your brain to pay a little more attention to? Take your next meeting. If your primary concern is to get your point across, you'll probably find yourself noticing every instance of being interrupted, and every moment of airtime that others take up. You'll probably lose some of the thread of the conversation, without realizing it, because you'll be focused on your desire to tell people what you want them to hear. You're not being willfully closed-minded; your automatic system is just efficiently prioritizing informa-tion that relates to your state of mind. Turn all this around, and the reverse is true, too. For example, if you instead decided to focus on finding new opportunities for collaboration or on hearing useful input from your colleagues, chances are you'd discover more of *that*. As we change our intentions, our brain's filters change, and the facts can appear to change with them.

## SET YOUR INTENTIONS, SET YOUR FILTERS

The point behind all of this is clear: we miss a big opportunity if we simply let the day happen to us.

We *can't* control everything (there are different types of books for those who believe that's possible). But we *can* tweak the way our working hours feel, by being more deliberate in setting our perceptual filters. And that's where it helps to have an intention-setting routine, one that has us pay explicit attention to the priorities, concerns, and mood we're carrying into the day.

Here's an approach I like. It involves taking just a moment to look at something from three angles (each beginning with "A," conveniently):

➡ Aim: Think about each of the most important of today's activities— the people you'll meet, the work you'll do. What really matters most in making them a success? That's your real aim.

➡ Attitude: As you think about the upcoming workday, take a moment to notice and acknowledge the concerns that are dominating your thoughts or your mood. Do these concerns help you achieve your real aim—and if not, can you set them aside for now?

➡ Attention: Given your real priorities, where do you want to focus your attention? Figure out what you want to see more of, and then make sure you look out for it.

Most people I've worked with find it's ideal to think about these questions before the day gets under way, either in the morning or even the night before. But because the whole routine takes no more than a couple of minutes, it's never too late to set your intentions as you're flying from one thing to the next.

For example, how differently might my meeting with Lucas have gone if I'd taken a moment to consider the "three A's" just before walking into that conference room? I might have had these things in mind:

➡ **Aim:** "What really matters to me is to help the team get off to a strong start with our new clients, by encouraging a collaborative tone and helping everyone feel good about the prospect of working together."

➡ **Attitude:** "I admit that I'm feeling grumpy and tired right now. I can't make myself less tired. But I can decide to set aside my irritation at the way the project is set up, in favor of focusing on the real priority: making the team a success."

➡ **Attention:** "I want to spot opportunities to help the team gel, by highlighting common ground in their ideas. I want to look for chances to inject warmth into the meeting."

Going over this mental "aim-attitude-attention" checklist would have taken me no more than a few moments as I stashed my coat on my way into the videoconference room. (And yes, ever since that day, I've made sure to do this before embarking on anything that matters to me.) It simply doesn't take much effort to focus your filters more firmly on the kind of day you want—especially if you can make it a regular part of your daily schedule.

To see a great example of someone who knows the value of setting intentions, let's meet Martin, the strategy director of an aircraft manufacturer. Alongside this role, he somehow finds time to sit on the board of several technology companies and provide advice to high-tech entrepreneurs seeking to get their start-ups off the ground. He's thoughtful, focused, and successful—partly, he says, because he's learned to be as strategic about his daily personal intentions as he is about his business.

What led Martin to establish an intention-setting routine? "Well, I've always had a problem with concentration," he says. "I'd get into the office and immediately get pulled into low-value tasks, chatting to colleagues, checking news websites, and so on. I started to realize my days weren't as good as they could have been because I was just drifting through them." One morning, by accident, Martin discovered how to give his day more direction. "I was sitting on the bed before going to work, feeling kind of overwhelmed by everything I had on my plate," he says. "For some reason I just started thinking about what really mattered to me. I picked up a notebook and I just wrote and wrote, about why I was doing what I was doing, and how I wanted to do it. I wasn't writing full sentences; it was more of a visual map of things that were important for me. It was incredibly clarifying." He was struck by how much more upbeat and purposeful he felt afterward, with his intentions so much more crisply and constructively defined.

Naturally, Martin wanted to inject more of that intentional direction into each day. He realized he couldn't sit on his bed and write for hours every morning, but he came up with a short version of the routine that he could fit into every day. "Before leaving for the office, I spend a moment clearing my head, just breathing deeply. Then I ask myself what's most important today, given what I'm trying to achieve at work, and make a few notes about where I want to focus my attention. It's that simple. And things come to the surface that I hadn't realized were there until I stopped to think. Often it means deciding to take a particular approach to a challenge at work, like thinking longer-term and being more tolerant of delays."

Martin says the payoff has been clear. "My first hour at work used to be all over the place, very unproductive. Now I'm 100 percent ready to go when I arrive. I'm calmer and in a better mood." Moreover, throughout the day, he makes a point of recalling his intentions, to help him stay on track. "It reminds me what my real priorities are for the day, if—*when*—I start to feel frazzled."

### Make Your Intentions Positive (or: "Snark In, Snark Out")

When you're contemplating a particularly challenging day, it can be easy to find yourself coming up with intentions that are a little sarcastic or negative, like: "What really matters to me is never again creating a two-hundred-page document for a meeting." Or perhaps you find yourself thinking that your real aim is to persuade one of your colleagues to understand that he made a stupid mistake last week.

But making sure a co-worker realizes his stupidity? It's not the most uplifting way to articulate an intention. It's a little petty—and that will have your brain subconsciously prioritizing petty observations. If you genuinely want to have a good conversation, it's better to articulate a more generous intention that speaks to the bigger picture. Ask yourself what you *really* want to achieve. In the case of dealing with your error-prone colleague, a bigger intention might be to help him work out how to avoid making the same mistake again. Thinking bigger still, you might decide you want to improve your working relationship, so in the future you can be more honest with each other about how things are going.

Setting these more solution-focused intentions doesn't mean avoiding challenging topics with your errant colleague. But a less combative approach will make it easier for you to spot ways to resolve the situation when you have that conversation. It will also make it easier to avoid triggering a defensive fight-flight-freeze response, whether in his brain or in yours—meaning you'll both be smarter and better able to reach a useful outcome.

## ONE MORE THING: CHECK YOUR ASSUMPTIONS

To make our positive intentions an even stronger base for the day we want to have, there's one more step we can take, which is to check and challenge any negative assumptions we're carrying into the day.

Like our priorities, concerns, and moods, our assumptions are another selective attention filter that our automatic brain uses to simplify our experience of the world. It works like this: If we encounter some information or behavior that matches what we're expecting, our automatic system will probably make sure we're aware of it. If, however, we encounter something that runs counter to our expectations, our automatic system will tend to disregard it. Known as *confirmation bias*, this is a cognitive shortcut that saves us considerable mental energy, since it stops us from having to develop a new mental model about the world every time we run into evidence that contradicts our beliefs.

### It's Bananas

In fact, confirmation bias doesn't just cause us to filter out information that might challenge our expectations; it can even distort the things we hear and see to match our expectations. Scientists have designed countless clever experiments to demonstrate this, and a favorite example of mine involves bananas. (Yes, I admit this could be construed as another gorilla-related experiment.) When volunteers looked at a black-and-white picture of a banana, tests showed they saw it as slightly yellow—even though in fact it was purely gray. The researchers demonstrated this by asking the volunteers to adjust the background on a screen until it was the same color as the banana shape. Without realizing it, the volunteers selected a background with a slight yellow tinge.

They had such a strong presumption that the banana would be yellow that their brains decided it actually was.[6]

If confirmation bias can affect how we see a tangible object like a banana, you can be sure it sways our subjective judgments of situations at work. In my case, it would have been a great start to set the right personal intentions for the project meeting with Lucas—for example, to inject warmth rather than frustration into the room, and to look for opportunities to build team spirit. But I also had a deeply held assumption that it's impossible for a new team to bond properly in a videoconference, as opposed to a face-to-face meeting, so my confirmation bias had me quietly looking for evidence that the videoconference wasn't working. Sure enough, that was a big negative factor in how I experienced the meeting; for Lucas, not so much.

Of course, this doesn't mean we should discount our past experience completely—we may have good reason to feel wary or worried. We just want to notice whenever we're feeling strongly attached to some negative expectations about a situation or a person, and recognize that our attachment may cause us to filter out any evidence to the contrary. That flash of self-awareness can be just enough to remind ourselves to be a little more open to taking in new information.

### Absolute Language

One helpful sign that you may be falling victim to confirmation bias is when you catch yourself using what I call *absolute language*: words like "never," "always," "completely," "totally," "absolutely," or "definitely," perhaps with a dash of "terrible" or "awful." The author Theodore Sturgeon once wrote, "Nothing is always absolutely so," and he was right—very little in life is truly completely good or bad.[7] So the use of absolute language is a flashing neon sign that you're probably seeing only part of the picture. Martin, the aviation strategy director, agrees. "I tend to overexaggerate the negatives, saying things like '*Nothing's* working.' It feels so good to wallow in your extreme language. I'm getting better, though, at catching myself saying these sorts of things, and asking myself, 'Hang on, is that really true? How about checking that?'"

So if you find yourself using strong words as you think or talk about the tasks ahead, or the people involved, take that as a helpful cue to check your perspective. Ask another "A" question:

➡ What negative assumptions do you have about this person or activity?

And then take one more step back, and ask yourself:

➡ What are you likely to focus on to confirm your assumptions?

➡ If you had to challenge your negative assumptions, what would you say?

➡ What counterevidence can you look out for, to help you keep an open mind?

Here's how I would have answered those questions if I'd acknowledged my negativity on the morning of the ill-fated project meeting with Lucas:

➡ Assumption: "It's going to be a terrible meeting because it's a video-conference."

➡ Confirmation: "There will probably be some technology glitches, and I'll tend to get fixated by them (and any signs of annoyance in other people) if I'm not careful."

➡ Challenge: "Lucas knows the clients and their preferences better than I do. It would probably have taken longer to find a date for us to meet in person. Video technology is better than it used to be."

➡ Counterevidence: "I can choose to notice what actually works well in the setup. I can look for ways to get the meeting back on track if the technology stutters."

And with that kind of small hike in open-mindedness, our positive intentions become far easier to bring to life—even when things don't go to plan.

## STARTING YOUR DAY THE NIGHT BEFORE

Now let's meet Audrey. She runs a widely respected government-funded agency that helps small companies get the advice and support they need to innovate and grow. An average day might see her delivering a new training course, negotiating for more funds, or encouraging mom-and-pop firms to take full advantage of the resources her agency offers. She's deeply committed to her work and has a strong sense of what these businesses need, since her own parents have run a small business for some years (an actual mom-and-pop, you might say). Like most leaders, she finds she has to be thoughtful about prioritizing her attention. Otherwise, she says, "I'd just end up doing whatever was most urgent."

So, like Martin, she has a daily intention-setting routine—but Audrey prefers to start her routine the evening before, on the train home. "I first reflect on the day I've just had. I go over what went well, what didn't, why, and what I could have seen coming. Then I look ahead to the next day, to think about what I want from it and what deserves the most attention." She jots down some notes, then starts the next morning by rereading them. "I remind myself of what's most important, and add anything that has occurred to me overnight. And as I go through the day, I refer back to them, especially just before I dive into the biggest things."

Audrey takes particular care to think ahead to the most demanding task of the next day. In her role, that's often a challenging conversation. She gives an example of how intentions have helped her there. "For a long time, I worked with someone who was passive-aggressive, though she could become 'aggressive-aggressive' if rubbed the wrong way," she laughs. "I'd often have to ask her to do things she wasn't keen to do, and she usually responded by listing all the things that could go wrong. When I didn't prepare mentally, I'd respond instinctively and see her behavior as a personal attack." Once Audrey started setting more positive intentions, her relationship took a turn for the better. "When I explicitly decided that collaboration was my aim, I'd see the same conversation quite differently. I found myself able to interpret her comments less personally, seeing them as an expression of her own frustrations or even of her desire to get things right. And you know, maybe she was still being a pain. But I found time and again that my state of mind made such a difference to my perception of her behavior, and therefore my reaction to her."

For Audrey, much of the breakthrough came from challenging her assumptions. "One of the big shifts for me was managing to get out of the habit of assuming ill intent. I used to have a very competitive mindset and expected everyone else to be competitive, too—which meant that was exactly what I saw. I'd pay a lot of attention to signs of potential sabotage, like someone sending a nasty email to my boss about some work I was involved in," she says. "But now, if I see bad behavior from someone, I don't assume they're a bad person—I consider the possibility that they're just having a bad day. Your assumptions really color what you see and how you react."

With practice, Audrey has also found she can reset her intentions in the middle of a tough situation. "I've realized that even when things are going down the wrong path, I can take a step back and do a version of what I should have done beforehand. That passive-aggressive colleague of mine used to tug her ear when she was getting stressed—so as soon as I saw that, I'd use it as a prompt to pause and say to myself, 'Time to rethink.' I'd shift in my seat to give myself a second to reset and remember what I really wanted from the conversation. I'd sometimes even say out loud, 'Give me a second—what are we really trying to do?' It didn't always allow me to have the conversation I'd have had if I'd prepared beforehand, but it meant I could usually make the situation better."

## CHOOSING YOUR FILTERS

Take a moment to think about the day ahead, or an important conversation you have coming up. Ask yourself these intention-setting questions:

➡ Aim: What matters most in making this a success, and what does that mean your real priority should be?

➡ Attitude: What concerns are dominating your thoughts or your mood? Do they help you with your priorities—and if not, can you choose to set them aside for now?

➡ Assumptions: What negative expectations do you have going into this? How might you challenge those expectations? What counterevidence might you seek out?

➡ Attention: Given your real aim and your assumptions, where do you most want to direct your attention? What do you want to make particularly sure you notice?

# TWO

# Setting Great Goals

So far, I've discussed how taking a few minutes to deliberately set our intentions is a splendid way to prepare for a good day. Now, I want to talk about the next few minutes of preparation, which is all about complementing your big-picture intentions with specific goals for the day ahead.

If you've ever held down a job, you probably already do some sort of practical daily planning—whether it involves writing a to-do list or just looking at imminent deadlines and figuring out what they require of you. But whatever your current approach, I'd like to share a few science-based tweaks that can add real power to your goal-setting routine.

First, I'll make the case for complementing your usual task-oriented to-dos with a few behavioral goals to bolster your intentions. Second, scientists have found that the way you articulate your goals makes a surprisingly big difference to your chances of success—so I'll show you four tips that will improve your hit rate. Third, if you manage your task list in a way that's kind to your brain, your brain will learn to love your task list—or at least like it a little more—and yes, you'll get more done as a result.

## SET BEHAVIORAL GOALS TO SUPPORT YOUR INTENTIONS

When it comes to setting specific goals for the day, most of us think about them like this:

- ☑ Get in touch with person
- ☑ Prepare for meeting
- ☑ Think about that thing

If you're an artist or an artisan, your goals might look a little different, but the essence is the same—it's stuff you need to get done. Conversations to have, things to learn, outputs to create. And getting clear on exactly what you want to do today is a very good idea. Four decades of research by Edwin Locke and Gary Latham (psychologists at the University of Maryland and Rotman School of Management, respectively) suggest that people who bother to articulate a specific goal boost their performance significantly, typically by 15 percent on tasks where it can be quantified.[1] Clear-cut goals help us stay on track for at least a couple of reasons. They go even further than intentions in focusing our attention, helping us resist the distractions of the working day. And they encourage us to be more persistent, because making progress toward a goal feels highly satisfying for the brain's reward system. That small buzz when you tick something off your to-do list is your brain quietly saying, "Right on."

Given the power of goals to boost our performance, it makes sense to apply that power not only to your practical tasks but also to your broader intentions for the day, by asking yourself:

➡ **Personally:** What can I shift in my own behavior to help make my intentions a reality?

➡ Specifically: What does that shift look like in practice—and what actions will I take today?

Let's say, for example, that your intention for today involves finding a way to move a project forward. Progress has been inexplicably slow, and it's been irritating you. But today, you've set a more upbeat filter for your attention: you're going to look out for any opportunity in the day's meetings to take small steps forward, rather than focusing on the snags. Great. Now, what can you *personally* do to make progress more likely? Perhaps you could involve your colleagues more, rather than trying to push the project through on your own. Even more *specifically*? Perhaps you could use your slot in the first meeting to lay out what you're seeing as the biggest roadblock, and ask for colleagues' ideas on how to get around it. Maybe you'll also bring donuts, to thank them for their input. Frankly, the things you can do to support your intentions are often obvious once you take a step back to think about it—but we often don't take the time to set these kinds of tangible behavioral goals.

In my own example of the videoconference with Lucas in the last chapter, I mentioned that my real priority had been to help the new team gel, so I should have been on the lookout for signs of common ground between people. When I took the time to set that more positive intention for subsequent team meetings, I also decided on two specific behavioral goals to support it. One was to make sure that I said something to appreciate each person's contributions at some point during the meeting. The other was to point out whenever someone's ideas nicely connected to something another person had previously said. (Good goals for any meeting, I've discovered, even those that aren't in a dark video conference room.)

So when you're looking at your aims for the day, don't just set yourself task completion goals. Set at least one or two goals for your own behavior, and make them as specific as you possibly can, to magnify your chances of having the day you intended.

## FIND A WINNING ARTICULATION OF YOUR GOALS

Now let's shift to the evidence on how best to articulate our goals— whether they're task-related goals or behavioral ones—if we want to boost our chances of success. Research suggests that we should aim to describe them in a way that is positive, personally meaningful, feasible, and situation-specific. Let's take each of those four attributes in turn.

### Approach Goals, aka "More of a Good Thing"

Our goals are usually framed in one of two ways. Either they're about doing more of something good, or they're about doing less of something bad. A wide range of research suggests that the first type (known as "approach" goals) are better than the second ("avoidance" goals) at encouraging high performance—even if they're pursuing the same broad outcome. In fact, when psychologists Andrew Elliot and Marcy Church worked with a large group of students at the University of Rochester to track the effects of different types of personal goals on the students' grades, they found that avoidance goals ("I want to avoid doing poorly") *depressed* performance about the same amount as approach goals ("I want to do well") improved it.[2]

To see how this applies in the workplace, think back to Audrey, the director of the innovation agency we met in the last chapter. She says that she often finds herself setting an intention to stay focused on building constructive relationships, rather than scoring short-term points in her difficult conversations. What specific goals might she then set for herself? As she prepares for her next challenging meeting, here are two things she might say to herself:

➡ Avoidance goal: "If we go off track, I'm not going to lose my cool; I'm not going to get obsessed with his petty comments; I'm going to do my best to stop this meeting from going wrong."

➡ Approach goal: "If we go off track, I'm going to remind myself what really matters; I'm going to remember to smile; I'm going to ask great questions, to make sure he feels heard."

Both are ways of describing what she wants. But merely reading the words creates a different vibe, doesn't it? The first makes me feel slightly worried about Audrey, frankly. The second leaves me feeling more optimistic about her chances of having a good meeting. And those instincts are correct.

Why? It goes back to the discover-defend axis that I described in The Science Essentials. When we're thinking hard about something undesirable that we need to avoid—in Audrey's case, the need to avoid getting into an argument with a colleague—it flags a potential threat that our brain needs to defend against. And since that defensive response is a drain on mental resources, it leaves us a little less smart and less capable of achieving our aims. But if we instead frame our goals as wonderful things that we want more of, it's easier for us to stay in discovery mode—even if we're doing something challenging. And by keeping us in a more open-minded, intelligent state of mind, that improves our chances of success.

Martin, our airplane strategist, previously worked for a company where everyone seemed driven by fear of failure rather than excitement about possible success. "Everyone was constantly on the defensive. I kept on falling into what I call my 'negative mind-trap'—telling myself, 'If this fails, I'll have no money.' It had a big impact. I was often depressed coming to work, and it was hard for anyone to do their best work." He was struck by the difference on days when he framed his goals more positively. "There were some days when I managed to think more about the prize, the possibilities, and it would flip my mood and my productivity very quickly—things would move fast for a day or two. I'd really feel like I was getting things done."

Here are some practical ways to reframe your goals to keep you in discovery rather than defensive mode:

➡ Ask yourself: "What positive outcome am I seeking? And what do I need to start doing, or do more of, to get that ideal outcome?"

➡ If any of your goals are about avoiding something, turn them around and ask what good thing you'd need to do more of to achieve the same outcome. (For example, instead of saying "Find a way to stop losing customers," try "Find a way to make our customer proposition irresistible.")

As a no-nonsense type, Martin is keen to add this advice on setting approach goals: "Framing things positively doesn't mean you have to be fake. I had a boss who was a horrible person but walked around with a big smile plastered on his face. That's not what this is about. It's just about articulating your goals in a way that helps you achieve them, in your own genuine style."

### Find a "Personal Why"

In The Science Essentials, I mentioned that researchers have found a sense of autonomy to be a crucial component of human motivation. If we're to exert effort, we generally like feeling we have a degree of control in what we're doing, and some choices to call our own. Correspondingly, scientists have found that we're more likely to achieve a challenging goal if we've decided for ourselves why it's worth succeeding. Or to use psychological terminology: *intrinsic* motivation—where we're doing things because they feel personally meaningful or satisfying—tends to lead to higher performance than the kind of *extrinsic* motivation that comes from seeking to meet other people's expectations.[3] In fact, extrinsic and intrinsic goals work so differently that they're processed in different parts of our brain. Requests from other people activate brain areas strongly associated with self-control and self-discipline; by contrast, goals we set for ourselves engage areas associated with our desires and needs.[4] They feel like things we want, rather than things we have to do.

The upshot? Not everything on our to-do list can be an act of personal passion. But the science tells us that we're more likely to get something done if we take a moment to think about why it matters to us personally. Going back to the example earlier in the chapter: if you've decided that you should ask your colleagues to help you unblock progress on a project, you might first ask yourself "Why does it matter to me to get them involved?" Perhaps that question reminds you why you cared about the darned project in the first place—which in turn encourages you to take the leap and ask for help in this morning's meeting. (Likewise: Why did it matter to me to help Lucas's team gel? Because it's my personal mission to help everyone have a good day at work. And so on.) Reconnecting with the "personal why" can be just enough to give ourselves an extra push toward action when we need it.

Of course, when we're handed a task by someone else, the "why" may not be as immediately clear to us. But even then, it's usually not too hard to find a way to link an assigned task to things that matter to *us*, even if it's a tangential connection. We can still ask:

➡ "What bigger aspiration or value of *mine* does this task speak to?"

➡ "How does this request support something that matters to *me*?"

I once heard a nice example of this kind of "personal why" from a community hospital CEO. David was new to his organization and still not a familiar face to staff, so he decided to spend a day working undercover as an anonymous orderly to get some insight into how it felt on the front lines of his organization. David busied himself ferrying patients from the emergency room to wards and from wards to operating theaters, learning a little more about his hospital with every step. At one point he came across a guy who was prodding a swinging door with a screwdriver. David asked the handyman what he was doing. The man looked up and said, "I'm fixing the hinge so it opens more easily. It's too stiff, so when you're pushing patients on gurneys through the doors it gives them a nasty jolt. That's not going to help them get better, is it?" Of course, the handyman had been handed a task list for the day by his boss, and he was steadily working through it. It could have been dull, a grind. But in his mind, the goal was not just to fix the door. It was to reduce harm to patients. And making the connection to something he cared about encouraged him to treat the tasks more like his own intrinsic goals, giving him more satisfaction and—all the evidence suggests—resulting in better performance, too.

## Bite-Sized Chunks

When you're planning your day, it can be tempting to come up with a laundry list of ambitious to-dos. But research suggests we achieve more when our goals are focused and achievable. To see why, think back to how our brain's reward system works. While achieving goals rewards us with a spike of motivating pleasure, *not* achieving them does the opposite. So it's usually better to break your big audacious goals into a series of small step-by-step goals that are within your reach. That way, the neurochemicals in your reward system will motivate you to continue, rather than dousing you with de-energizing feelings of disappointment.

For example, having "learn French" as a goal is unlikely to result in much progress today; it feels too big and amorphous to be on anything but the "someday" part of your to-do list. But you could probably break the goal down into bite-sized chunks that are genuinely feasible today, such as "do fifteen minutes of Internet research to find best-rated local French classes" or "call Nicole to ask her advice on learning French." And this kind of disaggregation is a good recipe for getting things done.

Martin, the aviation strategist, has a bold vision for what he's trying to achieve in his work, and many of his projects are large and long-term in nature. But he's learned to set small daily aspirations that give his brain a constant flow of reward. "I have a spreadsheet that lists the projects I'm working on, and for each one I've identified the *very next thing* to do on each of them. So I always know the small next step that I need to take. I've found that if you break one goal down into three smaller ones, it feels more doable and you get three times the pleasure of scratching them off the to-do list." For example, Martin's work often involves writing project proposals, something he says is "the least fun part of my job." To keep himself motivated, Martin never just sets a goal to "write a proposal." He splits it into "gather data," "create budget," "do a rough outline," and so on. "And each tick, tick, tick gives me a sense of progress," he says, which neatly spurs him on to the next task.

### Implementation Intentions, aka "When-Then" Plans

Finally, to make sure we accomplish our goals, it helps to get very specific about what we'll do and when we'll do it. Just compare these two versions of Audrey's goal, for example:

➡ "I'm going to be more collaborative in my conversations today."

➡ "When the other person frowns or raises issues, then I'll stop to listen properly and then ask questions to find out more."

Which leaves you with the clearer idea about what she should actually do? The second is much more tangible, much easier to imagine her succeeding at, isn't it?

That's because it contains a clear "when-then" rule, which says, "*when* X happens, *then* I will do Y." This kind of rule—known to scientists as an *implementation intention*—takes much less effort for our brains to handle than an abstract concept like "being collaborative," since it leaves no doubt about what to do when the time comes. By bridging the gap in our brain between abstract hopes and concrete steps, the "when-then" formulation creates a well-known recipe for meeting our goals.[5] Psychologist Heidi Grant Halvorson, at Columbia's Motivation Science Center, found in a review of more than two hundred studies that setting implementation intentions makes people as much as *three times* more likely to achieve their aspirations.[6]

Here's a small "when-then" example that has helped me achieve a daily goal. I'm not a morning person, and I've only ever been productive in the early hours because I had colleagues expecting me to show up. So when I set up my own consulting business and became my own boss, I knew there was a real risk I'd waste the first part of the day. My husband suggested that I get into a new habit of taking a brisk morning walk to wake up my mind before starting work. It sounded like a good new routine to adopt. But when I tried it, I'd often end up dawdling sleepily in the kitchen while reading email. So I wheeled out the "when-then" guns, and set myself some rules: "*When* I wake up on a weekday morning, *then* I will throw on some clothes and go make coffee to put in my travel mug. *When* I leave the house, *then* I'll pick up the spare keys next to the door and go for a twenty-minute walk. *When* I get back, *then* I'll check email for the first time."

To you, this little routine may seem like nothing. But these extremely specific and practical "when-thens" helped me to change the habits of a lifetime. And they're a wonderful way of making sure that your own goals get a little armor plating before going into battle.

## CREATE A BRAIN-FRIENDLY TO-DO LIST

Once we've got positive intentions and clear goals, most of us choose to keep ourselves on track by writing ourselves a task list of some sort. And there are many ways to create a to-do list; you might favor a fancy app, a treasured notebook, or scribbles on the back of your hand. Whatever works for you, works for you. But there are some to-do list essentials that we should all know if we want to help our brains navigate the day, based on the science of working memory, motivation, and goal pursuit. I don't always see people applying these brain-friendly essentials, so here's a checklist for you to consider:

➡ **Write it down as soon as it comes to mind.** Never waste your brain's precious working memory by trying to hold your tasks or ideas in your head. Use your intelligence for getting things done, rather than trying to remember what you need to do. That means having a process for capturing to-dos as soon as they occur to you, even if you then end up transferring them to a master list.

➡ **Only keep today's tasks in view.** You might have a grand list of tasks you'd like to complete in the coming weeks or months. But once you've decided what you really need and want to get done today, work off *that* list, and hide the rest. As long as your longer-term items are visible, they'll use up a little of your brain's processing capacity—and may even depress you a little if your long list is very long.

➡ **Make it satisfying to check off.** If you're online, give yourself a box to check, and a ping or a swoosh to hear. If you're working on paper, give yourself the satisfaction of a big bold line through everything you've done. The more rewarding it feels to track your progress, the more your brain will tend to spur you toward getting things done.

➡ **Be realistic about what you can do in a day.** Progress feels good to your brain's reward system; failure doesn't. Do you have five things you'd like to tackle today, but know you probably only have time for three? It's better to feel great about nailing three tasks. If you succeed and find you've got more time, you'll be flushed with motivation to seek out one or two more tasks.

➡ Include mind-body maintenance. Put exercise, rest, and other physical health goals on your list alongside your other tasks. If you take a moment to put "take a walk" on the list, you're way more likely to build it into your day rather than let it be crowded out by other demands—just as defining goals for anything makes it more likely you'll get it done.

## Setting Great Goals

Take a moment now to think about your priorities for today.

➡ Set some behavioral goals. *Personally,* what behavior of yours will support your intentions for the day? *Specifically,* what tangible actions can you plan to take? Put these on your to-do list along with your regular tasks.

➡ Articulate your goals for the win. Phrase them so that they're positive, meaningful, feasible, and situation-specific.
  • Create "approach" goals. Make sure your goals are about doing desirable things, or doing more of them, rather than avoiding bad things happening. If they're negative in tone, turn them around.
  • Find a personal why. Can you articulate why the goal matters to you or how it will benefit something you care about?
  • Break off bite-sized chunks. If the actions to take are unclear, break your goal down into smaller, bite-sized chunks. Get especially clear on the very first step to take to make progress.
  • Make a "when-then" plan. Define clear situational prompts (*"when* X happens, *then* I will do Y") to increase the chances that you'll get your most important goals met today.

➡ Create a brain-friendly to-do list. Whichever approach you take to task management, make sure you don't overload your brain's working memory and that you feed your reward system.

# THREE

# Reinforcing Your Intentions

You're now set to take a much more deliberate approach to your day, one that acknowledges that your aims, attitude, and assumptions can deeply influence the way you experience the world. Your goals are clear, and they're articulated in a way that's going to give you the best possible chance of success. Now I'm going to show you how to raid the scientific toolbox for techniques that will help you stay true to your good intentions as you tackle the most important or elusive of your priorities. The three tools are mental contrasting, priming, and mind's-eye rehearsal.

## MENTAL CONTRASTING

An excellent way to reinforce your positive intentions, strangely enough, is to make sure you spend a little time on the negatives. By this, I mean thinking honestly about what's likely to get in the way of achieving your goals, so you can address those obstacles head-on. It's a technique that's called "mental contrasting," because you're comparing your ideal outcome with the pesky reality of day-to-day life. (Perhaps some of you have been itching for this, after all that Pollyanna positivity.)

It's reminiscent of a phenomenon that Jim Collins termed the "Stockdale Paradox" in his business book *Good to Great*. The paradox takes its name from a two-sided coping strategy adopted by U.S. Navy Vice Admiral James Stockdale, who survived eight terrible years as a Vietnamese prisoner of war while many around him lost hope and perished. Stockdale observed that it wasn't just the pessimists who had lacked the psychological strength to endure; it was the blind optimists, too, because of the continual disappointment they experienced when their positive assertions (e.g., "We'll be out by Christmas") failed to materialize. Stockdale described it like this: "You must never confuse faith that you will prevail in the end—which you can never afford to lose—with the discipline to confront the most brutal facts of your current reality, whatever they might be."[1]

Today's psychologists have confirmed that this type of realistic idealism is just the ticket for ensuring we turn our intentions into actions. We're not facing challenges as awful as staying alive as a POW, thank goodness, but every day we face hurdles such as uncooperative technology or unexpected last-minute requests from colleagues. Gabriele Oettingen and Peter Gollwitzer, experts on the psychology of motivation at New York University, discovered that people are far more likely to achieve their goals if they think hard about both the *outcome* they want and the *obstacles* they're facing, and plan for both. Their twenty years of research have found this to be true across multiple spheres of life, including professional endeavors, academic test scores, and even romantic relationships.[2] They found that mental contrasting works especially well with the kind of goals I described in the last chapter—those that are broadly achievable and framed positively—since they're the sort of goals that naturally help you feel good about what you're trying to do. That means you won't be daunted by the small reality check that mental contrasting provides.

To benefit from mental contrasting as you're making your own plans for the day, ask yourself:

➡ What's most likely to get in the way of you succeeding in meeting your goals for today?

➡ What's your "when-then" contingency plan to prevent that obstacle from getting in the way?

In the last chapter, I talked about the way that the "when-then" technique had finally helped me achieve a cherished goal: to go for a morning walk before starting work. But I bulletproofed that morning walk even further when I acknowledged that bad weather ("Ugh, it's raining, maybe I won't go") and the temptations of a hot shower ("I'll just have a quick shower . . . oops, too late to go now") were serious potential obstacles to taking that walk. So I added a couple of when-then plans to deal with each one:

➡ "*When* I'm tempted to shower, *then* I will tell myself to just throw on yesterday's clothes, remind myself that I'm not going to meet anyone I know, and tell myself that I'll have an extra-long shower as a reward after the walk."

➡ "*When* it's raining, *then* I'll wear my waterproof jacket and peaked hat, which I'll keep by the front door for easy access."

A little of this kind of contingency planning will go a long way toward guaranteeing your success, too.

## PRIMING THE PUMP

Do you have a favorite song that always perks you up? Or a place where you always seem to do your best thinking—perhaps an airy room or a cherished window seat? On the flip side, maybe some things are guaranteed to make your heart sink—like hearing the phrase "two-hour conference call," for example. How is it possible that such tiny prompts have such a palpable effect on us? Are we imagining things? Probably not. Not entirely, anyway, thanks to the highly associative nature of our brains.

Every one of your thoughts, feelings, and actions corresponds to a network of neurons firing electrochemical signals in your brain. One batch of neurons fires when you think of the color red; a slightly different batch of neurons fires when you encounter something orange. Other groups of neurons come to life when you hear a particular song, snag that precious window seat, dial into a conference call, and so on. And each of those networks is in turn linked to many others, representing all the things you associate with that song, seat, or call.

For example, your neural network for the word "orange" is probably linked to your network for the word "red," given that they're both colors. And "red" is in turn connected with a whole number of other associated thoughts and memories in your mind, including perhaps "fire engine" and "sunset." To illustrate this, University of California psychologist Elizabeth Loftus created the following simplified example of the sort of neural maps that many of us might have in our brains, reflecting a lifetime of associations between various objects, experiences, and ideas.[3]

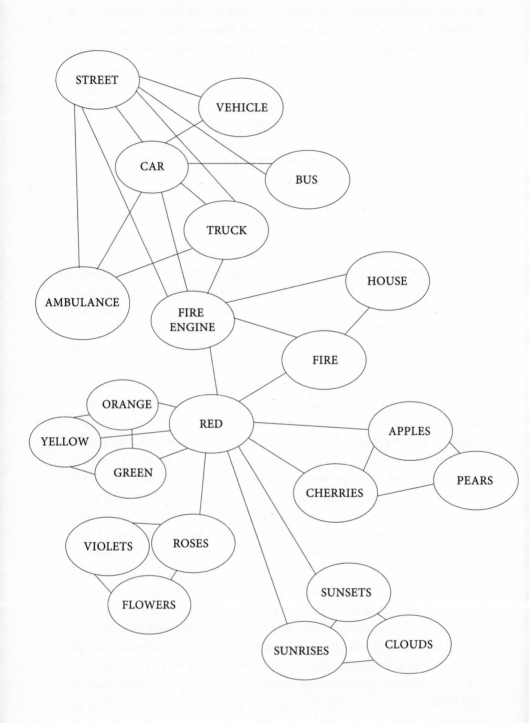

And here's the thing. Once one small corner of a neural network gets activated, it can act like a falling domino, prompting a cascade of activity in connected neurons. So if you were the owner of the neural map shown in the illustration above, and you encountered the color red in any form, you might find that it unexpectedly triggered a vivid memory of a gorgeous vacation sunset. Seeing a fire engine might unaccountably make you feel like buying cherries. A thought like this can pop into your consciousness seemingly out of nowhere, if you encounter a cue that your brain somehow associates with that specific thought—a phenomenon known to scientists as the *spreading activation effect.*

So if you once spent an afternoon cranking out great work while settled into that window seat, your "window seat" neural network might be connected with the one representing "extremely productive and focused behavior." As a result, you might find yourself getting a subtle efficiency boost whenever you sit there. Meanwhile, your neural network representing "conference call" might be connected to the network for "feeling bored"—which means you might find yourself feeling weary merely at the thought of dialing the phone number. An upbeat song might connect to the memory of a fun evening with friends where that song was playing, which in turn connects to your brain's network related to a happy mood. Recalling one aspect of that evening—the song—might end up rebooting other parts of the memory, including your emotional state. So you listen to the song as you're heading into work, and you feel happy—perhaps conscious it's because of that fun evening, but perhaps not.

You'll notice I'm saying all these connections *might* get made. They're not guaranteed. As you'll know if you've ever struggled to remember someone's name, neural connections don't always fire up on demand or in predictable ways. But neurons are more likely to connect if they've often done so in the past—which is why it's easier to remember the name of our spouse than that of a casual acquaintance. There's a saying in neuroscience that "neurons that fire together, wire together," reflecting the fact that neural connections get stronger the more they're used.[4] So in the case of our uplifting song, the more we associate it with feeling good, the stronger our brain's connection becomes between "that great song" and "feeling happy."

That's my excuse for humming Donna Summer's "I Feel Love" to myself before client workshops. The song does a good job of firing me up before I speak to a roomful of people, because it's associated in my mind with a Blue Man Group show I enjoyed some years ago. I found their performance hugely energizing, and "I Feel Love" was the high-octane song they played in their finale. So whenever I hear it, a small part of my brain launches the "feel energized" routine. It's a nice little nudge toward being ready for action.

And that's the basic mechanism behind a large body of research that suggests quite small cues can push our thoughts, feelings, and actions in one direction or another. For example, in one study, pairs of volunteers were asked to play a two-person game where each player got to choose between a collaborative strategy or an individualistic strategy. When the exercise was introduced to them as "The Community Game," two-thirds of the volunteers chose the collaborative strategy. But when it was called "The Wall Street Game," two-thirds chose the individualistic one. Why? Because the words triggered a bunch of associations in people's brains, rightly or wrongly, and those associations influenced (or "primed," as scientists say) the choices they felt like making.

Similar effects have been found with physical and visual cues, too. In one experiment, the mere presence of business-related objects—a briefcase, a boardroom table—made people more hard-nosed in negotiations with another volunteer, without any mention of Wall Street.[5] Another study found that after people were shown a picture of a library, they went on to speak more softly.[6] In a third study, where volunteers were given a test to measure their concentration, those who were asked to wear a lab coat made half the number of errors of those who wore their street clothes—presumably thanks to an association between lab coats and high academic performance. Sure enough, when the coat wearers were told that the white coat belonged to a painter (rather than a scientist or doctor), their scores dropped.[7]

These experiments would seem to present clear recommendations on how you should start every morning: put on a *doctor's* lab coat and dunk inspirational objects in your coffee. Of course, it's not that easy (if it were, this would be a very short book). No single experiment can prove that a particular cue will inspire particular behavior, not least because each person's brain has different associations with a given cue. For example, fire engines might have been yellow rather than red in the town where you grew up. You might hate Donna Summer and find nothing but positive connotations in the idea of a two-hour conference call. But there's little disagreement that the cues around us can provide small but sometimes useful nudges to our state of mind—especially if we're *deliberately* exposing ourselves to influences that we know are likely to trigger helpful associations in our brains (like my Donna Summer trick).

To apply this in your everyday life, think back to your intentions, and consider the kinds of thoughts and feelings you want to encourage in yourself today. Ask yourself:

➡ Which words or phrases might help remind you of those intentions?
  • Try writing a "note to self" that prompts you to keep this language in mind today.
  • Consider using that language on your to-do list, or in your meetings and emails.

Your language doesn't need to be poetic to be an effective prompt. Ever since political strategist James Carville coined the phrase "It's the economy, stupid" during Bill Clinton's 1992 U.S. Presidential campaign, politicians of all stripes have used variations on that blunt phrase to remind them of whatever they need to keep top of mind while talking to voters. Clichés are fine, too, as long as they speak to you. For example, if you've got an intention to say less and listen more in a meeting today, scrawling "less is more" in your notebook might be an excellent cue to lodge in the corner of your field of vision.

➡ Can you make your surroundings a metaphor for your intentions? Choose a particularly apt place to work, or consider whether you can tweak your regular workspace. For example:
  • To encourage open-mindedness, consider finding an open space to sit and think. (Perhaps even go outdoors to walk and talk, if you're having a conversation.[8])
  • For creativity, you might try to sit in a place that's full of art or quirkiness.
  • To have a relaxed discussion, choose a cozy space rather than a boardroom.
  • Need to think particularly clearly today? Clear your desktop or workspace. Brighten the lighting.

Martin, our aviation man, thinks a lot about how his surroundings can either detract from or support his intentions. He has a general day-to-day goal of remaining undistracted, and he vouches for the last of the examples above. "I always had a cluttered desk. But I discovered that when I was struggling to stay on track with the intentions I'd set in the morning, it really helped to literally remove everything from my desk. Clear the space, and I suddenly feel clearheaded. The effect is nothing short of miraculous."

## MIND'S-EYE REHEARSAL

If you play a sport like golf or tennis, have you ever tried to imagine yourself hitting a perfect shot before you swing your arm? If you think it helps, research suggests you're probably right, for two reasons. First, our brains activate in much the same way when we're visualizing something as when we're experiencing it for real. Researchers have found the overlap to be between 60 percent and 90 percent.[9] Second, the more we rehearse a particular behavior, the stronger the associated neural pathways become in our brain—making it easier for us to summon that behavior when we most need it. It's why practice makes perfect. So when we take the time to visualize ourselves handling a situation with aplomb, we're effectively giving our brain the chance to rehearse—making it easier for us to fire up the right neural connections when we're in the heat of the moment.

There's a great deal of research confirming the power of this kind of mind's-eye rehearsal. I especially like an experiment by Harvard researcher Alvaro Pascual-Leone and his colleagues, where two groups of beginners were taught to play a sequence of notes on the piano, then asked to practice it for a week, and tested throughout the week for their accuracy. The twist was that one of the groups was only allowed to "practice" in their minds. They would sit in front of a keyboard for two hours a day, but they weren't allowed to touch it; instead, they visualized themselves playing the notes. The other group was allowed to actually play the notes, rehearsing for the same amount of time. The result? Both groups learned to play the sequence. On day three, they were equally accurate. On day five, the physical practice group had edged ahead. But giving the "visualizers" just one hands-on practice session allowed them to catch up with the group that had played every day.[10]

Doug, the CEO of a major online retailer in China, uses mental rehearsal a great deal in his professional life. "It's become hugely important for me whenever I'm going into a challenging situation such as a big presentation," he says. "Of course I do the normal type of preparation—bullet points on cards and so on. But on the morning of the day I'm giving my talk, I also take a moment to imagine how I want the session to go. Then I think back to a previous difficult presentation that went well, and I remember how I handled it. I take a deep breath, and I think about each aspect of that successful memory and also the physical sensation of that past experience. The process relaxes me because it makes me feel sure that I have the resources to deal with the challenge ahead."

Note that effective visualization isn't the same as the kind of affirmations espoused by those in the New Age "positive thinking" movement. Doug wasn't just muttering "Believe you'll achieve it and you will." He was doing some mental contrasting and practical when-then planning. He imagined the specifics of the challenge ahead, and visualized exactly how he would address and overcome those challenges, based on his past experience. Likewise, the pianists didn't just talk about or imagine themselves as successful musicians; they steadily worked through each note in their mind. The scientific evidence on visualization supports the benefits of realistic mind's-eye rehearsal, not untethered wishful thinking.

I'd also highlight that mind's-eye rehearsal, when done well, takes advantage of as much sensory information as possible: visual images, yes, but also sounds, feelings, smells, even tastes. Doing this helps to activate a richer set of neural connections in our brains. So when Doug prepares to give a presentation, he pictures a room where he gave a great speech in the past, *and* he also brings to mind as many other details of that positive experience as possible: the sound of his voice, the things others said, and the feeling in his chest. Perhaps even the snack he ate before giving the speech.

Doug adds this advice for making maximum use of the technique: "What ideally happens is that over time you build up a playlist of successful memories to call on. You might call on one memory for 'I want to do a good presentation,' and another memory for 'I need to be supremely patient and tolerant today.' With some practice, I find you can visualize those memories just a moment before you need them—literally as you're walking into the situation."

Here are some practical step-by-step ways to use mind's-eye rehearsal to reinforce your intentions:

➡ **Relive past glories.** Think about the positive intention you have for the day. Identify an example from your past, where you behaved and felt just as you'd like to today. Then find a quiet place where you can close your eyes and sit comfortably.
  - Take a few deep breaths. (It will help you engage more of your brain if you can also notice how your body feels, acknowledge any sounds you can hear around you, and observe any patterns on the back of your closed eyelids.)
  - Now think about your positive past experience. In your mind's eye, look around, recall what you and other people said, what you were thinking; notice any feelings or sensations you remember.
  - Once you've reexperienced that memory fully, open your eyes. If you can, write down what stands out in your recollection. Note any images or phrases that might help you quickly reconnect with the scene.

➡ **Rehearse today's challenge.** Vividly imagine yourself walking through the situation.
  - Think about your intentions and goals for the challenging task, conversation, or meeting you're preparing for. Consider which aspects of the situation may be difficult.
  - Then, close your eyes and visualize yourself handling it all beautifully, from start to finish. Play the full movie in your mind, with the sounds, sights, and sensations you expect or want to have.

## BRINGING IT ALL TOGETHER:
## BEING DELIBERATE ABOUT THE DAY

Russell is the brand director for a large hotel chain, responsible for the company's marketing and publicity, as well as a part of their product development process. Recent "products" have been as big as a city hotel concept and as small as a slightly improved pillow; judging by the enthusiasm with which he talks about both, it's clear that he loves his job. His hours are long, though, so Russell works hard to make the most of the time he puts in. And that starts with the way he sets up his day.

"In the evening, I always think about the two or three things that really need to happen tomorrow," he says. "Then, in my first hour in the office, I think about what I want to achieve with the day, what I need to bring to the meetings I'm having. Which might be an idea or some analysis, but it's also about visualizing who I want to 'be' in front of the people I'm meeting—what I want to project in how I behave—as well as how I'm going to overcome any obstacles in my path. I do that thinking in the morning, because once I'm into the day I'm back-to-back and it's like running a ten-hour marathon. And I find that this small amount of preparation makes the most of everything I do later in the day. You've got limited energy and attention, so you really want to make sure you're putting it in the right place. You've got to make some conscious decisions about what matters."

He also checks his assumptions about the situations and people he's about to encounter. "I remind myself to go in expecting the best. I know it will affect my perceptions of the day," he says. Sometimes the unexpected happens, of course. "You do have to allow for left-field stuff. You need to have the capacity to handle the unexpected. But it's easier to respond in a way you'll feel proud of if you've decided before-hand what your North Star should be, so you know your real priorities and what you want to stand for."

He's not shy about reinforcing his intentions with a few priming cues. "I admit I sometimes choose my clothes the night before, depending on how I want to feel the next day. Sometimes it's just a question of deciding not to wear a tie. But I remember once I wore red laces on some black shoes and I was amazed how much people remarked on it being a creative thing to do. So now, if I know I'm going to meet people where I want to feel like a creative type, I might throw that into the mix."

Russell says his highly intentional approach to life has made his career far more enjoyable and successful over the years. "Frankly, I think it's allowed me to spot opportunities I would otherwise have missed, because I always take that time to get clear about what I want."

## REINFORCING YOUR INTENTIONS

Consider taking a moment now to revisit your intentions and goals for the day ahead. For the most important of them:

➡ **Mental contrasting.** What's most likely to get in the way of you achieving what you hope to do? What can you do to reduce the chance that this obstacle derails you—ideally by making a specific "when-then" plan?

➡ **Priming.** What cues can you use to remind yourself to stay on track today? Are there words or phrases that will help remind you of your intentions? How can you make your surroundings a good metaphor for your intentions?

➡ **Mind's-eye rehearsal.** Take a moment to visualize the most important part of your day going exactly as you hope. What will you be doing to overcome the challenges in your path? How will that look and feel? Can you recall a time in the past where you behaved just as you want to behave today, and bring that vividly to mind?

# PART II

# Productivity

## Making the Hours in the Day Go Further

The main thing is to keep the main thing the main thing.

—STEPHEN COVEY

Once you've set your intentions, established motivating goals, and taken steps to reinforce those intentions, how do you best organize your time and effort to achieve your aims? How can you fit it all into the hours you have, so that at the end of the day you can look back with satisfaction?

Let's start by acknowledging a basic truth: most of us have too much to do. Between the 1970s and the 2000s, the average American added nearly two hundred hours of work to his or her year—a whole extra month.[1] And our working hours aren't just longer; they're more hectic, too. We're handling more informal demands on our time than before, thanks to the steady, always-on flow of messages and alerts we now receive. Whether it's a witty instant message from a colleague or a "check this out" social media recommendation, every interruption steals a moment of our attention.

So we work hard, yet never seem to end up with a to-do list that's shorter than the length of our day. We focus on whatever is blinking most brightly, rather than on what's truly important and in line with our intentions for the day. And thanks to our long hours, we're probably not functioning at our best. There's evidence to suggest that our productivity and cognitive performance decline once our working day stretches beyond eight hours, which means our ninth, tenth, and eleventh hours make a progressively less satisfying dent in our workload.[2]

A couple of years ago, all this juggling and striving came to a head for Anthony. A digital marketing expert with two small children and a serious running habit, these days he seems full of an enthusiastic energy that makes him look younger than his years. But back then, he was ground down by his day-to-day life. "I was working too much, always overcommitting, and dealing with endless emails. I tried to take control, but failed. At my company, there was a sort of cultural 'presenteeism'—you needed to look like you were always present, always working. It was toxic." He ended up burning out. "I was completely exhausted, and I realized it wasn't sustainable. I decided something had to change."

Anthony had been doing his best to cover all the bases by multitasking and skipping breaks. But as he learned more about the science of personal productivity and prioritization, he realized that there was a better way to manage the demands of his professional life—one that didn't involve chasing his tail quite as hard, or swearing quite as loudly.

In this part of the book, I'll share what Anthony and others have discovered after putting this science into practice. I'll show you how to plan your time in ways that will make you feel less tired, more alert, and more in control. I'll also talk about what to do when you're overloaded or when you really, finally, truly want to stop procrastinating. After incorporating these ideas into your working day, you should find that the same number of hours will suddenly go a lot further, leaving you with a better feeling of accomplishment and balance at the end of the day.

# FOUR

# Singletasking

We tend to believe that by doing several things at once, we can fit more into the day. So we try to have a phone conversation while we're reading a document or clicking our way around the Internet. We scan our messages during a meeting, or even during dinner. We chat to passing colleagues while trying to write an overdue report and scarfing our lunch. "Busy, busy, busy," we think to ourselves.

As well as making us feel that we're working hard to stay on top of things, this kind of multitasking can give us a secret little kick. The brain's reward system likes novelty and human contact, especially when it's unexpected. So each ping and buzz of our favorite device carries the promise of a potential reward; every interruption brings the possibility of an interesting or amusing tidbit. Even if it usually ends up being spam, it's hard to resist.

And yet research unequivocally shows that multitasking damages our productivity—which means, to put it bluntly, it lengthens our days. Trying to do more than one thing at once not only slows us down, but causes us to make more mistakes—with the resulting rework slowing us down even more. We *feel* busier, but we're doing less, and doing it less well.

The toll that multitasking takes on our work isn't marginal, either. René Marois, director of the Human Information Processing Laboratory at Vanderbilt University, showed that people doing two tasks simultaneously took up to 30 percent longer and made twice as many errors as those who completed the same tasks in sequence—findings that have been replicated time and again by other scientists.[1] Other research has found that multitasking also hurts the quality of our decision making. For example, one group of volunteers was asked to select the best location for a warehouse after assessing the pros and cons of various options. When they had to juggle a new request for information—the sort of thing that happens to us frequently at work—the volunteers took longer to decide, and ultimately made poorer choices.[2]

Meanwhile, a study of Microsoft employees found that after they were interrupted by an email, it took them fifteen minutes to fully regain their train of thought, whether they replied to the email or not.[3] Instant messages weren't much better; it still took more than ten minutes to get back into the groove. Just multiply that loss of focus by the number of interruptions you get in your average day, and you begin to see why it might not be good for your productivity to be constantly online.

Why does multitasking cause such a loss of speed, accuracy, and wisdom? It goes back to the limitations of our brain's deliberate system. While we might think we're processing tasks in parallel, our deliberate system is actually rapidly switching our attention between each activity. Switch on "reading email," switch off "listening to our colleague." Switch on "colleague," switch off "email." And each of those switches costs our brain a little time and energy.[4]

To see this switching cost in action, try this basic exercise:

→ Say "abcdefg," then immediately after that say "1234567." Notice how long it takes you to do this. Perhaps even time yourself.

→ Then, interleave the two: say "a1b2c3d4e5f6g7." Notice how much longer it takes you to do the same amount of "work" while switching back and forth between letters and numbers—and how much more mental effort it requires from you.

So it's no wonder we say things like "I can't hear myself think" when people are talking at us and our phone is ringing. We make it harder for our brain's deliberate system to do its job when we ask it to juggle. And since emotional regulation—staying cool and collected—is also part of the deliberate system's job, loading it more heavily tends to affect our composure, too. One study found that while people naturally get a little anxious when asked to handle a brand-new task, they report twice the increase in anxiety if they're interrupted while trying to complete it.[5]

The upshot? While having a day full of variety can be energizing, you don't want that variety from minute to minute if you want to work fast, stay sharp, and feel calm. Multitasking can feel like a stimulating and efficient way to deal with having lots to do, but we're actually far more productive if we *singletask*—that is, if we do one thing at a time.

## But Aren't There Exceptions?

Unlike our brain's deliberate system, the automatic system *is* capable of parallel processing. So if one of your tasks truly requires no conscious thought from you, it's possible to do something else at the same time. Driving a car is often cited as a good example of an automatic task, which is why we're able to chat with a passenger at the same time as driving along quiet stretches of road where nothing surprising happens.

But as soon as that simple task becomes more complex—if, say, another car pulls out suddenly in front of us—driving is no longer an automatic task. It requires conscious attention from our deliberate system. And at that point, we can't chat *and* react safely to the changing situation in front of us. That's why one in every five serious crashes is caused by a distracted driver, and why police reports suggested that traffic accidents fell by 40 percent in Abu Dhabi and 20 percent in Dubai when BlackBerry's networks in those places failed briefly in 2011.[6]

There is some evidence that a tiny, single-digit percentage number of people have brains that seem to work differently. David Strayer, a psychologist based in Utah, has been looking at the very rare phenomenon of "supertaskers," and they do exist. But frankly, you're either one of these people or you're not, and the stark truth is that most people—even readers of this book—are not. Multitasking more frequently doesn't make you better at it, either. In fact, habitual multitaskers have been found to take *longer* to switch between tasks than occasional multitaskers—perhaps because they've lost the knack of focusing for any length of time.[7] And ironically, research suggests that people who are most confident of their ability to multitask are in fact the worst at it.[8]

## BATCH YOUR TASKS, ZONE YOUR DAY

So let's understand what an ideal day looks like for our singletasking brains. The first implication of the research is that you can work fewer hours, and work less hard during those hours, by batching your tasks more effectively. By batching, I mean grouping together similar tasks, so you spend less time and energy switching between different types of activity. In the "a1b2c3 . . ." exercise I mentioned earlier, it's like handling all the letters first, in one batch, then handling the numbers together, in a second batch. Applied to your tasks, that means spending time on email. *Then* on deep thinking. And not mixing the two.

Anthony has successfully lightened his workload by applying this batching technique to his daily tasks as much as possible. For example, part of his work involves finding and sharing interesting articles with his clients. "You think it's one to-do, but it actually involves several different types of activity," he says. "There's the task of *gathering* information, which means my mind needs to be wide open and in scanning mode. Then there's *digesting*, which means I have to stop and think. Then there's *sharing*, where I have to make some decisions: what's worth passing on, to whom? And gathering, digesting, and sharing require different mental states." Anthony used to mix them together, but, as he says: "I used to get distracted as I went back and forth, because I was using different apps to gather and to share. I always had lots of windows open on my laptop, and each one was an invitation to go off at a tangent. So I found it's much better to chunk the different types of activity and tell myself, 'Now I'm *gathering* and I'm entirely focused on that'; 'Okay, now I'm *digesting* and I'm focused on that.' It takes a lot less time overall, and what I do is better-quality."

Anthony also decided to create some standard "zones" in his schedule each day: at least one chunk of time to think about the trickiest tasks of the day, and a couple of "email zones" when he handles as many incoming messages as possible. Sometimes he has to be opportunistic in deciding where to fit them, by looking at the slices of open space in his calendar. But knowing that he has dedicated time to tackle his inbox twice a day makes it far easier for him to focus on his other tasks in between, Anthony says, allowing him to reap the cognitive and emotional benefits of singletasking throughout his day.

Here are some suggestions on how to try this yourself:

➡ Batch your tasks into different types of work. What types of tasks do you have to do today? Which to-dos fit into which category? Here are some groupings you might try:
  • In-depth thinking or creative work
  • Responding to emails and messages

- Reading and researching
- Meetings (virtual or in-person)
- Personal projects
- Administrative tasks

On the last category, Anthony says he borrows Benjamin Franklin's approach of describing the benighted "admin" category as "putting things in their places," or PTITP. "Everybody's heart sinks when they think of admin. But 'putting things in their places' sounds like the sort of thing any sensible person would want to do. Someone else I know calls it 'consolidation time,' for similar reasons."

➡ Then, identify your uninterrupted blocks of time. Look at your schedule for the day, and work out where you can identify blocks of uninterrupted time to devote to different types of tasks. Try to ringfence blocks of at least twenty to thirty minutes, as well as some longer ones of sixty to ninety minutes. If your schedule is highly fragmented, with meetings and calls scattered throughout the day, try to batch those interactions more closely together by asking someone to meet/talk a little later or earlier in the day. It's often possible to move appointments in this way, but typically we don't dare or bother to ask—and it's worth shooting someone the question if it means you can create a stretch of uninterrupted time somewhere in the day.

➡ Next, decide which batch of tasks fits into each block of time. The aim is to do less zigzagging across different tasks, with less jumping from writing a document to answering an email to picking up the phone. If you do nothing else, create one zone for more in-depth thinking/ creating, and one or two zones to crank through your messages. Give your biggest and best chunk of time to a task that needs deeper thinking, something that you know will take time to get into.

You'll also want to experiment with what times of day work best for different "zones" of work. Don't be too swayed by people who assert that there's only one time of day to do certain types of tasks. For example, some say you should *always* do creative tasks very early in the morning. This advice comes from the fact that there is indeed something special about the fluid kind of thinking that you have when you first wake up, and it's good to have a pad by your bed or shower to capture those thoughts. But you have to know yourself, and tune your schedule accordingly. If you're a night owl, your ideal routine is simply not going to be the same as that of the lark who loves to get up before 6:00 a.m. Whatever your "chronotype," late or early, recognize which time of day sees you at your best, and use it to work on your most complex tasks.[9]

## REMOVE DISTRACTIONS

The next big breakthrough for Anthony came from training himself to stay focused in the face of potential distractions. He knew that whatever activity he was busy with—a call, a chore, some writing—he would do it more intelligently and quickly if he could focus all his mental energies on the single task at hand. And, of course, the same is true for you.

Here's how I suggest you remove unnecessary distractions, to concentrate your brain's precious attention on whatever matters most right now:

➡ **Turn off alerts.** Once upon a time, the only alert we had to deal with was the ringing of a telephone. Imagine that! These days, we surround ourselves with devices clamoring for attention, from the buzzing and chiming of our smartphone to the visual pop-ups on our computer screens. As long as you have these notifications coming in all day long, you're not going to make best use of your time, since processing each ping takes a bite out of your brain's working memory, whether you respond to it or not. It's easy to turn them off when you really need to focus—for example, you can use your phone's airplane mode or turn off your computer's Wi-Fi access. For added IQ points, you can also permanently switch off the least valuable, most intrusive notifications in your device settings.

➡ **Remove temptation.** Every visual distraction uses another bit of your working memory and makes it a little more tempting to veer off into multitasking mode. So when you need to do some focused work, close your email program entirely. Close your browser, or at least the tabs you're not using. In the days before wireless Internet access, the author Jonathan Franzen locked down his focus on writing his novel *Freedom* by working on a computer that was unable to connect to the Internet—because he had glued an Ethernet cable into his laptop's network port, and then cut it off. More modern versions of Franzen's trick exist for the wireless age, in the form of apps that can block your access to certain websites for designated blocks of time (without requiring any glue).

➡ **Store stray thoughts in a "parking lot."** Even when you're doing your best to focus on one task, you may find that other thoughts pop into your mind as you're working, and some of them are too valuable to lose. Rather than using up mental space trying to hold on to these stray sparks, or being drawn into exploring them, get into the habit of immediately recording them (maybe on a sticky note or in a voice memo) so that you know you can come back to them when the time is right.

➡ **Build up your stamina.** Most of us are now unused to focusing our attention on one thing at a time, so it can feel hard at first. If that's true for you, start with just five minutes of undistracted time. Then acknowledge what you were able to get done in that time, and make sure to pat yourself on the back—perhaps by keeping a tally of the total amount of time you've managed to spend offline today. It's important to give yourself a small reward like this, because you need to compete with the minor thrill your brain gets from the constant stimulation of being online. Over time, gradually extend the length of your focused sessions until you're able to concentrate for longer without feeling antsy.

➡ **Time yourself.** When you're working on an important task, decide how long you want to spend properly focused on it. Then set a timer that counts down that number of minutes. It gives you a physical point of focus and allows you a burst of satisfaction when the timer runs down to zero and bleeps approvingly at you.

Anthony now gives himself different lengths of time for different types of tasks. "I read some research that said ninety minutes was optimal for focused, deep thought. So when I'm doing some harder thinking I set a timer to count down from ninety, and people can see that I'm in the middle of something. They can interrupt if they have to, but they know what it means." He says that sometimes he peters out after sixty-five or seventy minutes, "but that's okay, I've learned not to worry

about that." For less weighty work, he prefers twenty-five-minute seg-
ments. "Whatever length of time you choose, I find the timer makes
you feel more focused once you start, because it reminds you that it's
not going to stretch forever."

## What if the Boss Needs You?

Min is an executive in a telecommunications company, and she often
finds herself dealing directly with the company's global CEO. She describes him as "one of those perpetually hectic types, always firing
questions and demanding answers." She'd recently read an article that
helped her understand the perils of multitasking, and she was doing
well at changing some of her habits. She was checking her messages
in several defined batches each day, which meant that nobody waited
more than a couple of hours for a response from her. But it did mean
that people didn't necessarily get a response within minutes of trying
to reach her. And that included the CEO, who grumbled about it.

Min was tempted to cave in and set a customized alert on her
phone that would ping only when he got in touch. Before resorting
to that, however, she decided to try explaining what she was doing. "I
told him I was deliberately trying to be an email 'batcher' rather than a
'grazer,' because of the scientific evidence on multitasking. I explained
I was checking emails in four or five batches each day, which would still
allow a fast turnaround time." She says he nodded, almost persuaded,
but then asked, "What if I need to reach you really urgently? Checking
your email four times a day still means I could be waiting three hours
to get hold of you." Min thought for a moment. "How about I make
sure my assistant can reach me if you really need me?" He agreed.

Min reflected on the power of having that short conversation. "We
rarely take the time to talk about how we schedule our day, and why we
do it the way we do. But discussing it explicitly with my boss reduced
stress on both sides. It made a big difference to both of us."

## SINGLETASKING

Look at your schedule for today, and organize your tasks to allow your brain to work at its best (and get more done as a result). Try the following:

➡ **Batch your tasks.** Group together similar tasks (e.g., email, calls, and reading), so you're not constantly switching from one mental mode to another.

➡ **Zone your day.** Decide on the best time of day to tackle each batch of tasks, including one or two "email zones." Create longer blocks of uninterrupted time for your most important work. Can you move some appointments to create clearer zones?

➡ **Remove distractions.** Minimize interruptions, to help you focus your attention on the task at hand. Which alerts can you switch off? Can you use an app to block access to certain websites? Decide on a good "parking lot" technique to allow you to capture stray thoughts before they derail your focus.

➡ **Plan small rewards for good behavior.** How can you reward yourself for remaining focused while you singletask—for example, by setting a timer, or keeping a log?

➡ **Share your wisdom.** Can you be proactive in explaining your scheduling choices to colleagues? (Feel free to try the "a1b2c3 . . ." exercise with them, to demonstrate why you've been keen to multitask less these days.)

# FIVE

# Planning Deliberate Downtime

You look at the clock. Where has the time gone? You've got so much to do. Your eyes burn and your mind wanders. You can't even remember the last time you stretched your legs. But you have to keep going, you tell yourself, to make the most of the hours in the day.

Or do you? Do you really squeeze more productivity out of yourself by powering through your weariness? Since I'm posing this question, you probably know where this is going: the answer is no. It might go against our instincts, but making the most of the day doesn't mean churning away nonstop. In fact, the science shows that we're more productive if we give ourselves periods of downtime between our bursts of hard work.

There are two aspects to this argument. The first is that your brain's deliberate system needs regular breaks and fuel to keep it fully functional. The second is that when you're "resting"—that is, not actively engaged in a task—your brain is in fact busy helping you learn and reach new insight. Let me explain those two points a little more, before talking about what this means for you in practice.

## DECISION FATIGUE

Our days are full of small decisions. For example, if we hear someone say something we don't entirely agree with, we need to make a call: do we speak up and disagree, or smile and nod? If we decide to disagree, what should we say (and just how diplomatically should we say it)? Even these sorts of simple moment-to-moment choices involve evaluating the pros and cons of different options, computing how those options compare, and determining what we should do next. So decision making requires a lot of mental energy from our brains. And the more decisions we're asked to make, the less cognitive capacity we have available to assess alternatives and make good, nuanced choices—a phenomenon known to scientists as *decision fatigue*. It's something you'll be familiar with if you've ever redecorated an apartment and found yourself worn down by the endless choices of paint color or faucet design; perhaps you ended up saying, "I just don't care."

In the workplace, the effects of decision fatigue can be quite serious. In a study by behavioral scientist Shai Danziger and colleagues at Tel Aviv University, researchers looked at more than a thousand decisions made by ostensibly objective judges sitting on an Israeli parole board.[1] Throughout the day, the board would rule on whether to grant prisoners early parole or not, after hearing them plead their case. Their day was organized into three blocks, punctuated by two breaks. And the researchers found a very clear pattern in the decisions the board made. If a prisoner's case was heard at the beginning of one of the blocks of time, when the judges were mentally fresh after taking a break, the prisoner had a 65 percent chance of getting parole. But if a prisoner's case was heard toward the end of the session, before the judges were due to take a break, the chance that the judges would be willing to revisit the sentence dropped to almost zero, whatever the merits of the case. This pattern was inescapable—a peak after each break, followed by a steady decline. Nothing apparently mattered more to the outcome of a prisoner's plea than the timing of when it was presented to the board, and whether the judges had the energy to engage with the case.

Studies have also shown that people make poorer purchasing decisions when they're tired, whether they're shopping in a mall or buying a new car.[2] They're also less likely to make the right ethical decisions or follow safety regulations. A University of Pennsylvania study of hospital workers found that working long hours without a break made staff less likely to follow basic hygiene rules that they knew to be important.[3]

What lies behind all these lapses is the fact that when our brain's deliberate system is overworked, it can't do its job properly. That means we have less insight, less self-control, less concentration, and less effective forward thinking. Instead, when we've gone too long without a break, our automatic system takes over. And that means we tend to reach for the easiest payoff—the quick solution, the black-and-white answer, the short-term boost, the standard option, or the status quo—rather than the choice that's necessarily best.

These lapses are even more likely when we're hungry, because part of our deliberate system's capacity gets diverted toward monitoring the increasingly pressing need of our empty stomach and strategizing about how to deal with it ("Are we going to stop soon? Should I excuse myself? Are there any cookies left within reach?"). Like the rest of the body, our brain also needs blood sugar to function—but unlike other parts of the body, it can't store much of it, so eating regularly helps us stay cognitively sharp.[4]

Given all that, it's no wonder that even hardworking, committed people start to flag when they've gone too long without a break. It's simply not possible for us to sustain our brain's highest-quality attention and analysis indefinitely, even if we would like to. That's why so many meetings end in a slightly irritable fog: people who haven't taken enough breaks rarely have the mental energy needed to finish strong.

### THE HARD WORK OF RESTING AND REFLECTING

Even when our brains aren't busy with a task—when they're in what neuroscientists call a "resting state"—they are highly active.[5] What they're doing in this state has become the focus of an exciting emerging field of research. Researchers are finding that when we allow our brains to take a break from a task, they appear to do important work in encoding and consolidating the information that we've just absorbed—and this reflection time results in enhanced learning and insight.

Neuroscientist Saber Sami, of Birmingham University and Harvard Medical School, is one of those seeking to map the activities of our "resting" brains. In one of his experiments, volunteers were asked to lie inside an MRI scanner while holding a keypad, and then were asked to push buttons that matched various images flashing before their eyes. They were given several rest periods during the task, during which their brains were scanned. Everyone got faster at the task over the course of six hours, and the researchers could see which brain areas were engaged as they got better at it. But the key finding was that researchers saw new and stronger connections developing between those brain areas during the volunteers' rest periods, suggesting that their brains continued to process all that they were learning while not actively engaged in the task.[6] In other words, they didn't just improve because they had more practice. Their downtime played an important role in their improvement, too.

In Sami's study, volunteers weren't aware that they were reflecting on the task during their breaks. But a two-part study by Giada Di Stefano and her Harvard Business School colleagues neatly demonstrated the power of *consciously* taking a step back to gather our thoughts. The researchers first asked volunteers to complete puzzles where they had to find the two numbers in a given set that added up exactly to ten. Which sounds easy, but the challenge was that the numbers ran to two decimal places. The researchers found people were better at the task after being asked to take a moment to reflect on which strategies were working for them.[7] That was already interesting.

Then, working with employees in a call center in India, Di Stefano and her colleagues found real-life results that were even more marked. At the call center, new employees were given an initial four weeks of training. They all received the same training, but some of the new hires were asked to spend fifteen minutes writing about two or more key lessons they'd learned that day. The result? The employees who took the time to pause and reflect did 23 percent better on a post-training test. A small amount of reflection resulted in a big boost to performance.

In fact, giving our brain the chance to step back from a task and consolidate our experiences is a little like what happens when we're asleep, according to cognitive neuroscientist Jessica Payne, head of the Sleep, Stress, and Memory Lab at the University of Notre Dame. As she says, "It's clear that it's helpful for us to go online and then offline in bursts, if we're to maximize the brain's ability to make good use of the information we're absorbing."[8]

### YOUR "PIT STRATEGY"

All of this means we make better use of our mental energy if we carve out a little time to recharge and reflect during the day, rather than pushing ourselves from appointment to appointment without any breathing space in between.

There's a car racing metaphor I find helpful when I'm trying to remind myself to look up from my laptop and take a break. When I was a child, I visited the maintenance pit of the famous Silverstone Formula One racetrack, and of course it was fascinating to learn about the tire switches and refueling that mechanics were able to do in just a few seconds. But what stayed with me most was the idea that success was determined not only by the car's speed on the track, but also by the "pit strategy"—the race team's scheduled pit stops. Each stop was a tactical investment in performance, a deliberate slowing down, to enable the car to speed up afterward. Pit stops are not wasted time—they're an essential part of an efficient, well-planned race. And your brain is like that race car. Downtime is as important to your work as every other part of your day, and you need to make sure you get enough of that time throughout the day. Plan for it, protect it, respect it.

Now, let's get specific on the components of a good daily pit strategy: smart breaks and reflection time.

## SMART BREAKS

In the last chapter, I talked about zoning your day, by grouping together similar types of tasks. Now, as you look at your schedule:

➡ Plan to take a brief break between the different task "zones" in your day. For example, if you're spending an hour catching up on email, give yourself a few minutes to stand up and clear your head before you jump into a meeting or a spell of analytical or creative work.

➡ Never let more than ninety minutes pass without doing something to refresh your mind and body—if possible, by stretching your legs and getting a brief change of scene.

Why do I suggest ninety minutes? Florida State psychologist K. Anders Ericsson has spent years examining the characteristics and daily routines of deep experts—including world-class athletes, chess players, and musicians—to understand the patterns underpinning their elite performance. Ericsson found that the highest performers typically work in focused blocks of ninety minutes, with breaks in between.[9]

That rings true to me. In the last fifteen years, I've spent a lot of time designing agendas for board meetings, and observing what happens when I facilitate those sessions. Beyond the ninety-minute mark—sooner, if people are coming into the meeting already tired—attention scatters and energy peters out. If I ignore the need for a break, smartphones take control of the room as everyone looks for a stimulus to wake up their weary brains. But I've found that if I give people a fifteen-minute break at that point, they return full of resolve and focus, making it possible for us to continue productively for another ninety minutes.

Anthony, our digital marketing expert, now makes sure to get up and have a snack, a drink, or a short walk between tasks and meetings. The productivity benefits are obvious to him—and to his colleagues. "It's become a collective thing in the office, to go for a walk and talk about things. We've decided it's a legitimate use of time because we often get so much done when we've had a change of scenery." Anthony is in no doubt about the processing his brain seems to do when he steps away from a challenging task. "If I'm working hard on something, and then I bugger off and go for a walk, I find I can ace it in thirty minutes or less when I return. If I try to push straight through without a break, it takes me much longer overall." Anthony even has a name for the quietly productive time he spends away from his tasks—he calls it his "liminal state," the state of being in-between. Result: more insight for less work.

## Make Decisions at Peaks, Not at Troughs

It is especially wise to have a pit strategy for times that you're working on mentally taxing tasks. So when you're planning the day, ask yourself:

➡ What important decisions do you need to make today (whether they're analytical or creative choices)?

➡ How can you make those decisions when you're mentally fresh, rather than drained?

If you know you have a lot of decisions to make—perhaps it's a day of performance appraisals, or you need to review and edit a long document—it is especially important to plan to take regular short breaks, even if they only last for a few seconds. You also need to make sure that you don't let hunger undermine your ability to concentrate. Anthony says he knows when his blood sugar is too low to make smart choices. "I can tell, because I get a bit irritable and insistent in my views. At which point, a colleague will often tell me to 'eat some nuts or something.' Which I do."

## Create Breathing Room with Smarter Scheduling

➡ Plan meetings and calls that are shorter than the standard thirty or sixty minutes, whenever possible, to give your brain five to ten minutes to recharge between commitments.

➡ Wrap up commitments slightly early whenever you have the chance, to give yourself (and everyone else) a few moments of downtime.

Think about how we usually schedule meetings. If they're informal, we might say, "Let's chat at three this afternoon"; if they're formal, we might send an invitation that specifies a meeting time of "3:00–4:00 p.m." We then think we're free from four o'clock onward. But if you go from your three o'clock appointment straight into a four o'clock commitment, you have no downtime. And, as we now know, that's going to erode the quality of whatever you're doing after four.

Saku Tuominen and Pekka Pohjakallio run 925 Design, a consultancy specializing in helping companies create effective workplaces. Their idea is to apply sound design principles to the way we approach our daily work, to achieve the kind of elegance and efficiency that a beautifully wrought chair or phone can give us as consumers.[10] After they had analyzed the schedules and routines of more than a thousand professionals, one of their solutions was this: why not schedule forty-five-minute meetings, rather than defaulting to the tyranny of the full hour? The same went for arranging twenty- or twenty-five-minute conference calls, rather than allowing them to take up a full thirty-minute slot. When they worked with a range of companies to implement this idea, the result was clear. People found they could get more or less the same amount done, yet with the enormous added cognitive benefit of regular breaks.

Of course, we're not always in control of our schedule. But we usually have more wiggle room than we recognize. Instead of telling someone, "I'm free at three o'clock," for example, try saying, "I'm free from three to three forty-five." We can be practical and upbeat, with phrases like this: "I need to finish by three forty-five, but I think we can get everything done before then." And we can block out five to ten minutes in our diaries at the top of every hour. It may not always be possible to protect that breathing space, but it's such a transformational practice that even if it works half the time, you'll find it immensely worthwhile.

And you may also find colleagues love you for it, even if you simply make it a goal to wrap things up a little before you have to. I remember some advice I was once given by Sir Michael Barber when we were colleagues at McKinsey, after he'd stepped down from his role as a senior advisor to the British government. He said that he always aimed to end meetings early, because giving back those few minutes of time delighted everyone he worked with—especially the prime minister, Tony Blair.

## REFLECTION TIME

Finally, after completing big tasks, learning something new, or finishing up a meeting:

➡ Amplify the value of the experience by taking a moment to step back and reflect on your insights. What struck you most? (What will you do differently as a result?)

➡ If you're with others, invite them to do it, too.

Robyn is a social entrepreneur whose ventures include founding an organization that teaches computer programming and business skills to ex-convicts, enabling them to restart their lives with new purpose. She is one of those energetic people who seems to never stop moving— except she does stop, quite deliberately, several times a day, to do precisely this kind of reflection. Immediately after each major experience of the day—a conversation, something she's read—she takes thirty seconds to write down whatever important thoughts it's provoked. "It might be the tone in someone's voice, or the way that one simple suggestion sparks many others, or an idea planted in my mind by a passing comment." And, she says, each time she applies this thirty-second rule, "it gets a little easier and a little more helpful."[11]

Every evening, Robyn also uses a quick reflection practice that she invented, which she calls "DATE," an acronym that reminds her to think back on her day and recall what she's *discovered* ("which could be an interesting fact or lesson learned, or perhaps something I'll do differently tomorrow"), something she *achieved*, one thing she's *thankful* for, and something she wants to remember that she *experienced*, whether in her work or beyond. As Robyn says, "I've found this reflection time helps me make each day, good or bad, as valuable and significant as possible."

## Planning Deliberate Downtime

Look at your schedule for today and tomorrow, and plan for the following:

➡ Take smart breaks. How can you make sure you take regular breaks, at least every ninety minutes and between each "zone" of tasks in your day?

➡ Make decisions at peaks (not troughs). Which tasks will require you to make a lot of choices? How can you make them when your brain is freshest?

➡ Schedule breathing room. Can you schedule meetings or offer your time in blocks of twenty-five or forty-five minutes (instead of thirty or sixty minutes), to create micro-breaks between commitments? For commitments that are already scheduled, can you aim to wrap up a little early?

➡ Allow reflection time. At the end of each task or meeting, take thirty seconds to capture your biggest insights. Try an end-of-day reflection practice such as DATE (discovered, achieved, thankful for, experienced).

# SIX

# Overcoming Overload

Although Anthony has become pretty expert at designing his day to make the most of his time and effort, his workload is heavy. His digital marketing company is growing fast, and he says, "I hit pinch points in every week. I often end up with a Monday that's totally packed, which leaves me starting the week feeling exhausted. It's bad pacing for the rest of the week." Anthony says that feeling overloaded is a sure way of putting his brain on the defensive. "Sometimes I feel like throwing my hands up in the air and saying, '*Enough!*' I immediately feel my brain seizing up when I do that. Then, instead of being smart in handling the workload, it's easy to make bad decisions," he says. "You can end up catastrophizing, worrying about worst-case scenarios like missing deadlines and even losing your job. None of which helps you think any more clearly." It's a good description of how stressful it feels when our brain's deliberate system gets swamped with demands, and how the resulting tumble into defensive mode makes it hard to be our most sensible selves.

Some of this pressure is part and parcel of modern working life. But another reason so many of us often feel overloaded is because of something called the *planning fallacy*.[1] This describes the fact that we typically expect tasks to take less time than they actually do, because we base our estimates on one standout memory—our *best* past experience—rather than the *average* time it's taken us to do similar tasks in the past. (That's one of the brain's common automatic shortcuts, to rely on a single example rather than bothering to calculate an average across multiple data points.) As a result, we tend to set excessively optimistic expectations for ourselves. If we're already busy, that means it doesn't take much to unbalance us: a colleague who's on vacation, a looming deadline, an unanticipated problem, or simply say-ing yes to something we really should have dodged.

There's some obvious advice that flows from acknowledging the ex-istence of the planning fallacy: when you're estimating the amount of time a task is going to take, balance your brain's natural optimism by imagining a scenario where things don't go entirely your way. Then plan for something close to *that*. The fallacy exerts such a strong pull on our brains that this will probably leave you with an estimate that's fairly accurate. (And imagine how great you'll feel if you finish it sooner.)

But for situations when you're already too overloaded to be able to plan your way out, I want to show you some techniques for rediscover-ing a sense of Zen-like control—without hurling your smartphone to the ground.

### THE MINDFUL PAUSE

Anthony knows when he's hitting a wall. He recognizes the tension in his muscles and his snappish comments, as well as the feeling that he's not thinking straight. But he has a reliable routine for getting his brain back into discovery mode.

When he notices the tide of stress rising, Anthony says, he pauses, takes a deep breath, and then asks himself, "Do I want to feel like this?" He explains: "I know the way I'm feeling is just a symptom of too many demands on my brain, and that there are plenty of practical things I can do to help my brain cope. And I've found that asking this simple question reminds me that I have some choices in how I decide to react. It starts to reengage rational thought, without fail. It's like pinching myself in a dream."

He uses a specific technique for taking that deep breath. "When you're panicking, you can feel short of breath, but you're actually over-oxygenating yourself by breathing fast. So I use a technique called 'triangular breathing,' where you breathe in for a count of three, then breathe out for a count of three, then pause for a count of three. By slowing your heart rate, you're sending a signal to your brain that the threat has passed, so it reduces the other signals of stress." It's a great example of the kind of mind-body loop I mentioned in The Science Essentials.

With this, Anthony is basically using mindfulness as his first-line tactic to handle workplace overload. As a result, he's reaping some of the compelling neurological benefits that research has found to be associated with mindfulness practices, including sharper thinking and better resilience. Perhaps his short routine doesn't sound like mindfulness—but it is, in effect. The counting involved in his breathing exercise gives his overloaded mind a clear and uncomplicated point of focus for a little while, allowing his brain a few minutes to unpack and reorganize everything it's trying to keep track of. As Anthony says, "It slows and calms things down very, very quickly."

If you want a quick, discreet way of taking a mindful pause when you're swamped at work, try this:

➡ Find a way to sit (or stand) as comfortably as you can. Try putting your feet squarely on the floor. Close your eyes if possible, or just look downward into your lap.

➡ Next, choose an easy point of focus. Try one of these approaches:
- Concentrate on your breath. You can try Anthony's technique, or just count 1–2 on the in-breath and 3–4 on the out-breath. It can help you focus if you put your hands on your stomach to feel its rise and fall as you breathe.
- Notice how each part of your body feels, working up from your toes to the top of your head.
- Count down from one hundred to zero in your mind.

➡ If your mind wanders, don't worry—that's normal. Don't judge yourself. Just notice that you've drifted, then bring your focus back to where you were before.

If your moment of overload is hitting you in the middle of a meeting, you can use miniature versions of all of these suggestions to pause and bring your smarter self back online. Take just one or two mindful breaths; count down from ten (rather than one hundred); take a second to notice how your feet feel on the floor. Nobody will notice except your grateful brain.

## OUTSOURCE YOUR MEMORY

Because our brain's working memory is tiny, even small distractions can make it difficult to concentrate. And thinking about incomplete tasks and concerns qualifies as a serious distraction, especially if you're trying to keep track of them all in your head. You burn a little of your deliberate system's mental energy every time you tell yourself, "I must remember to pick up the dry cleaning today." That's why psychologists E. J. Masicampo and Roy Baumeister, at Florida State University, found that people do less well at solving anagrams and logic problems when they're aware of another activity that's yet to be completed.[2] There's even a term for this phenomenon: the "Zeigarnik effect," named after the Russian psychologist who discovered it.

The key to overcoming the Zeigarnik effect is outsourcing some of your basic memory tasks to a recording device other than your brain to free up space for real thinking:

➡ Develop a habit of immediately getting worries and work-in-progress thoughts out of your head and down on "paper"—whether real paper or the electronic version—so that your brain no longer has to expend energy on remembering them. (This echoes my advice in Chapter 2 on writing down even your smallest to-dos.)

➡ Consider keeping a notepad or voice recorder anywhere that you find thoughts often come to mind. Personally, I have a waterproof pad in the shower, as well as a regular one by my bed and a well-used notepad function on my phone.

You still have to consider later what to do with each item you write down—but your work will feel easier once you're not wasting mental horsepower on trying to keep everything straight in your mind. Unfinished tasks are like screaming kindergartners—much easier to handle when you get them to sit down quietly.

## MOST IMPORTANT THING FIRST

Some years ago, a haiku-like phrase was posted on a now-dormant Twitter account, badged as "productivity in 11 words." It said: "One thing at a time. Most important thing first. Start now."[3] It wasn't written by a behavioral scientist, but it might just as well have been, given the research on how readily the brain's deliberate system gets overloaded.

But what *is* the most important thing? If you could do only one thing today, what should it be? One January day in New York, I was coaching a high-powered businesswoman about to leave for the World Economic Forum's annual gathering of world leaders in Davos, Switzerland. There's no doubt that Valerie was entirely overloaded with things to do. She was in the middle of changing jobs, had promised a dozen favors to friends and acquaintances, and had a big speech to write about the role of business in society. She was listing all her tasks out loud as we walked in the snow.

Eventually, during a break in the conversation, I said: "That's a lot, yes. So, out of all that, what's really the single most important thing to do today?"

Her eyes widened. "That's it."

I looked at her blankly.

"What you said is so clarifying," she explained. It was hardly the most sophisticated question in the world, but it was enough to make her realize that "the most important thing" was to get personal invitations sent out to some key people for her speech in Davos. It meant a lot to Valerie to make that session a success, and it was approaching fast. Feeling overwhelmed had made it hard to see the obvious; posing the blunt question made it clear again, by reducing the noise in her head (or, to be specific, reducing the load on her brain's working memory).

It's a simple trick that Anthony uses time and again when he hits his weekly pinch points. "After I've taken a breath and gotten my head back on straight, I look at all the things on my plate and say, 'Okay, what *really* needs to happen by the end of the day?' That clarity can be quite de-stressing." What if there are multiple urgent things to do? "If I ask myself honestly, there's always one thing that's really top priority, usually because other things depend on it or there's really more at stake in the longer term. And the other things can be deferred or delegated or dropped if I really analyze it."

Looking at your to-do list, try these clarifying questions:

➤ What really matters most right now? (It may help to revisit your intentions for the day.)

➤ What really has to happen today, if nothing else?

➤ Project forward to the end of the day. What will you be most glad or relieved to have done?

## THE SMALLEST FIRST STEP

You're now clear on what's most important. But if it's a complex or daunting task, you can still feel stuck. So the next simple question to ask is this:

➡ What's the smallest first step you can take to move things forward?

This deceptively simple question soothes your brain for a couple of different reasons. First, it guides you away from worrying about the scale of the challenge you're facing, toward something that you know you can do. Your brain anticipates the reward that comes from success, which helps to move you out of defensive mode and toward a discovery state of mind. The "smallest step" question also reduces the load on your brain by redirecting effort from something it finds difficult (conceiving of an unknown future) to something it finds easy (thinking about an immediate action to take).

Angela, an attorney, works for a firm where managers are elected by their peers rather than appointed. It's an approach that rewards candidates who have great ideas and people skills, and Angela had plenty of both. But every time she thought about putting herself forward for a management election, she ground to a halt. Almost every day, she had an item on her to-do list called "start prep for election." It was always her "most important thing," but the task felt too large and complex to tackle in the middle of her busy days.

So we talked about the smallest first step. Angela says, "I realized that the first thing was just to have coffee with my boss, whom I know and like, to talk to him about my ideas. So I wrote that on a yellow sticky note. Then I called his assistant, and went and did it. After that, I took the same approach for the next step, and the next. It was very freeing." Moreover, it worked. After her colleagues elected her to a managerial role, Angela used the "first small step" technique to attack all her difficult tasks. "It *always* works. There's always something tiny you can do to feel you've made progress. It's an infallible way of keeping things moving forward when things feel unmanageable."

## YOUR COMPARATIVE ADVANTAGE

Sometimes you've worked out what's most important and your first steps are clear, but you're still left with too much to do in the hours available. For this problem, let's turn to an old economic concept called *comparative advantage*, first articulated by economist David Ricardo in 1817—but often misunderstood.

Here's how it works. Imagine England and Portugal can both make cloth and wine (and imagine that you're Portugal, while England is one of your colleagues). Portugal is a better producer of both products. So should Portugal just do everything, while England does nothing? No, because Portugal has got limited resources. (Just as you have limited hours in your day.) And it's not that England can't make cloth and wine at all. It's just not quite as good at it as Portugal.

Should both countries make both products, then? Well, no, not if they can trade with each other. England is "okay" at making both wine and cloth, but Portugal is "exceptionally excellent" at making wine and merely "very good" at cloth. The gap between Portugal's and England's prowess is larger in winemaking than in cloth production, so we say Portugal has a *comparative advantage* in wine (and not in cloth). The upshot? With limited resources, Portugal should focus on what it's most uniquely talented at doing: making wine. If Portugal does that and England focuses on cloth, Ricardo showed, the two countries will together produce more cloth and wine by specializing than if each tried to do both.[4]

This logic of comparative advantage can be a great help in prioritizing our work when we're overloaded. We so often get pulled into tasks that we should, by rights, be asking others to help with. We tell ourselves that they're not quite as experienced or knowledgeable as us, or that it will be quicker if we just do it ourselves. But there's a massive cost to this way of thinking. By being unwilling to delegate tasks that others could reasonably help with, we fail to make progress on the important or tricky things that *only* we can do. U.S. president Teddy Roosevelt knew this. He could type faster than his personal assistant. But however good his typing, his comparative advantage lay in more presidential duties, where his capabilities were more unique. So that's where he focused his attention, while delegating his typing to his assistant. The result was better for the country, without a doubt.

So look at your work for today, and ask yourself:

➡ Which tasks truly fall into the category of those only you can do?

➡ Which tasks could someone else do moderately well (even if not quite as well as you)?

Anthony works hard to isolate the things that don't really need his talents. "Everything in life can *feel* important, but you can't do everything. So I had to learn to let go of things, and it was ridiculously hard to do at first." He says that what made it easier was talking openly with his colleagues about what was on his plate, what was on theirs, and discovering where they could divide and conquer more effectively. "I realized there were things I enjoyed doing and was good at, but that others could take on—like writing the company's blog, or posting company tweets. Meanwhile, there were other things on my to-do list that only I could do, that hadn't been getting done. Finally, I had the space to work on them."

## THE "POSITIVE NO"

We've talked about how having limited hours in the day means you can't do it all. Every time you say yes to a request, you're effectively saying no to something else. So you want your yesses to be focused on the things that matter and that you're uniquely placed to do. But there's a common obstacle to focusing our time, which is a desire to avoid difficult conversations with people who are making requests we have to decline. "I don't like conflict or feeling like I'm letting people down," says Anthony. "So I find it hard to say no, and I get tense before making the call or walking into the meeting where I need to do it."

That's where the "positive no" technique comes in. If you find it difficult to extricate yourself from low-priority commitments, then learning how to deliver a positive no is like discovering a new superpower—it gives you the ability to make everyone feel better about the choices you're making (including yourself).

First articulated by William Ury, the co-founder of the Harvard Program on Negotiation, it's a technique that fits very neatly with the neuroscience of our discover-defend axis. Remember that our brains are constantly scanning for anything that promises to be a potential threat or reward. When people are responding to a threat, their brain diverts activity from sophisticated thought to blunt and rapid responses, a little as if they'd suddenly discovered the building was on fire.

Now think about our usual way of gracefully declining a request. We start with "I'm really sorry, I'm not going to be able to come to the meeting/take on the project/paint the self-portrait you commissioned . . ." It sounds polite. But starting with the negative signal of "I'm sorry," however well meant, puts the other person on high alert. Their brain immediately goes into defensive mode: "You're backing out! This is a threat!" And in this mode, people don't have the mental capacity to be expansive or generous in their thinking like they do when they're at their best. You might have been hoping for the other person's sympathetic understanding of your priorities, but you're unlikely to get it while they're on the defensive.

To give yourself a better chance of engaging with someone whose brain is in discovery mode, you instead want to start with something positive, rather than something negative. Like this:

➡ **Start with warmth.** First, acknowledge and show appreciation for the person's request.

➡ **Your "yes."** Then, instead of starting with "I'm sorry . . . ," begin by enthusiastically highlighting whatever your positive priority is right now, and why it's interesting, important, or meaningful to you. Consider picking out a reason that will also resonate with the person you're talking to.

➡ **Your "no."** Explain that this means, with regret, that you can't do the thing they've asked you to do.

➡ **End with warmth.** Perhaps there's a suggestion or offer you can make without detracting from your real priorities, such as an introduction to other people who could help. At the very least, offer some warm wishes for success in their project. It's an important closing sentence that often gets dropped when we're focused on our own discomfort at saying no.

Anthony offers a recent example of a positive no that helped him manage his workload. One thing that takes time out of his life is long-distance travel; he's often saying yes to trips that are interesting but not

critical. Recently he agreed to a trip to Kuala Lumpur before he realized just how difficult it was going to be to make time for the visit. He
didn't think he could back out of the trip, but the alternative was worse:
doing a mediocre job on projects that were important for the future of
his company. Ultimately, he realized that he had to tell the organizer
that he was withdrawing, so he could reclaim the time in his schedule.

Normally Anthony would have written something like this:

"I'm so sorry, but unfortunately I'm no longer going to be able
to join you on the trip to KL. We've recently taken on three big
projects and I'm finding myself swamped with all that entails. As
a result, I just can't carve out the time to make it possible, despite
my best efforts. Huge apologies again."

By comparison, his positive no went something like this:

"I was honored that you invited me to KL. The work you're doing
is fascinating and impressive [warmth]. As you might know, our
side of the business has also grown enormously in the past few
months. We've taken on three exciting new projects that will
really change the way our clients think about marketing. I'll be
setting up the projects in the coming month, and it's my responsibility to make them the success they deserve to be [his yes]. To
do a good job, though, I'm having to let go of a lot of things. And
sadly, one of them is the chance to come to KL. I'm disappointed,
as I was looking forward to it [his no]. Please let me know if it
would be helpful to connect you with people who might take my
place and add value to the group—I have a few ideas. In the meantime, I wish you all the best for a fruitful trip [warmth]."

The two responses feel very different to read, don't they? The content of his positive no was essentially the same as his conventional
no—a decision, an explanation, and an apology. And as soon as the
trip leader started reading Anthony's more positive version, it's likely
she guessed the reason for his email. But there's no mistaking the fact
that the tone of the second email feels quite different from that of the
first. With the positive version, her reward-hungry brain will have been
a little buoyed by Anthony's upbeat comments about his new projects.
Sure enough, despite her disappointment, Anthony ended up with her

understanding and respect. And this has generally been his experience. He used to fear that he'd damage relationships by saying "no thanks," but it hasn't happened since he began deploying the positive no. And he realized that "it's far better to convey a clear, sincere message that I'm not in a position to give my all, instead of doing a half-baked job because I'm stretched too thin."

## SET YOUR BOUNDARIES

There are days when it feels as if other people's demands are pressing in on us from all sides. Kristen certainly felt like that during much of her early career. She's a sharp-minded HR director for a global pharmaceutical company, with four children, a long commute, and a busy job. She initially struggled to find her balance as her family grew.

"When I came back to work after my third maternity leave," she recalls (slipping into the present tense), "I'm feeling like I haven't slept in four years. I'm three months behind because no one did my work while I was gone, and I'm way overloaded. I'm sitting in my office, feeling so mad, and I wanted to articulate who I was mad at. Initially I directed it at my company. I was mad because they were making me come to meetings really early, and they were making me stay really late. But then I thought, who is 'the company'?" And in that moment, she says, "I had this epiphany, because I realized I was mostly mad at *me* and my lack of boundaries. I'd let things get out of control and I was trying to find someone else to blame. But if I didn't have boundaries, who else was going to give them to me?" She laughs and shakes her head. "Did I think the company was going to say, 'Oh, Kristen, you're a new mom, poor you, don't work before eight, don't stay later than six'? No, it was up to me. Perhaps it shouldn't have been, but it kind of always is."

So she decided to take control. "I wrote on my notepad what my boundaries were: 'I don't accept meetings before eight. I don't stay past six. Between noon and one I'm going to be at my desk and I'm going to eat lunch. When I'm home, I'm home; when I'm at work, I'm at work.'" It was a very short list. "If it had a negative impact on my career, so be it, I thought. I couldn't carry on the way I'd been going. The irony is that after I instituted that list of boundaries, my career skyrocketed." Why did she think that happened? "Because it made me calmer and more effective. Also, I wasn't an executive at the time, but I think it showed that I had the capacity to be one, that I knew how to manage myself."

One of the actions Kristen took was to simply state when she was available, and when she wasn't, without drama. "I used very clear language: 'I have a hard stop at 10:00 a.m.,' for example. It's all I ever said." She didn't tie herself in knots trying to explain why she needed to leave the meeting on time. "And no matter what, that's when I would leave."

This kind of unruffled communication of boundaries is powerful because people's brains treat ambiguity and uncertainty as a threat. By contrast, clarity is strangely calming, even if the message isn't exactly what people would like it to be. "I decided I just couldn't go through my life being mad at everyone else," Kristen adds. "I had to know what I could and couldn't do, and I had to be willing to articulate it, and enforce it." And she continues to get promoted.

## AUTOMATE THE SMALL STUFF

Decision making is tiring for your brain's deliberate system, whether the stakes are big or small. Without realizing it, you can fritter away a fair portion of your mental energy on the day's minor choices: what to eat, what to wear, when to exercise, when to sleep, whether to answer the phone, and whether to prioritize this task or that one. So there's an argument for "automating" a few of your less weighty everyday decisions, by setting up simple rules that require no thinking. It can create head space for thoughts that matter more.

That's why a number of world leaders choose to minimize the amount of time they spend worrying about their wardrobe. In an interview, President Barack Obama once explained: "I wear only gray or blue suits. I don't want to make decisions about what I'm eating or wearing. You need to focus your decision-making energy. You need to routinize yourself."[5] In a similar vein, German chancellor Angela Merkel is famous for wearing just one jacket design, made up in multiple colors and fabrics.

Aliceson works in executive search, and her wardrobe certainly contains more than one jacket. But like Obama and Merkel, she's found it helpful to automate some of her daily prioritization decisions. "I've tried to turn as many things as I can into daily habits," she says. She cites her efforts to exercise and study French as examples. "I do a few minutes on each every day, rather than agonizing over whether it's happening today or not. I just do it. I find committing to a small daily task takes less mental space than planning to study a few times each week, and then wondering when or whether to make time." As a side benefit, she says it also means she's done some form of exercise almost every day since she was sixteen, even when the demands of her workload mean she's fitting it in by walking to and from meetings while making calls.

So if you're feeling mentally exhausted, or if you're going through a period where your work is particularly stressful, consider whether you could make like Merkel. Ask yourself:

➡ Could you decide to do something at the same time or in the same way each day?

➡ Could you set yourself a simple response rule, to reduce the amount of time you spend deciding how to react to common, low-importance situations?

For example, I used to ponder whether to answer the phone when I received calls from unidentified numbers. I'd spend three seconds wondering whether to pick up or not—seconds that would often irretrievably distract me from the work I was doing. But the great majority of these calls were spam, and real callers always left voicemail, and the time spent on the decision was a pure waste. So I set myself an automatic rule: "never answer the phone if I don't recognize the number." The result: a small but useful win in the battle to make the most of the minutes in the day.

102 HOW TO HAVE A GOOD DAY

## Overcoming Overload

Next time you're feeling overloaded, try these strategies—in fact, why not try them right now?

➡ **Mindful pause.** Give your brain's deliberate system a chance to fully engage, by pausing to focus on your breath (or scanning your body, or counting back from one hundred) for five minutes.

➡ **Get it out of your head.** Write down everything that's swirling around your mind, even the tiniest to-dos.

➡ **Most important thing.** What really matters most right now, either because it has to happen today or because it has the biggest impact?

➡ **Smallest first step.** What's the very first step you can take toward doing that most important thing—something small enough to do today?

➡ **Comparative advantage.** What are you *uniquely* well placed to do—and what could others do, even if not as well as you? Focus on tasks where the gap between your capabilities and other people's is biggest.

➡ **Positive no.** For a commitment that you need to delegate or decline: start with warmth; say what you're saying "yes" to; say your "no"; end with warmth.

➡ **Setting boundaries.** If you could set one boundary in the way you organize your time, what would it be? What's the clearest, cleanest way to communicate this preference to others?

➡ **Automate small daily decisions.** Consider whether you can do something at the same time or in the same way each day, to spend more of your mental energy on the things that matter.

➡ **And finally:** remember that you'll lessen your feeling of being overloaded if you also take the **singletasking** advice from Chapter 4 and the **downtime** advice from Chapter 5, since both will boost your mental performance and productivity.

# SEVEN

# Beating Procrastination

Doesn't it feel fantastic when we reach the end of the day and can look back with satisfaction on the things we've achieved? It feels great to get things done; it makes our brain's reward system very happy indeed.

Yet most of us have a list of important tasks that we're avoiding—emails unwritten, projects not started, things we're putting off despite the fact that they aren't going to be any easier to do tomorrow (or the day after tomorrow). Even a Nobel Prize–winning economist like George Akerlof procrastinates. When Akerlof was living in India years ago, he was bemused that it took him a full eight months to mail some clothes to a friend in the United States. Like most of us would have done, Akerlof beat himself up for sitting on the task for so long—but that didn't make him do it any sooner.

Akerlof was so struck by his inability to go to the post office that he wrote an important research paper on procrastination, helpfully unpacking the reasons that it exerts such a grip on most of us.[1] I'll draw on his insights, and those of other behavioral scientists, to show you a number of strategies for overcoming the allure of *mañana*.

Elta is someone who's thought a lot about how to beat procrastination. A soft-spoken Texan, she's a senior manager at a global research company, where her work focuses on food policy—not the kind that's about deciding what to have for lunch, but the kind that's about the steps governments can take to protect the food chain. She's good at her job. But there's a core part of her work that she dislikes, which is giving presentations. Elta often found herself leaving the preparation until the very last minute. "It's hard for me to agree to speak in public," she says. "And then, once I'm on the hook, I'll spend endless time avoiding thinking about what I'm actually going to say." Now, though, she's learned some techniques to make sure she doesn't find herself speechless in front of a room of people. These tricks all stem from the same central idea: rebalancing the way her brain compares short-term costs with long-term benefits. Let's look at why that's so important for overcoming procrastination.

### "JAM TOMORROW"

Most of the tasks we avoid are ones that promise long-term benefits—better relationships, career success, personal satisfaction—while requiring immediate effort from us. In Elta's case, doing more public speaking will strengthen her reputation and build her network over time, and preparing well will pay off when she stands up to speak. But the work she needs to put in to write a good speech—well, that's today's problem.

This short-term/long-term trade-off is at the root of our tendency to procrastinate. It's easier for our brains to assess the known present than to consider the unknown future, so our automatic system, always looking for shortcuts, will tend to give more weight to what's happening now rather than what might happen in the future. As a result, we generally prefer to have a tasty treat today, rather than tomorrow or next week—after all, who knows whether the prospective treat will actually be delivered? In other words, we all have what economists call *present bias.*

Present bias served us well as our species evolved. Life spans were not long, and danger was all around. Early humans focused their limited mental energy on protecting themselves from real and present danger: the saber-toothed tiger stalking the camp, the question of whether a berry was poisonous or not.

Today, most of us don't face such immediate pressure to survive, but we still find it hard to make a sacrifice *now* for a benefit *later.* We can do it, but only with significant effort; it taxes sophisticated neural networks in our brain's deliberate system, those associated with self-regulation and planning. Meanwhile, plenty of immediate rewards tempt us, like chatting with colleagues, browsing websites, or crossing off the easy tasks on our to-do list. So our automatic system, always keen to expend the least amount of mental energy possible, reaches for those rewards instead.

How, then, do you become less myopic about the more elusive items on your to-do list? The answer lies in rebalancing the stakes.

Left to yourself, you'll automatically tend to overweight the immediate downside of making an effort and underweight the long-term upside of getting something done. The key is to make the net benefits of taking action feel bigger and the net costs feel smaller.

## PICTURE THE BENEFITS

UCLA psychologist Hal Ersner-Hershfield has thought a lot about what it requires for us to take actions that don't pay off immediately—in particular, how to get people to save more for their future. He and his team found that we feel quite different about saving when we're shown photographs that make our future self more real. In a series of four experiments, he and his colleagues showed that when people saw a picture of themselves digitally aged, they saved more than twice as much ($172 vs. $80) when asked how much they would choose to save out of $1,000.[2] "To people estranged from their future selves, saving is like a choice between spending money today and giving it to a stranger years from now," Ersner-Hershfield says. But seeing a picture of their age-progressed self seemed to help their brains conceive of that future person as real.

It's relatively easy to apply this technique to the task on our to-do list that we've been avoiding. If we can paint ourselves a vivid mental picture of the future benefits of getting it done, we'll be more motivated to get started. Elta certainly finds it motivates her to think about the way it will feel to have aced the presentation. "It's helpful to think about the fact that people in the audience will remember me if I do well," she says. "And then my advice will be more respected whenever they next see me, because they know that I have sensible things to say. I'll feel more credible, and that's important to me." Imagining these benefits feels good, she says, and immediately makes her feel more drawn to the task.

Elta also takes careful note of any positive feedback she receives, since she knows it will help her visualize the benefits the next time she has to prepare a talk. "When someone in the audience tells me they liked what I said, I don't just smile and thank them. I really pay attention, and ask what made it useful for them, if I can. For example, someone once said they liked that I'd put the key message of each slide in a box. The next time I didn't feel like bothering with preparing my slides, it was helpful to remember that."

This "picture the benefits" approach helps with the many tinier moments of procrastination, too. When there's a call you're avoiding making or an email you're putting off replying to, you give your brain a helping hand by imagining the virtuous sense of satisfaction you'll have once it's done—and perhaps also the look of relief on someone's face as they get from you what they needed.

### Plan a Short-Term Payoff

For those challenging tasks that bear fruit only after many days or weeks of effort, where the future benefits may feel too distant to be alluring, it can help to promise yourself shorter-term rewards for finishing each small piece of the project.

A sporty ex-colleague of mine rewards herself with a bicycle ride when she nails a task she's been avoiding. A rather intellectual acquaintance allows himself an episode of a trashy TV program after tackling something especially difficult at work. I saw someone else install an app on his phone to count the number of times he exercises, so that he can award himself a beer for each gym visit.

Of course, all these people might have ended up doing some of these pleasant things anyway—but by *planning* these treats as rewards for effort expended, they were helping to stack the cost-benefit analysis in the direction of overcoming procrastination. In moderation, it adds up to a smart and enjoyable approach to productivity. (As long as it doesn't result in any drunken bike rides.)

### TIE THE FIRST STEP TO A TREAT

In Chapter 6 on overcoming overload, I talked about the calming power of identifying the smallest first step when feeling daunted by a task. When we're procrastinating rather than panicking, applying that "first step" technique can also be helpful, because it reduces our sense that there's a big short-term cost to getting started. And we can add a twist that makes it even less likely that we'll procrastinate: we can link that first step to something we're looking forward to doing today. In other words, tie the task that we're avoiding to something that we're *not* avoiding.

Taking this approach has made a huge difference to Elta's willingness to prepare for her talks. "I really want my audience to walk out thinking they've learned something. So my first small step is always to take ten minutes to decide what I want my one memorable message to be." And she weaves those ten minutes into the most enjoyable part of her day. "I'm always looking for ways to connect the things I do for pleasure and the things that feel like hard work. I like to walk through a park on my way to work, so that's when I think about whatever I'm avoiding, like deciding the key message for my next presentation. Because I'm in a good mood, I seem to be able to connect more readily with what I need to think about."

Elta is effectively adding some pleasure to the when-then goal-setting formula I talked about in Chapter 2. She's saying, "*When* I'm walking through a lush green park that lifts my spirits, *then* I'm taking a little time to think about whatever task I'm avoiding." For similar reasons, it can be a good idea to allow yourself to read lowbrow magazines or books when you're at the gym, because the guilty pleasure helps dilute your brain's perception of the short-term cost of exercising. Likewise, you might muster the self-discipline to complete a slippery task if you promise yourself you'll do it in a nice café with an indulgent drink in hand. By making the immediate task feel more enjoyable, all these examples reduce the amount of work that your brain has to do to make your short-term effort stack up against the eventual benefits.

## CHECK THE DOWNSIDE OF INACTION

Sometimes we weigh the pros and cons of doing a task. But how about the pros and cons of *not* doing the task? What are the implications of letting the status quo persist? That's something we typically don't evaluate at all. Known as *omission bias*, this phenomenon is another source of procrastination, since it often makes the choice to do nothing look more attractive than it actually is.

I asked Elta how she saw the pros and cons of *not* doing her public speaking preparation until the last minute. On the advantages of avoiding it, all she could come up with was the fact that she'd feel less stressed. It sounded a bit lame, and also untrue: it would lighten her load today, but it certainly wouldn't reduce her anxiety in the hours leading up to her talk. Then came a moment of insight for Elta, when she focused on the potential disadvantages of deferring her preparation. As she played it through in her mind's eye, she realized it was her worst nightmare. She'd be jittery as she stood up, she'd do a bad job, and she'd actively harm her reputation. It was oddly galvanizing for her to consider the downside of inaction for a moment or two.

## PRE-COMMIT

In case thinking about the costs of the status quo isn't enough, research suggests there's an effective way of making inaction look even less appealing: by making a public commitment to getting something done.

Oxford University neuroscientist Molly Crockett has shown that, even when there's no public pronouncement, pre-commitment works better than willpower alone when people are trying to resist temptation; in other words, it's easier to resist watching cat videos when you've thought ahead and blocked several of your favorite cat video sites.[3]

And it's even more powerful to *publicly* commit to getting something done, because our brain's threat-perception and reward systems are so highly responsive to our social standing. It matters to us whether we're respected by others. So by telling people about our plans, we add social costs to not following through; none of us much wants to look foolish or lazy to other people. That's why people sign up for marathons and tell all their friends; it's why I tell my husband that I'm going to choir practice on days when I know I'll be tempted to skip it. It's even better if you can involve other people directly by making shared plans, because then you risk *really* annoying your colleagues and friends if you don't show up.

Elta confirms that she uses social pre-commitments to motivate herself. "First of all, I'll force myself to formally sign up to do a presentation, even though I don't want to." Why? She doesn't want to leave an audience hanging without a speaker, or get a reputation for being flaky. Then, to add impetus to her preparation, Elta involves a friend or colleague. "I tell them 'I'm going to practice my presentation on you.' For example, when I was working at Berkeley, I had a good friend who knew how I felt about speaking. So we'd agree to meet in coffee shops, and she'd listen to me practice. We didn't work together—in fact, she was in a different field—but committing to meet her meant I had to prepare beforehand." So not only did Elta get to the end of the day feeling good about her productivity and diligence, but she also got to see a friend—providing a neat short-term reward for her social brain.

## TRY THE "FIVE WHYS"

Sometimes we find ourselves returning to a task repeatedly, but we still seem unable to take the first step. Perhaps we mean to set our intentions every morning, but somehow never find the time. Or we'd like to stop multitasking, but find we never go offline for longer than a couple of minutes. We hear a little voice in our head saying, "Yeah, good idea, but . . . no." In these situations, unless we get to the bottom of the "but," it's hard to make progress.

What can we do? The first thing is to acknowledge the "but" rather than brush it aside. So much of our daily behavior is driven by our brain's automatic system. Deeply coded needs and fears drive our choices in a way that's largely invisible to our conscious mind. If we get stuck in a behavioral loop that we don't like—such as avoiding tasks we genuinely want to get done—it's a good cue for us to pause and reflect. By definition, we can't know all the inner workings of our automatic system, otherwise it wouldn't be doing a good job of being automatic. But we can ask some nonjudgmental questions to try to understand what the real blockage might be.

For a quick way to do this, I like the technique of the "five whys," where you patiently ask yourself a series of "why" questions to unearth the roots of your reticence; the name of the exercise refers to the fact that the true cause of your issue generally surfaces by the time you ask the fifth "why" question (and in my experience, you often hit gold by the time you reach your third or fourth "why"). The technique originated in the auto manufacturing sector, where it's used to work out why a production process has gone wrong. It's certainly not a substitute for psychotherapy. But it's always striking to me how quickly the "five whys" can help to uncover the root causes of many day-to-day difficulties.

This approach worked for Elta when she still found it hard to knuckle down to preparing presentations. "I stopped and asked myself a few questions," she says, "starting with '*Why* do I feel reluctant to do this?' Then '*Why* do I say that?' and '*Why* is that a problem for me?' and so on."

First she discovered a quiet voice in her head saying: "The reason I can't be bothered to prepare is that I'm always going to screw up my presentations—so why bother?" She wondered where on earth that was coming from. "I pushed myself to articulate *why* I thought I was going to screw up. I finally realized it was because I was afraid I didn't have anything to say, that I wasn't good at what I professed to be good at." But where was that feeling of inadequacy coming from? After another "why," she realized it was a legacy of her unusual career path. "I had always felt like I didn't match a traditional job category. I wasn't a quant analyst. I don't have consulting experience. I was just an academic who got interested in public policy. And I was interested in food, which was peripheral to what my company does. So I didn't know where I fit in. That's where my anxiety was coming from."

Once Elta discovered the real reason behind her avoidance of the task, she had a way forward. She could challenge the concern she'd unearthed, and then—if needed—do something to address it. "I asked myself, 'Is it realistic that I'd be seen as incompetent?' And the answer is no, not really. I can talk to you all day about food policy. I reminded myself that I'd won projects for my company, and that colleagues are asking me to join their projects. There's plenty of evidence that I know my stuff." To reinforce this further in her mind, she decided to have a conversation with her bosses to discuss her contributions to the company's work. After that, Elta hit the procrastination buffers a lot less often.

The blockages you uncover with the "five whys" aren't always as existential as Elta's; they can be quite practical, arising from competing commitments or routines in your life. For example, suppose you were indeed finding it hard to set daily intentions in the morning. A few "why" questions might highlight that the challenge really stems from your commitment to eating breakfast with the family. Once you've made that conflict more explicit in your mind, it's more likely you'll find a way to overcome it—perhaps experimenting with setting your intentions the night before or during your commute to work. As Elta says, "If you don't work out what the real blockage is, you can go round in circles feeling bad about yourself. But once you do work it out, you can deal with it and get things done." And getting things done generally leaves us feeling very good about our day.

## BEATING PROCRASTINATION

Think about the item on your to-do list that you've been avoiding for a while. (If you don't have one, please take a bow, and skip to the next chapter.)

➡ **Picture the benefits.** What will be better as a result of getting this done, for you and for others? How great will that feel? Think back to the last time you got something like this done—what was the upside?

➡ **Plan a short-term reward.** How could you plan to reward yourself for today's progress toward the end goal, if it's a long haul?

➡ **Tie the first step to something you like.** Identify the first small step you need to take. Then find a way to link that to something you are definitely going to do today and that you enjoy doing.

➡ **Amplify the downside of inaction.** How can you sharpen your sense of the costs of not getting it done? What pre-commitments can you make, ideally involving other people?

➡ **Ask the five whys.** If you're still finding yourself reluctant to make progress, ask yourself five "why" questions. What surfaces as the real blockage? What can you do to address *that*?

# PART III

# Relationships

## Making the Most of Every Interaction

Most of the great triumphs and tragedies of history are caused not by people being fundamentally good or fundamentally evil, but by people being fundamentally people.

—TERRY PRATCHETT AND NEIL GAIMAN

In all the empirical studies on psychological well-being, one thing emerges as a reliable foundation for happiness: the quality of our relationships.[1] And given that we spend a third of our life at work, or thinking about work, it's not just our family and friends who matter. Our interactions with colleagues and customers are also hugely important. A good conversation at work can encourage us, amuse us, or fill us with pride and purpose. It can make all the difference to the way each day feels.

That's because our highly social brains are wired to constantly assess the state of our affinity with others, and the strength of our identity within the group.[2] An enormous amount of our inner dialogue includes ruminations about other people—what they did, why they did it, what they think of us, how we compare with them, et cetera. Meanwhile, everyone else we meet is running the same kind of calculations about *us*. The soap opera of our social minds never stops, and it's central to the way we experience our working lives.

And as in any soap opera, even when we're surrounded with talented, likeable people, there can be misunderstandings. Sometimes our co-workers are a dream to be around, and sometimes they're not; some people are pleasant, and others make us tear our hair out. We usually assume this is something we simply have to roll with each day.

In reality, our own actions and attitudes have a huge influence in shaping other people's behavior. We are far less at the mercy of others' moods than we often assume—and that's what I'll show you in this part of the book. I'll show you how to create a great foundation for any interaction by building strong rapport from the start. I'll help you understand the motivations that tend to be uppermost in other people's minds, making it easier for you to understand where they're coming from and how to get the best out of them. And if tensions arise, I'll also show you some foolproof ways to handle challenging interactions with wisdom and self-assurance. At which point each episode of your soap opera should have a happy ending—or at least a productive one.

# EIGHT

# Building Real Rapport

When we really connect with someone, however fleeting it is, we all know how great it feels. There's the click of mutual understanding, and a sense of being on the same page. We can enjoy an easy laugh and a confidence shared. It can happen with a clerk in a store, or with a colleague, or with our spouse (certainly we hope we have it with our spouse). This feeling of affinity and openness makes everything feel easier, even when you've got serious stuff to talk about.

Is rapport a question of chemistry? Partly. But research also points to several human factors that can quickly increase the level of warmth and trust between two people. They involve the quality of our intent, the level of our curiosity, our ability to find things in common, and our own willingness to open up.

## SET COLLABORATIVE INTENTIONS

Let's first revisit the importance of our intentions in the context of our interactions with others. We know from Part I how subjective our experience of each day really is—how our aims, attitudes, and assumptions determine much of what our brain notices. So once we have certain expectations of an interaction, our brains will scan for evidence that matches those expectations and tend to filter out any signals that contradict them. If we go in looking for opportunities to collaborate, we stand a reasonable chance of finding them. If we go in spoiling for a fight, we'll tune in more to slights and disconnects. Because this filtering happens at a subconscious level, we'll swear that we're being objective. But the effects are real.

That's exactly where Peter's interpersonal challenges started. As the head of a consultancy that advises businesses on IT issues, Peter often parachutes into fraught situations after a huge project has started to go off track, well beyond the point where "shut it down and reboot" is helpful advice. He's good at his job and quick to smile. But Peter was finding that tensions often ran high with both his clients and his colleagues. He often felt disappointed or unimpressed by the people around him. And in turn, they weren't racing to spend time with him. In fact, just before Peter reached out to me for help, he'd had a contract terminated because of what he called "office politics." But, he said, "I'm a nice guy. I'm not a jerk. I need to understand what's going on."

As we talked, we realized that Peter's sense of self-worth had long been tied up with being smart, spotting problems, and moving fast to solve them. Over the years, he would engage in conversations with a clear (if unspoken) intention: he wanted to show he was right so that he could demonstrate his usefulness. And showing that he was right, in his mind, meant showing how other people were wrong.

Those intentions ended up badly skewing his interactions. Peter would keenly spot every opportunity to prove his point of view, marshaling data and charts to display his understanding of the situation. He'd see wrinkled brows and become frustrated that others seemed confused; meanwhile, he'd miss signals that his clients had valid questions to raise, or useful perspectives to share. Gradually, every conversation turned into some form of intellectual combat.

And yet, behind Peter's battle-readiness lay a more noble intention. Deep down, he had an overwhelming desire to be helpful, and a belief that he usually *could* do something useful if given the chance. But he began to see that if he was to have the effect he wanted, he needed to express that desire in a more collaborative manner. With that in mind, he started to recast his intentions for client meetings, using these guidelines:

➡ Aim: First, decide what collaborative outcome you'd really like from the conversation. Make sure it's one that is good for both of you, and that speaks to what matters most for your relationship.

➡ Assumptions: Second, check your negative expectations regarding the other person, because they'll shape what you notice. Instead, decide to look for something positive or interesting about that individual.

Peter's answer to the first question ("What do you *really* want from the conversation?") was obvious once he stopped to think about it. He needed to build a trusting relationship with his clients so that he could speak openly with them about the difficult work they were doing together. He wanted his clients to feel good about working with him, and to look forward to meetings with him rather than dreading them. And as to the second point, Peter realized he needed to stop assuming that his clients just didn't "get it."

The first big experiment was a dinner with the CEO of a business where he'd already made some enemies while working for the head of IT. The CEO was fairly new in his role and Peter was, as usual, tempted to quickly label him as being out of his depth. In the past, Peter would have highlighted all the ways that he was more knowledgeable than his client so the CEO would see just how much he needed Peter around. But instead, Peter set a clear, collaborative intention for the dinner, which was to better understand the CEO's hopes for the new role, and where he saw the biggest opportunities and concerns. "I found it really difficult not to wheel out my data, to show him how badly his business was doing, but I held back," Peter said. And it was worth it. "It really was a great conversation, much better than I expected." Peter also found that when he invested upfront in building rapport, he earned the right to show off a little. "Near the end of the dinner, the CEO actually did ask me for my views, so I had a chance to strut a bit of my stuff. And he seemed to like it." So much so that it marked the start of a better relationship between Peter and the CEO's company.

## ASK QUALITY QUESTIONS

Isn't it annoying when people don't really listen to what we're saying? There's the "mm-hmm" conversation, when the person we're talking to is obviously thinking his or her own thoughts—sometimes coupled with a dash of smartphone eye-flicking. There are times when the other person just talks and talks, leaving the exchange feeling distinctly one-sided. There's the "I know exactly what you mean" brigade, who are desperate to make clear that nothing you're experiencing is unique. And then there are the many routine conversations where both of you are just skating on the surface, exchanging autopilot pleasantries.

Unfortunately, we're all a little like this. Our heads are full of our own concerns most of the time, leaving us with less space to contemplate where other people are coming from. In fact, our brain's automatic system saves a lot of mental effort by using the shortcut of assuming that other people are fairly similar to us. Not identical, obviously. But we tend to assume that others share our preferences and perspectives, and that everyone understands and values things just as we do. This *projection bias*, as scientists call it, means that we don't always listen that closely to what others are saying. And if we're thinking about what we're going to say next, that diverts even more attention away from what the other person is saying, as we pause to reload our next salvo of comments and ideas.

None of this is great for rapport. If you recall the last time you had a conversation that made you feel you'd deeply connected with someone, chances are that it involved the other person showing some real curiosity about your life or your views. He or she probably gave you space to talk and made you feel heard. Being invited to share your thoughts and experience makes you feel interesting. All of this provides wonderful rewards for a social brain.

And research bears this out. In a recent experiment, Harvard psychologists Diana Tamir and Jason Mitchell gave volunteers small cash rewards for answering three types of questions: factual ones (e.g., "Leonardo da Vinci painted the *Mona Lisa*, true or false?"), invitations to speculate about other people (e.g., "How much does the president of the United States enjoy winter sports such as skiing?"), and opportunities to offer their own views about a subject (e.g., "How much do you enjoy winter sports such as skiing?"). In general, people preferred to talk about themselves—to the point that they willingly gave up money to do so, since the cash reward for talking about yourself was 17 percent lower than the other two options. By looking at brain scans, the researchers confirmed that talking about their own likes and dislikes activated the volunteers' neural reward systems, while speculating about the likes and dislikes of *other* people failed to have the same effect.[1]

So if we show some real curiosity about other people, they're going to find it rewarding to talk to us. And that's a fine footing for a good conversation. What does it mean to show real curiosity, though? Does it just involve asking questions? Well, that's a start. But it's not the whole answer, because most questions don't convey real interest in the other person. If you listen hard to your next group conversation at work, you'll notice that most of the questions that get asked are one of three types: they're superficially oiling the wheels ("Did you have a good weekend?" "Yes, you?"), they're factual inquiries ("How long till launch date?"), or they're platforms for conveying a hypothesis ("Have you thought of XYZ?" "Could you make things better by delegating more?" "Is the reason you're struggling because this is all new to you?"). We mean to be helpful when we're asking this sort of question, but our focus is to get our ideas across rather than find out what's in the other person's head.

The kind of question that signals genuine curiosity is quite different. First, it's an open question—one that can't be answered with a yes or a no. Second, it invites people to share their thoughts, motivations, or feelings, rather than merely facts. Third, you actually intend to listen and reflect on the answer. I call them "quality questions" because they immediately shift the quality of a conversation. For example:

➡ Not "Have you thought of XYZ?" but "How are you thinking about this?"

➡ Not "Is the reason you're struggling because this is all new to you?" but "What's making it feel hard?"

➡ Not "Could you make things better by delegating more?" but "What would the ideal situation look like for you?"

➡ And if you want to ask about people's personal lives, you could get beyond the normal "How was your weekend?" with a question like "What do you do outside work? How did you develop an interest in that?"

All of which can be followed with a simple invitation to share more, before you jump in with your own comments. Merely by saying "Tell me more about that," you'll be in the top percentile of listeners that anyone will meet today.[2]

Peter is on a mission to replace all his "here's my smart hypothesis" questions with quality questions that show true interest in his clients. It didn't work immediately. In a recent meeting with a new prospective client, Peter remembered to start by asking some questions to get to know the guy. But, he said, "I wasn't getting any interesting answers!

That rattled me, and so I quickly defaulted to my old approach and started to deluge the client with my ideas." Which didn't go so well. "He looked dazed and overwhelmed, and the meeting kind of fizzled out." In retrospect, Peter realized that his questions were "still quite superficial. They were either yes-no questions or just fact-gathering about his career. And I wasn't really listening to the answers. I was just waiting to tell him what I knew."

I asked Peter when he'd found it easiest to show genuine curiosity in recent conversations. He remembered an occasion when a meeting with an Italian client had been rescheduled so many times that by the time they met, there were no longer any pressing issues to discuss. As a result of having no fixed agenda for the meeting, Peter realized, he'd found it easy to ask genuine questions about his client's business and personal life, and to pay attention to the answers. Sure enough, the client sent a note afterward saying that it was one of the best professional conversations he could remember ever having.

Peter decided he could replicate the conditions of that meeting with other people, too. He wrote himself a list of reminders:

➡ Don't be too attached to a personal agenda (trust that you'll eventually find an opportunity to share your thoughts).

➡ Decide to find the other person interesting in some way.

➡ Ask truly open questions, rather than making suggestions masquerading as questions.

➡ Properly listen to the answer. Notice what seems most striking, and ask more about that.

With all that in mind, Peter got back in touch with the client he'd overwhelmed. "I apologized for having talked *at* him before, and told him I wanted to find out more about his thinking. And when I saw him, I took this completely different approach, asking real questions. I was surprised how it was possible to get back on track after that bad start. But it worked fine after I changed tack."

## THAT "IN-GROUP" FEELING

Whenever we meet people, our brains do some fast work to decide how to react. Do we recognize their face? Are they a threat to us? What are their most obvious characteristics? Are they like us, or not?

This last question is critical. In the absence of any other information, we lean toward seeing strangers as potential threats. "Better safe than sorry," say our brain's survival circuits. But as soon as we get a sense that the other person is similar to us in some way—politics, background, interests—we begin to relax, and subconsciously treat them as a potential ally. Scientists describe this as seeing someone as part of our *in-group.* And this small shift in social calculus has major effects on our interactions. First off, we're no longer in defensive mode, which makes us altogether more charming to be around. Research has also found that seeing someone as part of our in-group means we're immediately more likely to feel empathy for that person's pain, or share in the joy of his or her success.[3] And in general, brain scans suggest that when we think about people who seem similar to us, our neural activity looks a lot like we're thinking about ourselves.[4] So it's no wonder that we're so generous and attentive with people who seem to be part of our tribe. We're treating them a little like extensions of ourselves.

This has a real impact in the workplace. For one thing, we're more likely to hire people who look and act like us. Lauren Rivera, a sociologist at Northwestern University, found that 74 percent of recruiting managers at prestigious firms reported that their most recent hire had a "personality similar to mine."[5] How did they decide they were "similar"? It wasn't a particularly deep assessment. One of the most important factors was having familiar leisure pursuits, such as a shared interest in sports or technology.

And that tees up the good news here, which is that research confirms that it takes very little to create a tribal sense of "us." Experiments have shown that it's instantly created when people are randomly assigned to be on the same team.[6] Researchers even found that volunteers were more likely to help a stranger after they'd been asked to tap along in time to the same tune.[7]

I'm not suggesting that you walk down the hall picking people at random to be on your team, or start drumming your fingers on the table in your next meeting as you hum your favorite song. But you can quickly create powerful in-group benefits by asking enough questions to find small things in common with other people—such as a shared interest, taste, goal, or bugbear—and then taking the time to discuss them a little.

It can be tempting to skip this investment in building a sense of an in-group when everyone's busy and under pressure. It can feel like needless small talk. But that's often when it matters most, because research suggests that stress otherwise readily weakens people's ability to feel empathetic.[8] Under pressure, other people are more likely to treat us as a potential threat, less likely to care about what we think, and more likely to resist our ideas or appeals for help. So when we're up against a deadline or caught in a drama, it's even more important to find ways to connect with the person on the other side of the table.

Francesco is an accountant, and one day he was walking into a meeting where he would normally have gotten straight down to business—in this case, negotiating terms in a contract. He was expecting the discussion to be challenging. But Francesco and I had recently talked about this in-group research, so he decided to try something radical: "I started instead by treating the other guy like a normal person, rather than the enemy." Francesco asked him about his work and his background, and quickly found that they'd worked for the same accounting firm a long while ago. They talked briefly about that. When they came to the negotiation just a few minutes later, Francesco recounts, his opposite number said, "Don't worry, I trust you—your proposals look fine." Says Francesco, "I'd tried this approach in other meetings and it had worked well, but I hadn't expected it to help in a high-stakes situation like this. I guess he just needed to know that I wasn't trying to trick him in some way, and discovering our common ground seemed enough for him to trust that I wasn't trying to undermine his position."

Here are some suggestions for rapidly creating an in-group feeling with someone you're talking to:

➡ **Find a shared interest.** Look out for anything that signals interests or preferences that resonate with your own, however small they are. Music, gadgets, clothing, and hobbies are all fair game. Be willing to comment or ask about it, and to share your own experience.

➡ **Highlight a common goal.** This creates a deeper connection, because it usually signals shared values. To elicit shared goals, ask, "What matters most to you in this?" and "What do we both hope to achieve?"

➡ Talk about a common complaint. Be careful how you use this, because negativity can nudge people out of discovery mode. But it's an easy conversational gambit to complain about bad weather or traffic. A little "us against the world" (or against competitors or corporate headquarters) can help to create a feeling of being on the same team.

➡ Echo the other person's words. Not only does this help people feel you're on the same wavelength, but playing back someone's turn of phrase shows you've really been listening. The effect can be striking, even when you're merely echoing statements of fact; one study found that waiters get higher tips when they repeat an order back to customers.[9]

## RECIPROCAL DISCLOSURE (AKA "GIVE A LITTLE")

There's a branch of economics called game theory, which seeks to understand the way we make decisions when multiple people are involved—how we second-guess other people's motives, and what we choose to do as a result. It can feel like working through the moves of chess or dating—"if I do this, then maybe they'll do that, which means . . . oh, I probably shouldn't do this after all." And advanced game theory proves what psychologists have suspected for years, which is that reciprocity is very important to us as human beings.

To demonstrate this, economists use a famous game called the Prisoner's Dilemma, involving two partners-in-crime being held in separate prison cells. These two "players" each need to decide whether to collaborate or to cheat, without being able to communicate with each other. "Collaboration" means sticking to their pre-agreed story, which would allow both players to get off with a light sentence. "Cheating" means snitching on the other player in order to walk completely free, while leaving the other player to serve a long sentence. The game's payoffs are constructed to encourage both players to cheat on the other, to create an interesting dilemma for the players. Researchers have staged the game many thousands of times over the years, using different stories to explain the same basic set of tradeoffs. And their results show that the classic "cheating" solution is actually appealing only when the game is played just once. As soon as the Prisoner's Dilemma is set in more real-world terms—by allowing players to interact more than once, with each person having a chance to adapt his or her behavior to the other's, as in a real relationship—researchers found that a very different dominant strategy emerged: *reciprocity*, also known by economists as "tit-for-tat." That is, if you cheat this time, I'll cheat next time; if you collaborate this time, I'll collaborate next time. Not exactly Mother Teresa, but not Gordon Gekko, either.[10]

Neuroscientists examining brain scans of people playing Prisoner's Dilemma (and other similar games) have also seen evidence of our preference for reciprocity. They found that when one player chose to cheat rather than cooperate, it made the other player tense up and activated the part of his or her brain that deals with conflict resolution and self-control. When a player chose to cooperate, this activated the reward system in the other player's brain. And when they *both* cooperated, there was a happy buzz in both players' brains. In other words, reciprocity feels good.[11]

That's why charities give out buttons and pencils when they're trying to raise funds. It's why someone telling us some juicy gossip ("I heard that . . .") is quite likely to draw some nugget of information out of us ("Well, *I* heard . . ."). It's one reason that it can feel awful to say "I love you" to someone and be met only with a smile rather than an "I love you, too." Reciprocity is a powerful force for social harmony.

So how does this affect our ability to build rapport? Some years ago, I discussed the importance of reciprocity with a group of partners from a private equity firm. Their business involved buying underperforming companies and turning them around, so they could resell the companies for more money some years down the line. They appointed experienced executives to run the companies they owned, and they wanted these executives to keep them in the loop about all the issues they were wrestling with. And for that, they knew they needed to build trust. But it was proving mighty hard. It turned out that their hand-picked executives didn't much feel like pouring their hearts out to the owners, and the owners weren't entirely sure why.

After speaking to some of their executives, I realized what was going on. The executives didn't really see the private equity guys as real people. In their eyes, they were simply corporate overlords, to be avoided if possible, and certainly not to be confided in. The private equity partners were shocked and disappointed. But when I asked them what they'd shared with the executives of their *own* thoughts and concerns about work or life, they looked bemused. They were certainly ready to spout advice or ideas. But talk about their own personal worries with these executives? "Why on earth would we do that?" they asked. Because, I said, they were expecting the executives to do exactly that. And it wasn't fair to expect something from others that they weren't prepared to do themselves.

So, gradually, the private equity partners accepted the idea that showing a little of themselves might encourage more openness from the executives. It was new to them, but the results were quick and stark. One of them, Johan, was a burly man who rarely spoke about his feelings, and he certainly didn't relish the idea of opening up about concerns in his professional life. But he decided that he would feel comfortable talking about the worries he had about a construction project on a beach house of his. It wasn't particularly deep, but it was a good first step. The next time we met, Johan was beaming. "I was in the car with an executive after a meeting, so I thought, 'This is my chance,' and I started talking about the beach house. It was very surprising," Johan said. "He started talking to me about all sorts of things. We eventually did discuss how things were going at the company, too. It's the best discussion we've had." Of course, it wasn't the beach house that tripped the switch; it was the fact that Johan was willing to open up about something on his mind.

Arthur Aron, a psychology professor at Stony Brook University, wouldn't have been surprised to hear Johan's story. His research has showed that less than an hour of reciprocal disclosure is enough to create remarkable closeness between strangers. On a scale of 1 to 7, hundreds of volunteers rated their "deepest" relationship as a 4.65 for closeness. After talking about their answers to personal questions for forty-five minutes, random pairs rated their closeness as 3.82—not all that much lower.[12] The upshot: if you're trying to build rapport, be willing to reveal a little of yourself.

## POCKET THAT PHONE!

One last thing I should mention: technology keeps us connected—but it can also undermine rapport if you let it subtly compete for your attention, however much effort you're putting into asking quality questions, creating a sense of in-group, and using reciprocal disclosure. In a study by British psychologists, merely having a phone visible on the table led people to feel less of a connection with a stranger they'd been asked to talk to. They were less likely to agree with the statement "It is likely that my partner and I could become friends if we interacted a lot."[13] So if you're keen to have a meeting of minds, put away your phone and be fully present in the conversation.

### BUILDING REAL RAPPORT

For your next conversation where rapport is important:

➡ **Set collaborative intentions.** Set intentions that focus on improving the quality of the relationship, not on your agenda. Check your negative assumptions. Decide to find the other person interesting.

➡ **Ask quality questions.** Get really curious about the other person. Turn some of your regular closed, factual questions into open questions that invite them to share their thoughts and feelings about a topic (and that can't be answered with a yes or no). Show that you're listening by following up with a "tell me more" about one thing they said.

➡ **Create a sense of in-group.** Look for points of similarity or connection—shared goals, gripes, or interests—to create a sense of in-group that means the other person's brain sees you as friend rather than foe.

➡ **Use reciprocal disclosure.** If you'd like the other person to open up to you, think about what you're willing to show and share of yourself.

➡ **Pocket that phone.** If you need to stay reachable while having an important conversation, make your ringtone loud enough to hear from your pocket or bag.

# NINE

# Resolving Tensions

Rubbing shoulders with the rest of the human race can be hard at times. Everyone is living their own life, with their own goals and needs. As we all pull in different directions, we can easily find our days cluttered with annoyances. Sometimes they're small, like the irritable push of fellow commuters or a snappish comment in the corridor. Sometimes the grievances feel bigger. We might find ourselves having an argument that escalates, being excluded from an important discussion, or working with someone who repeatedly fails to follow through on their commitments.

When tensions bubble to the surface in this way, it's unlikely that we can control the whole situation. But we can choose how we want to react. And in this chapter, I'll show how much difference that can make. By focusing on what *we* can do to make things feel better, we can usually resolve or at least reduce the impact of tense situations, even when it's someone else who's triggered the tension.

## FIND COMMON GROUND

Let's start with the situation where we have a straight disagreement with someone. In some ways, it's surprising that arguments don't happen more often, given that the filters of our automatic system—including inattentional blindness and confirmation bias—make the reality we experience a highly personalized one. You only need one of your colleagues to have had a rough morning for that colleague to see things differently than you while you're sitting in the very same meeting (as I discovered with Lucas back in Part I). And since none of us ever has the whole picture, it's possible that both of you are right *and* wrong on certain aspects of the topic. We all see different "gorillas."

Mathematical psychologist Anatol Rapoport showed that recognizing this fundamental truth—that it's unlikely either side is 100 percent wrong—is the key to resolving conflict. In his classic book *Fights, Games, and Debates*, Rapoport demonstrated the power of developing what he called "empathetic understanding" of each other's point of view and what I simply call "common ground." It means showing that we've understood where the other person is coming from, and highlighting the similarities between us. From that common ground, mutually acceptable solutions are much easier to find, because the process helps to nudge our brains out of defensive mode, allowing us to think more creatively and approach compromise more openly.[1]

Here is the five-step process I've evolved based on his research:

➡ **Step 1: Describe the other person's point of view as if you really like it.** Be as compelling and generous as you can. The philosopher Daniel Dennett once put it like this: "You should attempt to re-express your target's position so clearly, vividly, and fairly that your target says, 'Thanks, I wish I'd thought of putting it that way.'"

➡ **Step 2: Identify all the things you agree on.** Recognizing the areas where you *do* agree, even if they're few, will help build a sense of in-group. Get the ball rolling with your own suggestions, then make it a collaborative effort by asking: "What else do we both believe to be true?"

➡ **Step 3: Isolate and understand the *true* disagreement.** Define precisely where you differ. Then go deeper by asking: "Why do we each feel or think differently about this specific issue?" Surfacing the experience or assumptions that shape your perspectives helps you understand the nature of your respective "gorillas." You may even learn from each other.

➡ **Step 4: Explore how both of you could be correct.** Now, you may "agree to disagree"; it feels easier to do that once you can see where you're aligned and why you disagree. But you can also ask: "Is there any way that both of our perspectives could be somehow correct?" It's often the case that you're each partially right—but perhaps in different situations or circumstances.

➡ **Step 5: What can you do now, based on your common ground?** There's always something. And the prospect of progress will help both of you feel good, making it easier to resolve or accept whatever is left on the table.

For example, suppose you're having an argument with a co-worker on the right way to get useful customer feedback. You think your company should invite anonymous comments from customers, because you think they'll be more candid that way. But your co-worker holds an opposing view: that customers should put their real names on their comments. So you first show you understand their side of the argument by outlining the advantages of their approach: customers will be less tempted to engage in trash talk and will only complain if they have a genuine grievance, and the company will be able to follow up with them directly if necessary.

Next, what do you both agree on? The benefits of soliciting more input from your customers, and that online is the way to do it, and that you want to get a process in place this month. The only thing you actually disagree on is whether customers should be anonymous. After a few "whys," it becomes clear that this is because you have different views on how readily customers speak their mind: you fear people won't speak up without anonymity, while your co-worker fears that people will speak up too much under the cloak of anonymity. Why? Your co-worker's been burned by a terrible social media campaign that backfired.

How could you both be right? Well, customers aren't all the same. You're probably each right regarding different types of customers. This part of the conversation germinates a few new ideas. It might be possible to design a survey that gives both options. Perhaps you could get people to proactively opt for anonymity so that it's not the default option. You could test out both approaches for a week each, and see what emerges.

Once you've found this common ground, it's clear that you can get moving on designing the majority of the process. The anonymity question can be resolved later; there's no need to hold everything up because of that. That seems obvious now. But when people's brains are in defensive mode, it becomes harder to see common sense. Small disagreements can end up holding back progress beyond reason. By contrast, focusing on your agreements leaves each of you better able to access your wisest selves—and get things done as a result.

## POSITIVE CONTAGION

In challenging interactions, the next thing you can do to set a constructive tone is to take advantage of a phenomenon called *emotional contagion*. That's the term used to describe the way our highly social brains are wired to sense the emotional state of other people around us, and to sync up with them.[2]

Social psychologists like Ron Friedman have found that merely being near someone in a good mood can be enough to lift people's motivation (and therefore their performance), and being near someone grumpy can do the opposite. Friedman and his colleagues at the University of Rochester showed that this happened even when people were working on completely different tasks—and it happened within five minutes, without any conversation.[3] Stress leaks, too. Other researchers found that asking people to do some unexpected public speaking not only made the speakers twitchy, but also raised the cortisol levels of people who'd been assigned to listen to them.[4] And it doesn't take much to provoke this contagion. German researchers found that merely looking at photos of people smiling or grimacing was enough to provoke measurable feelings of happiness or sadness, even when the viewers saw the photos for just half a second.[5]

So when there's tension at work, the mood we choose to carry into a conversation can throw either inflammatory fuel or soothing water on the fire. I remember facing that choice one day in a long coaching session with four hard-nosed corporate lawyers. I'd been told that one of the attendees would be very late, so we began the meeting without her. The conversation quickly picked up an inspiring momentum, full of mutual support and shared advice.

After a couple of hours, our tardy member finally breezed through the door and flung herself into a chair, the stress almost visibly rippling around her. She launched into a diatribe about how packed her schedule was, and then barked a question about future dates for the coaching program. I reminded her mildly that there was just one more long-agreed-upon session scheduled for a couple of months later. As she spluttered, "But I can't do that, it's not in my diary, I can't possibly . . . ," I watched in amazement as the other three, previously happy and energized, changed their demeanor entirely. Earlier they'd been sure they were coming to the next meeting, but now the room filled with grumbling: "Where's my phone?" "It's not in my calendar, either."

"I don't think I can make it." "How annoying." The cranky virus was on the rampage.

I had some choices. I could project the concern and irritation I was beginning to feel. Or I could try for something more positive. I thought about my real intention for the meeting: what mattered most here? The answer was clear: I wanted to restore the supportive group dynamic. So what emotion did I want to somehow radiate? This was all happening in a split second in my head, and so I had to work with whatever emotion came to mind, which was "love." Try not to groan. It was simple and strong, though I wouldn't have dared say the word out loud to any of them.

I knew I couldn't just grit my teeth and tell myself, "Feel loving, dammit"; I had to find a genuine warmth to project into the room. So I called to mind all the things I had really loved about working with them so far. With that in mind, it wasn't too difficult for me to smile at them benevolently, to nod and answer their questions calmly. Within a few minutes, I felt an easing in the air around us, a settling. We were back on track, and able to make good use of the rest of the time.

So when you're walking into a tense conversation or you feel the atmosphere sharpening around you, recognize that you can be a subliminal force for good in the room. You can't always change the direction of the conversation, but you can help to set the tone. To do this:

➡ Go back to your collaborative intention for the conversation, and ask yourself which emotion you'd like to be projecting.

➡ Think of times you've felt that emotion in the past, or of people who reliably put you in that mood. Visualize those situations or individuals in your mind, to harness a little of the mind's-eye rehearsal benefits we encountered in Chapter 3.

And if you're able to do this mental preparation *before* the meeting, so you can walk in full of infectious energy, so much the better.

## ASSUME "GOOD PERSON, BAD CIRCUMSTANCES"

At this point, we know that our assumptions about other people can dramatically influence our interactions with them. Confirmation bias means that if we're anticipating that someone's going to be dumb or annoying, we'll subconsciously pay disproportionate attention to the dumb or annoying things they say or do—and even twist those observations a little until they confirm our hypothesis (remember the gray/yellow bananas in Chapter 1). But it goes further than that, because if we then respond negatively to those perceived provocations, showing frustration or irritation, it's a sure way of putting the other person's brain into defensive mode—which makes it *harder* for them to be brilliant and charming, and *more* likely that they'll behave dysfunctionally. When it comes to other people, our negative assumptions can quickly become a self-fulfilling prophecy.

And psychologists have found our habitual assumptions about other people aren't terribly forgiving. When we think about ourselves, we know that certain aspects of our behavior are constrained by the circumstances we find ourselves in. For example, if we get less work done today than we should have, part of the story might be that we're short on sleep, or we're not feeling well, or we're waiting on some essential feedback from a colleague. But if we see someone *else* doing less than we would expect, we tend to assume it reflects something fundamental about that person's capabilities or character—that they're incompetent or lazy, rather than tired or delayed. We rarely spend a lot of time considering the reasons he or she might not be on their game today, especially if we don't know them very well. This tendency to attribute others' weaknesses to character rather than circumstances is something psychologists call the *fundamental attribution error.*[6]

Why do we judge others so much more harshly? Well, our brain's automatic system finds it simpler that way. It takes less mental energy to assess someone once and then pigeonhole him or her forever—"Aah, Person X is not very smart"—rather than analyze what might be going on with Person X every time we see them. On high-stress days when our brains are overloaded with other things to worry about, researchers have found that we're even more likely to take a shortcut by making this kind of generalization.[7]

Early in her career at Harvard, Teresa Amabile and colleagues ran an experiment that shows how the fundamental attribution error can harm colleagues who are struggling at work. They took 120 people and nominated some of them as "questioners," who were asked to compose a series of difficult general knowledge questions based on things they themselves already knew. Another group, the "answerers," was to do its best to answer the questions. The interaction was watched by a third group, the "observers." Afterward everyone was asked to assess the intelligence of people they'd interacted with. Here's what's startling: even though it was clear that the questioners had made up questions based on their own esoteric interests, and this was why the answerers struggled to get many questions right, all three groups rated the answerers as less smart than the questioners. And the answerers were even harder on themselves than the questioners.[8] Nobody seemed to accept that the answerers performed less well because of the situation they'd been randomly placed in, rather than because of their innate intelligence.

So we make big assumptions about other people's personalities and capabilities based on very limited observations. When we find ourselves labeling someone as dumb, lazy, or annoying, it should raise a red flag. How much of that person's behavior is driven by circumstance, and how much is driven by character? Asking yourself this question doesn't mean the other person isn't being irritating *right now*—but it can lower the tension considerably if you can conceive of him or her being a good person in bad circumstances.

Here's what I suggest when someone has infuriated or disappointed you:

➡ Step 1: Get clear on the "true facts." All facts are true, right? Well, by *true* facts, I mean the things you truly do know for sure. Remember how even our factual perceptions are subjective, thanks to the filtering of our brain's automatic system. So the first step is to strip away as much subjectivity as you can, by focusing on what actually happened, without interpretation or emotion. For example, in an interaction where you felt ignored by your boss, saying "She ignored me" assumes her actions were deliberate. That's an interpretation—something you don't know for sure. What *can* you say for sure? "She didn't say anything to me when I saw her this afternoon, or at least I don't remember her saying anything." Boom. That's your true fact.

➡ Step 2: Assume "good person in bad circumstances," and consider potential explanations for his or her behavior. Assume the person is essentially decent, and turn your "What the heck?" into "What could be going on with them?" "What could have triggered their defenses?" (For guidance, see the box "Common Defensive Mode Triggers," on page 136.) "What might they be feeling or fearing?" Come up with two or three possible reasons for the behavior you've observed. You don't have to believe those explanations; the mere idea that there *could* be circumstances behind this behavior helps reframe the situation from one where they're an aggressor to one where they *could* be a victim. And that reduces the sense of threat they're presenting to your brain, making it easier for you to be your best self in handling the situation.

Armed with your potential alternative explanations, you can proceed in a more tolerant frame of mind—perhaps to find out what's really going on with that person by asking some sympathetic questions, or simply assuming the best in him or her and proceeding accordingly.

Russell, the hotel brand director we met in Part I, swears by this "good person, bad circumstances" approach. It's part of his responsibility to make sure that unhappy customers get their issues resolved—which means he often finds himself in the middle of challenging conversations with colleagues. He says: "People might act like jerks, but you often don't know what's really causing it. That insight came to me years ago, when I was wheeling a suitcase down the middle of a road because the sidewalk had terrible potholes. A car came up behind me, and to the driver I obviously looked like an idiot. Why on earth was I walking in the road? Then I had a lightbulb moment. I realized that from the car, he couldn't see that the sidewalk was impossible to navigate. Since then, I've used that as a metaphor for the fact that nobody ever has the whole picture. If someone doesn't seem to get where I'm coming from, I remind myself, 'He's just in his car.' But often I'm the one that's 'in the car,' when I have to remind myself there's probably a good reason that someone's doing something that to me looks annoying."

In general, therefore, Russell says he reminds himself to go into challenging conversations assuming the best about people. "I presume most people are trying to do a good job. I think that's a way of taking control of a situation, to decide to attribute good intentions to someone. If you treat apparently difficult people as if they're coming from a good place, you see more of the good things they do. And they can sense it, which means they're likely to respond well, which fulfills your expectations."

Russell gives a recent example. "I had a colleague who seemed to be jockeying for position. He'd invited himself along to a brand strategy meeting that I chair, and in the middle of it he questioned the actual purpose of the meeting—why it existed, how it related to other parts of the corporate strategy process. Instinctively I interpreted it as a power grab. I thought he was trying to undermine me. But then I realized that I was 'in the car,' attributing bad intentions to his behavior. So I decided instead to assume that he was raising a genuine question. I drew him a diagram to show how the meeting would feed into the broader strategy process. He appreciated it, and told me afterward that he'd really enjoyed the meeting. It could have gone down a very different track if I'd assumed he actually had bad intentions."

## Fits All Sizes

Once you're in the habit of thinking like this, you can apply the "good person, bad circumstances" technique in seconds whenever you're disconcerted by someone's behavior. For example, suppose you sent an email request a few days ago to someone who hasn't replied. It's easy to assume this signifies a problem—that the recipient is ignoring the message, perhaps because they don't like the request, or don't like *you*. You're about to send a slightly tense email to chase a response. But what are the "true facts"? You sent the original email seventy-two hours ago, and you have not seen a reply. Then, assuming "good person, bad circumstances," the possible explanations include: she replied and it's in your spam folder; she's really busy; she's on vacation and didn't set an auto-responder; she's thinking about your request and is not yet sure what to say; she's totally disorganized and about to declare email bankruptcy. With even one of those alternative explanations in mind, the chances are that you'd write a more generous email, or perhaps pick up the phone, or at least stop worrying for a while. (And if you're the one not replying to other people's email, do take a look at Appendix B at the back of the book.)

## COMMON "DEFENSIVE MODE" TRIGGERS TO WATCH OUT FOR

When you encounter someone behaving in a way that seems dysfunctional—whether it's a sharp comment, surprising stubbornness, a turf grab, or general unresponsiveness—it's likely that something has put him or her into defensive mode. But what? Well, there's a pretty clear set of "threats" that will trigger the average person, usually involving a fear that some fundamental human need isn't being met. Several needs are social in nature: inclusion, fairness, and feeling respected. Other needs are more about an individual's self-worth: autonomy, competence, purpose, and security. There's also a more basic need for rest and refueling, reflecting the fact that when we're exhausted, either mentally or physically, we become more sensitive to *all* potential triggers. Being familiar with the following list of common needs and fears will help you become more adept at figuring out what could be pushing someone's hot buttons—and whether you're inadvertently the one doing the pushing.

| Social Needs | Common Triggers to Watch Out For |
|---|---|
| Inclusion | Has the person been excluded from something, such as a meeting, a process, or an email thread (whether inadvertently or deliberately)? |
| | Could the person feel isolated, perhaps because they're from a different background or have different views, values, or experience? |
| Fairness | Could your actions (or those of others) be perceived by the person as unfair? |
| | Could the person feel they're giving a lot without receiving anything in return, violating the principle of reciprocity? |
| Respect | Could the person feel they've been publicly undermined—for example, by being criticized in public or by having others disagree with his or her views? |
| | Is the person getting enough recognition and praise for their efforts? Have they recently received negative feedback? |
| | Does the person feel they're being listened to? Do they often get interrupted or ignored? |

However, if you read this list and are still thinking "I have *no* idea what this person's problem is," take heart. There is a silver bullet, and it's this: show them some appreciation. Telling someone that you recognize the efforts they're making—or indeed sharing any kind of compliment—speaks to many fundamental human needs, by helping people feel more competent, valued, and fairly treated. That's a recipe for cutting the tension quite quickly. Your sentiment doesn't have to be expressed lavishly to have an effect, either. In a study by Japanese researchers, volunteers in a brain scanner were told that total strangers had characterized them as "sincere" or "dependable." It was uninformed praise, but it still activated the volunteers' reward systems to the same degree as a financial incentive.[9] So if in doubt, find something appreciative to say to the person, and go from there. (In fact, go specifically to the next section on the "notice-acknowledge-offer" technique.)

---

## Potential Solutions to Explore

- Acknowledge the exclusion, and explain the reasons for it (if it was intentional).
- Highlight where the person is being included in *other* important activities.
- Consider whether you can give the person a defined role that makes them feel part of the team.

- Emphasize your similarities more than your differences. (Review the advice on creating a sense of "in-group" in Chapter 8.)
- Encourage connections between them and others in the group.
- Explore whether there's a chance for your group to learn from the person's perspective.

- Be transparent with him or her about the rationale for what's happened.
- If you've had to make difficult choices, open up to them about the dilemmas you faced. (See the section "Come On, Be Fair" in Chapter 10.)

- Make sure they're receiving credit for their contributions to a team or group effort.
- Find something you can give back or help the person with. Ask what support they need to perform at their best.
- Highlight any support they're already getting, if it's behind the scenes and unknown to them.

- Visibly rebuild their sense of status, perhaps by saying positive things about him or her in public, giving them new desirable responsibilities, or asking their advice.
- Convey to the person that their views are valuable, even if they were overruled. If you can, show how they helped enrich the debate.

- People hear criticism far more vividly than praise—so be more vocal in showing appreciation for the things they're doing.
- When you do need to give someone feedback, always use the techniques in the section "Brain-Friendly Feedback" in Chapter 10.

- Even if you don't agree with what the person is saying, make sure they know you've understood their point, by repeating what you think they're saying, and checking with "Did I get that right?"
- If you notice someone being talked over, pause the conversation and invite them to make the point he or she was trying to interject.

| Individual Needs | Common Triggers to Watch Out For |
|---|---|
| Autonomy | Has the person had something presented to them as a fait accompli? Have they been told to do something without having much say? |
| | Could the person be feeling micromanaged? |
| Competence | Might they be feeling out of their depth? |
| | Do they face a real chance of failure in their work (whether anyone's admitting it or not)? |
| Purpose | Has anything happened that might feel like a violation of his or her personal values (e.g., equality, honesty, trust)? |
| | Is the person working on something that might feel pointless, thankless, or dull? |
| Security | Will proposed changes take away something the person is used to having, such as a resource or a routine? |
| | Is the person facing a lot of uncertainty in their role? Are their responsibilities unclear? |
| | Have you failed to do something you promised to do? (Or could it be perceived that way?) |
| Rest | Could the person be physically exhausted, or stretched by family or health issues? |

## Potential Solutions to Explore

- Find some specific choices that you can let them control, however small—like the timing of a deadline or the location of a meeting.
- Make sure the person feels properly consulted on next steps.

---

- Get clear where they truly need your input, and give them more space to act on other topics—even if they don't do things exactly as you would.
- Try the "extreme listening" and "coach, don't tell" techniques from Chapter 10.

---

- Check what the person feels well equipped to do, and where they're feeling less confident.
- Where possible, emphasize the places where they're in good shape.
- Help them see how to access support on the areas where they're less confident.

---

- Ask where the biggest risks lie, and help the person identify ways to mitigate them.
- Show them that it will be possible to learn from failure, if it happens—and that you will help them do so.

---

- Have an open conversation with the person about their values. Explore the possibility that the same value may be interpreted differently by different people.
- Consider whether there is anything that can be done to respect those values more fully.

---

- Show them how their work contributes to something bigger or more meaningful. Help them see who benefits from what they're doing.
- Help the person see how they might play to their strengths or interests, even in work that's less than fascinating.

---

- Highlight what they will get in its place. Make that benefit feel as real and personal as possible.
- If there are no benefits to them, at least be transparent on the reason for the change.

---

- Help him or her work out what *is* stable or known amid the uncertainty.
- Outline the process by which uncertainty will be resolved (even if the outcome is still unknown).
- If you've been sitting on a request from this person, at least send a holding response if you're not able to engage fully with their question.
- Help them clarify what they're responsible for delivering, and where the boundaries with other people's jobs are.

---

- Explain precisely why things turned out differently. Apologize for the resulting impact on them (even if it's not your fault). Explain what you can definitely now commit to doing.

---

- Signal that it's okay to talk about the demands he or she is facing.
- Help them find a way to recharge their batteries, or to balance those demands with their workload.

## NOTICE-ACKNOWLEDGE-OFFER

If someone's in defensive mode, we can often improve the situation merely by considering what might have triggered his or her behavior. Empathy can shift the tone of our responses just enough to stop the tension from escalating. But if you suspect there's a real problem, it's obviously best to have an actual conversation with the person about whatever has triggered that reaction.

Why? For one thing, when you acknowledge what someone's feeling, their brain will stop trying to telegraph their needs and fears quite so frantically. For another, there's a chance we don't actually know what's put the person into defensive mode, in which case we might try to solve the wrong problem. For example, you might guess that a colleague is being prickly because they weren't copied in on an important email discussion, when the real issue is that a treasured member of their team has applied for a job opening in your part of the organization. Or their bad temper might have nothing to do with you at all. And if you start copying them in on every single email you send, it's not going to make them any happier to see you.

So if you sense that someone is upset or irritated—whether with you or someone else—and you can find a way to talk to him or her directly, try this simple "notice-acknowledge-offer" routine:

➡ **Step 1: Notice.** Tell the person what you've noticed and then ask for their perspective. Focus on a factual observation and phrase it in neutral terms. For example: "I noticed that the board went with option X after all. What's your view on that?" Or "I noticed that you frowned when I made that suggestion. Can I ask what was on your mind?"

➡ **Step 2: Acknowledge.** Once they've shared their feelings, show that you've understood by saying, "I'm sorry, that must be frustrating/concerning/annoying" (select an appropriate sympathetic word). This step signals that you're not dismissing whatever is bothering them. It doesn't matter if *you* think they shouldn't feel frustrated, concerned, or annoyed. If *they* think they have cause, their brain will be on the defensive. Making them feel heard helps to reduce the state of alert in their brain. And the word "sorry" is helpful even if you've done nothing wrong—it conveys that you care (just as it does when you say "sorry for your loss" to someone who's been bereaved).

➡ **Step 3: Offer.** Ask, "Is there anything I can do to improve the situation?" Often the answer is no, but if the answer is yes, it's good to know. It's important to ask even if you didn't cause the problem; you may see a way to help, and if you want the person's dysfunctional behavior to stop, it's worth the effort.

Lucy is the chief operating officer of a payroll and pension services company, and over the years she's seen the value of being able to have honest, supportive discussions about workplace irritations. "I've been in three jobs where I had to sort out a major relationship issue that was having real business impact. Tensions build up, and it's amazing to me that very few people really do anything to resolve things by having a real conversation about the issue." To have those conversations, Lucy is a big fan of the notice-acknowledge-offer technique.

"Once, I was responsible for managing a global alliance we'd formed with another company. There were four different regions, and one was headed by someone who was notoriously unsupportive of the alliance. It wasn't clear why. He was very effective, always hit his numbers, but had a reputation for being obstructive." So Lucy went to see him. "I said: 'This is what we're trying to achieve.' Then I opened up a bit and said, 'I've noticed you're not on board, which obviously worries me. Tell me—what's working, and what's not working?'

"His immediate response," says Lucy, "was, 'You're already halfway there, because you've bothered to come to see me and ask what I think!' It turned out that he wasn't against the alliance. But he'd been feeling that he was being ordered to attend meetings, which he often couldn't make because nobody had checked his availability before scheduling them." And Lucy saw that this was an example of something broader— that he felt he'd been *told* what to do throughout, rather than being engaged in a discussion of what should happen. "By contrast, I was now asking for his views, including and involving him, and showing that he was respected. After that, we met once a month, and I made sure that he was included in all operational discussions." And, says Lucy, there was no more "obstructive" behavior.

## MANAGE YOUR OWN BAGGAGE

We've talked about the other person in the interaction being the one who's in defensive mode, and how you can be smarter in working out what's triggered him or her. But I'm hoping that at this point, you're also considering the fact that you're part of this equation. Tension, by definition, requires two sides pulling tight. There wouldn't *be* tension if you weren't also at least a little triggered—whether by the other person or by something related to them. And sometimes it's hard to know where tension starts, because the evidence on emotional contagion tells us how quickly stress can be mirrored between two people. It's not always obvious who "caused" the situation. So it's worth examining the baggage you're bringing into the conversation, and handling it with care.

Let me pick out three things you can do to become better at this—all of which are centered on deepening your self-awareness. First, understand your "hot buttons," the things that are most likely to trigger you. Second, know the early warning signals that you're slipping into defensive mode. Third, have a simple go-to routine that allows you to step back and hit the reset button. Together, these three things add up to really skillful self-management when you're under pressure.

### Know Your Hot Buttons

All of us have some kind of reaction to the common triggers set out on pages 136–139, but most of us have specific situations that are especially guaranteed to fire us up. For example, maybe you just hate being talked over (violating your need for respect and perhaps also reciprocity). Or maybe your pet peeve is dealing with someone very flaky (causing you uncertainty, and possibly challenging your competence if his or her unreliability affects your own ability to deliver); meanwhile, someone else might see a talkative, flaky colleague as rather vivacious and spontaneous. We're all different in our intolerances, because the things that really rile us often harken back to past sources of hurt or annoyance that have settled deep into our long-term memories. Our brain's survival circuits draw on those memories for clues that we're facing a threat, reacting strongly if they find a match between the present situation and a past negative incident.

But if we can see a pattern in the things that bug us, we can get faster at spotting when we're in the grip of a defensive response—and that means we can launch our "step back and reset" routine before the conversation goes too far south. It also makes us more adept at anticipating conversations that are likely to trigger us, allowing us to plan accordingly.

To get a clearer picture of your hot buttons, take a few minutes to make some notes on the following:

➡ Think about a time you got irritated or upset with someone (whether you showed it or not).
  - What were the other people saying or doing that you found difficult?
  - What were you thinking—*and* feeling—as a result?
  - What really felt at stake for you? What did you stand to lose?
Repeat the exercise with another couple of situations.

➡ Look across your examples. What comes up more than once in your answers? What does that suggest might be a particular hot button for you? (Refer back to the list of common triggers for inspiration if it helps you to articulate what you're reacting to.)

*Bonus question*: what happened in your past to make you especially sensitive to this? If you can answer this, it may highlight how the situations you face today are not like the original one that got under your skin, which might help to reduce the strength of your reaction.

➡ Look ahead to any important conversations you have coming up at work in the next week or two. Do any of them run the risk of including this hot button? If so, what collaborative intentions can you set for the conversation, to help keep you on track throughout?

### Know Your Early Warning Signs

Forward planning is helpful. But our automatic brain works fast to put us on the defensive. So fast, in fact, that we can be triggered before we even consciously realize what's going on. So it helps to recognize the early warning signs that your deliberate system is going offline. For example, I know that if I haven't smiled for a while and my face feels set and frozen, it's a sign that I might be in fight-flight-freeze mode. For you, the most obvious physical signal might be a change in the pitch of your voice, your chest tightening, sweaty palms, or a pounding heart. You might also have some signature phrases you tend to say when you're in defensive mode. So think again about those past situations where you were wound up. Walk through them again in your mind. Notice:

→ The way your body or voice changes when you're getting uptight

→ Any pointed phrases that you find yourself saying when you're annoyed or upset—to yourself, or out loud

→ What other people might notice in your tone or demeanor if they were watching you

### Know How to "Step Back and Reset"

When you feel the temperature rising—either you've spotted your favorite trigger, or you've spotted an early warning sign—you want to have a simple go-to technique to help you step back and reset. You're effectively giving your brain's deliberate system a moment to catch up with the faster automatic system that's put you on alert. But you need it just at the point that you're feeling the pinch. So it needs to be something easy, that you can do quickly and without much thought, when you're in the middle of a tense interaction. (In Part VI, on resilience, I'll show you some more techniques for rising above difficult situations, but "step back and reset" is the core of what you need in the middle of a conversation.)

Try doing some thinking now about the right technique to deploy in the heat of the moment.

→ Step back. Decide on a small personal routine that helps you stop and take a deep breath. If that sounds a little like the "mindful pause" idea in Chapter 6, on overcoming overload, you're right. What worked for you when you're feeling overloaded might also work for you in the middle of a tense conversation; Anthony uses what he calls his "triangular breathing" technique for both situations (breathing in for three, out for three, pausing for three). Since my early warning sign is a frozen face, my "step back" usually involves me smiling broadly. For a client of mine, it involves holding her pen between both hands and examining it while she rolls it between her fingers a couple of times.

➡ Reset. Ask yourself a question, to reengage your brain's deliberate system and encourage some of the curiosity and exploration that's characteristic of discovery mode. Again, it helps to have a go-to question that you can remember at times of stress. Here are some I like:
- "What was/is my real intention for this conversation?"
- "What's really going on here? What's triggering this tension in me, in them?"
- "When I look back on this, what will I feel good about having done?"

When Peter (the IT consultant we met in the last chapter) thought back over his most tense conversations, some clear habitual triggers emerged. "One definite hot button for me is a situation where I don't feel I'm getting my point across. I've taken the time to explain something well, and the other person still doesn't accept what I'm saying. That annoys me without fail." Situations like this challenged Peter's desire to feel valued, and they were usually accompanied, he says, by a feeling of "wanting to fix something and not being able to do it. Feeling like I have to be a sledgehammer." What early warning signals would enable Peter to spot that he was about to behave like a sledgehammer? "There's something about my shoulders tensing up. My voice gets louder, too." There were also certain phrases that told him that he was about to lose his balance. "I hear myself think, 'I know I'm right!' followed by 'Why don't you get it?'"

With this self-awareness, Peter became much better at predicting when he would go into hammer mode. And as soon as he noticed his tension levels rising, he used a specific phrase to help him step back. "It's something a very laid-back friend of mine says at stressful times: 'Easy does it.' I say that to myself and it reminds me of him, and reminds me to relax." For the next step, reengaging his deliberate system, Peter finds that "asking myself 'What really matters?' is a good reset question for me. It stops me trying to pound the person with my point of view, by reminding me that's not actually my aim. A better relationship is the aim."

## Midflight Correction

If you find it too difficult to "step back and reset" in the middle of a tense conversation, don't despair. You've got at least a couple of other options. One is to simply excuse yourself for a few minutes. Everyone needs to go to the bathroom from time to time, so just use that as a convenient excuse to regroup.

The second option is to perform your "step back and reset" out loud. In the middle of a conversation, Peter was still occasionally finding himself thinking: "Oh no—I *know* I'm triggered, because of the way I'm behaving, but I don't know what to do! I must plow on!" But he discovered it was perfectly possible to say, "I'm sorry, I realize I'm having a reaction to something we've just discussed. Can we pause for a moment?" Not only does this kind of candid disclosure give you a chance to reset your approach, but it can also—as we saw in Chapter 8 on building rapport—deepen the level of trust and openness in the conversation.

## HOW TO RAISE DIFFICULT ISSUES WITH SKILL

Occasionally, all the social intelligence and self-awareness in the world can't get around the fact that someone has done something to wind you up. You try to rise above it, but every time you talk to that person there's a cloud lingering over your exchange. What should you do? Continue to try to smooth things over, or tackle the issue?

You can guess where I'm going with this. There's a strong case for clearing the air, for several reasons. First, as long as you're tense, your deliberate system is unlikely to be mustering your best social skills, even as you're supposedly smoothing things over. Second, far from lowering the ante, trying to suppress negative emotion has been shown to make the brain's defensive response even more pronounced.[10] Third, confirmation bias means that you're likely to see ever *more* sources of annoyance in this person over time, rather than being able to move on, because your expectations of this person now have a negative slant. Fourth, you might hope to avoid conflict by trying to pretend nothing is wrong, but emotional contagion will have you communicating your quiet simmering in subconscious ways. So you might think you're protecting the relationship by keeping your mouth shut, but there's a good chance that you're only making things worse.

The challenge is that very few of us relish conflict, and "clearing the air" sounds like code for "awkwardness." So here's a technique you can use to get things off your chest while also putting your relationship back onto a stronger footing. I've taught it to CEOs to help them raise difficult issues with their boards, but it works in lower-stakes situations, too.

As always, the starting point is the intention you set for the conversation. Although you might be unhappy with the other person's behavior, having a goal for the conversation of "I want to show her what's what!" is not going to reduce conflict. I was once working with a real estate advisor named Simon who was upset with a prospective client. The issue was that the client had assured Simon that he was likely to win a project that he'd bid for, but then she had failed to award him the work—and this had happened several times in a row. When I asked Simon to articulate his goal for his conversation with her, the first word that came to his mind was "revenge." He laughed, but it was only slightly funny, because it was obviously somewhat true. So I asked him what he *really* wanted from the conversation. "A good result would be if she saw me more as a person, less as a disposable service provider. And I'd like to understand where she's coming from in deciding who to give work to."

Once your collaborative intentions are set, I can all but guarantee that you'll safely navigate the conversation if you walk through the following steps. It helps if you can take five or ten minutes to jot down some notes before you go into the conversation, so you're clear on what you want to say in steps 2 and 3 in particular:

➡ Step 1: Ask permission. Don't just dive in. Say: "Our relationship is important to me, and there's something on my mind—can I talk to you about it?" If it's a bad time, you don't want to choose this moment for your chat; if it's a good time, you've signaled your collaborative intent.

➡ Step 2: Describe what you observed. The trick here is to focus on the true facts, again without emotion, interpretation, or generalization. Don't blurt out phrases like "You let me down" or "You're no good at . . ."; these statements are debatable, because the other person can say, "That's not true." Instead, aim for something that feels more like "What I noticed was [fact, fact, fact]." For example, Simon said: "What I noticed was that when we met two weeks ago to discuss the outline

of our proposal, I recall you used the phrase 'you're front-runners'—
but then we didn't make the short list." (He did not say "you gave us
false hope.")

→ **Step 3: Say how the facts made you feel.** Next, describe the way the person's behavior made you feel. The power of this step is that, again, it's not disputable, and it humanizes the issue that you're raising. For example, Simon said: "It made me feel confused, because I'd had positive feedback from you, and then we apparently didn't even do well enough to make it to the next round. It makes me feel worried that I'm not understanding what you need or want from us."

Here, it helps not to use dramatic language. For example, Simon was tempted to say that the experience made him feel "incredibly angry." But before the meeting, he asked himself which of the common triggers he was reacting to, and he realized his anger was sparked by a concern that he was letting his team down. It was a competence issue. This was something he could safely talk about.

If you can, it also helps to add a sincere explanation of why this matters to you, to convey that this isn't about you whining. You are speaking up because you feel this is important enough to merit discussion. For example, for Simon: "I care about that because it's my job to make sure that we're delivering the best possible service to you. If we're not doing that, I really want to find out why."

→ **Step 4: Ask for the other person's perspective.** Of course, we know by now that we never have the whole picture in any situation, thanks to our brain's *selective attention*. So don't forget to ask: "How do you see it?" Then pay attention to the answers, without arguing or trying to inject solutions. In Simon's situation, it turned out that his client had no idea that her encouragement was seen as a rubber stamp. Her goal had been to solicit as many good proposals as possible. It's possible Simon was misinterpreting what she'd said, or maybe she'd genuinely overdone it. Either way, he now had an understanding of where she was coming from. His ballooning anger was being nicely deflated.

→ **Step 5: Do some joint problem solving.** The final step is to decide together how to make things better. If you're giving feedback to someone junior to you, it's easy to make this a moment where you tell him or her how to improve. Resist that temptation. Ask them for their thoughts first, and then build on their suggestions. (Remember the importance of autonomy as a motivator.) In Simon's case, his client suggested they have a more in-depth discussion about the things her company was looking for in a supplier, so that Simon could better understand their business needs. She was impressed that he'd raised the issue with her so thoughtfully. And by this point, revenge was very far from his mind.

## HOW TO DEAL WITH UNSPEAKABLY DIFFICULT PEOPLE

We've learned that when we encounter bad behavior in another person, it typically reflects some kind of defensive reaction unfolding in their brain. By addressing whatever may be posing a threat, we can usually nudge that person back into the arms of their better angels. But with some particularly challenging people, it can be difficult to sustain the effort required to unearth their goodness. (Key words: psychopath, narcissist, serial jerk.) In that case, you might decide to set a more modest goal: making your interactions manageable rather than marvelous.

Here's how to use the principles in the book to do that:

➡ Play back what they've said. Where possible, repeat what you think they're asking or saying, and check "did I get that right?" It makes them feel heard, which can calm them. And playing back their unvarnished words can occasionally highlight their unreasonableness.

➡ Talk about observable actions, not their attitude. You can have factual conversations about actions—for example, about whether something was done or not done, by whom, at what time. They can deny they have a bad attitude. It's harder to deny the facts of what's happened.

➡ Be crystal clear in your communication. Remember you each have different cognitive filters. What you say may not be what they hear. So: use simple language, clearly define what success looks like, and set obvious deadlines. Make sure it's captured in writing if possible.

➡ Focus on solutions. You can help both of you stay in discovery mode if you focus as much as possible on the ideal outcome of whatever you're working on. This might require you to let go of points of debate or annoyance, in order to focus on the prize that matters most.

➡ **Show appreciation.** If you can stomach it, feed their psychological need for recognition. Find something specific that you can tell them you appreciate about them.

And to help you be your best self through these interactions:

➡ **Get some distance.** The activation of our own brain's defensive system drops when we adopt a distanced perspective on the situation (see Chapter 17 for more on this). So, imagine what you'd say if you were giving advice to someone else dealing with this person. Think about what will make you look back in the future and say "I rose above it and handled it pretty well."

➡ **Concoct a story to explain their behavior.** A disastrous childhood? A marital drama? Maybe, maybe not. But just considering the possibility that they're a victim of circumstance can help to reduce the sense of threat they're presenting to your brain.

➡ **Talk to people who can support you.** Remember that social connection feels like a reward for our gregarious brains, so it usually helps to talk to someone you trust about the situation.

➡ **Cut your losses.** If you've tried all the techniques here and they're still being unconstructive, it's okay to minimize the exposure you have to them (see "Ditch Your Sunk Costs" in Chapter 18 to see why). Keep your interactions short, businesslike, and polite, without investing much more of yourself.

## RESOLVING TENSIONS

If there's someone who's causing you stress at the moment, try one or more of these techniques:

➡ **Find common ground.** If you disagree on something, use the following process: articulate the other person's perspective as if you truly believe it; identify what you both agree on; isolate the real disagreement; explore how you could both be right; and decide what you can do based on what you agree on.

➡ **Spread positive contagion.** Your own mood can be infectious. Decide what emotion you want to project into the conversation, and visualize something that can quickly put you in that state of mind.

➡ **Assume "good person, bad circumstances."** Get clear on the "true facts": what you know for sure. Then assume that the other person has good intent, and imagine the circumstances that could be causing his or her behavior. (Refer to the list of classic defensive mode triggers for inspiration.)

➡ **Notice-acknowledge-offer.** If you can have a direct conversation, use the "notice-acknowledge-offer" approach to check that you understand the issue and to move things forward. Invite the person to talk ("I noticed that . . ."), show empathy ("I'm sorry, that must be challenging . . ."), and offer support ("Is there anything I can do?").

➡ **Manage your own baggage.** Identify your hot-button patterns—triggers that you particularly respond to—and your early warning signs. Decide on a quick "step back and reset" routine, including a question to fully engage your deliberate system (e.g., "What really matters here?").

➡ **Raise difficult issues with skill.** Set your collaborative intention. Then, in the conversation: ask permission, make your factual observation, share your feelings (and why the issue matters to you), invite the other person's perspective, and jointly discuss a solution.

   Side note: if you find yourself repeatedly putting off a difficult conversation, revisit Chapter 7, on procrastination, for techniques that will help you take action.

# TEN

# Bringing the Best Out of Others

Whether you're a manager with hundreds of direct reports, an entrepreneurial one-man band, or part of a team of equals, it helps to know how to bring out the best in other people. Life is generally far more fun when our colleagues are in good form. Just think about how wonderful it feels when someone steps up and takes responsibility for his or her work. What a thrill it is when someone you're counting on comes through with some great ideas. How refreshing it is when someone accepts our comments in the entirely helpful spirit in which they're meant.

It might seem that our chances of experiencing this kind of healthy collaboration depend squarely on the character and capabilities of our colleagues. But, as always, our own behavior plays a major role. There's a lot we can do to help other people fully inhabit the smartest, most resourceful and flexible version of themselves. Obviously, the advice in the previous two chapters will help you build rapport and manage tensions. But this chapter covers another four techniques for bringing the best out of the people you work with, whether you're the boss or not. In fact, these tools can help you see the sunniest side of your family and friends, too. Planning a vacation together will never feel quite as challenging again.

### EXTREME LISTENING

In Chapter 8, I showed how you can strengthen rapport with others by asking high-quality questions and truly listening to the answers. But there's another type of listening that can also serve you well in your relationships at work, since it's a great tool for helping other people think clearly and take initiative.

It involves us redefining what it means to be helpful when someone mentions that they have something on their mind. For most of us, the highest form of helpfulness is to step in and offer suggestions. But when someone is telling us about a problem and we leap in to offer advice, a paradox arises: it's all too easy to leave the other person feeling bombarded rather than soothed. "Have you done this? What about that?" we say. Inadvertently, we can even make the other person feel judged, as if they should have spotted the answer themselves. If that happens, their brain is likely to register our well-intentioned help as a kind of threat—which makes them less creative in their own thinking about the problem. By the end of the discussion, instead of saying, "Wow, I feel motivated and empowered now," they're mumbling, "Well, I guess I'll go and do all those things, then."

So what's the alternative? Instead of racking your brain to come up with solutions and ideas, you create the best possible space for *the other person* to think effectively about the problem. The approach is called "extreme listening," a term coined by educationalist Nancy Kline.[1] It works by doing two things: it boosts the other person's feelings of autonomy and competence, which helps to keep their brain in discovery mode; and it encourages them to step back and reflect. As we've seen earlier in the book, both discovery mode and reflection time create a fine foundation for good thinking and high performance.

Here's how to do some extreme listening:

➡ **It's not about you.** First, let go of your need to feel helpful by making comments and suggestions. You're giving the other person something at least as precious: the encouragement and time to think clearly. You can provide more traditional forms of help later on, if needed.

➡ **Let the other person set the topic.** If it's not already obvious what he or she is struggling with, ask, "What would you find helpful to talk through?"

➡ **Don't interrupt.** Let them talk at length; aim for at least five minutes. It's sometimes hard not to fill the gaps when the other person pauses to think. But don't jump in. Listen intently. Make encouraging noises. Nod. Wait.

➡ **Maintain eye contact.** Even when the other person glances away, keep your eyes on them. Stay present and responsive.

➡ **Keep them talking.** When the other person runs out of steam, invite them to continue. Ask: "Is there anything else you're thinking about this?" If the answer is no, that's fine. When they're done, ask, "So what do you think you'll do now?" Don't feel you need to offer anything clever beyond that.

➡ **And once again, remember:** it's about the other person, not you. Your thoughts, ideas, and suggestions will be bubbling up inside you. If they threaten to boil over, remember that you'll have a chance to share them some other time, and bring your focus back to the other person.

Once when I was demonstrating this technique to a group of senior executives, they sat transfixed by the unfamiliar sight of one of their colleagues being listened to carefully rather than having to fight for airtime. After we stopped to discuss the technique, one of the executives started giggling. "But it's just like flirting!" he said. It was so rare for him to witness anyone paying undivided attention to another person that the only reference point he had was the experience of wooing his spouse. And he was right in a way: flirting tends to make us feel good precisely because the rapt attention of the other person makes us feel interesting and smart. But this workplace example of extreme listening seemed perfectly professional to the volunteer. When we asked him how it had felt, he said, "Great, actually. I felt like I had time to think, and that you cared about what I was saying, even though you weren't commenting. And I got somewhere useful."

Ros is a senior healthcare executive who now sees extreme listening as a vital management tool. Her work involves leading complex projects that seek to improve the quality of patient care, involving huge numbers of people—often including family doctors, insurers, government officials, hospitals, and community groups. She can be successful only if she's helping other people do their best work. But how to do that? Ros says she'd gone through most of her life "trying to solve people's problems," a habit she developed while growing up in a large family, and she had always assumed this was the best way to support colleagues who asked for her help. But it was tiring, and she knew it wasn't helping people to get better at doing their jobs. "So I tried out some of this extreme listening with Alex, my deputy." He had an issue he wanted to talk about, and normally Ros would have tried to fix it for him. "But instead," Ros says, "I let him talk without interruption, and I actually explicitly told him the 'rule' I was following, that I wasn't going to interrupt his train of thought. I nodded, encouraged him, and asked 'What else?' when he flagged. Within five minutes he'd literally solved the whole thing himself. We both laughed so hard. It absolutely worked, and I didn't have to do anything." Alex went on to use the technique with his colleagues, and now they both use it frequently. As Ros says: "I realized one of the biggest gifts you can give someone is to make them feel capable of handling things themselves."

## COACH, DON'T TELL

What if the other person still isn't sure what to do, after we've done some extreme listening to help them clarify their thinking? What if we want some reassurance that the person is going to approach the issue in a sensible way? In cases like this, we might feel the need to shift gear and take a more active part in shaping whatever happens next.

At this point, we have to achieve a delicate balancing act. On the one hand, if our colleague is doing something important, we want to be helpful and we want to be sure they're going to deliver. We might have ideas to share and deadlines to convey. It's tempting to look over his or her shoulder and do our best to keep them on track.

But psychologists have shown that autonomy is one of the most fundamental motivating forces in life.[2] Give someone space and responsibility, and they feel competent and respected; take it away, and their enthusiasm collapses. Many managers know this instinctively, and research confirms that this can make all the difference to people's performance, especially when tackling challenging tasks that require perseverance. Autonomy even helps when people are trying to quit smoking, a notoriously difficult thing to do. In a study of patients who were seeking medical help to quit, researchers showed that those whose doctors were "autonomy-supportive" as opposed to "controlling" (as assessed by expert observers listening to audiotapes of their interaction) were more likely to be smoke-free, both six months later and thirty months later.[3]

So if we're trying to equip other people to do their best work, we should strike a balance that falls somewhere between micromanaging the heck out of the situation and delegating it so completely that we relinquish all control.

Ndidi is a senior manager who's worked hard to find that balance in recent years. An executive director responsible for the regional operations of a global educational charity, she says she used to be overly hands-on. She recalls: "My check-ins with staff always involved me saying, 'I think you should do this or that.' I meant to be helpful. But I realized my micromanaging was setting up a dynamic where my staff thought, 'Oh, Ndidi knows the answer, so I won't bother to work it out—I'll just ask her to tell me what to do.' As a result, they weren't learning to think strategically. They'd bring the same issues to me again and again. Yet they're highly skilled people. They just didn't feel that I trusted them to think for themselves."

The good news for Ndidi, and for us all, is that there is a sweet spot between total micromanagement and total delegation, where you can both respect people's autonomy and ensure that they have the guidance they need to get the job done. One of the surest ways to strike that balance is to ask a simple set of coaching questions that help the other person reach their own insights. By doing this, you leave the other person with the sense of autonomy and ownership that psychologists have found to be so important for high performance. You still get to guide and challenge their thinking, but in a way that gives you confidence that they'll succeed. It's the best of both worlds.

So what are these magical coaching questions? They're based on something known as the "GROW model"—because they walk people through steps called the *goal, reality, options*, and *way forward*:

➡ Goal. What does the ideal outcome look like?

➡ Reality. What's the current situation—the good and the bad?

➡ Options. What are the options for moving forward? (Always start with the other person's ideas. Tell them you're happy to add yours, but that you want to start with theirs.)

➡ Way forward. What is their first step going to be? When will they take it? What help do they need?

"When my staff come to me with issues now, I literally GROW-model it," Ndidi says. To get clear on the *goal*, she likes to ask, "What's going to make us feel that this has been a success?" She says the "us" in her question makes sure they explicitly agree on the right end point.

"If we can get aligned on the ideal outcome, in some detail, I've found I can worry a lot less about how they get there." As a result, she says she often spends longer on the goal part of the discussion than on any of the other three steps.

To help them confront *reality*, Ndidi tends to ask, "What does the ideal situation look like, and what are the barriers to getting there?"

She has a few ways of drawing out their thoughts about the *options*. "What's one route you could take?" she asks first. And then, to encourage them to explore more than one idea, "If that doesn't work, what else could you try?" Once a few ideas are on the table, Ndidi might make an observation if something big seems missing—saying, "I notice you haven't mentioned X"—before letting her colleagues react. Then, to narrow the field of options, she asks, "Which route do you want to go down?"

Finally, as they discuss the *way forward*, Ndidi always asks, "Is there anything specific that I can do to help?" It's a good way of signaling that support is available, even though the GROW model means her colleagues have done their own problem solving. And she concludes by "making sure we're crystal clear on who's accountable for doing what, by when. You don't have to be soft just because you're not telling them what to do."

Apart from using the GROW model as a backbone to her conversations, there are a few other things Ndidi has found helpful in reminding herself to "coach, don't tell." "I have a phrase on repeat in my head: 'Don't tell them the answer!'" she says. "I also physically lean back. In the past I've always tended to hunch over the table, leaning toward them and writing down what they should do. So for me, sitting back is a metaphor—something I associate in my mind with being in coaching mode."

Ndidi remembers using the GROW model for the first time with one of her direct reports. "She came to me with a problem about an all-day meeting she was planning. Several people who would be attending were unhappy about a particular topic, and she was worried that their concerns would end up derailing the whole thing." Ndidi reminded herself to sit back in her chair, and started her coaching with this goal-focused question: "What's your vision of the ideal outcome for this meeting?" "At first, my colleague was floored by it," she says. "I realized, sadly, this was probably the first genuine question I'd ever really asked her. But then she relaxed, started thinking, and came up with solutions I would never have come up with myself, like creating an open-space session at the beginning of the meeting, where attendees could raise all their questions. And it was hands down the best conversation I'd ever had with her. She glided out of the room on air."

Ndidi says this coaching approach has shifted the performance of her team. "Now my staff behave like leaders. They're not afraid to speak up, with me or each other." It's also created more breathing room in her own schedule. "If you coach someone rather than telling them the answer, you usually don't have them coming to you with the same issue ever again, because they know how to solve it next time around. Plus you don't have to come up with all the answers yourself. So I'm less tired. This is part of my time management arsenal now."

## BRAIN-FRIENDLY FEEDBACK

However effective your coaching, getting the best out of people sometimes means that we have to give constructive feedback to improve their performance or get a situation back on track.

Yet personal criticism, however well intended, naturally puts most people's brains on high alert. In fact, it's a perfect example of a nonphysical threat: it can undermine the recipient's pride and social standing, and possibly their job security, so it's hard to stop their brain from going into defensive mode when they're told that something they've done is wrong. Even if they know it's not the grown-up thing to do, their brain is contemplating a snappish comment (fight), a cowed withdrawal (flight), or a hope that the problem might just go away (freeze).

So how can you encourage someone to accept your suggestions without triggering that kind of defensive response? The trick is to express your views without making the other person *wrong*, by finding ways in which they could be (partly) right and building your suggestions around that. This helps them to stay in discovery mode, allowing you to have a more intelligent, open-minded conversation about the issues you'd like them to consider. None of this means you sidestep any shortcomings; it just means calling them out in a way that's going to make things better, rather than worse. Here are three ways to give this kind of brain-friendly feedback:

## Technique 1: "What I Like About That Is . . ."

➡ Tell the other person: "What I like about that is . . ." Give meaning-ful, specific examples—more than one if possible. Aim for as many specific positive examples as you can before you give suggestions for changes.

➡ Then say: "What would make me like it even more is . . ."

If this seems familiar to you, don't skip over it too quickly. Most of us already know that it's helpful to say something positive before we relay criticisms, but the details here make this far more effective than the usual "praise sandwich."

The deliberate formulation of *"What I like about that is . . ."* requires you to give specific examples of the things you appreciate. This is really important, for two reasons. First, it's much easier for people's brains to process and remember specifics than to handle abstract ideas. Second, people are wired to be more sensitive to threats than to rewards. Over the millennia, that hypersensitivity undoubtedly kept the human race safe in the face of charging mammoths and attacking tribes. The com-bination of those two factors means that if you just make a general positive statement ("It's great! You're great!") followed by a list of spe-cific things they should change, their brains will discount that splash of praise and focus entirely on the negatives.[4] So you need to be as tangible and forthcoming in your praise as you are about your criti-cism; not just saying "it's great" but what specifically is "great" about it. That's how you make sure they hear that you genuinely value aspects of whatever they've said or done.

Then, when you introduce your suggestion for improvement with the phrase *"What would make me like it even more is . . ."* you're fram-ing your comment as an idea that—if explored—could take the other person from good to great, rather than something they were really dumb not to have done. You're still making your point, but it feels much less threatening to people's competence and self-respect than the usual "You should do this differently."

Taken together, these two sentences greatly increase your chances of keeping the other person in open-minded discovery mode as you give them feedback, making it far more likely that you'll have a pro-ductive and good-natured conversation. The "What I like . . ." feedback style can help you, too, because being forced to find something you like—however hard it is to find this golden nugget—often reveals something useful that you might have missed had you led with your criticisms.

### Technique 2: "Yes, And . . ."

➡ Avoid the joy-killing phrase "Yes, but . . ." when you spot a problem with someone's suggestion.

➡ Instead, try "Yes, and . . . ," to signal that you're adding your perspective *alongside* that suggestion rather than in conflict with it.

For example, if someone is keen to launch a new project that you think is ill-timed, instead of saying "Yes, great project. *But* it's the wrong time," say "Yes, great project. *And* we also have the annual strategy round about to launch." Then invite discussion: "What can we do about that timing?"

The "yes, and" approach allows you to introduce important considerations without closing down the other person's ideas. I like it a lot, because it allows more space for the possibility that you don't have the whole picture. Remember the subconscious filtering that your brain's automatic system does for you, ensuring that you never see all the information and options around you? So perhaps you've seen the "gorilla" that your colleague missed—but perhaps they've seen one that *you* missed, and that's why they're saying what they're saying. And by encouraging you to build on what your colleague has said, the "yes, and" approach is more likely to help you see scope for compromise, if it exists. In fact, "yes, and" turns out to be one of the fundamental tenets of improvisational comedy, because it's such a reliable way of encouraging creative collaboration. (If a normally tense feedback discussion ends up dissolving in laughter, that may mean you're doing it right.)

### Technique 3: "What Would Need to Be True to Make That Work?"

➡ Instead of saying "That won't work because of this, that, and the other . . . ," try saying "What would need to be true to make that work (well)?"

The hypothetical phrasing sets an exploratory tone rather than a critical one, and the question encourages a feasibility check without making anyone look silly, or badging anything as "wrong." It was a device much used by my colleagues at McKinsey when teams discussed competing ideas, since it helped ensure that each proposal received a fair hearing even if it didn't initially sound appealing. And it meant that every team member felt included in the decision on what to do next, even if his or her preferred option didn't make the cut.

Peter's IT consulting job puts him in a delicate situation a lot of the time. He cares about doing a good job, and what he really wants to say to his clients is, "You know that big project that's costing you millions? The way you're going about it is a disaster. Trust me, I've seen hundreds of these." And that was broadly what he was saying in his proposals and meetings, albeit more diplomatically. He would lead with the challenges of this kind of IT work, and how his firm could ensure that things didn't go wrong. In projects that were under way, he would boldly call out the blunders that nobody was willing to admit. He called it "telling the truth," and there were clients who told him they appreciated it.

But, inescapably, Peter was effectively criticizing what the clients had done before they hired him. So of course it was hard for them to avoid becoming defensive. He didn't want to lose his critical edge. But after we talked about the effect he was having, he settled on a new approach using these brain-friendly feedback techniques. For example, when he was hired to review the status of their IT systems, he would lead with what they were doing well. It sometimes required some generosity on Peter's part, but he was always able to find something to say. "Even when I didn't agree with the specifics of what they'd done, I was often able to say positive things about the high-level strategy." Then he'd go on to suggest how they could build on their successes to date. In doing so, he says, "I tried to avoid saying the word 'wrong' at any point and used as many 'ands' as I could. I said, 'Here's what would have to be true to make your strategy work . . . *and* here's another approach, with these benefits.'"

With this new approach, he says, he started to have what he called "unexpectedly great" meetings. He still got the chance to talk about the risks and all the ways to mitigate them, but it happened without the clients' brains being in defensive mode. He stopped getting thrown out of meetings and started winning new work. He remembers a potential client saying to him, "Now, *this* is what I want. This is a real conversation."

## COME ON, BE FAIR

Fairness is a powerful social force. When it's present, it helps us feel good about being part of society, makes us willing to contribute and compromise. When it's absent, we struggle.

Colin Camerer and Richard Thaler, behavioral economists from Caltech and the University of Chicago, respectively, have demonstrated the importance we place on fairness in a well-known experiment called the Ultimatum Game. It works like this: Imagine you've been given $10, and you're told to offer a stranger anything between zero and $10. If the other person accepts whatever you offer, you both get to keep your respective shares of the money. But if he rejects your offer, neither of you gets anything. Without social brains, you might offer the person a few pennies, and he would accept it because it's better than nothing. But to human beings with a deep-seated psychological need for fairness, that feels like a derisory offer. And sure enough, in experiments, most people reject this highly unequal deal—leaving both sides with no deal and no money. The deal typically gets done only once offers reach $2.[5]

This is mirrored in the findings of neuroscientists like UCLA's Matt Lieberman and colleagues, who have scanned the brains of volunteers while they are playing these kinds of social games. Their work shows that fair offers activated people's reward systems, while unfair offers required people to engage their brain's self-control circuitry to overcome their annoyance and swallow the unfairness.[6] In other words, people's brains had to divert some precious deliberate system capacity to staying calm in the face of the injustice. (And that's when there's just $2 at stake.) The bottom line? Ensuring that colleagues feel that workplace decisions are fair not only keeps their reward systems happy, but leaves people with more mental energy to focus on other things.

You would never set out to be unfair in your dealings with colleagues, I know. But I highlight the topic because managers are often on the hook for making decisions where there are winners and losers. Some people get promoted; others don't. Some divisions get more resources; others don't. And for those on the losing side, it's all too easy to see those decisions as unfair.

You can't avoid the fact that decisions sometimes benefit certain people more than others. But you can demonstrate that the *process* behind the decisions is fair. That means being as transparent as possible about the reasons for your decisions when you're navigating difficult waters. Like this:

➡ Explain the factors being weighed, and why they are relevant criteria for the decision. Show how the options are being assessed against those criteria.

➡ Discuss any dilemmas you face in making the decisions, and how you're handling them.

Your colleagues might not like the eventual outcomes of your choices, but behavioral science suggests that they'll be far more supportive if they can see that your decision-making process was fair.

### Bringing the Best Out of Others

Think about someone who's doing some work for you—or someone you want to help. Experiment with these techniques:

➡ **Extreme listening.** Improve the quality of the other person's thinking by listening to him or her unusually closely, without interrupting.

➡ **Coach, don't tell.** Use the GROW questions to guide the other person through clarity on the *goal*, the current *reality*, the *options* they see (add yours only after they share theirs), and the *way forward*.

➡ **Give brain-friendly feedback.** Use one or more of these three techniques next time you want to provide input or challenge someone's ideas:
  • "What I like(d) about that is . . ." and "What would make me like it even more is . . ."
  • "Yes, and . . ." (rather than "Yes, but . . .").
  • "What would need to be true to make that work?"

➡ **Be fair.** Be as transparent as you can in explaining the process for making tough decisions. Be alert to anything the other person might perceive as unfair, even if you don't see it as such.

# PART IV

# Thinking

Being Your Smartest, Wisest, Most Creative Self

The difficulty lies not in the new ideas, but in escaping from the old ones.
—JOHN MAYNARD KEYNES

Sometimes we have days when we just nail it: we have great ideas, make smart comments, and maybe even make people laugh with our searing wit. But on other days our mental engine is running more slowly than we'd like. We get bogged down in a task, pushing hard but failing to make much headway. We think of something clever to say in a conversation, but it comes to us hours after the moment has passed. We might even find ourselves making a dumb mistake, whether it's one that prompts an immediate cringe or one that comes back to bite us later.

Of course, all sorts of things can block our brilliance from shining through on occasion. Our work might be harder than usual—or perhaps we're just not firing on all cylinders after being up late the night before. Whatever the cause, Part IV will show you some techniques for raising your game and giving you more of the creativity, wisdom, and insight you need to ace your day. And if you're already feeling sharp and ready for anything—well, these techniques will take your performance to a whole new level.

# ELEVEN

# Reaching Insight

We all recognize the feeling of getting bogged down in a task. You might be an accountant trying to figure out why your numbers won't add up, or an artist whose muse has gone missing—very different jobs, but a similar sensation: you're stuck in a loop with ideas that aren't working, and you can't see a way out. To make progress at times like these, we need the kind of breakthrough that comes from *insight*: that "aha" flash of understanding that results in our suddenly seeing a new solution.

Peggy, a successful freelance art director in Chicago, is someone whose work requires a lot of those "aha" moments. As an independent contractor, she's frequently pitching for interesting jobs at advertising agencies, making it particularly important for her to be able to impress people quickly with her creative ideas. What's more, she's found that "really good work often looks like nothing I've done before," she says. "Tweaking what's worked in the past only gets you so far. Making big leaps usually requires a different approach to the problem, where you connect the dots in a new way."

The scientific evidence suggests she's absolutely right on this. Our efficient brains have automatic routines for dealing with everything from writing emails to brushing our teeth—and given half a chance, our neural networks will also save effort by continuing to think along existing pathways, coming up with incremental variations on old ideas. As a result, psychologists have long observed something they call the *Einstellung effect*, where having an existing solution in mind makes it harder for us to see a radically different but better way to solve our problem.[1] So if what we want is *new* thinking, we need to help our brains get out of a rut, to stimulate lots of *new* connections. What can we do to give ourselves the best chance of that? Plenty, it turns out.

## POSE A QUESTION

So we want to signal to our brain that we want it to go explore, rather than rehash the same old thinking. Surprisingly, doing that can be as simple as framing our knotty task as a question rather than a weary statement.

In one odd little study, psychologist Ibrahim Senay and colleagues at the University of Illinois demonstrated the benefits of this approach.[2] Their volunteers were first told that they were doing a handwriting test, and were asked to write some words on a piece of paper. Certain people were asked to write "Will I," while the others were asked to write "I Will." Then they were all asked to solve ten anagrams. Those who had written "Will I" (with its subtle suggestion of the question "Will I solve these anagrams?") went on to solve nearly twice as many anagrams as those who wrote "I Will." The Illinois researchers connected this result to wider research findings which suggest that being asked a question (rather than being told to do something) leaves us feeling more in control, less defensive, and consequently more open to new ideas.[3] Questions seem to encourage our brains into discovery mode, by piquing our curiosity and instilling a feeling of "Ooh, I wonder what the answer might be," rather than "I must crack this darned thing."

How can we apply this to tricky tasks at work? It can be as simple as framing the task as an open question—simply pausing and asking, "What's the right way to solve this, ideally?" When I feel frustrated by a lack of progress, I often find that's enough to put me in a more exploratory mindset.

I also like rhetorical questions that invite us to set aside barriers that might be narrowing our thinking. For example: "If you knew the answer, what would it be?" Or "If you had no constraints, what would you do?" Questions like these usually make my clients do a double take. They push back, chuckling and telling me, "That makes no sense at all" or "But I *do* have constraints, that's precisely the problem." But then they try it, and discover that these sorts of questions loosen up their thinking. They seem to help us think more creatively by helping our brains feel less threatened by the challenge.

On a recent project, Peggy, our freelance art director, was looking for ideas on how to market a new air freshener, one that not only smelled good but had the added benefit of killing germs. All the ideas that she and her colleagues had proposed seemed a little stale, like the air the product was supposed to freshen. So Peggy started asking questions to open up their thinking. "One question I like to ask is 'How does this product fit into people's lives?' It encourages exploratory thinking even when the product doesn't seem that exciting." Peggy also has some crazier questions in her kit bag. "I also asked everyone: 'Let's say the product knocked on our door and we opened it. What would we see?'" She says the immediate answers were a little weird: "It's sort of big, and green, and speaking German." Silly, of course. But, she says, "asking such an obviously nonthreatening question shifted something in the way we were thinking." It got Peggy and her colleagues out of their narrow "gotta fix this" mentality and into a more creative frame of mind, where better ideas started to flow.

So when you feel as if you're banging your head against the wall, don't just exhort yourself to bang harder. Instead, try leading your brain into a more exploratory state with an expansive question, like:

➡ "What would be a totally different approach to this?"

➡ "What would be a great way of going about solving this?"

➡ "If I knew the answer, what would it be?"

➡ (And sure, by all means: "If the solution knocked on the door, what would it look like?")

## REFRESH AND REBOOT

"I often find that problems are best solved by not thinking about them for a while," Peggy says. "I'll deliberately plan to step away from a tough task after spending some focused time on it, to work on something else for a while. When I come back to the original thing, I come back at it in a different way, and I'll often get a eureka moment. I think there's value in trusting there's a better solution and telling yourself you just don't know what it is yet, but that it's out there if you just give yourself the space to process it."

Everything we know about the brain suggests that Peggy is spot on with this observation. In Chapter 5, on the value of planning downtime, I highlighted that a great deal of further neural processing happens when we stop consciously thinking about a topic. Our subconscious connects the information we've just absorbed to the older memories stored in our brain—and those new connections are just what we need for fresh insight. So when we return to the original task after shifting our attention elsewhere, we often find ourselves able to see new ways of approaching the problem.

But what if you're in the middle of a meeting, or you're up against a deadline, and it's simply too fanciful to think of taking a break right now? Research suggests that even briefly shifting your focus to another serious task can be enough to refresh your thinking. That's Peggy's experience, too. "If people are getting stuck and maybe a bit negative, with everyone bagging on an idea, I'll suggest we change gear and brainstorm another part of the project just for a few minutes. When we come back to the original topic, it always helps us see something we hadn't previously seen."

A number of cognitive scientists have demonstrated that it doesn't take long to get some of this subconscious processing benefit. Studies have found that shifting attention from a complex problem to another task for just two, three, or four minutes can help people make better decisions when they return to the problem.[4]

However, the research does suggest that two things are needed to make sure we reap the full benefits of this cognitive shift. First, we need to intend to come back to the task at hand.[5] Otherwise, our brain will assume it's not necessary to continue processing the information at a subconscious level; it will just move on to thinking about other things, like what we're having for lunch. Second, researchers have found that it helps to tackle a different kind of task during those moments when we step away from the problem.[6] If we're working on a spreadsheet full of numbers about product sales, looking at another grid of numbers isn't going to be as mentally revitalizing as engaging in conversation about, say, the product's new marketing campaign.

So for a complex task where the way forward isn't obvious:

➡ Stop and tackle a different part of the problem or a different issue for a few minutes, to allow your brain some time to do some background processing before you return to the issue.

➡ If you can, plan to split your work on the topic into two working sessions rather than trying to complete the task in one sitting.

Important side note: for those tempted to see this as a license to multitask, resist! What the science suggests is that you can revitalize your creativity by *deliberately* stepping away from the toughest part of your task for a while, before reengaging deeply with it. We're talking about a careful shift, from focusing on one topic to focusing on another, not frantically flitting across the vast realm of your to-do list in the hope that it will inspire you. (Scattering your attention only increases the load on your brain, making it harder to think creatively.) So it still pays to do one thing at a time, even when you're mixing things up.

## SWITCH VIEWS

Here's another tactic for increasing your chances of finding a new solution: portray your challenge in a different way, to engage parts of your brain that haven't yet been invited to the party. For example, if you've been thinking about a problem in terms of numbers, try describing it visually—or vice versa.

I saw this work well for a group of executives I was working with on a leadership development course in Norway. As leaders get more senior, they often report a sense of loneliness that arises from feeling that they have fewer people they can openly ask for advice and support. The group gathered in Norway was no different, and we were discussing how they could build a network of more supportive relationships to sustain them through challenging times. Most of them had quite fixed ideas of what it meant to improve their network. They associated it with dull conferences and dutiful drinks. They were writing lists of people they thought they should contact, and then feeling guilty about not doing it. It was hard for them to get beyond their negative associations with the idea of "networking."

To help them think differently, a McKinsey colleague of mine suggested they draw visual maps of their existing professional networks, with themselves at the center and a web of links to people around them. The executives raised an eyebrow or two at the suggestion, but then gamely settled into the task. The group sat with large pieces of paper and drew with colored pens for fifteen minutes, coding the relationships in terms of their quality and proximity. They drew lines that were thicker for stronger relationships, or dotted lines for weak ones; they used arrows to show the direction of support being given in each relationship.

Each person drew a rather different type of map, reflecting his or her own professional reality. One executive drew herself surrounded very tightly with lots of people, leaving the outer edge of the page quite blank, which led to an admission that she felt suffocated rather than supported. Another had split the page into "colleagues," on the left, and people "outside the company," on the right. The right-hand side was virtually empty, which sparked a discussion of how his whole team was stuck in a rut without any new ideas. As they compared their maps, the tenor and quality of the conversation changed entirely, becoming far more constructive. Suddenly the discussion wasn't about transactional LinkedIn invitations, but about the real issues they wanted to address in their relationships. As a result, each executive ended up with a useful plan and the enthusiasm to put it into action.

Time and again, I've seen these kinds of useful breakthroughs when people find novel ways to articulate a challenge they're working on. Mapping things out visually, with lines and boxes, can give us a better overview of the whole picture as well as helping us see new connections in a situation, often highlighting consequences or shortcuts that weren't previously obvious. Writing about a potential solution in longhand—something most of us rarely do these days—can also encourage new insights. In fact, researchers from Princeton and UCLA found that students who took handwritten notes performed better when asked conceptual questions after a lecture than those who typed (often verbatim) notes. As the students wrote down what struck them, they were already sifting and interpreting the lecturer's ideas, connecting them to what they had previously learned and developing more nuanced insight.[7]

With that in mind, what can you do to see your challenge from a completely different angle? Here are some specific things to try:

➡ **Write in longhand.** Take a notebook and pen, and start writing down your thoughts about the issue. Most of us do this so rarely that it's a quick way of getting into a different state of mind and allowing novel connections to form. Set a timer and write for ten minutes. If you run out of steam, it's okay—just ask yourself what else you have to say about the topic, and wait till something else comes to mind. It always does.

➡ **Explain your issue to someone else.** If you've spent a while wrestling with an idea, try explaining what you're doing to someone else. In software engineering, this process is sometimes called "rubber duck-ing" because even explaining your work to an inanimate object (such as a rubber duck) is a reliable way of reaching new insight. It works because articulating your thoughts in conversation activates differ-ent neural networks than solo thinking does. Explaining what you're doing to someone who's not an expert in your field can also require you to use metaphors or examples, which in turn can encourage new thoughts.

➡ **Map it out.** Create a physical map of the key aspects of the project or problem you're working on. Here's how:
1. On a sticky note, write your central issue in a few words, preferably as a question (e.g. "How can we launch our new product on time?").
2. Brainstorm the big factors that affect your issue (e.g. "software bugs," "product manufacturing," "beta test feedback," "having enough good programmers"). Write each on a sticky note and paste them around your central question.
3. Group together any factors that are closely related (e.g. you might create different clusters for hardware, software, and marketing is-sues).
4. Then enrich your map. Try these ideas:
   a. Look for causal linkages between your ideas, and draw arrows to show these linkages (e.g. maybe "software bugs" feeds into "cus-tomer focus group feedback"; "having enough good program-mers" might affect "software bugs").
   b. Try some color coding. For example, put a green dot on things that are currently helping you, and a red one on the factors that are holding you back.
   c. Move anything that seems to be in the wrong place. Fill any ob-vious gaps.
5. Step back and look at your map, and notice what's striking in the patterns you see. What now seems the most important or interest-ing thing for you to address? (In the example I've described, I would bet that incentivizing the best programmers quickly becomes a more obvious priority than it was before the exercise began.)
    Tip: You can do all of this on a flipchart, or even on a large piece of regular paper, but you may shift your thinking more if you give yourself real space to move your notes around, by using a blank wall or a large whiteboard as a backdrop.

## FIND AN ANALOGY

One more way to spark new thinking is to seek out stimulating analogies for the issue you're working on, by making use of interesting things you encounter outside your normal frame of reference—whether you're observing an unfamiliar workplace or wandering along a new street. A few simple questions can help you extract ideas from the strangest places, once you get into the habit of asking them more often. Whenever you come across something thought-provoking, ask yourself:

➡ How is this thing you've noticed *similar* to the topic you're working on?

➡ What's *different* about it? And what's most striking about that?

➡ What might that suggest as an idea for you to explore?

For example, suppose the issue on your mind right now is the excessive workload your team's currently facing. Everyone's worn down. You're catching your breath while having dinner in a buzzing restaurant with an open kitchen, and you reflect on those analogy-seeking questions while you're waiting for your food. First, you notice that the kitchen staff are deluged with customer orders, like your own team. What's *different* is that staff in the restaurant seem pretty calm, despite the demands they're facing. And while your team allocates work depending on who's got spare capacity, each person in the kitchen has a clear job to do: some make salads, others hot food or desserts. What does that make you think? You consider that maybe you could do more to tag each team member to particular types of requests, so that everyone isn't flipping from one thing to another all the time. You remember the advice on "batching" tasks from Chapter 4, and realize that this might reduce people's stress. An idea takes shape in your mind.

Peggy, the freelance art director, finds that certain websites often inspire her when she browses with those analogy-seeking questions in mind. "I find it useful sometimes to flip through certain blogs, Getty Images, GigPosters, that sort of thing. I like to see what thoughts they provoke." One day, as she was looking for a final piece of inspiration on her air freshener ad campaign, she came across an old-fashioned botanical rose diagram. The rose connected with the traditional idea of a scented spray, but it was a very technical diagram. It wasn't initially obvious how it related to her campaign. But something made her pause. She noticed the leaves of this particular rose looked like boxing gloves. That in turn sparked a memory of the last time she'd been pruning her own roses, in which she remembered them bobbing and diving in the wind. Suddenly she had a much better idea for her air freshener advertisement: a rose with boxing gloves, combining antibacterial power and scent. "I knew I'd got it. Sometimes it just takes looking at the issue in a completely different light, and being open to whatever develops."

So how did Peggy's work on the air freshener ad campaign end? She smiles. "The account director told me the rose with boxing gloves was 'award-winning work.' And as a freelancer, *that* is the kind of comment that leads to job security."

## Reaching Insight

When you need a flash of inspiration on a thorny topic, try the following:

➡ **Pose a question.** When you're feeling blocked, ask yourself: "What would be a totally different approach to this?" "What would be a great way of going about solving this?" "If I knew the answer, what would it be?"

➡ **Refresh and reboot.** Try shifting your focus to a different type of task for a while, before returning to the original issue.

➡ **Switch views.** Try a different way of describing or looking at the issue you're working on, and notice what patterns or insights come to the surface:
  • Write about it in longhand for ten minutes.
  • "Rubber duck" it: explain the issue to someone unfamiliar with it.
  • Create a physical map of your issue, e.g. using sticky notes.

➡ **Find an analogy.** Expose yourself to a different type of stimulus (e.g. observe another organization's ways of working; view websites or images from fields different from yours), and ask yourself: How is this *like* the topic I'm working on? How is it *different*? What new idea does that suggest I could explore?

# TWELVE

# Making Wise Decisions

If the last chapter was about creativity—the process of opening up fresh ideas and possibilities—wisdom is its complement: narrowing down the field and making shrewd choices between options. And although wisdom might seem a grand word, it isn't necessarily about making bet-the-company decisions. If you think about it, our days are full of opportunities to make wise (or foolish) choices. When tackling your next piece of work, for example, where should you start? Whom should you get involved? Which approach should you take? Choose rashly, and you can end up with complaints and setbacks that take the shine off the day. Choose sagely, and the chips will tend to fall your way. Your colleagues might even be moved to say, "Hmm, that's a good point," or "My goodness, you handled *that* well." Bravo you.

What does behavioral science tell us about how to achieve this kind of everyday wisdom? Basically, this: we need to take care to engage our brain's deliberate system when we're dealing with things that matter. Remember that the deliberate system is the network that's responsible for analyzing, exerting self-discipline, and thinking ahead—and those are the skills we need when we're trying to exert good judgment. If we don't consciously engage our deliberate system, our automatic system will quietly take control and rush us to the easiest answer available. Which might mean saying the first thing that comes to mind in a delicate meeting, or blindly copying what's always been done in the past. After all, it's the job of our brain's automatic system to minimize the amount of mental energy we expend—but often, the easiest choice isn't the right one.

## SIGNS THAT YOUR AUTOMATIC SYSTEM IS IN CHARGE

A good first step toward making smarter choices is to become adept at recognizing when your automatic system may be taking charge. In my experience, if you catch yourself saying or thinking anything like the following phrases, then the chances are that your automatic system is trumping your deliberate system:

➡ "It's obviously right (or obviously wrong)."

➡ "I recently heard XYZ . . . therefore . . ."

➡ "Everyone agrees."

➡ "I understand it—so I like it!"

➡ "Let's just stick with what we know."

➡ "There's only one real option."

These are all versions of your automatic system confidently yelling, "I don't care that the world is complicated—I'm making things simple for you!" But each phrase represents a slightly different type of common mental shortcut. (Of course there are many more beyond this; these are just some of the ones I hear most in the workplace.) So let me say a little more about each one, to improve your chances of spotting them before they trip you up.

### "It's Obviously Right/Wrong"

One way that your automatic system saves mental energy is to seek out evidence that confirms what you already believe, while ignoring any evidence that contradicts it. That saves your deliberate system a lot of work. It means you don't have to rethink your assumptions and expectations, and it reduces the uncertainty and ambiguity that's taxing for our brains. Our automatic system is even willing to reinterpret reality, if the evidence can't be made to line up perfectly with our preexisting views. In Chapter 1, I explained how this *confirmation bias* can result in us seeing gray bananas as yellow. And the same applies to decision making. We're capable of unconsciously twisting the facts until they fit what we're expecting to see.

So if we're anticipating that something will be a bad idea, we'll tend to notice all its weaknesses and none of its strengths—and we might even invent some criticisms that aren't really fair. It goes the other way, too, when we get ourselves attached to an idea we love and find ourselves blind to its downsides. The result? A black-and-white view of the world. Things that seem "obviously right" or "obviously wrong."

A recent study by psychologists at Yale did a good job of highlighting the grip that confirmation bias can exert on our brains. Researchers asked a group of volunteers about their political views, and then had them analyze some data on gun control. Those who had identified themselves as conservatives made significantly more numerical mistakes when asked to analyze data that seemed to indicate that gun control worked. And the liberals became equally innumerate when they were faced with figures suggesting gun control did *not* work.[1] It's just that little bit harder for our brains to think clearly about evidence that goes against our views—and the brain's automatic system doesn't like hard work.

This isn't a question of intelligence, by the way. We're all susceptible. Investment expert Warren Buffett has spoken admiringly of Charles Darwin's determination to overcome confirmation bias, saying: "Now, there was a smart man, who did just about the hardest thing in the world to do. Charles Darwin used to say that whenever he ran into something that contradicted a conclusion he cherished, he was obliged to write the new finding down within thirty minutes. Otherwise his mind would work to reject the discordant information, much as the body rejects transplants. Man's natural inclination is to cling to his beliefs, particularly if they are reinforced by recent experience."[2]

### "I Recently Heard That . . . Therefore . . ."

Which leads us to the next big shortcut: we're often disproportionately swayed by information we've recently been exposed to, even when it has nothing to do with what we're deciding.

Put yourself in the shoes of visitors at the San Francisco Exploratorium, who were asked to estimate the height of the tallest redwood tree in the world. First, some visitors were asked whether it was "more or less than 85 feet tall"; others were asked whether it was "more or less than 1,000 feet tall." That was a warm-up question. Then they were asked to estimate its actual height. On average, volunteers exposed to the smaller initial number (85 feet) guessed that the tallest tree in the world was 118 feet high. In the group exposed to the higher number (1,000 feet), their estimates were fully seven times higher.[3] The visitors thought they were being objective, but their brains had latched onto that first number as a guide. This phenomenon is called *anchoring*. It occurs when our automatic brains don't bother drifting too far from an initial suggestion, like a ship tethered by an anchor.

We can be susceptible to this kind of influence even when the initial anchoring information is plainly irrelevant. In a well-known experiment, Duke behavioral economics professor Dan Ariely asked people to recall the last two digits of their Social Security number, and then to bid on a number of products that he offered for sale: a book, some chocolates, IT equipment, and wine. Within each bidding round, there was a significant correlation between those who wrote down higher Social Security digits and those who made higher bids.[4] It makes no sense. But those two irrelevant digits were fresh enough in mind for people's automatic systems to grab the cue and make use of it.

The effect extends into non-numerical situations, too. *Recency bias* describes the way that we're disproportionately influenced by anything that has just happened, saving our deliberate system from the harder work of looking back over time and working out longer-term patterns. It's why for every 20-degree increase in a day's temperature, researchers found that car dealers sell 8.5 percent more convertibles.[5] "It's been sunny in the last few hours, so a convertible is the right investment for me," goes the logic of your shortsighted automatic system.

### "I Understand It, So It Must Be Good"

Another shortcut we take is to assume that if something is easy to understand and remember, it's probably correct. (Behavioral scientists describe this as a preference for *processing fluency*.) As a result, we tend to be attracted to ideas that are clear and simple, while subjecting difficult-to-understand ideas to more in-depth analysis and criticism.

That explains a study conducted at the University of Michigan, where psychologists Hyunjin Song and Norbert Schwarz found that people fell for a trick question more often when it was made easy to read. Try this: "How many animals of each kind did Moses take on the ark?" (Answer: None. It was Noah who was on the ark, not Moses.) When this question was printed with sharp contrast and in a large font, readers were often fooled by the question. But seeing the words printed in tiny, hard-to-read font made readers pause for a moment, making it more likely they'd spot the trick.[6] It's as if adding the extra step of asking "*What* does that say?" is enough to wake up the brain's deliberate system.

### "Everyone Agrees"

When we're surrounded by people who have already formed an opinion about the right thing to do, it's easy for our brain's automatic system to decide that no further thought is required—a shortcut known as *groupthink*. There was probably an evolutionary benefit to this, once upon a time. Being part of a tribe helped keep us safe over the millennia, and agreeing with our tribe helped us belong—much as fitting in at work tends to make us feel more secure in our jobs.

Psychologist Solomon Asch ran some seminal experiments demonstrating this as far back as the 1950s, in which he found that most people were willing to say that a line on a card was the same length as one on another card next to it, even though it was very clearly longer or shorter. Why? Simply because all the other people in the room did.[7]

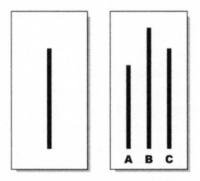

Asch asked volunteers to say which line on the right-hand card (A, B, or C) was the same length as the line on the left-hand card. One-third of all answers was incorrect, and three-quarters of participants were willing to give a wrong answer at least once.

In the workplace, we discuss topics that are far more subtle than the length of a line. So our tendency toward groupthink is harder to spot; it can easily look as if we're simply part of a team that's harmoniously on the same page. In her book *Mindset*, Stanford professor Carol Dweck recounts a story about Alfred P. Sloan, once the CEO of General Motors, and a leader who knew groupthink when he saw it. When addressing a group that seemed happily aligned on the right thing to do, he said: "I take it we are all in complete agreement on the decision here. . . . Then I propose we postpone further discussion of this matter until our next meeting, to give ourselves time to develop disagreement and perhaps gain some understanding of what the decision is all about."[8]

### "Let's Just Stick with What We Know"

Next up is the *endowment effect*, the fact that we tend to overvalue things we have—even when they hold no sentimental value. In one famous experiment (conducted by giants of behavioral economics including Richard Thaler and Daniel Kahneman) people were given a choice between two gifts of equal value: a mug or some chocolate. When people were allowed to choose freely between them, roughly half chose each gift. But when people were first allocated either a mug or some chocolate, *then* immediately asked if they wanted to swap, most refused: 86 percent of those starting with mugs stuck with their mugs, and 90 percent of those who started with chocolate kept their chocolate.[9]

Why are we so unwilling to let go of what we have? The reason seems rooted in our *loss aversion*, the fact that losses loom larger in our minds than gains of the same size. You might be excited about being given a nice office; if it's taken away from you once you have it, studies suggest that your disappointment will outstrip your original excitement.[10] So it's important for us to know that when we're making decisions, we—and others—will instinctively tend to overvalue the status quo compared with new options, unless we stop to think properly about how splendid the unfamiliar thing might really be.

### "It's the Only Real Option"

Finally, if we encounter an option that seems workable, we'll be inclined to think it's perfectly good, without really questioning it. "Someone's made a suggestion? It looks okay? Fine by me, then," says your brain's automatic system: "Why on earth would I waste mental energy by asking my deliberate system to analyze this further or look at alternatives?" This is known as *default bias*, and it's perhaps the easiest shortcut to spot, because it's in play anytime you've only got one option on the table. It can be a helpful time-saver if the decision has no consequences. ("When shall we meet for lunch?" "Twelve-thirty?" "Great.") It's not so helpful if you're making an important choice, and the only reason for your course of action is that it's the only option you were aware of.

## ADOPT A CROSS-CHECK ROUTINE

So the upshot is this: to lighten the load on our brains, our automatic system is almost always trying to keep us from seeing the whole picture. Sometimes that's okay, because speed and simplicity are all we need. But when we're doing anything where good judgment matters, we need to widen our field of vision. That means being willing to look for contradictory evidence, see beyond recent events, and take a second look at apparently obvious choices. And we certainly want to consider more than one option—even if it means we come back to the original idea.

But our shortcuts are fast and instinctive—so how can we possibly know what we don't know? Some behavioral scientists are pessimistic about our ability to outthink the automatic system, and I understand that point of view. But in the workplace I've seen one technique that generally succeeds in improving our average level of wisdom: adopting a go-to cross-check rule that's simple enough to become part of your routine anytime you're doing something important. Here are five cross-check rules that I've seen people deploy effectively: "Don't Default," "Devil's Advocate," "Mandate Dissent," "Never Say Never," and "Pre-mortem."

### Don't Default

If you're making a decision that has consequences, you always want to pause if you're faced with just one option—even if it looks appealing. Like this:

➡ Hit the "pause" button and give yourself a moment to think about alternatives. Ask yourself and others: "If we *had* to think of other possibilities, what would they be?"

➡ Look hard at the advantages of the other options, and use what you discover to test or refine the original proposal. Perhaps the first option is still the right way forward, but you might see ways to improve it once you've forced yourself to consider other possibilities.

One person that Charles Darwin would probably respect for his efforts to overcome cognitive shortcuts is Nayan, the chief financial officer of a global bank. During the day, Nayan makes complex business decisions about the right way to manage the bank's finances. At home, he paints Hindu mandalas. His colleagues have nicknamed him "Yoda," the epitome of wisdom and calm.

As with most senior managers, many of Nayan's decisions revolve around people issues rather than balance sheets. "When I first joined the bank, I was told that one of my first tasks was to fire someone. The decision about this guy had been made before I came on board, and I was the new line manager, so it fell to me." It would have been easy for Nayan to just accept that default instruction. After all, he was new, and of course he didn't want to rock the boat. But despite hearing some strong language about this person's behavior—he was apparently "arrogant"—it wasn't clear to Nayan what substantive evidence sat behind that accusation. So he decided to do what he would normally do when making an important decision: he asked a lot of questions.

First, he acknowledged that the default option—to fire the guy— might still be the correct one. "But I wanted to map out all the options." There was obviously "fire him" and "don't fire him." But under the "don't fire him" option, Nayan mapped out a few different possibilities. "I think people were seeing this as a 'do nothing' option. But there were lots of potential ways to improve the situation, like coaching him or moving him to a different role, that didn't involve him losing his job."

Then Nayan gathered more information. "I spoke to a cross-section of his co-workers, and asked about his good points and bad points." What did Nayan discover? "The guy was bright and decisive. Sometimes too decisive. But his team loved him and he was a great mentor to them." As a result, Nayan believed it would be worth holding on to him if he was willing to do more to build bridges and work collaboratively. "The decision that was handed to me was based on perceptions more than evidence—some of his peers simply didn't like his style," Nayan said. When Nayan approached him, he was mortified to discover what people thought of him, and grateful to have a chance to put it right—which he did, within three months.

### Devil's Advocate

It's not always easy to challenge our own assumptions. We know we have blind spots but, by definition, we don't know exactly what they are. So when we're making important decisions, it's helpful to ask a devil's advocate to test our reasoning.

➡ Think of someone you respect but who tends to approach things differently than you do, perhaps because of their personality or experience. Maybe you've even disagreed with them in the past. (Think of more than one person who fits the bill, if you can.)

➡ Ask your devil's advocate(s) about the situation:
  • What do they see differently than you do? What do they think you're missing?
  • What assumptions would they challenge in your thinking?
  • What advice would they give you?

**Side note:** If you can't have a live conversation with them, you can still benefit from imagining their answers to those questions; it's strangely easier to see holes in our arguments when we put ourselves in someone else's shoes. Just take five minutes to write what you'd imagine each devil's advocate would say to you about the issue at hand.

➡ Now suppose there's a good chance they're right. What information should you seek out, to make a better decision?

Attendees at the 2013 annual meeting of Warren Buffett's company, Berkshire Hathaway, got to see a live demonstration of this devil's advocate approach. Buffett is well versed in the behavioral science of cognitive shortcuts, so he's always looking for ways to seek out what he calls "discordant information" that will challenge his assumptions. On this occasion, he invited Doug Kass—a vocal critic of his firm's investment approach—to ask him tough questions in front of the whole audience. Kass confronted Buffett about Berkshire Hathaway's investment strategy, governance, and succession planning, while Buffett parried amiably.

Luckily, you don't have to do this in public to reap the benefits. Nayan often gets his devil's advocate perspectives from informal conversations with people around him. "I work in a fast-changing environment, so I often find it helpful to run my thinking past other people to make sure I've seen all the angles." Nayan doesn't just turn to senior people, either. "I have a young colleague who is always three steps ahead of me on technology issues. I like talking to him about my work even when it's not directly connected with his field, because I've noticed he always challenges and shifts my thinking. He asks good questions."

### Mandate Dissent

In a group setting, you shouldn't need to seek out devil's advocates in the same way—there should already be several different viewpoints in the room. But as I said earlier, groupthink is a hidden force in most group discussions—so while one or two people may walk in with genuinely different perspectives, they'll have a tendency to fall in with the majority view (whether they're aware of it or not). And even if some minority viewpoints do make it into the open, confirmation bias will lead the majority to undervalue those alternative views. Nobody's trying to make bad choices; it's just how we create harmony and simplicity in our minds.

So in groups, it's actually valuable to invite *everyone* to be a devil's advocate. If you make it okay to share contrasting perspectives—or even require everyone to do so—research suggests that your group will make better decisions.[11]

What does that look like in practice? Eric Schmidt, executive chairman of Google, says, "What I try to do in meetings is to find the people who have not spoken, who often are the ones who are afraid to speak out but have a dissenting opinion. I get them to say what they really think and that promotes discussion, and [then] the right thing happens."[12]

When I'm in a group that's discussing an important issue, I actually like to go one step further. Whether or not I'm chairing the meeting, I suggest that *everyone*—even those who've already spoken—answer a thought-provoking question, such as:

➡ "If there were something we were missing here, what would it be?"

➡ "If there were a completely different way to see this, what would it be?"

➡ "If there were one thing that worried you about this, what would it be?"

The "if" framing of the question is important, because it allows people to be more speculative and less worried about being "right" before they speak up. And asking everyone to raise at least one concern makes it entirely acceptable to surface doubts and queries. That means people don't get labeled as difficult for daring to differ. Then, once all the issues are on the table, the group can have an explicit discussion about how to address each issue and move forward. It's still possible to make a mistake—but much less likely.

Peggy, the advertising art director we met in the last chapter, always makes sure she invites a range of people to provide input on her most important work, and welcomes their views even when they don't jibe with her own. "We all have our biases, so it helps to discuss an issue with people from different backgrounds—a planner, an account manager, a creative director, or a writer. It's sometimes hard to accept their comments, but I've learned not to say 'I don't agree,' and to ask some questions instead. It often happens that someone will make a suggestion that makes no immediate sense to me, such as adding text to that very visual air freshener ad I came up with. I don't think the words are needed, personally. But then I discover it's because the client has said they're worried that the technical germ-killing benefits of the air freshener won't be clear to customers. And honestly, I hadn't realized that was a worry for the client." Once Peggy's heard and understood the views of her dissenters, she says, she always does better work.

### Never Say Never

In a complex situation, it's rare that something is very obviously the right thing to say, do, or choose. When we're making any meaningful decision, whether it's how to run a meeting or where to invest a big chunk of money, there are usually some pros and cons to every option. So when you notice yourself feeling very strongly attached to an idea, or very strongly opposed to one, it's a good sign that you might be falling victim to confirmation bias.

186 HOW TO HAVE A GOOD DAY

In Chapter 1, I suggested that you watch out for "absolute language" as a signal that confirmation bias is affecting your intentions; it's equally useful when you're evaluating options and ideas. Look out for phrases like: "We *have* to do this!" "That will *never* work!" or "I have *absolutely* no clue why anyone would want to do that!" Step back and ask:

➡ "What am I/are we assuming or asserting here?"

➡ "What if that isn't 100 percent true? Is it never/always/absolutely/definitely the case?"

➡ "What do the exceptions tell me/us?"

In Peggy's case, the fact that she sometimes catches herself asserting that it's "never" a good idea to add more words to an advertisement is a good signal that she should consider when that might not be true—for example, when the words explain the product's more complicated benefits. In Nayan's case, his colleagues' assumption that it was "absolutely necessary" to fire someone prompted him to check whether it *was* "absolutely" the only option. Hyperbole is an excellent red flag on the route to real wisdom.

### Conduct a Pre-mortem

Finally, here is a last-ditch tool to maximize your wisdom and minimize your blind spots before pushing ahead with a decision. Recognizing that we can never see the whole picture, we can force ourselves to explore the one perspective that we'd never willingly adopt: that we are completely, catastrophically wrong in the way we're going about things. Psychologist Gary Klein, senior scientist at MacroCognition, named this technique a "pre-mortem," as opposed to the "post-mortem" examination that sometimes happens *after* a project has failed.[13] Uncomfortable, perhaps, but liberating, too—and far better than having to do an actual post-mortem further down the line. It works like this:

➡ Think about what you're trying to achieve with the decision you're making.

➡ Think forward to an alternate future when your decision has played out, and played out badly.

➡ Imagine yourself now picking up the pieces. Ask yourself: Why did it go wrong? What was it that you failed to think about when you first made the decision?

I remember asking these questions one day when I was working with a big, established company that was about to take over a smaller firm with a younger, zippier culture. I'd spent a day with the integration team who were charged with making the acquisition a success, and they were doing some advance planning for the merger. Their conversation focused on "timelines" and "deliverables," and it had been pretty productive. But the problem with planning for mergers is that a lot of it is done in secret, behind closed doors, before it's announced to the public. That makes it even harder than usual to uncover your blind spots. It's easy to believe your own version of the world is correct when you're not exposed to the thinking of outsiders.

So I posed an exercise that began: "It's ten years from now, and the merger is widely described in the business press as a failure. Why didn't it work out?" At first they laughed amiably. But then they threw themselves into the task. Their headline answer was this: "We didn't take steps to preserve the small firm's culture, the thing that made them attractive to us. Stifling their culture made it impossible for them to be as creative as they'd been in the past." I asked them to be more specific. "Well, we assumed they should adopt all our business processes, didn't we?" This was indeed what they'd spent the previous hour planning, in some depth. I asked what a wiser approach would have been. "We would have been more nuanced about which processes we truly needed them to adopt, and where we could have let them be different. And we would have asked them to tell us how much space and support they needed to allow them to continue being agile and innovative." And with this pre-mortem completed, what were they going to do differently now? "Well, we're not going to impose all our processes on them. We'll work out which we think are really critical for us to have in common, and then we'll discuss it with them." That sounded a lot wiser.

## WATCH OUT FOR SYSTEM FATIGUE

When we're tired, either physically or mentally, it's harder for our deliberate system to exert control over the choices that our automatic system makes. That's why we're more likely to make a mistake when we're short of sleep, after we've been making lots of decisions, or if we have been trying to stay focused for a while. In short, anytime we're working hard. So paying attention to signs of exhaustion in our deliberate system is important if we want to be our smartest, wisest selves.

Vivek is an entrepreneur whose work demands a lot of his brain's deliberate system. He owns an international business that helps companies better understand the way their customers feel about their products. "It's complex," he says. "Many of my clients are biotechnology companies, making cutting-edge medications and devices. So I have to learn the technicalities of those products to be able to lead an intelligent conversation about them. I need to design the right interview questions and interactive exercises to elicit authentic responses from the customers. Then, when I'm meeting the customers in person, I have to keep the conversation flowing naturally while paying close attention to the subtext of people's comments, so that I can go deeper when needed."

He's become quite adept at recognizing when his deliberate system is out of juice in the face of those demands. "When it's overloaded, even simple tasks feel difficult, like responding to a client email or being disciplined about the amount of time I'm spending on Facebook." And in those moments, he knows it's more likely that his brain's automatic system will take control. He reels off a list of things that have happened when his deliberate system was exhausted, including making not-very-tactful comments and taking the subway to an old office location instead of his new one.

So what does Vivek do to refresh his brain's deliberate system when he notices that it's flagging? "I step away. Most often, I do breathing and mindfulness exercises. I just sit back and close my eyes. Even ten or fifteen minutes can clear my mind. I also go for a run if I can. If I can't do any of that, I try to focus on tasks that won't tax my brain too much, like watching a video from an online course. I'm still making use of the time, but it's relatively passive, and it allows my deliberate system to reboot."

Vivek uses some of the cross-check routines in the previous section to make sure he's not on autopilot when it matters most. "But I also have one or two other tricks that help me be extra careful that I'm engaging my deliberate system when I'm doing something important," he says. "For example, as soon as I start writing an important email, I make sure that I top and tail it with proper greetings. For me, typing 'Dear Whoever' triggers a reminder that I need to take a careful approach. It reminds me to slow down, engage my brain in the right way, and check what I'm doing."

To be as thoughtful as Vivek in noticing when your deliberate system needs refreshing, look out for these signs that it's not functioning at its best:

➡ You're feeling impatient or irritable.

➡ You're finding it hard to concentrate or think straight.

➡ You start making small mistakes or saying clumsy things.

And then do one or more of the following:

➡ Take a proper break, if you can, ideally involving some physical movement. Failing that, give yourself the kind of "mindful pause" I covered in Chapter 6, on overload: give yourself a few minutes to focus on your breathing (or some other simple point of focus).

➡ Shift your focus to a routine task that needs doing but is less mentally taxing.

➡ Take extra steps to review what you're doing, using one or more of the five cross-check techniques I described earlier in this chapter.

## RESOLVE DILEMMAS WITH (GREATER) EASE

Let me close this chapter by adding some advice for handling situations where wisdom can feel especially elusive: times when we need to choose between two valid courses of action that are so different that they're hard to compare. The Greeks called this a *dilemma*, meaning "two premises," because it involves two quite different models of what's best. For example, suppose you've been given a free ticket to a conference in your field. You'd love to go, because it would enable you to publicize an important project. But you have a close colleague who's told you he's trying to build his network by attending more conferences. What should you do? Should you give him the ticket, or not? One option is good for your project, the other is good for your colleague. They both matter. Argh—what to do?

Economist Ting Zhang and her Harvard colleagues, in a series of experiments, found that one subtle shift better enabled people to find ways to resolve dilemmas like this. The shift was this:

➡ Don't ask, "What *should* I do?"

➡ Instead ask, "What *could* I do?"

Why did Zhang find that a "could" question worked better for people trying to square the circle?[14] Her finding makes sense when we keep our discover-defend axis in mind. Just thinking about "shoulds" can set us on edge, by making us feel constrained and obligated. The resulting negative tone shifts us a little toward defensive mode, impairing our ability to think expansively and creatively about options. The word "could," however, primes us with a sense of possibility, autonomy, and choice. By keeping us in discovery mode, it encourages us to summon our wisest, most insightful selves.

So instead of beating yourself up as you think, "*Should* I give him the ticket?" you might instead wonder, "*Could* I ask for a second ticket?" Or perhaps you realize that it's unlikely you'd attend for the whole day, so you ask whether you could split the ticket between you and your colleague. Both are options you'd be less likely to come up with while you're busy feeling guilty. So next time you're feeling stuck in a moral dilemma, skip the "should" and try a "could."

## MAKING WISE DECISIONS

Next time you have a choice to make, whether big or small:

➡ Notice when your automatic system is talking. "It's obviously right [or obviously wrong]." "I recently heard XYZ ... therefore ..." "Everyone agrees." "I understand it—so I like it!" "Let's just stick with what we know." "There's only one real option."

➡ Adopt a cross-check routine. Try each of these cross-check questions, and decide to make at least one of them part of your personal routine:
  • Don't default: "What would be another option, and what do its advantages tell me?"
  • Play devil's advocate: "What would be another way of seeing this?"
  • Mandate dissent: "If you had to raise a concern, what would you say?"
  • Never say never: "Is it always/never/absolutely the case?"
  • Conduct a pre-mortem: "If this goes horribly wrong, what will have caused that?"

➡ Watch out for system fatigue. If you feel impatient, distracted, or clumsy, give your deliberate system a mindful pause. Shift your focus to more routine tasks. Take extra cross-checking steps to compensate for your automatic system's shortcuts.

➡ Resolve dilemmas with greater ease. Ask "What *could* I do?" rather than "What should I do?"

# THIRTEEN

# Boosting Your Brainpower

In this chapter, I'd like to share a collection of techniques to help you approach any task with the best of your mental faculties—whether your work requires insight, wisdom, or any other intellectual feat. First I'll show you three ways to frame your task in a way that will help you do your best thinking. Then I'll show you how some of the concepts we've touched on earlier in the book can be deployed to boost your performance.

## START WITH POSITIVE FRAMING

Our most important or interesting tasks often involve solving problems—something that can be an energizing experience when we reach a good outcome. But when it's not immediately obvious how to address an issue, it's easy to feel a little tense. And when we're worried about a challenge, or we're put on the spot with a question we don't know how to answer, our automatic system may identify these situations as threats to our sense of competence and social standing. If we're not able to prevent the fight-flight-freeze response that follows, we can find ourselves getting a little dumber—more black-and-white in our thinking, or more reckless in our actions—just when we want to be thoughtful and wise. In other words, our deliberate system deserts us just when we most need it.

So how can we improve the quality of our thinking when we're wrestling with tasks that matter? The trick is to neutralize the sense of threat, so we operate in discovery mode rather than defensive mode. And it doesn't take a lot to encourage that—we just need something appealing to focus on for a moment. In fact, some researchers found that when volunteers were given a puzzle where they had to navigate a little mouse out of a maze, all it took to lift their performance by 50 percent was seeing a picture of some cheese next to the exit instead of a menacing owl.[1] For us, the metaphorical "cheese" might take the form of thinking about the positive aspects of the job at hand, acknowledging progress to date, or even just remembering the best parts of the day so far. All of these are ways to shift our brain's focus from threat to reward, so that we're better able to access the full range of our cognitive resources.

Ros, the senior healthcare executive we met in Chapter 10, starts every meeting with this in mind. "We've got a huge project where 95 percent of it is going fine, but three things aren't going so well," she says. "We're getting a lot of questions about those three things, and I can see my team tensing up whenever we talk about them. So now I always begin our meetings by talking about what we've recently achieved. And you can see how it calms everyone down and helps people think more clearly." She's keen to emphasize that "it's not about trying to spin or gloss over the problems. But beginning with what's working well puts everyone in a more open frame of mind, meaning we can look at what's *not* working without people getting defensive."

Notice that the aim is not to make everyone so relaxed that they ignore the issues they're facing, or forget to check for the kind of cognitive blind spots I mentioned in the last chapter—confirmation bias, groupthink, default bias, recency bias, endowment effect, and processing fluency. If our shortcuts go unchecked, we're more likely to make bad decisions. But if we can explore difficult topics without putting ourselves and others into defensive mode, it's easier to discuss those potential blind spots in a constructive way. And then you have the best of all worlds, intellectually speaking: you'll be relaxed enough to be expansive in your initial thinking, but still rigorous enough to kick the tires on your ideas.

Here are some practical ways to make sure that you're tackling even your most challenging, crisis-ridden work in discovery mode:

➡ Before you get into your task in detail, take stock of recent positive events. You can do this on your own, or with others at the beginning of a meeting. For example:
  • Take a moment to recall one or two good things that have happened today, or in the past week. (It's fine if these are tiny wins or are unrelated to your current work. Perhaps someone brought you a coffee

this morning when you weren't expecting it. Quite literally, it's the thought that counts.)

- If it's something you've worked on before, review recent progress and identify what has helped you achieve those wins.

➡ **Imagine the ideal outcome of the task or project.** If you've got a tough task on your plate, it's easy to get uptight if you focus purely on the hurdles you have to overcome. Try setting them aside for a moment, and ask yourself:

- "What does the ideal outcome look like?"
- Then: "What first steps would take us toward the ideal outcome?"

"I always make sure to begin each piece of work in a good mood," says Peggy, our advertising art director. "It's just very difficult to come up with anything smart when you're upset, angry, or tired. You can't work when you feel under threat." A favorite technique of hers before she dives into a task is to take a moment to appreciate one thing she likes about her job. "For example, I think about the way it gives me the chance to do different things every day. I like to learn new things, and I've been able to work on projects in pharmaceuticals, soft drinks, beer, you name it." That moment of appreciation helps her set her mood and put her into discovery mode, so she's in good shape for the challenges of the day.

## DRAW AN ISSUE TREE

You're tired. The work is hard. You're trying to think straight, but your mind is foggy and you don't feel like you're getting anywhere useful. It's making you irritable, or anxious, or maybe both. That's often how it feels when your deliberate system is overloaded. But you can give your overworked brain a helping hand by applying some structure to your task, so that you're handling just one part of it at a time rather than trying to tackle the whole issue at once.

Let me give you an example. Imagine you're a landscape gardener, and you're not bringing in the profits you'd hoped when you set up your business. You're not sure what to do to improve the situation before the bank starts breathing down your neck. One option is to stop using the services of a hired hand who helps you out occasionally. (Let's call him Frank.) But you know you sometimes need help for the heavier work. You'd have to stop taking on the bigger projects, the sort that bring in the healthiest revenues. Already your brain feels tired.

So instead, you start to think about the issue in stages. First, you write down the question you're wrestling with: "How to increase profits?" Logically, then, what are the different routes you can explore? Profit is revenues minus costs. So you can increase revenues or you can reduce costs. Or maybe both. You write that down as a tree with two branches coming off your big question. Okay. It's not going to win the Nobel Prize in economics, but your head feels a little clearer already.

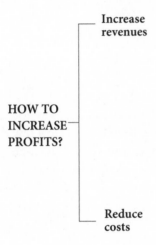

Now set aside the "reduce costs" branch for a moment, and just focus on "increase revenues." What are the basic ways of bringing in more money? You can charge higher prices for the same amount of work. Or you could increase the amount of work you do.

Then, you turn your attention to the "reduce costs" branch. One of your major costs is your hired hand, but other categories include your materials, your transport costs, and your marketing. You draw those branches.

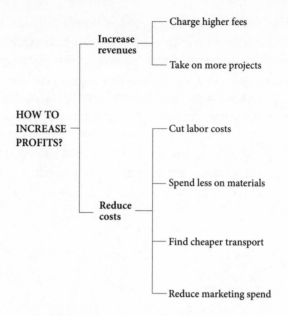

At this point it feels like there might be a few different avenues to explore. With less brain swirl, you could now take each branch in turn and break it down further, if you wanted.

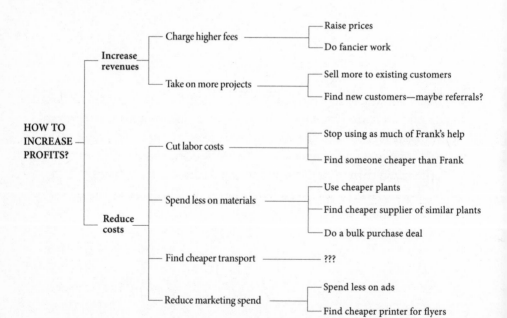

Now you've got a rich list of ideas to test out. You don't like all of them, and there are some holes. But your head feels clearer, because at each stage you're thinking about only one or two things at once. And as a result, you start to see that you have some good options. For example, you might look into buying your supplies in bulk, asking existing customers to recommend you, and checking competitors' rates to see if you're underpricing your work.

This is one of the tricks of the trade that my colleagues and I used at McKinsey. The consulting firm is famed for being able to wrestle complex topics quickly to the ground, and this kind of issue tree was often one of the first tools we used when beginning to think about a daunting topic. And sometimes you don't even need to draw yourself a whole tree. Sometimes the first or second branch is all you need for inspiration. In the last chapter, I described how Nayan (the bank CFO) was faced with a difficult decision about a colleague. For him, merely drawing the "fire him"/"don't fire him" branches of the issue tree made it obvious that there were a host of options open to him under the "don't fire him" branch. Being systematic in breaking down the issue was enough to make it easier for Nayan to see his options.

## HARNESS YOUR SOCIAL BRAIN

As I said in Part III, human beings are deeply social, and even the most curmudgeonly of us devote a surprising amount of cognitive energy to assessing other people's motives and perceptions. Chattering away in an internal monologue, our brains are constantly saying things like: "Is that person wearing the neon hat a construction worker, or is that some new fashion? Why is he wearing it in the elevator? What kind of person is he?" And we're not just noticing people's clothing—we're observing their demeanor, judging the context, deciding what we think of them, and predicting what they'll think of us. All before we've even opened our mouth to say "I like your hat."

So our brain's capacity for social calculation is very well developed, to the point that we actually recall and process information better if it's socially encoded—that is, if the facts are set in the context of the way people behave and feel.[2] That's why we tend to remember gossip easily, with its juicy human interest, while we have to make an effort to remember telephone numbers or long lists of instructions. Correspondingly, we can often give ourselves (and others) a better chance of understanding thorny topics if we find a way to weave a human story around or through them.

I noticed this whenever I found myself explaining a complicated training exercise to clients or colleagues. Whenever I gave the instructions in abstract terms—for example, asking people to get into groups of three, so that two people could each ask different types of questions of the third person for fifteen minutes before rotating the roles—the sequence was entirely clear in my own head. But it often wasn't clear to anyone else, and their eyes would glaze over. That is, until I said exactly the same thing using real names and motivations. "Imagine you, me, and Princess Diana get into a group and sit down together," I'd begin, and all would be suddenly clear.

There's even evidence to suggest that we do better on pure logic tests when they're given a social context. Researchers have used a puzzle known as the "Wason selection task" to demonstrate this.[3] In the puzzle, you're shown four cards and told that you need to check whether the following rule is being observed: if a card has a D on one side, then it has to have a 3 on the other side. Which card(s) do you definitely have to turn over in order to check the rule holds?

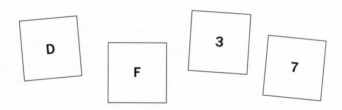

Got it? The answer isn't D alone. And it's not D and 3, because the rule doesn't say that a 3 has to have a D on the reverse. The answer is D and 7: if you turned over the 7 and it had a D on it, you'd show the rule had been broken. If that's not obvious to you, don't worry—at least 75 percent of people get it wrong.

Now try this: You're a bartender. You have to make sure that anyone drinking beer in your bar is over twenty-one, or you could lose your license. Each of the cards below represents information about four of your patrons. One side of the card shows what they're drinking, and the other side of the card shows their (real) age. Which card or cards

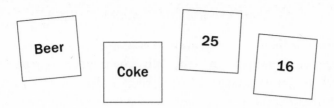

do you need to turn over to see if the twenty-one-and-over rule is being violated?

The answer? You need to turn over the cards for "beer" and "16." In other words, if you saw someone drinking beer, you'd check their age; if you saw someone who looked underage, you'd check what they were drinking. It's the same structure as the previous test, but roughly 75 percent of people get this version right (and you probably did, too).[4] That's three times as many correct answers, just by adding some social context.

You can apply this insight in your own work when you're wrestling with a tricky analytical or conceptual challenge, by recasting it in social terms. Here are some things to try:

➡ Turn the components of the problem into real people, and imagine them interacting. For example, if you're trying to work out how Factory A's output should feed into Factory B's production schedule, try thinking of the factories as Anna and Bob, who are trying to coordinate their workload.

➡ Imagine a real person walking through the situation or process. For example, if you're looking for ways to improve customer service, picture a friend going through each step of the interaction with your company. What would he or she find frustrating or difficult?

This kind of social framing might just give you some extra brainpower to play with, or at least reveal perspectives you hadn't previously considered.

## LOOK AFTER THE SMART BASICS

There are four themes I've mentioned earlier in the book that I'm going to recap here, since they're especially powerful in sharpening your mind when you need to rise to a challenge. They involve scheduling blocks of deep thinking time, engineering your environment, prioritizing your sleep, and doing a short burst of aerobic exercise.

### Undistracted Thinking Time

In Chapter 4, I talked about the importance of reducing distractions, given the way that multitasking increases the number of errors we make. So if we want to be on our game, we need to give ourselves un-interrupted time to work on our most intellectually challenging tasks.

But, you might be thinking, doesn't exposure to new information make us more creative? In Chapter 8 we saw how fresh thinking comes from encouraging the brain to explore new perspectives and make new connections. But it depends on *how* you take in that new information. Genuine insight isn't helped by piecemeal attention. Teresa Amabile and her colleagues at Harvard Business School evaluated the daily work patterns of more than nine thousand people working on projects that required creativity and innovation. They found that the likelihood of creative thinking was higher when people focused on one activity for a chunk of the day. Conversely, when people had highly fragmented days, their creative thinking decreased significantly.[5] This probably relates to something that neuroscientists call the "preparatory period" just before we have a moment of insight, when our neural activity actually goes strangely quiet.[6] If you get a pinging email alert at that moment, your mental quiet evaporates—along with the chances that you'll hold on to the big breakthrough you were about to have.

Like many people, Peggy, our advertising art director, often finds herself working in open plan offices, where it can be harder to avoid interruptions. Her solution? "I go to a conference room if I can. And even if I can't, I eliminate a lot of distractions by turning off alerts and putting my phone on 'do not disturb.'" Peggy also realized that her daily calendar quickly gets filled with meetings. "That leaves me doing my thinking around the edges of the day, when I'm often tired. So instead I decided to start scheduling my thinking time just like any other meeting, to give it proper priority."

If you carve out some focused thinking time and successfully manage to protect it, it's worth explicitly rewarding yourself in some way after you finish—perhaps with a walk or a talk with a favorite colleague. The reward will make it easier for your brain to repeat your virtuous focused behavior next time around.

## A Good Thinking Environment

In Chapter 3, I talked about the way that small environmental cues can nudge us to stay on track with our intentions, thanks to the way our highly associative brain readily reboots old associations given half a chance. For example, if we have a connection somewhere in our brain between having a clear desk and a clear head, tidying our desk may provide a small nudge toward clearer thinking. Peggy says, "I am very interested in how different surroundings can affect my work. I've found that I do think more expansively if I literally feel like I have space to think, so I like to keep my work area uncluttered. I like a bright environment; it makes me *feel* bright. I like to have a pen in my hand, because it tells me that I'm ready for ideas." These small workspace cues help Peggy create openness, readiness, and focus in her mind, because she associates them with the kind of thinking she does when she's at her best.

She even pays attention to what she's wearing. "As a contractor, I often work from home, and it would be easy to sit at home wearing pajamas. What does it matter, right? But I make sure to get dressed as if I'm going into the office, every day. Shoes, hair, the works. If I'm in my pajamas, I feel sloppy and I don't feel fully awake. If I have real work clothes on and I sit at a desk, I feel mentally ready." For Peggy, it's another useful trigger to encourage high-performance thinking. (For scientists, it's a nice example of something they call "enclothed cognition.")

So consider which workplace cues you particularly associate with good thinking, and find a way to surround yourself with a few of them. And remember that what brings out the best in you is entirely personal. In contrast to Peggy, you might associate pajamas and darkness with creativity (perhaps that's how you once did your most innovative work). In which case, turn off the light and put on your inspirational bathrobe.

## Sleeping Yourself Smart

I mentioned at the beginning of the book that our brain's deliberate system needs to be well rested to function at its best. Sleep well, and you give your brain the best chance of being able to marshal all of your intelligence when you need it. Sleep badly, and you lose a few IQ points. Matthew Walker, who runs the Sleep and Neuroimaging Lab at the University of California Berkeley, has conducted several studies illustrating this stark truth. One experiment found that a solid night's sleep made people twice as effective at working out complex patterns in information.[7] In another experiment, people solved 30 percent more anagrams after periods of rest that included rapid eye movement (REM) sleep—which we get more of the longer we're asleep.[8]

That's not to say we can't muster the energy to plow on when we're exhausted, as I'm sure you know all too well. As long as we're only dealing with familiar or predictable challenges, we can just about get by on autopilot.[9] And if we're truly riveted by what we're doing and are willing to put in extra mental effort to stay focused, we can rally our deliberate system for a brief boost. But as soon as we're handling anything that isn't either entirely routine or utterly riveting—most of normal working life, in other words—we don't have the mental flexibility to perform at our best when we're tired.

Moreover, we need decent sleep if we're to make good use of what we experience each day. Overnight, we move through several sleep cycles lasting 90–120 minutes, containing periods of light sleep, deep sleep, and REM sleep in turn. Each type of sleep plays a slightly different role in helping us process our experience of the world: reviewing the day's events, recalling the things we've learned, reinforcing neural pathways around new information to make it easier to remember in the future, or connecting that new information to previously encoded knowledge.[10] A night's sleep with plenty of those cycles leaves us with a better chance that we'll wake up with deeper understanding of what happened the day before. A short night, meanwhile, means we create fewer long-lasting memories and insights. In other words, we remember less and learn less.

Yet many of us persist in believing that it's okay to burn the candle at both ends. Everyone can imagine how a sleep-deprived driver might crash a vehicle, but there's a tendency to think that purely intellectual work is somehow immune. Long nights remain common in some professions, because there's a belief that staying awake is better for meeting deadlines (and gaining badges of honor) than getting some rest. But nobody's immune to the workings of neurobiology. Big errors of judgment get made. Andrew, an investment banker, told me about mistakes he saw colleagues making when they'd been ordered to stay in the office without sleep in the middle of big deals. "They were so exhausted that they were sending sensitive emails and making calls to the wrong people, or telling the buyer highly confidential things that they should have been telling the seller, with disastrous results."

Peggy's learned to prioritize sleep, even when she's up against a deadline. "I'll be working late to try to get something difficult done, and I'll think, 'I just want to push through and finish this.' But it's not a recipe for good work. There always comes a point where I know that if I got some sleep and then picked it up in the morning, I'd nail it in a fraction of the time it's taking me as I'm sitting here, late and frustrated."

Sometimes we intend to get a good night's sleep, but we don't make it easy for our brains to get what they need. We all know the usual reasons we fall short—long working hours, getting up early to get the kids ready, interminable commutes—but an often overlooked cause is that many of us now use phones and tablets in bed. This exposes us to light that's rich in blue wavelengths, something that makes our brains think it's the middle of the day because it suppresses melatonin, the hormone that signals to our brains that it's time to sleep. Naturally, that makes it harder for us to drop off. In fact, Harvard's Division of Sleep Medicine found that people's bodies released melatonin a full ninety minutes later when exposed to bright light rather than dim lighting before bedtime—effectively shortening their night's sleep by that long, too.[11]

Here are some suggestions on how to sleep smart:

➡ **Prioritize it.** It doesn't matter how well you think you're getting by— you'd be sharper if you weren't short of sleep. So if you're working late and not sure whether to push on: go to bed. You'll be faster and smarter in the morning—more in control of the facts, and more able to see new linkages.

➡ **Make it darker.** Expose yourself to as little light as possible before bedtime. Try not to use your phone as an alarm, to reduce the temptation to look at its screen. If you like reading e-books, use a device that has diffuse light.

➡ **Develop a sleep routine.** It's easier to fall asleep more quickly if you have a routine, because your associative brain starts to associate the bedtime ritual with "it's time to sleep." The ritual ideally includes going to bed at the same time each night, with a fixed pattern of activity leading up to the moment when you climb under the cover.

Finally, if it's truly impossible for you to get all the sleep you need (thanks to work schedules or family responsibilities), there's encouraging evidence on the usefulness of naps in improving the clarity of your thinking. NASA has conducted multiple studies on the effects of what it calls "strategic naps," one of which found that a twenty-five-minute nap boosted performance by 34 percent and alertness by 54 percent.[12] And naps of sixty to ninety minutes have been found to be long enough to improve memory.[13]

That's why companies like Google, Huffington Post, Cisco, Nike, and Procter & Gamble have set aside nap rooms for their employees. It's still comparatively rare to find workplaces that are well set up for naps, of course. But I often carry earplugs and an eye mask with me, and have been known to rest my head on my desk to grab a nap; I know other people who sit in their cars or book themselves into small conference rooms to snooze, sometimes using special nap pillows (yes, such things exist). According to an international survey by the National Sleep Foundation, a third of us are regularly using naps to top up our sleep—and our smarts.[14] That includes productivity expert David Allen, author of *Getting Things Done*, by the way. He told me that he aims for a nap of twenty-five to forty-five minutes every afternoon, which he says is "much better than coffee."[15]

## Aerobic Exercise (Just a Little)

Finally, a reminder of a simple way to quickly boost your smarts: jumping around. A wealth of research shows that exercise improves our focus and our memory, quickens our response speed, and improves our ability to learn and plan.[16] That makes us better at handling complex tasks. One set of experiments demonstrated this using something called the Stroop test, where subjects have to look at a word like "red" printed in blue ink, and answer correctly when asked what color the ink is—which is not as easy as it sounds. And studies have shown that just one bout of exercise makes people score higher on the test. The only thing that exercise doesn't seem to do is actually answer all our emails for us—although a workout does make it more likely that we'll whiz through our inbox more efficiently when we get back to it.

So exercise sharpens the saw. But how much do you have to sharpen it? Do you have to run? Get breathless and sweaty? The great news is that there is lots of evidence that you can get most of the intellectual benefits of exercise with just twenty to thirty minutes of moderate aerobic activity—and researchers from the Arnold School of Public Health found that this can be done in two or three bites, for example with a fast walk to and from a meeting. They conclude: "Some activity is better than none, and more is better than some. Even light-intensity activity appears to provide benefit and is preferable to sitting still."[17] So you don't need to do anything too fancy to reap some quick cognitive benefits when you're in the middle of a challenging task.

For Peggy, her go-to mental boost involves jumping on her bicycle. "After one especially bad meeting I went for a two-and-a-half-hour bike ride around Los Angeles. That enabled me to say, 'Okay!' and get back into it. But usually I don't have to go for all that long. A few minutes can help me come back to the task with more focus."

### Boosting Your Brainpower

In your next big task, try the following techniques to help you think as clearly as possible:

➡ **Start with positive framing.** Think about something positive before getting into the tough stuff. For example: review recent progress or positive events; start with the ideal (and work back from that).

➡ **Draw the issue tree.** Break a complex task down into its constituent parts, step by step, to allow you to focus on one thing at a time and reduce the load on your brain.

➡ **Harness your social brain.** Imagine parts of your problem as people; imagine a real person you know walking through the issue you're wrestling with (as a user or customer).

➡ **Look after the smart basics.** Remove distractions; surround yourself with cues that you associate with good thinking; don't skimp on sleep; do some physical activity.

# PART V

# Influence

## Maximizing the Impact of All You Say and Do

Don't worry about people stealing an idea. If it's original, you will have to
ram it down their throats.

—HOWARD AIKEN

Every day sees us writing and talking and tapping, working to communicate our thoughts and directives to the rest of the world. On good
days, our words have instant impact. Our ideas flow confidently, and
we get the outcome we were after—whether it's a lunch date with that
special person, backing for a big idea, or an agreement that we really
do deserve a raise. But on other days, all the traffic lights seem to turn
red as we approach them. We're as smart and charming as ever, but our
message somehow doesn't get through.

So this part of the book is about how we can more effectively communicate what we believe, need, and want. I'll look at how to get our
views across in a compelling way, so that even busy people pay attention. I'll discuss how to get colleagues on board with our proposals,
and how to be persuasive in encouraging them to do something differently. I'll also present some techniques for conveying more of our
inner confidence to the outside world, to add extra impact to all we say
and do. And lastly I'll talk about how we can apply all this advice to
make sure our hard work gets recognized, so that everyone knows they
should come to us the next time they want brilliant results.

# FOURTEEN

# Getting Through Their Filters

We communicate for lots of reasons. Maybe we need to let colleagues know what's expected of them, or give people the information they need to make decisions. Sometimes we want to tell the world that we've had a big breakthrough in our work. Whatever our motivation, the first crucial step is always the same: the people we're communicating with need to stop and listen to what we're saying. But if you've ever sent an email or made a remark in a meeting and not gotten the exact response you wanted, you'll know that their full attention isn't guaranteed, no matter how good your ideas are.

Why is it sometimes hard to get our message through? In large part, it's because other people's automatic systems get in the way. For example, remember how confirmation bias works: the brain tends to prioritize information that matches its existing view of what's true or likely, while filtering out everything else. It's a good way of lightening the load on the brain's deliberate system. But it means that if we present an unfamiliar piece of information that doesn't fit with what our colleagues already believe or expect to hear, their automatic spam filter may simply block it out—however important or correct it is.

So people aren't always being consciously closed-minded if they're not responding as you hope; it's possible—even probable—that their brains are on autopilot. And research suggests that there are certain techniques to break through people's spam filters. The key is to use a communication style that respects the way the brain works, by appealing to its reward system, engaging its social radar, and reducing the amount of processing it needs to do. In this chapter, I'll show you how to use those techniques to help your ideas get the hearing they deserve.

## PROVIDE A REWARD
## (SURPRISE! NOVELTY! ANTICIPATION!)

Think about the last article you remember reading. What made it stick in your mind? Chances are that there was something that surprised or tickled you. That's an interesting thing about the brain's automatic spam filter. It tends to block information that people don't already agree with, but you can get through the filter with something that feels novel or intriguing. As I mentioned in The Science Essentials, these qualities delight the brain's reward system, perhaps because they speak to our social nature. It feels good to be able to tell others that we saw something unusual or startling; it makes us feel that we're offering something of value to our tribe. UCLA neuroscientist Matt Lieberman conducted a series of experiments showing that an idea is more likely to stick with listeners if they can imagine themselves telling someone else about it. It turns out that this is even more important than whether or not they even like the idea.[1] So a good general guide on whether you're getting people's attention is to ask yourself: "Are people going to feel like telling someone else what I told them?"

Greg is a crowdfunding entrepreneur who is creating new ways to raise money for healthcare research. A large part of his job involves explaining his ideas to potential investors and scientists, and he's always been thoughtful about ways to make his opening gambit as stimulating as possible. "I remind myself that it's like people who have headphones on. They can't really hear me—unless I do something that's interesting enough to get their attention," Greg says. "So whether it's a one-to-one meeting or a big speech, I try to make sure in the first two minutes that they know they're going to hear something a bit different, by breaking whatever pattern they're used to. For example, at conferences now, I'll often start by saying something like, 'I totally understand that you're not listening to me, that your internal soundtrack is full of "Who is this guy? Why would I support *him*?"' After suffering through thirty-eight PowerPoint presentations, they're not expecting that, and it always gets a laugh. And bam, they're actually now listening."

Greg remembers how one clever opener helped him develop a relationship with a major bank for his crowdfunding project. "Rather than being pushy in trying to persuade them to give us money, I told them, 'Of course, you really shouldn't be involved with us. We're disrupting the way that the financial sector works, while you need to protect it.' It was true, but the opposite of what they were expecting me to say, and it got them interested enough to pay attention. We had a very good conversation after that."

That was a bold opening statement for Greg to put out there. But your communication doesn't have to be as risky as that to get through people's spam filters. You just need to introduce a small dose of intrigue or novelty into what you're writing or saying. Here are a few options:

➡ Flag an interesting "reveal." In the modern world, this technique has been raised to a high (or low) art by websites that specialize in creating "you'll never believe this" headlines that can be difficult to resist. You might groan when you see the most blatant examples of this clickbait, but they're prevalent because they generally work, and they work because people like having their interest piqued. It's a technique we naturally use when talking to our friends, saying, "You'll never guess what happened today . . ." (rather than "I've got three key points to tell you about my day"). But it's pretty rare in communication at work, and it can be a simple way of getting people to engage. Try the following:

  • In your opening, hint at something intriguing (e.g., "I noticed something surprising/remarkable/startling . . .") It's even better if you can share an anecdote that gets people interested in how the story ends, since it sustains the anticipation for just a little longer.

  • When you want people to pay attention, use a simple marker phrase that creates a moment of suspense and promises an imminent payoff, for example: "Now, what's really interesting is this . . ."

➡ Try a different medium for conveying your information. Even in the most serious of settings, I've noticed that people who are used to reviewing thick documents suddenly become more engaged when given the chance to absorb information in a different way. I like turning presentations into large posters and inviting people to walk around the room to take notes and discuss. Peter, the IT consultant whom we met in Part III, had a breakthrough with a prospective client in the financial sector when he showed them a rough video he'd made on his phone, containing interviews with people on the street about their approach to personal finance. Meanwhile, an unpublished experiment at Stanford found that even drawing a chart live on a whiteboard was

9 percent more memorable than walking people through static slides that included the exact same content.[2]

➡ **Adopt an unusual vantage point.** Another method is to put the audience in the shoes of someone with a relevant view on the topic. Peter's *vox pop* videos did that by giving his client the perspective of the average layperson. Greg sometimes invites his audience to see the process of funding new cancer drugs from the perspective of a cancer cell. "It's a very different way for the audience to think about the topic. As a cancer cell, I tell them, 'I want as much time as possible to grow before I'm noticed. So when a clinical trial takes months to recruit volunteers, I like that; when it takes years for the trial to disseminate its findings, that's also great for me.' It's easy to show that our current approach to running clinical trials protects that little cancer cell, because it takes so long. And it really grabs them." Which means they're listening closely when Greg goes on to explain why there should be nimbler approaches to funding medical research.

## EMPHASIZE THE HUMAN ANGLE

Emma is a sparky, irreverent high school English teacher, and she's another person who has thought hard about how to get her ideas across—in her case, to her teaching colleagues. Her school's principal had hired Emma not only to teach, but also to help the school shift its teaching style from "chalk and talk"—where kids listen and absorb—to one that helps kids become independent learners, capable of working things out for themselves. "When I started talking to the other teachers about this new approach," Emma recalls, "I could tell they were thinking, 'She's young and enthusiastic, and she'll learn to pipe down.' They weren't unfriendly, but they just weren't that interested in what I had to say."

She knew she couldn't get their attention by promising immediate benefits. "We're so focused on tracking short-term measures of success in education, like test scores. I had to be honest that the old teaching methods do just fine in getting students to read *Jane Eyre* and pass an English exam. The real benefits of a more modern approach come through in the long term, by equipping students better to handle a fast-changing world." Emma needed to talk about *that* if she was to have any hope of engaging her colleagues. "So I asked them to put them-selves in the shoes of a child at our school, and imagine what they'd be able to do differently in thirty years' time, having learned to think in-dependently as a fifteen-year-old. Then I asked my colleagues: 'Did we get into teaching to help kids get high scores, or to help them get access to the world?' I could see them smiling and nodding—later, one said it really rallied them by reminding them of what teaching was all about."

Emma's approach was a masterstroke of communication, for sev-eral reasons. First, we achieve more impact with our message if it sparks some kind of emotion in our reader or listener.[3] People's brains form stronger associations around a new piece of information when it includes emotion as well as facts; there's more material for the brain to get its teeth into, so to speak.

Does it matter whether you use negative or positive emotion? Yes, actually. Negative emotions get our attention very quickly of course—just yell "Fire!" and you're guaranteed to have people at least glance in your direction. But there are some downsides to using negative emo-tion in business communication. First, remember that we generally seek to avoid threats, so we tend to prefer propositions that are framed positively. For example, in one study where people were told that there was a 90 percent survival rate for patients undergoing a specific type of surgery, they were far more likely to choose to have the surgery than if they were told that there was a 10 percent chance of dying.[4] Second, scientists have found that people don't recall details very well when a message is suffused with negative emotion.[5] Given all this, it won't surprise you to hear that researchers have found time and again that positive content gets shared on the Internet more often than negative content.[6]

So Emma was wise to reconnect her colleagues to their deep per-sonal sense of purpose as teachers, since it sparked some powerful positive emotions that helped her message get heard and remembered. And rather than saying "How can we stop our students being passive consumers of what we teach them?" Emma asked: "How can we create lifelong learners who'll be equipped to deal with life's ups and downs?" The same question, essentially, but framed to draw teachers' attention toward a positive prize.

Emma also talked about the likely effect of her new teaching meth-ods on named kids at their school, and also asked the teachers to put themselves in those kids' shoes fifteen years from now. That was smart, too, because we all remember information more readily when it's "socially encoded"—that is, if it's linked to stories about real people's motivations and feelings.[7] As I mentioned in Chapter 13, it's easier for most of us to recall a gossipy story than to remember a list of twenty things, even though the gossip probably includes far more than twenty bits of information. And research shows very clearly that charities raise more money when their communications highlight an identifiable person whose life will change as a result of donors' generosity. For example, one fundraising campaign that talked about a specific hungry seven-year-old girl named Rokia was more successful than one talking about broader statistics of her whole country's struggle with starvation.[8]

So human interest—people plus (positive) emotion—is an ingredient that makes it easier to engage our audience. That's why professional communicators tend to start speeches with an anecdote, and why media headlines are so often written with a prominent human angle. It's a recipe that leads people to click, read, follow, and share online articles. It's not just celebrity news websites we're talking about here, either. An analysis of the internal communications website at my old firm, McKinsey, showed that its staffers clicked most often on content that was personal, especially if it was also surprising and made them smile—precisely the factors I've talked about in this chapter.[9]

And yet, do we use this knowledge in everyday professional communication? You have to be kidding! (Dash of emotion judiciously placed there.) We mumble about not wanting to seem unprofessional, and push on with our dry reports and presentations and charts. But it's possible, and entirely professional, to put characters before concepts, just as Emma did. Lead with the human stuff, and you have a better chance of getting people to pay attention to any logical stuff—arguments, data, bullet points galore—that you want to present after that.

Here are some approaches to try:

➡ **Share a human example.**
  • Start with an anecdote or example that illustrates how your idea affects a real person—either someone in your audience, or someone they can relate to or care about. (Just as Emma talked about the effect of new teaching methods on the teachers' students.)
  • Find an individual who's a great example of what you're trying to say, and tell his or her story.

- If you're talking about something very dry, like a business process, you can still talk about how it makes life easier for somebody when it's working well.

➡ **Highlight the emotional side.** Here are two non-hokey ways to do it:
- Emphasize why the thing you're talking about matters to you and/ or to your audience. (Remember how Emma tapped into teachers' desire to make a lasting difference in their students' lives.) Don't be scared of the *F*-word, "feel." You can make people sit up and listen with simple phrases like "It makes me feel proud that . . ." or "we should all feel good about . . ."
- Invite your audience to put themselves in your shoes, or in others' shoes. For example: "You can imagine how I felt. I was really worried. That's when I had the idea to . . ." "Just think how it will feel to have been one of our students . . ."

➡ **Talk about a positive outcome.** Inspire your audience by painting a picture of the likely positive outcome that will result from addressing the issue you're talking about. Even if you're talking about a very negative situation, you can still describe what it would look like if the problem were solved, to leave people feeling energized rather than depressed: "Imagine if this were fixed . . ."

## MAKE IT FLUENT

If you're trying to get heard, it helps to make your communication as easy as possible for other people's brains to process. That's because the more effort people have to make in understanding what you're saying, the less mental energy they have left to engage with the information in any depth. And one rule of thumb that everyone's automatic brain uses (as I said in Chapter 12, on decision making) is to assume that things that are readily understood and remembered are probably correct.

There are lots of ways that this liking of *processing fluency* plays out.[10] In one example, Princeton psychologists Adam Alter and David Oppenheimer found that companies with names that were easy to pronounce outperformed companies with "disfluent" names on two stock markets.[11] Another study found that people trusted aphorisms when they rhymed; less so when they didn't. (Woes unite foes: sure. Woes unite enemies: really?)[12] Other research suggests that people tend to believe statements they find easy to remember, whether they're true or not.[13] Phrases they find easy to read—either because of the language used or because of the way the text is laid out—are seen as being more compelling and appealing than similar but less accessible information.[14] We process and recall concrete words that we can picture (e.g., "animal," "chair," "coffee") more readily than abstract concepts (e.g., "seniority," "justice," "patience").[15]

So processing fluency should be a primary goal in your communication, whether you're writing or speaking. Here are five ways to make your message easier for people's brains to process:

➡ 1. **Keep it as short as possible.** Recognize the limited processing capacity of people's working memory. Keep the language as simple as possible. Take out unnecessary detail or ~~verbiage~~ words.

➡ 2. **Provide signposts.** If you have a lot of information to get across, help people find their way through it with clear signposts. Say things like: "There are three things I want to tell you . . ." and "Now, turning to the third point . . ." Doing this means they're not devoting as much mental energy to wondering how much more you're going to say.

➡ 3. **Use sticky phrases.** Emma described her goal as replacing "chalk and talk" with "independent learning," and she spoke of her desire to help her students be "thinkers, not regurgitators." I found myself remembering those phrases months after I talked to Emma. Using memorable language can even get you a job under the right circumstances. Greg was sought out for his current role on the strength of the company's founder remembering a talk Greg had given about "passion capital" five years earlier. The phrase had stuck in the founder's mind as a reminder of what Greg stood for.

➡ 4. **Give concrete examples.** The more you can get beyond generalities and give specific examples, the easier it is for people to grasp what you're talking about. People might nod when you say, "We need to be more respectful of each other's time," but there's an entirely different level of engagement when you say, "For example, I'd like to suggest we start our meetings on schedule, rather than waiting for the last person to turn up."

➡ **5. Include a visual image to illustrate your point.** In 2012 the UK government's Behavioural Insights Team—a group dedicated to applying behavioral science to public policy—was trying to reduce the number of drivers who failed to pay their annual car tax. It was costing the government millions each year in lost revenue. They first tried rewriting the government's standard warning letters in plainer English, with a simple header: "Pay your tax or lose your car." This doubled the number of people who paid up in response to the letter. But when the letter was brought to life with a picture of the car in question (taken by a traffic camera), the number tripled.[16]

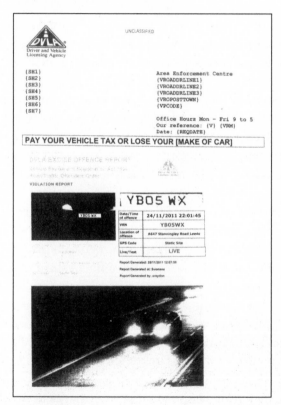

Source: Behavioural Insights Team

Why is a picture worth a thousand words (or so)? Because a huge part of the brain specializes in visual processing. So if you're able to use an image, you get more of your audience's brainpower engaged in chewing over your message.

## OVERCOME THE CURSE OF KNOWLEDGE

When we're trying to get a message across, we often think hard about what we want to say. But in our zeal to communicate, it's easy to forget to put ourselves in the shoes of the person we're trying to engage. If we don't stop to think about what they know or feel, our automatic system takes the *projection bias* shortcut, which means we generally assume that others see the world as we do. And that shortcut can cause us to suffer from what scientists call the *curse of knowledge*, where assuming that others know what we know leads us to overestimate how well we've communicated.[17]

That's how statements that seem totally clear to us can be interpreted differently by others. For example, if someone said to you, "Jo hit the man with the binder," what would you think? Would you decide that Jo had taken a binder and whacked a colleague on the head with it? Or would you assume instead that she'd punched someone who was holding a binder at the time? Both are valid interpretations; the only thing that's certain is that you might want to steer clear of Jo for the rest of the day. Yet when participants in an experiment were given this kind of ambiguous sentence to say to someone else (after deciding which interpretation they thought was correct), four out of five speakers overestimated the chance they'd be understood. The speakers had such a strong sense of their intended meaning that they believed that listeners would be able to hear things just as they intended.[18]

The curse of knowledge creates lots of potential for crossed wires in the workplace. Sometimes we know when a misunderstanding has occurred: "I'm sure I told you this was due on Friday. How was it not clear *which* Friday I meant?" But on many occasions, we never find out that our message failed to land as we intended. We simply don't achieve the impact we'd hoped, and we don't really know why. So to make your communication as clear as it is in your own head: never assume that others know what you know. As Greg says, "You've got to accept the other person's starting point. I work out how they're feeling and what they know, and I go from there."

In practice, that means:

➤ Before you open your mouth or start typing, always take a moment to put yourself in the listener or reader's shoes. Think about what that person is likely to know or feel about the topic at hand.

➡ If you're talking to someone in person, find out where he or she is starting from ("Before I launch in, tell me what you already know about XYZ"), and periodically check to see whether you're successfully landing the points you're trying to make ("Let me pause there before carrying on—does that makes sense? Is there anything I'm missing?"). Don't talk for more than five minutes without checking in. Find out what the other person wants to know next, and respond accordingly.

## GETTING THROUGH THEIR FILTERS

Next time you're intent on getting a message across:

➡ **Provide a reward: surprise, novelty, or anticipation.** Aim to get your audience to want to tell others what you said. Flag clearly the most interesting aspects of what you're saying, so they don't get buried, and promise a "reveal." Try a different medium for getting your information across (e.g., posters, videos, hand-drawn pictures). Adopt an unusual vantage point.

➡ **Emphasize the human angle, with the formula: "people plus positive emotion."** Show how your idea affects real people, and invite your audience to put themselves in their shoes. Explain why your message means so much to you or your audience. Inspire them by painting the picture of a potential positive outcome for everyone involved.

➡ **Make it "fluent."** The easier it is to understand and remember, the more compelling your message will be. So: keep it simple and short; use signposts; use sticky phrases; give concrete examples; if you can, include a visual image to illustrate your point.

➡ **Overcome the curse of knowledge.** Don't assume they know what you know. Ask what they understand and feel about the topic under discussion, and work from there. Stop to check their perspective as you're talking.

# FIFTEEN

# Making Things Happen

Much of the time, we need to do more than make sure the world hears and appreciates what we're thinking. We want our words to lead people to actually *do* something, whether to lend us their help, give us their time, or change the way they work.

And that's no small thing. People have well-established pathways in their brains that correspond to their routines, and their energy-saving automatic systems are geared toward reusing those pathways again and again, making them inclined to repeat past behavior. What's more, doing anything differently requires people to bear some uncertainty about what will happen as a result—and since uncertainty stretches the brain's resources, it's something the brain likes to avoid.

That's why the status quo can be hard to shift. It's why your colleagues may say a well-intentioned "yes" to a request, but fail to follow through when their old patterns prove hard to break. As Emma, our iconoclastic teacher, says, "At my school, most of the staff has taught in the same way for a long time. And they're good at what they do, so it's not obvious why they should try something different."

But if we knew how to make people feel good about trying something new, we could make our ask feel less worrying and more appealing to their brains. And that makes it more likely that we'll succeed in securing whatever it is we want or need from them. The techniques in the previous chapter will help you frame your request so that people pay attention; the techniques in this chapter will help you translate that attention into real action.

## PROVIDE SOME CONTEXT

A classic study by Harvard psychologist Ellen Langer tested three different ways of persuading people to do a simple thing: to let someone cut in front of them as they were about to use a photocopier.[1] She had the person who wanted to jump in line say one of these three sentences:

➡ "Excuse me, I have five pages. May I use the Xerox machine?" When hearing this, 60 percent of people were kind enough to agree to let them go first.

➡ "Excuse me, I have five pages. May I use the Xerox machine because I'm in a rush?" This time, 94 percent agreed. The addition of a reason meant that almost everyone said yes—quite a big change. People may have rolled their eyes, but they probably felt some sympathy for the person in a hurry. We've all been there.

➡ The most surprising thing happened when this third sentence was used: "Excuse me, I have five pages. May I use the Xerox machine because I have to make some copies?" This time, the "reason" given was a meaningless tautology—but 93 percent, about the same proportion, still agreed. Signaling that there *was* a reason—even if it wasn't a very good one—seemed to be enough to make the request feel acceptable.

What does this mean for you? Well, when you're asking people to do something, you'll probably get more cooperation if you give a brief reason, rather than merely asserting that it's what you want them to do.

You might have thought this was obvious, but I've observed that people often make requests of colleagues—asking an assistant to book a meeting room, for example—without any explanation. After all, if booking rooms is part of a colleague's job description, why explain the request? But taking five seconds to say "Because it's an important meeting for us at this point in the project" instantly makes it feel like more of a team effort and less of an order, which in turn translates into better support. In effect, you're helping colleagues stay in discovery mode, by treating them with more of the respect that everyone's social brain craves. So for the simple requests you're making each day, remember to give a couple of seconds of context rather than barking the kind of transactional order you'd make at a fast-food restaurant.

## MAKE IT EASY TO CHOOSE (AKA "NUDGE")

We know by now that people's brains like to take shortcuts. If they don't have to spend time thinking about an answer, they generally won't. So when there's a readily understandable and halfway reasonable option on the table, people are likely to choose it—or at least be swayed by it. As we saw in Chapter 12, this phenomenon is known by behavioral scientists as *default bias*. When you're the one making decisions, you want to be careful that you're not just choosing an option because it's easy. But now we get to turn the advice around: if you're sure that you have a good idea to propose to your colleagues, you want to make it as effortless as possible to follow your lead.

This concept gained widespread attention thanks to Richard Thaler and Cass Sunstein's book *Nudge*, where they showed how people could be nudged toward healthier, more sensible behavior once it was made easy to choose that course of action.[2] One famous example they cite relates to consent rates for organ donation. In countries where the default option is to donate your organs after death—that is, you have to make a conscious decision to opt out, rather than a conscious decision to opt in—donation rates are over 90 percent. In countries where it's not, rates are typically well below 30 percent.[3]

And as Thaler and Sunstein pointed out, nudging in this way doesn't mean depriving people of the right to choose. There are times when it's important to give people space to take ownership of their choices, especially when you're keen for them to feel a deep commitment to a complex idea (see more on getting people involved below). But where you know your suggestion is going to save people time, or there's an obvious smart choice, you can give a powerful boost to your persuasiveness if you recognize the value of making it simple to choose to do the thing you'd like people to do.

Here are three ways to apply this advice when you're seeking to influence others: remove the barrier, make the first concrete suggestion (perhaps giving a range), and provide visual hints.

### Nudge 1: Remove the Barrier

If you know what you really want people to do, ask yourself:

➡ What might stop people from doing what you would like them to do? How can you solve that problem for them, or make it simple for them to solve it themselves?

➡ Could you even make your desired outcome the "do nothing" option for them?

Mo is an experienced salesman in charge of Middle East and North Africa operations for a data storage company. "The first introduction I had to behavioral science was to learn about the power of asking open questions rather than closed ones," he says. "But once you've had a good discussion with the customer and it's clear that they're really interested, there's a technique called an 'assumptive close.' That's where you ask a closed question instead, saying 'Would you like to pay for this by debit or credit card?' instead of saying 'What would you like to do now?'" By offering two options that involve the customer buying his product, Mo is making it easy for the customer to choose to finalize the sale rather than agonizing further over the purchasing decision. Mo says that when salespeople use this approach, they win the sale about 75 percent of the time; when they don't, it's more like a quarter of the time.

While you may not be in sales, you can apply this insight in your own work. The trick is to consider what might prevent people from doing what you would like them to do, and then to be proactive in removing that obstacle for them. Your aim is to reduce the amount of effort required on their part. At the simplest end of the spectrum, that might look like including a prepaid envelope with a form that you're hoping someone will fill out and return to you. Or if you believe your colleagues think better when they're well hydrated, and want them to drink more water, you might put jugs on the meeting room table rather than having people get up to fetch a drink.[4] Make it effortless, and you're halfway to getting the behavior you want.

In some situations, you can even make your desired outcome the "do nothing" option. For example, say you're writing a report and you need to set a final deadline for comments from your colleagues. You'd prefer no last-minute input, but you want to give people a last chance to contribute. A common approach would be to circulate the document, saying, "Let me know if you're happy with it." But if you wanted to make your desired option (receiving no last-minute comments) the easiest one for your colleagues to choose, you could instead say: "If I don't hear anything back by close of business today, I'll assume you're happy with the document." You don't prevent them from providing input; you simply make it easy for them *not* to do so.

## Nudge 2: Make a Suggestion

Can you offer a practical, concrete suggestion before anyone else does? If so, you're likely to significantly influence the outcome of any discussion that follows. Even if people don't end up choosing your idea as a handy default option, your first suggestion creates an easy anchoring point in people's minds. As I explained in Chapter 12, once people have been exposed to an anchor suggestion, it subliminally exerts a drag on their choices—even when the anchor is plainly wrong or irrelevant.

For example, in one experiment, some volunteers were asked whether Mahatma Gandhi died "before or after age 9," while others were asked whether he died "before or after age 140." That question was enough to implant the numbers 9 and 140 as anchors in the minds of each group, respectively. Then all of them were asked to guess the actual age of Gandhi's death. The first group guessed (on average) that he died at age 50, and the second group at age 67. The 9 dragged the first group downward, while the 140 dragged the second group upward.[5]

The powerful drag of the first suggestion is helpful to understand not only in big negotiations—those involving budgets, salaries, and the domestic split of housework, for example—but also in the many miniature daily negotiations involved in setting deadlines and fixing appointments.

For example, if we want to propose a lunch meeting with a colleague or client, the usual approach is to say, "Would you like to have lunch?" But with default bias and anchoring in mind, you could make a more specific suggestion, such as, "Would you like to have lunch, perhaps on Wednesday next week? There's a great new pizza place across the street we could try." Your prospective lunch companion might not want to do precisely what you suggest, but you've anchored him on a date in the near future and a convenient nearby venue, so any countersuggestions he makes will tend to reflect those starting points. (I've found that making a concrete proposal can also reduce the amount of back-and-forth on email tremendously—and people are often grateful that they don't have to think up a suggestion for themselves.)

If you are actually negotiating numbers with someone—maybe you're trying to agree on a salary, or you're doing a deal with a customer—consider giving a range that allows you to provide *two* anchors. In a recent study of this kind of *tandem anchoring*, Columbia Business School professors found that sellers who wanted $7,200 for a used car achieved better deals when telling buyers "I want $7,200 to $7,600 for my car" compared with saying "I want $7,200 for my car." Giving this kind of modest range, including a bolstering (but still reasonable) top number, also worked better than pitching an unreasonably high starting point. And interestingly, the sellers stating a range weren't perceived as arrogant—they were seen as flexible.[6]

Charities are using a form of tandem anchoring when they give you guidance on "suggested donations." If they provide standard options of $100, $50, $30, and "other," they know they'll get higher contributions than if the options are $50, $30, $10, and "other." The $30–100 range is more likely to result in a donation of $30 than giving a suggested range of $10–50, even though $30 is contained within both.

So, if you can:

→ Make a specific suggestion as early as you can in any exchange where there's a joint decision to be made. If you don't want to sound too pushy, frame it with a "maybe," or signal your flexibility: "If that doesn't work for you, let me know what you prefer." You'll still have an influence on the outcome.

→ If you're talking numbers, try giving a range that spans your desired outcome and an even better (though still reasonable) outcome.

### Nudge 3: Provide Visual Hints to the Outcome You Want

We can also nudge in subtler ways, by giving visual clues to the outcome we'd like to see. For example, on escalators in many big cities around the world, there's a convention: relaxed people stand to the right to allow rushed people to thunder past on the left (in some cities it's the other way around, but with the same idea of separate fast and slow lanes). But visitors to these cities often don't know this, which leads to frustrated commuters and startled tourists. Recently, at my local station, I've noticed some escalators are now printed with pictures of two feet on the right-hand side of each step, giving visitors a subtle suggestion of what's expected. And it's worked beautifully, reducing tension all around.

How might you apply this in your communication? Here are a couple of things to try:

➡ Use visual cues (arrows, graphics, photos) to draw people's eye to whatever you'd most like them to focus on.

➡ Make the visual layout of your material suggestive of the kind of response you'd like from them.

On the latter, suppose you wanted to ask colleagues to share their ideas for improving your company's workspace. If you made an open request for input, it's fairly likely you'd hear between zero and one idea per person. But if you were to give people a form with three numbered boxes preprinted on it, you'd be more likely to get three ideas (or at least one or two) from each person. Just be sensible in how you use this; research suggests this works as long as your request is reasonable, so only put forty boxes on your form if you're sure people will be fired up rather than scared off by the suggestion that you're asking for forty ideas.[7]

## BRING THE BENEFITS TO LIFE

At a subconscious level, most people are reluctant to embrace the unknown. Everyone's brain has to work hard to process ambiguity, so their automatic system tends to place more weight on whatever's familiar and certain, versus uncertain future payoffs. From a personal perspective, as we saw in Chapter 7, this *present bias* is one of the reasons that we might procrastinate when we need to exert immediate effort on a task that only pays uncertain future dividends—like saving for our retirement, or writing the difficult email we've been putting off for a week. But it's also why it's not straightforward for a colleague to do something new or different, even if it involves a relatively minor change in behavior like sending you a regular weekly update. People's brains are generally geared to stick to what they know, because it's difficult for them to assess whether they'll benefit from what you're proposing and whether it will feel unpleasant or arduous.

Turn this around, however, and the advice is clear: you have a better chance of encouraging cooperation from your colleagues if you can make the benefits of that cooperation feel clear, vivid, and personally relevant. As soon as they feel that what you're proposing will be genuinely rewarding, you're encouraging their brains into discovery mode, where they'll feel more receptive to new ideas. And the best way to signal that is to give a tangible example of how life will be better for them once they've said yes to your request.

Emma's new pedagogical proposals seemed fairly abstract to her fellow teachers. The phrase "thinkers, not regurgitators" was memorable, so it got through their spam filter. But it wasn't completely clear what it meant in reality. So Emma did several things to make the benefits of her proposals feel more real in her colleagues' minds.

First, she asked some of the more supportive teachers to share stories of times when they'd gotten their students to do some independent projects, and how that improved the kids' focus and engagement in the classroom. Then Emma invited her colleagues to watch her demonstrate the new teaching techniques in a class. It took some courage for her to volunteer this, but she knew it was the best way for them to see what it meant in practice. The teachers got to see Emma doing more asking and less telling, for example, and they saw the galvanizing effect that this had on the children.

As well as boosting her colleagues' awareness of the payoff from trying something new, Emma also considered what might make the effort feel less burdensome. Quickly, she realized she needed to address the fact that her colleagues didn't like the idea of being evaluated as they experimented with these new techniques. It posed a threat to their sense of competence (one of the common triggers we saw in Chapter 9). But of course, they needed to get *some* feedback on their efforts. So after her demonstration classes, Emma invited her colleagues to share constructive observations with her. In those discussions, she proved that chewing things over could be an interesting, even enjoyable learning experience—which took the sting out of their fear, and helped them refocus on the benefits.

So when you're asking colleagues to try something new:

➡ **Bring to life what's great about your request—for them.** Spark their reward system by sharing a concrete example of how your ask will be beneficial for them, as well as you. If possible, find a way to demonstrate it to them, to make it feel as real as possible.

➡ **Proactively address any potential "threats."** Put yourself in their shoes—or ask them explicitly—and consider the concerns they might have. Do any potential threats arise from your request, for example to their sense of autonomy or competence, that might put them into defensive mode? Can you do anything tangible to allay those concerns?

## USE SOCIAL PROOF

"To really change anything at my school, it's not just one person you have to shift, it's the whole weight of the staff room," Emma told me. But if she spent time trying to persuade every single teacher individually, it would take forever. And she couldn't invite them *all* to observe her classes. Her teenage students would consider it, like, a total bummer to have crowds of teachers sitting at the back of the room.

So Emma decided to focus her initial efforts on a smaller group of colleagues, a committee that included one respected teacher from each department: mathematics, science, history, and so on. These were the people she invited to her demonstration classes to turn them into early advocates. Emma had sway within her own English faculty, but she was realistic about the fact that she wouldn't be the most credible advocate for teachers in other departments. By getting one person from each faculty on board, she knew that every teacher in the school would have one close colleague who was visibly enthusiastic about her new teaching approaches.

This allowed Emma to harness the power of something called *social proof.* We already know that our brains rely on shortcuts to decide whether something is a good idea or not, and one shortcut comes from the social signals we get from our in-group. In other words, if people similar to us are demonstrably in favor of something, we'll tend to support it, too. For example, Australian researchers found that people laughed more at a TV comedy when they thought the canned laughter track was a recording of people like them.[8] And when researchers from Harvard and Yale spoke to fifteen hundred adults about the arguments for and against HPV vaccination, they found the participants were much more willing to agree with medics who subtly signaled that they held similar political views.[9] The upshot: when we're seeking to persuade someone of something, it helps to emphasize that others in their "tribe" already think our ideas are fabulous.

To use social proof when making requests, try these approaches:

➡ **"Someone like you said yes already."** Tell your colleagues that one or more of their peers have agreed to what you're asking. (And— ahem—do make sure that this is true.)

➡ **Recruit the influencers.** If you're trying to reach a group of people, it's worth enlisting group members who have influence, so you can say, "People like *them* are on board." Here, I don't necessarily mean influence in terms of seniority. Look for:
  • Experts: people widely respected for their knowledge or skills
  • Hubs: social types who are well liked around the water cooler
  • Gatekeepers: people who control important resources or processes

Greg, our crowdfunding entrepreneur, is always keen to publicize the investors he's already got on board—with their permission—knowing that it will help draw others in. "It helps people feel validated," he says. "And I always work extra hard to convert the thought leaders and people with big networks. If I can get *them* to invest in funding new research, they'll want to tell their friends about it, and their friends will want to follow."

## GET THEM INVOLVED TO GET THEM ON BOARD

As you might suspect from the affection you feel for your pet projects, we tend to become attached to things that we've played some part in shaping. One of the most pointed demonstrations of this comes from another study by psychologist Ellen Langer, whom we met earlier in this chapter (in the line for the photocopier). In a famous experiment, she sold a bunch of office workers a lottery ticket for $1 each.[10] Half of them were handed numbered tickets at random, while the other half were allowed to choose their own ticket. A couple of days later, before the lottery draw was to take place, the ticket holders were approached with a request to give up their ticket for a price of their choosing. At this point, the *endowment effect* (which I talked about in Chapter 12) had kicked in, where people overvalue things they already own, even when there's no sentimental attachment involved. So people who'd been issued tickets at random now wanted about $2 to relinquish them. But the key finding was this: people who chose their own ticket asked for far more. They wanted a whopping $8.

Other studies have found similar effects in real-life settings. For example, when receptionists at two British doctors' offices asked patients to personally write the time and date of a follow-up appointment on a reminder card, rather than simply being handed the completed card, it led to an 18 percent drop in missed appointments.[11]

Why do people place more value on things they've participated in or contributed to, even if their input is minimal? Partly, it goes back to the importance of autonomy as a motivating force. Being involved gives people a soupçon of control, and that's highly rewarding for their brains.

This has huge implications for the way we communicate. It seems efficient to just tell people what we want or need to have happen—and that can be fine when the stakes are low or the negotiations simple, when it's good to apply my earlier advice on making the first suggestion. But if we've got ideas that require real buy-in and belief from our colleagues to be a success, the advice changes: we shouldn't foist our demands on other people. If we do, they're less likely to be positive and supportive than if we'd given them just a little space to come to their own conclusions about the wisdom of what we're proposing. You need to let people choose their own lottery tickets.

Emma took this into account when she set up a meeting to tell a larger group of colleagues about her new teaching techniques. "Usually staff training sessions are very dry. You want to shoot yourself by the end," she says. So she decided to run a very different type of meeting, one that left the teachers feeling that they had a hand in creating the project themselves. "I had people presenting their own ideas rather than having me lecturing them. I staged an event I called a 'village fair,' where ten staff who had excellent ideas on new teaching strategies each hosted a table and teachers wandered around each table to see them demonstrate their ideas." She let her colleagues discover for themselves what was interesting at each stop, and let them roam as they chose, and take notes about things they particularly liked. She let them talk to each other in small groups, to decide what they wanted to take away from it all. She created the frame for the conversations, and provided the information to guide them, but she let people take control of as much of the session as possible. "And after that, we built momentum very quickly," Emma says.

So how can you give people a sense of ownership, so they're more invested in whatever you're interested in doing or changing? Here are three suggestions for three different situations:

➡ **Situation 1: If you have a suggestion to make, connect your idea to their own views and concerns.**
  - Share the facts of the situation. (Without expressing your own views just yet.)
  - Ask for *their* reactions to what you're describing.
  - Then find a connection between their views and your suggestion: "Your comment about [xyz] links to something I'm thinking..."

Greg, the crowdfunding entrepreneur, says, "Even when you're desperate to get your point across, it's always helpful to first ask people about their views on the issue you're trying to address—in our case, shortfalls in medical research funding—because it draws the other person into the discussion. It makes it much less about me just going in demanding money, and much more about us figuring something out together."

➡ **Situation 2: If you need help, ask for their advice first.**
  - Ask: "If you were me, what would you do to make this work?"
  - Then, and only then, ask: "Is there anything you might be able to do to help with that?"

If you suddenly present people with a request, it's easy for them to feel stressed about having too little time to do what you're asking of them, and people are less generous when they're in defensive mode. Instead, try setting out your challenge and then asking for their advice (to which you listen closely, of course). By showing that you value their views, you provide a small social reward that helps to put people into discovery mode, where it's much easier for them to feel like helping you. As the nineteenth-century political advisor Arthur Helps quipped: "We always admire the wisdom of those who come to us for advice." And, crucially, the discussion allows them to reach their own conclusions about the kind of help they can give.

➡ **Situation 3: If you'd like cooperation with something that's fairly fixed, create options.**
  - Ask people to help you come up with options for ways to respond or move forward.
  - If you can't do that, at least give them some options to choose between, so there's a decision they can call their own.

Perhaps a decision has already been made—by you or others—and you're having to deliver the news. "We're having a reorganization and our reporting lines are changing," you say, knowing this is the third restructuring in three years and everyone's weary. But giving people choices can still provide some of the autonomy that their brains crave—which will help you to stop them from checking out completely.

And you don't have to use this technique only when you're delivering tough messages. It's a good general rule to follow where you want people to feel engaged in anything you're doing.

For example, I use this approach in every workshop I run for large groups of clients. I'm on the hook to teach a certain amount of material, and the objectives of the session are fairly fixed. But my work isn't a success unless clients love the ideas enough to use them in their everyday lives—and for that, it's important they feel ownership of what I'm teaching. Since I'm never in a position to throw the whole agenda open, what can I do? I give my clients choices—plenty of them. For example, if I've done some analysis to inform the session, I put the results in front of them and ask them to tell me what strikes them as most important—and reprioritize my material accordingly. If a discussion is getting heated, I give them options: do they want to carry on talking, or do they want to "agree to disagree" and move on? If we're running over time, I ask them whether they would like to skip some content, take a shorter lunch break, or finish later in the day. And so on. I need to roll with whatever they choose, but it's worth it. I know that what I teach will be more highly valued if it feels like *their* workshop, not mine.

## GIVE AS WELL AS TAKE

When we're focused on getting what we need from other people, it's important to remember that we're in a position to give as well as take. As I explained earlier in the book, reciprocity feels rewarding to people's social brains, while violations of reciprocity upset our sense of inclusion and fairness. (Most of us get riled if we're not thanked after giving way to another driver at an intersection, or if someone only ever gets in touch when they have a favor to ask.) So people will feel instinctively better about helping you if they sense that you're not just one of those "takers," to use University of Pennsylvania psychologist Adam Grant's term for those who systematically take more than they give.[12] So when you're approaching someone for help or cooperation:

➡ Ask yourself not only "What do I need?" but also "What can I offer?"

What if you're asking for support from people who are very senior or not that well known to you? What do you have to offer? Plenty, actually. At the very least, you can express appreciation for their work, ideally giving specific examples of things you've liked. That's rare enough to be a treat for most people. But it's likely you have something more concrete to contribute to even the most lofty of co-workers. Perhaps you can help them by publicizing what they're doing among your peers; perhaps you could volunteer some of your time to help them on a project. Greg, our crowdfunding entrepreneur, says, "One thing I can often offer is to introduce someone to people in my network, even if it's not directly connected with my work." Be thoughtful about ways you can be generous, and generosity is much more likely to come back at you.

## BRINGING IT ALL TOGETHER: PUTTING WORLD-CLASS INFLUENCING SKILLS TO WORK

Marcella is an immunologist, an expert in the way the human immune system functions. Her work is central to the global search for an effective HIV vaccine. As a senior scientist, she could have decided to focus on her own research, but she decided to step up to a far bigger challenge: persuading HIV laboratories around the world to use the same processes and standards so that their results could be compared and aggregated. It would help accelerate the discovery of that all-important vaccine.

But it was a huge undertaking, since most labs have their own culture and their own ways of doing things. Marcella had a mandate and funding from several sponsors to establish this "global quality system." But that on its own wasn't going to be enough to convince skeptical lab workers to change the way they worked. And since she had no direct authority over any of them, she needed a sophisticated approach, one that recognized where each lab was coming from.

She knew that once she had a few respected labs on board, others were much more likely to follow—an example of social proof in action. So she started with three from her own academic network. "They were each doing different things with their antibodies and cells. They'd simply never coordinated with anyone else." If standardization could be achieved across those three laboratories, she knew that it would send a strong signal that it could work for other labs. And within each laboratory, the same principle applied: it was important to get some key influencers on board. "We needed buy-in from the leadership group of each lab, for anything to change with their colleagues," Marcella says. "So I created a committee, with two leaders from each of the labs, to drive everything."

Still, not everybody in this inner circle was convinced by the arguments for the project. And even those who were intellectually supportive needed encouragement to take the leap and embrace a new way of working. "In the short run, we had to acknowledge that it might feel like standardization was slowing them down, but we showed that it would eventually benefit them hugely." Marcella painted a vivid picture of its future benefits, highlighting things that would help the labs do good work—for example, by strengthening their reputation, the standardization project would help them attract talent and funding. Marcella also took care to highlight the personal benefits for those involved. She told everyone that they'd be seen as pioneers, and that they could put this prestigious work on their CV. "For many people, that was a big thing." And of course, she emphasized the cause that they all really cared about. "We made sure everyone recognized that they were going to improve the landscape for HIV research for everybody by participating."

Marcella also made sure every lab felt they had ownership of the process, even when that complicated matters. "I got each lab to list their own existing standard operating procedures, and got everyone involved in creating templates for our standard processes. Of course, it meant we were swamped by documents!" But she knew it was better than a central team swooping in to do an impersonal audit and imposing ideas that did not reflect day-to-day operations in the laboratory. Marcella was also clear on where there was flexibility. "I told them that even once we've got the templates in place, deviations from standard processes aren't always a bad thing. Sometimes mistakes can teach us things. They just need to be recorded and documented so we can track them." Framing mistakes in this way was a great way to keep people in discovery mode, even if things went wrong.

It wasn't always fun. "It was hard on me at first. It was very intense, and I felt disliked by people at times, rightly or wrongly. But my husband said, 'You have the right kind of mind for this—embrace it.'" And it was worth it. "From a point where it was me working alone in an old building, to two of us working together, to a huge team of people—we've come a long way. Those original three labs connected with many more, spreading the new techniques to many other laboratories in the US, China, Thailand, India, South Africa, Uganda, the UK, and Germany. We created almost five hundred clear best-practice processes to follow. We have a unified system for quality control of specimen collection. And now our sponsor wants to take the HIV experience and apply it to other infectious diseases." It has been, and still continues to be, an inspiring example of international collaboration.

## Making Things Happen

When you next need help, support, or engagement from someone:

➡ **Provide context.** Give at least a brief reason for your request, to explain why it matters.

➡ **Make it easy for them.**
  - Work out what might prevent people from doing what you hope, and remove that barrier. (And because effort is a general barrier to action, make your desired option the "do nothing" option where you can.)
  - Make a concrete suggestion to "anchor" the discussion and reduce the amount of thought needed. (For numerical negotiations, try suggesting a range between your realistic desired outcome and an even better one.)
  - Provide visual cues that draw attention to the outcome you want.

➡ **Bring the benefits to life.** Don't assume that the benefits of what you're asking are obvious to others. Paint a picture that shows how it will help them personally (or causes they care about). Proactively address anything that might seem like a downside.

➡ **Use social proof.** Show how similar people have already done what you're asking. If you have aspirations to engage a lot of people, first find and focus on the (sometimes hidden) influencers: "experts," "hubs," and "gatekeepers."

➡ **Get them involved.** When your success requires full buy-in from other people, let them contribute in some way. Ask for people's views, and then connect your idea or request to their own thoughts on the topic. Ask for advice before you ask for help. Leave room for people to come up with options or make some of their own choices.

➡ **Give as well as take.** Respect the principle of reciprocity. Ask yourself what you can offer the person whose help or support you need.

# SIXTEEN

# Conveying Confidence

The advice in the past two chapters was designed to help you make the content of your communications more compelling and influential. Now I'd like to talk about ways that you can further boost your impact—and enjoy yourself more in the process—by projecting self-assurance in all you do.

It can be nerve-racking to stick your neck out and assert your views to people who don't already think you're marvelous. In fact, the Trier Social Stress Test, an ordeal that's designed to induce stress for research purposes, centers on just this kind of activity. In the test, people have to give a short speech to a panel to argue why they're the right person for a dream job. They're put on the spot in various ways, and the judges aren't allowed to smile at them. The experiment reliably boosts people's heart rate and levels of stress hormones, as their brains and bodies go on high alert. That's tough enough, but real life is often even more challenging than the Trier test, where at least the panel sits and listens. Most of us have had the experience of being in a room with highly critical or opinionated people who make it harder to get our ideas across, or where technology hiccups make it difficult to stay cool and push on.

So what does behavioral science have to tell us about projecting confidence in these kinds of stressful situations? First off, the research suggests that confidence does matter, because we do generally trust and follow those who remain poised in the face of life's challenges.[1] In the absence of any information to the contrary, the brain's automatic system takes another of its infamous shortcuts: "If someone seems to believe in what they're saying, they're probably right." Scientists call this shortcut the *confidence heuristic*. And in organizations, study after study shows how people tend to accord high status to confident individuals, giving special value to their contributions.[2]

But what *is* confidence? According to the research, one trait commonly associated with confidence is being proactive. When we see someone speak up and take initiative, we tend to assume we're dealing with a person of substance, someone with the power or expertise to have an impact. The same is true when we see someone who has the ability to convey certainty—or, at least, the clarity that passes for certainty in uncertain times.

But beyond that, there's no one right way to come off as confident. It can look different from one person to another, depending on their personality. We all know people who exude quiet confidence without being brash. They might not be the ones talking all the time, but when they talk, others listen. Greg, the crowdfunding entrepreneur, has decades of experience at the most senior levels of business and politics, and he says, "Real confidence is definitely not about swagger. And it's not always having a ready answer, either. To the contrary, it's sometimes showing that you're secure enough to pause, think about what other people are saying and say, 'That's really interesting.'" One study even suggested that speaking hesitantly was more likely to get you promoted in a collaborative culture, compared with a punchier take-no-prisoners style of delivery.[3]

So real confidence doesn't have to be about talking loudly. It's more about being the person we are when we're at our best, rather than trying to copy what we think self-assurance looks like in someone else. It's about staying in discovery mode when faced with stressful situations: being curious about what's happening rather than threatened by it, which in turn allows our brains to focus on being clever rather than defensive. In this chapter, I'll review some ways we can bring our boldest self to life.

## REFRAME YOUR NERVES AS EXCITEMENT

Let's start with the moment when we often most need to summon our confidence: just before we enter the fray to make our pitch, presentation, or request.

When our brain recognizes that we're facing something exciting or challenging, it readies us for action by pouring a cocktail of neurotransmitters into our neural pathways, blending chemicals that boost our level of motivation and attention, making it possible for us to spring into action. That's a process known by scientists as "arousal." Yes, stop snickering; it's also partly what's going on when we have the hots for someone. But arousal is also the word that describes the kind of mental readiness we need in our professional lives, for example when we're psyching ourselves up before giving a talk or asking for a raise. As we rise to meet the challenge, our brain is making sure we feel alert and alive. We might feel nervous, too, and two of those neurochemicals—adrenaline and noradrenaline—will probably have our heart racing a little. But as long as positive emotions are in the mix, we're still in discovery mode, and we're not panicking.

It's only if we interpret the situation negatively—perhaps as a threat to our competence or our ability to stay in control—that our level of arousal flips us into defensive mode. As we know, that's where our brain's survival circuits trigger a fight-flight-freeze response, boosting our levels of adrenaline and noradrenaline to battle-ready heights. In smaller amounts, those two neurochemicals do a nice job of motivating us and sharpening our focus, but at these much larger doses they make us skittish and give us tunnel vision. Interestingly, though, the really big guns of our threat response haven't yet fired. It's another twenty to thirty seconds before our adrenal glands respond, releasing yet *more* adrenaline and noradrenaline into our system, as well as the powerful but slower-acting hormone called cortisol.

And that's our window of opportunity. During that half minute between our initial alert and our adrenal reaction, it's still possible to dampen down our threat response fairly quickly and easily. In those few seconds after we notice that our heart has started pounding, we have a choice. We can interpret that as a sign that there's a threat looming, and allow our defensive response to unfold unchecked, or we can decide to interpret our case of nerves as a sign that our brain and body are ready to rise to a thrilling challenge. We can see it as "game over" or as "game on." And research suggests that choosing the second option can make all the difference in the way we perform under pressure. Psychologists Wendy Berry Mendes and Jeremy Jamieson, at the University of California, San Francisco, and the University of Rochester, respectively, have conducted a number of studies showing that people perform better when they decide to interpret their fast heartbeat and breathing as "a resource that aids performance." As they say: "Arousal is semantically and psychologically fuzzy. Our responses depend in large part on how a situation and our body's responses are construed."[4]

So the next time you notice you're getting keyed up:

➡ Remind yourself that this is your body and brain ensuring you're ready for what comes next.

➡ Try saying some version of this to yourself: "That's my brain and body getting me ready for this challenge. Let's do this!"

It should help steer you back toward discovery mode before you even open your mouth to speak.

## CONNECT WITH YOUR VALUES

Now let's talk about what you can do to boost your confidence well before the adrenaline kicks in. Another way to tap into your discovery-mode self is to take a step back from the task before you and spend a moment reflecting on the bigger things in life, such as your values and your sense of purpose.

Can something as simple as that really make a difference? Yes, measurably so. In a study at UCLA, psychologist David Creswell and his colleagues ran an experiment where they asked volunteers to take the stress-inducing Trier test I described earlier. Before the test, all the volunteers were given a survey that asked them to rank the values and issues that were important to them. Then some of them were asked questions to elicit their thoughts and feelings about the value they cared about most strongly. *Those* volunteers, the ones who spent time reflecting on an important personal value, had a different experience in the stressful parts of the test that followed. They reported feeling better able to cope and less anxious about the speech. And their brains and bodies apparently agreed, because the level of cortisol in their saliva was indeed markedly lower.[5]

How can you tap into your personal values to exude more confidence under pressure? Here are three things to try before you step up to the plate with a big request or bold assertion:

➡ Write a couple of sentences about your broader aspirations in life or work. A study by psychologists Gavin Kilduff and Adam Galinsky (at NYU and Columbia University, respectively) found that people who did this were subsequently rated as more proactive and leader-like by their co-workers, even when their tasks had nothing to do with the personal goals they wrote about.[6]

➡ **Remind yourself of the noble reason behind the thing you're about to do.** Who (apart from yourself) is going to benefit from whatever you're asking or advocating? Will it help your organization, society, or the people in your audience? One of the things that can hold us back from making a request is a feeling that we're being somehow selfish, or a concern that people will *perceive* us as selfish. That's why Greg periodically reminds himself that he's "transforming the future of healthcare," not just "asking for money." He knows he's more relaxed and confident when he adopts that perspective.

➡ **Focus on whatever you feel most strongly about.** To convey confidence when the stakes are high, even experienced communicators can benefit from focusing their message on the things they personally care most about. Patrick, a media company CEO, was working with a performance coach to prepare for a big press conference. He was a seasoned leader, used to being on the public stage. But each time he rehearsed his speech, he kept stuttering as he reached a particular point—which was strange, because he didn't have a stutter. Yet it kept happening every time he tried to talk about his "excitement" over certain new plans for the company. His coach asked him what the problem was. "The truth is," Patrick told her, "I'm not sure I completely believe that part of the speech." His coach asked him to try refocusing that section on topics that Patrick felt genuinely excited about. The result? No stuttering, and a widely lauded presentation.

## TAKE YOUR SPACE

I'd like to highlight an unusual technique that you can use to boost your confidence both as you prepare for your challenge and while you're actually in the midst of it.

In The Science Essentials at the start of the book, I highlighted the strength of the connection from body to mind and back again. This two-way flow manifests itself in an odd and useful way when it comes to assertiveness. Amy Cuddy and her colleagues at Harvard were intrigued by the fact that when we feel comfortable and courageous, we behave like gorillas: we tend to make ourselves bigger. ("Gorillas *again*?" you may be saying.) We stand tall; we spread out, with our arms behind our head, perhaps, or our hands on hips. And when we feel reticent or uptight, we tend to do the opposite. We hunch our shoulders. We fold ourselves into smaller shapes, by crossing our arms or bowing our heads.

Remarkably, both Cuddy's team and a Swiss-led research group have found that the mechanism works the other way, too. When people make themselves physically bigger—by standing straighter, planting their legs a little further apart, and throwing their shoulders and arms a little wider—it quickly boosts people's feelings of self-confidence.[7] It's as if a relaxed, let-it-all-hang-out stance is signaling to the brain that there are no threats nearby, so it's okay to emerge from defensive mode. And when volunteers spent a couple of minutes stretching their arms and legs to expand their physical space before giving a speech, Cuddy found their performances were more highly rated by independent observers compared with other people who'd been sitting around normally beforehand.[8]

Now let's meet Gemma, who used to manage the Romanian operations of a global agricultural products company, overseeing everything from local manufacturing to sales to public relations. She'd done this complex job well for some years and felt ready for a bigger challenge. But when she started talking to her boss about the possibility of promotion, she was told she wasn't considered to be "board material." When she pushed for more details, he didn't seem to have any issues with her performance. She just wasn't seen as having as much gravitas and assertiveness as some of her peers. Gemma felt confident in her capabilities, but her demeanor wasn't conveying it. She says, "I was competing in a game that I didn't even know was happening. I thought, 'Okay, now I get it. I have to step it up.' It's about attitude as much as anything else."

A key meeting was coming up where she needed to make the case to the board for securing extra budget for her country's operations. She knew it was a chance to show who she really was, and she decided to put power posing at the heart of her preparation. "I had this phrase running through my head: 'take your space.' I visualized myself being relaxed in the conversation, and in control of my turf." When the meeting came around, she says, "I inhabited that image completely. I sat squarely at the table, back straight, head up, with my shoulders and hands planted wide. Made my case. Looked everyone in the eye. And those words, 'take your space,' all the time in the back of my mind." Did it work? "The effect was electric. People were really listening.

Afterward, the chair of the board took me aside and urged me to put myself forward for bigger roles, and he said that he would support me. I use this 'take your space' reminder all the time now."

To try this for yourself before your next high-stakes conversation:

➡ Find yourself a space where you can spread out; an empty room, corridor, or restroom will do. Stand up straight, with your legs wide apart. Stretch out and swing your arms. Put your shoulders back and open up your chest. Plant your hands widely on a table, or behind your head.

➡ When talking with someone, try a more modest version of the same thing. If you notice yourself hunching over, sit back and breathe deeply, opening up your lungs. Uncross your arms and legs. Try putting an arm over the back of your chair, or planting the palms of both hands on the table.

## SCORE MORE PERSONAL RECOGNITION

Let's face it: in professional life, it's not always straightforward how to make sure you get due credit for your efforts. And yet we all want to feel useful and valued—as we saw in Chapter 9, getting this basic human need met helps to keep our brains in high-performance discovery mode. So let me share some graceful techniques for making sure the trophy has your name engraved somewhere on it.

Cristine spent the first phase of her sales career working for technology start-ups in Brazil, but for the past few years she's worked at a much larger company with tens of thousands of employees around the world. She's responsible for finding and managing clients for their business services division, and she's good at her job. But it takes effort to shine in such a huge place. As she says, "I wasn't really telling senior people what I was achieving. I felt that boasting about my successes wasn't my style. I tended to assume, 'They know what I do; I don't need to tell them.' But it turns out I *do* need to tell them. Even if they like you, people don't have time to dig into the detail and find out exactly how good you are. So they won't know what you have to offer unless you tell them something positive and memorable about your work. I'm in sales—I should know this!"

A new boss gave her some advice. "She said that every time I met someone senior, I should tell them one good thing I'd done recently. So I did. Initially it felt weird, really forced. But then it quickly became natural to say, 'Oh, you might be interested to hear that a great opportunity has emerged from a conversation I had with so-and-so last week.' It's more interesting than the usual small talk, and it turned out not to feel like a 'hard sell' at all."

There were a couple of things Cristine did to make it feel even easier over time. "First, I learned that the trick was to say something that was interesting specifically for the person I was talking to. So now I think about how recent work of mine might help his or her business, and say something related to that if I can. And of course that gets their attention. Everyone's interested in something that's relevant to them. You just need to cater to your audience."

She also invented a simple but powerful process to make sure she always has good news to hand. "Every Friday afternoon I block 5:00 to 5:30, which is often dead time anyway, and I write down in a spreadsheet the best thing I achieved this past week. I block half an hour, but in reality it just takes five minutes. As I'm doing it, I think about which person might be interested in hearing each example. And it also means I have a great database to draw on for my annual performance appraisal, because all the information is right there." Cristine gives a recent example. "A client had some confidential information leak, and I went the extra mile to help them turn the situation around. They were really grateful and I got a nice message from someone about five levels up from me. But honestly, in six months' time, I would have completely forgotten about this. Writing it down means I won't."

And the result? "I have earned the respect of people who wouldn't even have heard of me before. I feel like I'm building a personal brand, one that delivers results. Now it feels second nature to me. And my boss has even adopted my Friday afternoon process from me."

When you're next interacting with someone from whom you're seeking more recognition, try drawing on the advice from throughout Part V—as Cristine did—with these approaches:

➡ **Start where they are.** Find out what the person is most concerned or excited about in their own work. Show them how your work relates to those things.

➡ **Put a human face on it.** Talk about a specific instance where your work had positive impact on real people (customers or co-workers). Don't just talk about numbers or abstract ideas.

➡ **Keep it simple.** It's easier for people to recall a few big achievements rather than a long laundry list of all the work you've done. (You can always provide a backup list.)

➡ **Give context.** Explain *why* you've done the things you've done, signaling your good judgment. A little backstory helps fix the achievement in their mind.

➡ **Harness social proof.** Highlight warm feedback or support you've gotten from other people like them, or people whom they respect.

➡ **Involve them.** Ask for their advice on next steps, then tell them how you'll act on what they've said to you.

➡ **Give as well as get.** If you're looking for appreciation, make sure you're giving it out, too. Emotions are contagious, and people are wired to feel good about reciprocity. Even the most senior people like to know their efforts are worthwhile.

### CONVEYING CONFIDENCE

Think about the next time you know you're going to want to be your most confident self. Try these techniques:

➡ **Reframe nerves as excitement.** When you notice the physical signs of being keyed up, such as faster heartbeat and breathing, see them as evidence of your readiness for the challenge. Think "game on" rather than "game over."

➡ **Connect to your values.** What really matters to you in life and work? What's the bigger purpose of what you're asking or advocating? Keep that front of mind for yourself, perhaps by writing a note to yourself before your big moment. Focus your message on the things you most care about.

➡ **Take your space.** Plan to give yourself five minutes beforehand to stand straight, throw your arms wide, and square your shoulders. In the situation itself, make just as sure to "take your space" then, too, by sitting tall rather than hunching over with folded arms.

➡ **Score more personal recognition.** Apply all the influencing advice from Part V in the way you talk about your personal achievements, as shown in the list above. Keep track of your small day-to-day successes, so that neither you nor your boss has to rely on imperfect memories to recall all you've achieved.

➡ Do also revisit the advice from Chapter 3: **mental contrasting, priming,** and **mind's-eye rehearsal.** All those techniques can help boost your self-assurance when you're facing a challenge.

# PART VI

# Resilience

Sailing Through Setbacks and Annoyances

There is nothing either good or bad, but thinking makes it so.

—WILLIAM SHAKESPEARE, *HAMLET*

So far in this book, I've emphasized what you can control. But, of course, barely a day goes by without something unexpected happening—a deadline that moves, a decision that doesn't go your way, or a crisis unfolding out of thin air. Perhaps you've set your intentions for the day and are trying to pay attention to positive things, but then you realize you've made a huge mistake about something. Maybe someone fails to do what they promised, or just keeps you waiting for an answer you need. These kinds of uncertainties and unwelcome surprises cause us stress, but there's no avoiding them. They're part of life.

The good news is that we're surprisingly resilient in the long term. As Harvard psychologist Dan Gilbert has shown in his decades of research on *affective forecasting*, we have a tendency to overestimate the personal impact of every life event, good or bad. Even with the worst that life can throw at us, we have a remarkable capacity to adjust to new circumstances and get back to our former levels of happiness.[1] But when we do get derailed by disappointments and irritations, it can be scant comfort to know that someday we'll get over it.

So I'd like to add to your "good day" repertoire by sharing some reliable science-based techniques to help you get back on track quickly when you hit a bump or two. I'll talk first about ways to get back onto an even keel when you're hit by something unpleasant. Then I'll talk about ways to bounce back and move on from situations that have been dragging you down for a while. I'll show you how to deal with uncertainty and ambiguity gracefully and skillfully. And finally I'll cover some advice on the best way to handle a situation where someone else has let you down, so you can keep merrily sailing along.

# SEVENTEEN

# Keeping a Cool Head

As a young man, Bartek knew he wanted to work with food. But when he first arrived in London from Poland, he had to take the first job that came along: mopping floors in a hotel where he remembers "corridors so long you could see the curvature of the earth." His breakthrough came when he managed to persuade the hotel chef to let him try out for a job in the restaurant kitchen—and from that point, he built a flourishing career in the catering industry, eventually becoming a senior manager in a successful company making soup and stews. Bartek ran their day-to-day operations while helping the owners expand the business. But in 2012, disaster struck. He had decided the company should expand production capacity to meet an expected surge in demand from visitors flooding into London for the 2012 Olympics. But that wasn't how it turned out.

"Everyone had forecast that the Olympics was going to be amazing for businesses in London. Orders would be hard to fill because of the demand, and hard to deliver because the roads would be jammed with visitors. I devoted a lot of time to making sure that we were on top of it. We hired more drivers and leased more vans. We were so ready," Bartek says. "I thought we'd not just protect our existing business, but also pick up new business from restaurants whose suppliers hadn't planned as well as we had. Then the first day of the Olympics arrived. We all left home early to get to work on time, thinking that traffic would be terrible—but the roads were completely clear. Our fleet of delivery trucks completed their rounds and were back at the depot within three hours."

It was the first of a series of terrible days. Instead of booming, orders were down, and the business was losing money. "It was really tough. And personally, it felt like people were questioning everything I did." Bartek felt so bad about the situation that he was finding it hard to think straight. He could feel his muscles tightening up, which he realized was a sign his brain was on the defensive—something he was well equipped to recognize, thanks to his martial arts training. He knew he needed to find a way to manage his reaction, to chill out enough to bring his brain's deliberate system back online so he could figure out the right way forward. Luckily, Bartek knew just how to do that (which means I can reassure you that his story has a happy ending). Let me explain the kind of tactics he used.

## LABEL IT

A powerful way of quickly reducing our levels of worry, anger, or frustration is to do what behavioral scientists call *affect labeling*. Years of research suggests that if we can name the negative emotion we're experiencing and describe succinctly what's causing that feeling, we can reduce its hold on us.[1]

One study by UCLA researchers had four groups of arachnophobes confront a live tarantula and get as close to touching it as they could.[2] The first group were asked to articulate, or "label," their feelings about the ordeal, by saying things like "I'm anxious and frightened by the ugly, terrifying spider." (A response that certainly seems reasonable to most of us.) Another group used fighting words: "That little spider can't hurt me. I'm not afraid of it." A third group distracted themselves by talking about something completely different, while a control group said nothing at all. The results were striking: even a week later, the "labeling" group exhibited noticeably less fear than the other groups when they had to confront a spider again. Their palms were less damp and they managed to get closer to the spider.

That reduction in negative emotion is mirrored by what's going on in our brains when we use the labeling technique. Researchers have found that while activity in our survival circuits rises when we spot possible trouble, it calms down when we label what's going on.[3] That makes it easier for us to engage the sophisticated reasoning skills of our brain's deliberate system, so that we can see the bigger picture and—if necessary—find a way forward. It's almost as if acknowledging that there's a problem allows our brain to stop sounding the alarm: the cognitive equivalent of saying, "Yes, I heard you—so now what?"

Bartek used labeling to great effect in the midst of his Olympics crisis. "When I felt panic creeping up on me, I wrote down how I felt and what I was worrying about. In fact, I kept a diary of my concerns each day. As soon as I put my feelings on paper, it seemed to help massively." He points out, though, that labeling can seem at odds with the professional advice we often receive from colleagues. As Bartek says, "We're often told to 'just get on with it' or 'suck it up.'" There's lots to be said for that kind of can-do optimism. But if it comes at the cost of bottling up your concerns, research suggests it tends to make things worse, rather than better. Suppressing negative emotions has been found to backfire, *increasing* both physiological and neurological markers of stress.[4] So as Bartek says, "If you jump straight into solution mode before recognizing how you're feeling, you probably won't be doing your best thinking about what to do next."

Doug, the online retail CEO whom we met in Part I, agrees. "In the heat of the moment, one thing that reliably stops me from losing my cool is acknowledging what's bubbling up inside me. If I'm sitting in a meeting and someone's made a crass comment, or someone's denying responsibility for something they've done, I say to myself: 'This is annoying. You're right to be annoyed. Let's deal with it later.' So I acknowledge the feeling in my mind, but park it to think about later on. That often gets me through the moment."

What you'll notice about both Bartek and Doug is that they're not using affect labeling to wallow in their negative emotions. They're keeping it crisp and using it as a mental stepping-stone toward thinking more clearly about solutions. That's the approach you want to take, too. Here are some things to try:

➡ **Writing it down.** Write a sentence or two about how you're feeling, and what's causing those feelings ("I feel irritated/upset/let down right now because . . ."). You might also want to refer back to the list of common triggers in Chapter 9, to see if it helps you to label what's causing your feelings. Then review what you've written, without judging it. Finally, ask yourself, "Now what's the right thing to do?"

➡ **Structured venting.** If you find it helpful to talk to co-workers or friends about what's winding you up, ask them to hold back on giving advice until you've articulated what you're feeling and what's causing that feeling. It's not hard to do this informally by simply saying: "Can I just get this off my chest?" With a close friend, you might be even more explicit: "I don't need you to solve anything just yet. I just need you to nod and say, 'How terrible.'"

➡ **Calling it out.** Next time you're in a meeting where tension is obvious, try saying out loud: "This is feeling tough right now, isn't it? What can we do differently?" It's almost inevitable that the group will give a collective sigh of relief as your acknowledgment allows everyone's brain to calm down. And you'll be much better able to move forward from that point.

As the crisis unfolded in Bartek's company, he encouraged people to talk openly about what was going on. "I got us all in a room to talk about what had happened. I asked people what they were most worried about. At first we talked about what would happen to the product line and so on. But eventually someone cleared their throat and said what was really on their mind: 'I'm worried about my job.' And then everyone opened up, including me." Bartek and his colleagues did not lose their jobs—in fact, his ability to turn around the situation impressed everyone. But in the heat of the moment, as he says, "just talking about our most basic fears really helped."

## GET SOME DISTANCE

Have you ever noticed how giving advice to other people can feel easier than solving your own problems? I see this time and again when I coach clients in groups rather than one-to-one. They'll often give their colleagues great insights on a topic that they themselves are wrestling with, prefaced by a sheepish "I know this is ironic, but it's obvious to me that you should do X. I guess I should take my own advice, too." It's an example of what behavioral scientists call *distancing*, where we adopt a perspective that's different from our own; research confirms that it's another highly effective technique to deploy when you're under pressure.

Ethan Kross is director of the University of Michigan's Emotion and Self-Control Lab. In one experiment,[5] he and his colleagues gave a group of volunteers the Trier Social Stress Test we encountered in Chapter 16—the one where people have to prepare and deliver a speech on why they're an ideal fit for their ideal job. In this version of the Trier test, after they'd prepared the speech but before they'd given it, the volunteers were given three additional minutes to reflect on their anxiety. One group was asked to consider the question "Why am I feeling this way?" A second group was instructed to distance themselves by commenting on themselves in the third person: "Why is [their first name, e.g., Caroline] feeling this way?" When they finally spoke in front of a panel of impartial judges, the second "distanced" group received higher ratings on their performance. And they felt better, too. Researchers found they expressed less "this is horrible/that was terrible" negativity both before and after their speech.

Distancing has been found to help when the immediate threat has passed, too. Research finds that people feel calmer when looking back at a recent unpleasant event if they describe it as an observer would have seen it. And learning how to use distancing seems to have a lasting beneficial effect, making it easier for people to stay calm the next time something stressful happens.[6]

Here are some ways to adopt a distanced perspective when you're worried about something:

➡ **Talk to yourself.** Instead of saying to yourself: "*I'm* worried about this afternoon's meeting because . . . ," try "*You're* nervous about this afternoon's meeting because . . ."

➡ **Travel forward in time.** Ask yourself: "What will I think about this a month from now, or a year from now?" Simple, but it's a favorite of mine precisely because of that.

➡ **Wear someone else's shoes.** Think about what someone else would say if they were describing the situation from a neutral perspective, for example that of a stranger passing by.

➡ **Inhabit your "best self."** Think about the person you are when you're at your wisest, and ask what that "best self" would say about the situation. It's a twist on the "someone else" approach, but it allows you to tap into your own experience of handling stressful situations.

➡ **Advise a friend.** Gain some distance by asking yourself, "If I were giving advice on exactly this situation to a friend of mine, what would I say?"

That's not an exhaustive list, but they're techniques I've seen work. It helps to experiment until you find a distancing technique that's easy to tap into when needed. For example, Chloë, the operations director of a fashion business, has developed a go-to distancing question to use at times of crisis. She asks: "What would my 'best self' say about this when looking back on this in a week's time?" At a stroke, this question effectively combines at least two of the distancing techniques above— shifting the time frame and inhabiting the wisest version of herself.

Meanwhile, Doug, the retail CEO, likes to draw on a number of different distancing approaches. "I often ask myself, 'Honestly, in a year's time, how big a deal is this going to be?' Or I imagine that I'm observing the situation from the outside, looking in." In all cases, he says, "I think about what the voice of reason would be from a different perspective. And once I've tapped into that voice of reason, it's much easier to ask sensible questions like 'What's the worst that's going to happen?' or 'Is it *really* this person's fault?' when I'm annoyed with someone."

And Bartek? "A trick I use to get some distance is a twist on the 'see through the eyes of a child' idea from Buddhism. Going further, I ask the question 'What would a starving child think about this?' It's dramatic, but it works for me. When I was worrying during the Olympics about whether my avocados were going to go soft because we weren't selling enough soup, asking that question reminded me that the world wasn't going to end. It helped put things in proportion and lowered my anxiety, so I could think more clearly about what I needed to do next."

## ASK A REWARDING QUESTION

Many studies have found that it's easier to rise above unpleasant situations when we're in a positive frame of mind.[7] But how are you supposed to stumble upon a positive frame of mind when you're troubled by something at work?

That's where *rewarding questions* come in. They give your brain a reward of some kind—not a fleeting treat like chocolate or booze, but the more profound kind of boost we get from learning something new, feeling competent, or having a sense of purpose. By helping you tap into these three classic sources of motivation, rewarding questions help you get back into discovery mode, where it's easier to see how to jump the mental hurdles in your way. Try the strategies below, and see what works best for you next time you're feeling worn down by a situation at work.

### "How Fascinating! What Can I Learn from This?"

I'm sure you're familiar with the satisfaction of stumbling upon an "aha" moment, or the guilty pleasure of hearing a juicy piece of inside gossip. I've mentioned before that our brains find it rewarding to learn new things. That's why one of the best questions you can ask yourself when something has gone wrong is:

➡ "What can I learn from this?"

In fact, I've seen scores of executives make good use of the advice of orchestra conductor Ben Zander, who suggests going a step further. He famously counsels musicians to throw their hands in the air and say "How fascinating!" when they make a mistake in their playing, before asking themselves what they can learn from the experience.[8] The phrase helps to remind them of the potential joy of discovery, even if they often find themselves accompanying the exclamation with a wry smile and muttered epithet.

What did Bartek choose to find fascinating in his Olympic fiasco? "I learned to recognize that even though I'm a worrier and a planner, circumstances will always surprise me. I need to accept that I can't know or predict everything. That's quite refreshing." He also took away some more specific lessons from the experience. "I realized that I could have contacted caterers in previous Olympic cities to ask how things had worked out for them. It's a lesson for the future: I can do more to draw on the experience of others, rather than always trying to work things out for myself, which is my tendency." Fascinating indeed, and useful, too.

### "What Do My 'Crucibles' Tell Me?"

I talked in Chapter 10 about ways to boost your colleagues' performance by helping them feel capable of solving their own problems. Now let's apply that technique to ourselves. When something happens to make us feel frustrated or inept, it helps to remind ourselves of our accumulated skills and experiences, and how they can equip us to rise above the challenging situation we're dealing with right now.

Harvard Business School professor and former Medtronic CEO Bill George explains one way to do this in his book *True North*.[9] There, he writes about the bolstering effect of revisiting your "crucibles"—by which he means the big trials you've overcome in your life, that have helped to forge who you are today. They don't necessarily have to be in the professional realm—your crucibles might be testing times you've handled in your personal life, too. Ask yourself these three questions:

➡ "When have I handled a difficult situation well in the past?"

➡ "What personal qualities enabled me to overcome that?"

➡ "What does this tell me I'm well equipped to do in my current situation?"

Bartek found that revisiting his crucibles gave him more optimism about his ability to recover from his mistakes. "Probably the toughest point in my life was when I came to London with nothing." He remembered he was resourceful and flexible, willing to mop hotel floors as a route to get ahead. And he knew he still had those strengths in him now. "It made me think, 'Okay, been there, done that,' when I was worried about losing my job. I knew I was strong enough to cope if I had to. And that helped stop me from going round in circles with worry."

## "What *Really* Matters?"

Scientific research on resilience also indicates that having a sense of purpose tends to help people bounce back from adversity.[10] Sometimes the idea of "purpose" can feel too big to get our heads around—the meaning of life may not be obvious right here and now. But we can always take a moment to think about the bigger picture, by reflecting on the things that matter most to us and considering what that might tell us about the best way to react to a difficult situation. This takes us right back to the beginning of the book, in a way, since a simple first step toward restoring a sense of purpose is to revisit your intentions. Bartek says that it almost always helped him think more clearly when he did this, by asking himself:

➡ "What matters most right now?"

➡ "What do I really want to have happen here?"

Bartek says the answer was "sometimes about doing the right thing for our staff, or sometimes it was about being a good dad, if I was trying to find the right trade-off between work and family. It was always clarifying, and it made me feel less uptight quite quickly."

## DO SOME DIAPHRAGMATIC BREATHING

I mentioned the calming effects of breathing in Chapter 6 as part of the "mindful pause" advice when you're overloaded, and in Chapter 9 on the "step back and reset" technique to help you manage your reactions to a tense conversation. Why does it keep coming up?

One reason is that when we're under stress, the tangible shift that's often easiest to spot in ourselves is that our breathing becomes shallower and faster. If you notice this happening in the middle of a difficult meeting, it's a good sign that you're on high alert. And breathing is one of those mind-body loops where there's a two-way street between our physical state and our state of mind. Countless studies suggest that when we make our breathing more relaxed—deeper and slower, taking in plenty of air each time—our body seems to take that as a signal that the threat has passed.[11] Stress hormone levels drop, restoring an ability to think more constructively. Ninety seconds of deeper, slower breathing can be enough to start easing us out of defensive mode.

I'd like to add some extra advice here on technique, though, because there's a particular type of breathing that most effectively sparks this soothing change in your neuroendocrine system. It's known by some as "diaphragmatic breathing"; others simply call it "belly breathing." It involves opening up your lungs to their fullest capacity by sticking out your belly. Well, technically it means lowering your diaphragm, but that's a hard instruction to follow; what's easy to remember is to take a breath that's deep enough to inflate your mid-section.

Nayan, the bank CFO we met in Chapter 12, finds this kind of breathing helps him handle even his worst days. And he's had plenty of tough ones. During the last financial crisis, he worked with several institutions to help keep them solvent, and Nayan told me "there was a point where there were 'oh my gosh' moments every single day, mentally and emotionally. The issues we were uncovering were so complex, much worse than I'd realized. The number of hours I was working, the intellectual challenge of figuring out what to do—it was immense." To get through this period, he used pretty much all the tools I've discussed in this book, but one that he used every single day was his diaphragmatic breathing technique. He says: "My team asked me how I was keeping so calm in the face of everything," he says. "So I showed them what I did. I told them first to tune in to hearing their own breath, and then to start breathing slowly and deeply. I told them that if they could also close their eyes and relax their body, starting from toes upward, without trying to control their thoughts, they were basically doing a simple mindfulness exercise. And you can do the breathing part of it on a train, in a conference room, wherever."

My work rarely involves the kind of drama that Nayan was experiencing. But like him, I use the belly breathing technique almost every day, since I've found it keeps me serene when I'm facing travel delays or overcrowded streets. (And for those of you concerned about looking less than svelte as you fill your lungs: if you sit or stand up straighter so that you lengthen your torso as you breathe in, I've found that nobody can see you doing it.) It so quickly neutralizes irritation that I can't help wondering whether there should be billboards suggesting people try it before getting into their cars or onto mass transit. Meanwhile, I hope it improves your own commute.

## MASTER THE UNKNOWN

Our workplaces are full of uncertainties. Will you sell enough this month to make your target? Will you manage to win that big promotion or charm that new client? What did the CEO mean when he talked about the need to "find efficiencies"? While it's no fun to have bad things happen, our brain finds negative uncertainty as stressful as actual negative outcomes, and we'll seek to avoid it if we can.

Take this example, where you have to choose between two options. You can either be given $30 cash in hand or you can take a gamble where you have an 80 percent chance of winning $45 and a 20 percent chance of winning nothing. Which would you prefer? The second option is objectively more lucrative, since it yields an average expected gain of $36. But if you'd feel happier with the first option, you're not alone; most people agree with you. It's a phenomenon known to behavioral scientists as the *certainty effect*.[12]

Why do we prefer to avoid situations where we lack information? One reason is that they make our brain work especially hard, as we're forced to assess many possible scenarios—and we know how much our brain's automatic system likes to save us mental energy. Not knowing what's going on also makes us more sensitive to negative experiences; it seems to enhance the sense of threat. For example, in a study at the Wellcome Trust Centre for Neuroimaging in the UK, researchers found that people rated an unpleasantly hot panel as being markedly more painful to touch when they had less idea of the temperature they were about to experience.[13]

And yet sometimes we appear to enjoy uncertainty. We devour TV programs and movies that build suspense and keep us guessing. Research tells us that babies in every culture enjoy the game of peekaboo, where a person's face is revealed in front of them at unpredictable intervals.[14] But what's striking about the uncertainty we enjoy is that it's *bounded*. It's only about specific, defined elements of the situation. For example, when we read or watch a good thriller, there's plenty the writer has made sure we don't know—but we *do* know that all will be resolved within a countable number of hours, and we know that nothing life-changing is going to happen to us as a result of the surprise ending. And, as it turns out, the same is true for those small babies playing peekaboo. They only find it fun when there are some things they can rely on—that the person who hides is the same one who comes back, in roughly the same location. When someone new appears, or the person pops up in a completely different place, researchers have found that babies don't laugh nearly as much.[15]

That gives us the clue to weathering stressful periods of uncertainty. The more we place boundaries on the uncertainty—by acknowledging what we know for certain—the more manageable the remaining ambiguity feels to our brains. That in turn reduces the state of alert in our brains, allowing us to make wiser decisions about what we do next.

And however turbulent our situation, there are always *some* things that we can pin down. In the middle of a crisis, we can highlight the parts of our work that remain untouched by the upheaval. In the areas that are in disarray, we might realize we've got a good sense of how 80 percent of the situation will turn out. We can articulate and plan for possible scenarios for the 20 percent, and we might at least be able to find out *when* the uncertainty will be resolved. Also, we control our own personal response to the situation: what we choose to say, do, or feel about it. Research suggests that this approach—focusing on what we control rather than what's being imposed on us—can even help people be more resilient when dealing with highly stressful and chaotic situations like military combat and natural disasters.[16]

That was borne out by the experience of Jacquie, a college PR officer, who had to cope with a deadly earthquake that struck her New Zealand town in 2011. Jacquie was the media contact for the college, and journalists from around the world descended upon her while she and her colleagues were coping with chaos. Her team was trying to figure out what to do without power and water, while not knowing when the next aftershock was coming or even how their loved ones had fared.

Amid all that, Jacquie found it helpful to focus her attention on a few familiar and controllable things. First of all, she looked for connections to things she knew. For example, she quickly came to see that "making progress was still all about relationships—helping others cope under pressure, building trust with the media, giving people some optimism where possible, and being kind to one another." These were things she knew she was good at, even if the context was entirely unfamiliar. She also decided to see it as "the most profound professional development opportunity I'd ever have. I thought, 'If I can handle this, I can handle any crisis.'"

Focusing on those two small islands of certainty—her skills and her attitude—boosted Jacquie's resourcefulness and resilience through the difficult days and months that followed. With many buildings damaged, the college held a celebration for its graduating seniors in huge tents on campus, and Jacquie ensured that this precious "good news story" received national media coverage. It was seen as a remarkable triumph for the whole community. And at the end of it all, Jacquie and her colleagues won a much-deserved industry award for their post-earthquake work.

Try this approach for yourself when you're dealing with an uncertain situation, by asking these clarity-restoring questions:

➡ "Setting aside the things I don't know, what are the things I *do* know?"

➡ "What is there that's familiar to me, given my past experience?"

➡ "What is mine to shape or control in this situation?" (For example: "What attitude do I want to have about this?" "What do I choose to learn from this?")

➡ "What are some possible future scenarios?" (Include the best case, the worst case, and some variation on the extremes.) "What would I do in each of those scenarios?"

➡ "What are some 'no regrets' actions that I know I can take?"

## KEEPING A COOL HEAD

You can't know for sure when the next curveball is going to come your way. But you can do some preparation to make sure you have "stay cool" techniques ready for the next time it happens. Practice with whatever is most bothering you at the moment.

➡ **Label it.** Write down how you feel about this situation, and why.

➡ **Get some distance.** Try: talking to yourself in the second person, addressing yourself as "you"; looking back from the future; wearing someone else's shoes, perhaps those of your "best self"; imagining you're advising a friend.

➡ **Ask a rewarding question.**
  • Ask: "How fascinating! What can I learn from this?"
  • Think of a crucible moment, where you overcame a challenge in the past. Ask: "What qualities allowed me to overcome that? What does that tell me about my ability to improve *this* situation?"
  • Ask: "What am I really trying to achieve? How can I refocus on that?"

➡ **Do some diaphragmatic breathing.** Get used to the unfamiliar sensation of your lungs being truly full. Repeat a few times and notice the effects.

➡ **Master the unknown.** Consider the issue where you're facing most uncertainty at the moment. Work out what you *do* know or control.

# EIGHTEEN

# Moving On

Sometimes the difficult moment has passed—the tough meeting is over, the dodgy decision has been made—but we're unable to let go of our irritation or dismay at what's happened. We sulk about a person who has wronged us, or about the unfairness of a situation. Perhaps we entertain fantasies of redemption or revenge. Or we simply worry repeatedly about something we wish we hadn't done, as the repercussions play out around us.

While it's normal and healthy to reflect on what's going on in our lives, obsessive rumination isn't all that helpful. Apart from taking up precious minutes of the day, it keeps us in a negative mood that makes it hard for us to be at our cognitive best. So it's good to know about the techniques that research suggests will help you bounce back and move forward after a setback.

## REAPPRAISE THE SITUATION

Throughout the book, I've talked about how our conscious perception of the world is always incomplete, because the brain's automatic system filters out apparently "irrelevant" information before we're even aware it exists. That's why it's good to set intentions *before* each big thing we do, since they serve to tell our brain what's important enough to merit our conscious attention. But if our day still turns out to be unpleasant, the good news is that we can also edit our interpretation of reality after the fact, using a technique that scientists call *reappraisal*.

Reappraisal involves exploring alternative explanations for what we've observed, acknowledging that it's possible we may not have the full picture. It sounds simple, but research by many psychologists and neuroscientists has shown it to be one of the most powerful things you can do to improve your emotional resilience. Not only does using the technique reduce the intensity of your brain's defensive response when things don't go your way, but research has found that the benefits stay with you. Reappraise a rough experience at work, and you'll find it easier to roll with the punches the next time a similar thing happens.[1] In fact, people who learn to use reappraisal have been found to have better long-term emotional stability, interpersonal skills, and psychological well-being.[2] Reappraisal has even been linked to improvements in working memory and reasoning skills, probably because flipping between different perspectives helps us to develop our mental agility.[3]

So how do you do it? In experiments, volunteers are often simply taught to attach alternative stories to a negative picture. For example, they consider the possibility that a photo of women crying outside a church represents a wedding rather than a funeral, with the subjects shedding happy tears rather than sad ones.[4]

In real life, we usually need a bit more help than that. If a situation has already generated a negative reaction in us, it's highly unlikely that we're seeing it objectively, since negative emotion has a tendency to blur important details in our memory (as I said in Chapter 14). So from experience, I suggest these three steps to fully benefit from the power of reappraisal when you're upset or angry about a situation:

➡ Step 1: List the "true facts." You'll be good at this by now, because this was also a foundational step in the "good person, bad circumstance" technique for handling difficult behavior in other people (in Chapter 9). You'll remember that "true facts" are the things you truly know for sure. In this chapter, we're talking about a situation rather than another person, but the advice is similar: as soon as you catch an emotional tone creeping in, you're in the territory of interpretation rather than facts. For example, suppose you've had a performance review that isn't as glowing as you'd hoped. It would be easy to say "I've been shortchanged" or "They aren't recognizing my contributions." Is that true? Maybe, maybe not. What you know for sure is something more like this: "I was expecting to be rated a 5. I was rated a 4." It's dry—but that's the point. It helps take the heat out of the situation.

➡ Step 2: Highlight the assumptions you're making. Now you get the chance to think about your interpretation of those events. Write down a series of statements beginning with the words "I'm assuming . . ."

For example: "I'm assuming my performance was equivalent to a 5 rating, and they've failed to acknowledge it." "I'm assuming they're trying to take me down a peg. I'm assuming it's probably payback for ignoring their advice that I should close down my pet project." You get the idea. The trick is to check what you're assuming about all dimensions of the situation: the causes, the outcome, yourself, and anyone who's involved.

➡ **Step 3: Generate alternative interpretations.** Look hard at your assumptions, and turn the biggest ones on their head. It may help to know that they're likely to be the ones that are *personal, pervasive,* or *permanent.* That is, you're taking something highly personally, you're assuming that an issue has wide-ranging consequences, or you're assuming the impact will endure for a long time (or forever). For each assumption, ask yourself:

- What if that assumption wasn't correct? For example, what if the problem isn't personal, pervasive, or permanent?
- What would be another way of seeing the situation? What else could be going on? Don't shy away from creative ideas, even if they feel initially improbable to you.
- What evidence might support those alternative interpretations?

There are two basic approaches to generating alternative perspectives in Step 3. One is to minimize the negative interpretation: "I'm assuming this is a sign that I've fallen out of favor, but that's unlikely to be true because the face-to-face conversation I had with my evaluator was very positive." This approach can stabilize the negative emotional spiral. But you can also explore positive interpretations, something that experiments on appraisal suggest may boost your mood further.[5] In this example of the performance review, what would be a much more optimistic version of events? "They like what I'm doing. But they want to send me a message that it's not wise to ignore an experienced colleague's advice and that I need to be more collaborative. They intend this to be a learning opportunity for me." As you do this, it may dawn on you that at least some of this could be true.

What's remarkable about reappraisal is that entertaining a different interpretation of the facts actually changes how people experience and remember a tough situation—it's not just warm words. Scientists like Kevin Ochsner of Columbia and James Gross of Stanford, two of the most influential thinkers in the field of emotional resilience, have shown that there's less activation in the brain's survival circuits when people think about an unpleasant situation having attached a more positive story to it.[6] Adopting a different perspective shifts our neurological reaction to the original unpleasant situation, making our emotional experience genuinely different.

Reappraisal was an important tool for Bartek as he navigated his stream of bad days during the Olympics. "I was making all sorts of negative assumptions, seeing everything as doom and gloom, but then I realized I was in a kind of brain panic. I needed to see the facts as they really were, and stop over-extrapolating from that. So I learned to ask myself, 'What do I really know for sure?' and 'What am I assuming?' whenever I couldn't stop myself from worrying." Those questions revealed to him that he was making one big "permanent" assumption: that his ill-fated decisions were irreversible. When he challenged himself to think differently, he saw it simply wasn't the case. "In fact, we were able to downscale more quickly than I expected, and business eventually picked up from there."

Bartek says his use of reappraisal techniques has left him with a more resilient perspective on life: "I now feel much steadier when things go up and down." Which is exactly what Ochsner and Gross's research suggests: the more we learn to reappraise difficult situations, the easier it becomes for us to remain composed when things don't go as we expect. And that's a very useful talent to have in the modern workplace.

## DITCH YOUR SUNK COSTS

It was a relief for Bartek to realize that he could reverse his decision and downscale—but he did have one more psychological barrier to overcome in making that decision, which was kissing goodbye to the money he'd already spent on expanding capacity. He knew he needed to move on, but it was tempting to throw good money after bad, hoping that business would improve. It wasn't all that easy for him to let go. As he says, "Downscaling was a really tough decision to make, because we'd invested so much. *I'd* invested so much."

And it's not just Bartek. It's generally hard for any of us to walk away from all the time, effort, or money we've already sunk into a situation that has little prospect of improving. You'll recognize this if you've ever decided to keep watching a terrible movie because you tell yourself "I've already paid for the ticket" or "I've already given it half an hour," despite the fact that you'd have been happier if you'd walked out and saved yourself another hour of boredom. Professionally, maybe you have a dysfunctional project (or relationship) that you've been trying to turn around for a while. You sense that life would be better if you gracefully wrapped things up, but you don't want to quit because you've already put so much energy into trying to make it work. This difficulty in letting go of bad investments of time, energy, or money is such a human universal that economists even have a name for it—the *sunk cost fallacy*. We struggle with the prospect of losing those past sunk costs, even though we stand to gain more if we change course.[7]

So let's suppose you're dealing with a situation that's not going well. Perhaps it's the result of an earlier decision you made. How do you decide whether to stick with it or change tack and move on? Investment analysts and behavioral scientists wholeheartedly agree on what you should do. In short, you should:

➡ Imagine you're starting entirely afresh from where you are, as if all past events and outlays have been wiped off the slate.

➡ What are the likely future costs and benefits of investing further time, effort, or money in this situation?

➡ What are the likely future costs and benefits of extracting yourself from this situation?

➡ Compare the two, and ask yourself: should you stay or should you go?

As you compare the pros and cons of carrying on versus walking away, you can include any reputational or relationship costs that may be involved in extracting yourself from your commitment. But you should ignore *past* investments of time, effort, or money. As long as you're living in a world where time moves forward and not back, those past costs are sunk and gone.

If this still feels counterintuitive, psychologists have found that people are better able to think clearly about sunk costs if they make sure to pay close attention to the benefits of moving on.[8] Our natural tendency is to zoom in on our sense of loss—that's what economists call *loss aversion*—and ignore the benefits of letting something go. For Bartek, that meant it was hard for him not to focus on the ill-fated cash he'd spent on leasing extra trucks and buying vegetables, as well as the damage to his pride. But removing the extra production capacity was going to yield huge benefits. It would stop his company hemorrhaging five-figure sums each day, and would improve morale and productivity at a stroke. And once he thought about that, the idea of reversing his decisions felt a lot better.

Finally, if you're dealing with a situation where there aren't clear financial benefits to cutting your losses, it can be helpful to look at mistakes as useful experiments that will pay dividends in terms of life experience. That gives you a clear benefit to carry into the future: valuable knowledge about ways to handle similar situations if they ever arise again.

## WHEN SOMEONE ELSE SCREWS UP

We're often dependent on people over whom we have no control, whether we're toiling away on a virtual team in a large organization or we're a lone entrepreneur working with an incompetent supplier. And it's tough when they let you down. Obviously, you now have a full set of tools for staying cool, moving on, and coping with ambiguity—all of which can help you stay positive when you're at the mercy of others who aren't delivering on time or as planned. But you can also apply the tools from the last couple of chapters while you're talking to the person who's messed up, to make it more likely you'll both find a workable way out of the mess that's been created.

First, though, let me pull in some of the advice from Part III. It's often the case that the person who's screwed up is feeling embarrassed, worried, combative, or all three. And that means they're deep into defensive mode, where their deliberate system—the one responsible for reasoning, self-control, and planning—isn't going to be functioning properly. You might think they deserve to feel even worse than they do, but that won't help if you need their intelligent cooperation to find a good solution. So here are three ways to draw someone out of defensive mode—or at least avoid pushing them deeper into it—if you need them thinking sharp.

→ Acknowledge how it feels for them. That doesn't mean you shouldn't be annoyed or upset, but you're likely to make them feel less "triggered" if you can signal that you understand they (probably) didn't intend to cause the problem that's unfolding.

→ Assume "good person, bad circumstances." Talk about the actions they took to create the screw-up, rather than criticizing their character or morals. So, say "You delivered this three days late for the second time" rather than "You are always late and you are a terrible person." (The advice in Chapter 9 on raising difficult issues may also be helpful here.)

→ Focus on finding solutions, not on blame. Criticism is one of the surest ways of triggering a deep defensive reaction. So if you actually need to resolve a situation *right now*, the better immediate strategy is to focus on solutions. (Serious consequences can come later, if needed.)

Armed with that attitude, you can then deploy the resilience tips from the past couple of chapters to help move everyone forward.

George is the CEO of a large private-label clothing manufacturer, and he swears by this approach when dealing with other people's screw-ups. One day he discovered a long-running fraud at the staff restaurant. Tens of thousands of dollars had been stolen over several months. It was a huge breach of trust for a company with a generally friendly culture, and all his senior colleagues were upset. After the perpetrator had been dealt with, some executives directed their anger at the finance team. "The fraud should have been picked up way earlier than it was," George says, "because the finance team should have been conducting audits. One of my colleagues was in full-on accusation mode, asking them, 'Why didn't you do this or that?' The questions weren't entirely invalid. But the finance guys were already feeling bad, so shouting didn't help."

In fact, with everyone on high alert, there was predictably little clear thinking taking place. "It was a mud-slinging match," he recalls, "and it wasn't getting us any closer to knowing what to do next. The only solution people came up with was to close the cafeteria permanently." This is a classic example of the knee-jerk, black-and-white thinking that happens when people's brains are in defensive mode and their deliberate system isn't fully engaged. Luckily, George knew a little about the way that people's brains react when they're feeling threatened. "So

I was as furious as anyone, but I knew there was just no point trying to resolve the situation in that way."

George called a halt and adopted a different strategy. He deployed several of the resilience tips I've mentioned in this part of the book, starting with distancing. "When I personally have to deal with difficult things, I like to step outside the situation and look at it from the outside in," he says. "I imagine a situation where someone else is the CEO of the company, and ask myself what I would advise *them*. So I encouraged my staff to play that abstraction game, too. I asked them, 'What will we consider important when we're looking back on this, in five years?'" Then he encouraged them to let go of sunk costs. "I often say 'we are where we are' when something bad has happened. It's a basic phrase to remind us to stop looking backward, to get beyond blame, and look forward instead." And he asked them to recall crucible moments the company had previously faced. "I reminded them that when this or that bad thing happened in the past, we got through it. We're more resilient than we think."

Once his colleagues were calmer, he asked them another rewarding question: "What can we learn from this?" he wondered out loud, "and what should we do as a result?" Finally, once they were ready to get into detailed problem solving, he channeled some of the advice from Chapter 13, framing the task with a positive question to help them continue to think productively. "What's the ideal outcome we want to create?" he asked. "Those questions caused us to raise our game on risk management considerably," George says, "to the point that we went on to fix the issue so it never happens again."

So next time you're dealing with a crisis that's not of your own making—or even one that *is*—try asking these sorts of questions to lower the state of alert in everyone's brain and allow you to get to a solution:

➡ Distancing. "What do we want to be able to say about how we handled this situation when we look back in a year's time?"

➡ Rewarding questions. "When we've dealt with problems in the past, what's worked well?" Or "What can we learn from this situation?" Or "What really matters most right now?"

→ **Positive task framing.** "Set aside the current situation for a moment. What's our ideal outcome here?" And "What's the best first step to take right now?"

## MOVING ON

To practice the techniques from this chapter, pick a recent negative event that still annoys or upsets you when you think about it.

→ **Reappraise the situation.** What are the *true facts*? What are you *assuming*? (Are any of those assumptions personal, pervasive, or permanent?) What would be an *alternative* way of explaining the facts? What evidence might support that alternative interpretation?

→ **Ditch your sunk costs.** For a situation that's failing to improve despite your efforts, ignore sunk costs and look only at the future costs and benefits of investing more versus walking away. In the benefits of walking away, include what you've learned from the experience.

→ **Find a way through when someone screws up.** Avoid putting the person deeper into defensive mode: acknowledge they may not have intended to screw up; talk about their actions, not their character; focus on solutions, not on blame (for now). Use **distancing** techniques and **rewarding questions** (from Chapter 17) to reduce stress levels. Then work back from the ideal outcome you both want, using the **positive framing** technique (from Chapter 13) to keep everyone in discovery mode as you solve the problem.

# Staying Strong

When we're under pressure, facing uncertainty, conflict, or disappointment at work, it's not uncommon to grit our teeth and try to push through it without much regard for our physical well-being. We might decide we just don't have time to exercise, or to give ourselves a moment of calm, or to get the sleep we know our bodies really need. But at this point in the book, you're aware that our physical condition directly affects the way we think and feel. When we're tired and out of touch with our physical selves, we make poorer decisions in all we say and do, and we get more wound up by regular stressors.

I've touched on the benefits of better understanding our mindbody loops earlier in the book, especially in Part IV, where I talked about the way that sleep, exercise, and the "mindful pause" improve the quality of our thinking. Here I'd like to focus on their emotional resilience benefits, showing how sleep, exercise, and mindfulness can improve our ability to roll with the ups and downs of working life.

## SLEEP THE GOOD SLEEP

In Chapter 13, I talked about the clear cognitive benefits of getting enough sleep. But respecting our need for sleep also improves our ability to handle worrying or upsetting situations with aplomb. That's because several research teams have demonstrated what you might guess to be true: that you're more likely to overreact to negative things when you haven't slept well.[1]

Neuroscientists have observed this difference on brain scans of people shown upsetting images while lying in a scanner. Volunteers who hadn't slept showed much more activation in their brain's amygdala—in one study, 60 percent more—than people who were well rested.[2] In other words, a tired brain's survival circuits are more jittery, and more likely to launch a fight-flight-freeze defense in the face of something challenging or uncertain. The researchers also discovered that tired brains found it harder to calm down once they were agitated. And by observing lower levels of activation in their sleep-deprived subjects' prefrontal cortex, the researchers could also see that people's deliberate systems weren't doing as much as they might to reintroduce a more measured perspective. So no wonder skimping on sleep makes it harder to rise above setbacks with a smile.

Other researchers have confirmed the positive side of the equation, which is that getting decent sleep makes it easier to laugh things off the next day. Stanford researcher Cheri D. Mah found that when she got male basketball players to sleep ten hours a night—that sounds long, but these were kids in their teens and early twenties, doing a lot of physical activity—their mood and daytime energy both improved. Their hoop shooting performance also improved hugely, by an average of 9 percent, a result the players were probably more excited about than anything else.[3]

George, the clothing manufacturer CEO we met earlier, says: "Sleep is so underrated in the business world. Why do some people boast that they only need five hours? What I've read suggests that's unlikely—and the dysfunctional behavior I've seen when people are on five hours' sleep backs that up. If I run short of sleep, I'm not embarrassed to say that I crash the next day in some way, even if I look like I'm keeping going." George used to sleep much less than he really needed to, he says. But since becoming aware of the way that sleep boosts both his physical and emotional stamina, he's changed his habits and become more proactive in getting his quota. "I started measuring my sleep with a fitness tracker, and I've seen a strong correlation between low sleep averages in a week and my feeling particularly grumpy and irritable. So now I monitor when my average is slipping and will try to get extra sleep to make sure I catch up."

George spends a lot of time crisscrossing the globe as he visits customers and suppliers, so the combination of fierce jet lag and heavy workload does occasionally see him hitting the buffers before he can get himself caught up. He's found he can get a useful temporary boost from napping at his desk, even though it's not as good as a decent night's sleep. Research suggests that a short nap can provide just enough sleep to aid the brain's processing of negative emotional experiences and dampen our instinctive reaction to unpleasant situations.[4] That's in line with George's experience.[5] "I just put my head down and switch off for a while. I'm always clearer-headed afterward, and better able to face the rest of the day," he says.

So if you're dealing with a lot of ups and downs at work, do aim to follow the "smart sleep" guidance I shared in Chapter 13. Here's a reminder:

➡ View sleep as a key part of your professional armory, and prioritize it as much as anything else you do to prepare for challenging days at work.

➡ Recognize that your ability to sleep is strongly affected by the amount of light you expose yourself to. Allow some wind-down time in a dimly lit bedroom and don't look at lit screens before sleep.

➡ Experiment with taking more naps. Consider carrying ear plugs, an eye mask, or nap pillow with you (or failing that, some very dark glasses).

## EXERCISE YOUR MIND

Earlier in the book, I talked about how even a small amount of moderate exercise is enough to deliver useful intellectual benefits. But exercise doesn't just help us think straight and perform well. It's a reliable, high-caliber way to steady our mood and reduce anxiety when we're feeling stressed. In fact, studies suggest that it often matches antidepressant drugs in the treatment of mild to moderate clinical depression.[6] And although the positive effects of exercise get better with repetition, research has shown that even a single moderate workout can alter our neurochemistry enough to make us feel calmer. A really energetic workout goes even further, by feeding our brains endorphins—the body's own painkillers and mood boosters (the word "endorphin" effectively means endogenous morphine).[7]

Kira, a communications director, got plenty of endorphins when she was a student. She spent her spare time working as a lifeguard, and she played varsity volleyball. Then, like many of us, Kira fell out of her youthful exercise habits once the structures of college life dropped away. Her job was demanding, and there never seemed to be enough time to go around. Because she was working for a global firm, urgent requests flowed into her inbox at every hour of the day. It was hard to switch off, let alone take time to look after herself.

After years of just about managing to push through mental and physical exhaustion, she finally tweaked her routine to include some exercise and relaxation time. What prompted the shift? "Honestly, I realized it made me a better person when I did. It would mean the difference between yelling at people, or not. I was able to think more intelligently about my response to annoying emails, able to not write the angry reply, or at least better able to pause and rethink before sending it. So I started to pay attention to my body again, for the first time in many years."

What's her technique for fitting some physical maintenance into a busy schedule? "It starts right at the beginning of the day," Kira says. "When I'm setting my intentions for the day, I always ask myself, 'What three things would make today a great day?' and what I do is make sure that one of the three is a physical thing. Then I look at my schedule and work out when I can fit it in, and I view it like any other professional priority." The big shift behind these small changes, Kira says, is "realizing that my body is as important as my brain. That it is effectively an extension of my brain, and vice versa. So I treat it like a friend now, rather than beating it into submission."

Bartek added bursts of extra exercise to help him stay centered during his Olympic soup crisis: "When things are tough, I know it helps to pause and take my mind somewhere else. I do judo, and that was good because you simply can't worry about work when someone is about to throw you on the mat. But in the summer of 2012, I also started running for the first time. I found it allowed me to switch off the endless thinking for a bit, and it really helped me regain the logic of the situation."

Of course, it's one thing to know that exercise is a quick route to feeling good—but it's quite another to find the time for it. So as we learned in Chapter 2, on goal-setting, it helps to start with something achievable, an activity that readily fits into your day and that feels at least mildly enjoyable, so that your brain's reward system gets a kick out of it—a fast head-clearing walk on your way to or from a meeting, for example. (You might recall several of the interviewees in this book mentioning that this is part of their strategy for getting some activity into each day.)

And it's important to remember that exercise isn't time out; it's time invested. Ros, the healthcare executive we met earlier in the book, says: "I've got deeply held beliefs about what deserves my time, and exercising had never made it to the top of that list in the past. Yet it's obvious how much better I feel and think after I've taken more care of myself. I become more optimistic about my abilities and have more of a sense of possibility that I can make things happen." So now she thinks about exercise as "a practical investment in dealing better with everyday stress. Then it doesn't feel like an indulgence, or a chore, and I'm more likely to do it."

## MINDFULNESS MOMENTS

In The Science Essentials I talked about the evidence that the practice of mindfulness enhances all the functions of our brain's deliberate system by improving connectivity between key parts of the prefrontal cortex. That's a big deal when it comes to workplace resilience, because our deliberate system isn't just what enables smart thinking, insight, and focus—we also rely on our deliberate system for emotional self-control and flexibility. It's what stops us from shouting "That's not fair" when something manifestly unfair happens, and it's what enables us to reappraise our interpretation of a difficult situation. In fact, researchers analyzing brain scans of people using mindfulness have seen how it reduces their survival circuits' reactivity to negative events, so that there's less defensive behavior for them to overcome in the first place.[8] In other words, people who use mindfulness are harder to tip into defensive mode. So mindfulness is as powerful in boosting our emotional stability as it is in improving our thinking.

What do those benefits look like in a modern working environment? One group of researchers at the University of Washington recruited a bunch of HR professionals and then asked them to juggle multiple workday demands.[9] In the middle of the experiment, they gave some people basic mindfulness training. Others got relaxation training, while a third group got nothing. The tasks that people had to complete included scheduling a meeting with multiple attendees while facing limited conference room availability, and designing a creative agenda for the meeting. They received the information they needed through a flow of emails, instant messages, calls, documents, and comments from people dropping by unannounced. Some information was incomplete, and the meeting attendees changed their minds about their schedule (yes, the researchers were impressively committed to making the study feel like real life). Unsurprisingly, the volunteers reported feeling drained by the experience—that was the idea. But the group that got the mindfulness training coped markedly better, and reported less stress, than the other two groups.

So let's remind ourselves—what *is* mindfulness? It's centered on the following steps: *pause* for a moment; choose to *focus* on something with all of your attention; and if your attention drifts away, just *return* it to your point of focus without judging yourself. Most people who practice mindfulness choose to observe their breath, because it's entirely portable and something we never have to fumble for. So breathing exercises have come up several times in the book so far. But our single point of focus can be just about anything. We can pay close attention to a picture or a plant in our workplace, or each mouthful of the food we're eating. Whatever we choose to observe, we're being mindful of something that we might not have otherwise stopped to notice, and we're creating a moment of stillness in the daily whirlwind of our lives.

As the benefits of mindfulness become more widely known in business, eight-week mindfulness courses are proving increasingly popular. But if the thought of attending a course seems incompatible with the demands of your life, the good news is that you don't have to make a big commitment to get results. Neurobiologist Fadel Zeidan and colleagues at the University of North Carolina had volunteers practice twenty minutes of mindfulness for just four days, and in that short time great things happened. People reported less fatigue and anxiety, and had more self-control. Using a battery of puzzles and tests, the researchers also found that measures of their working memory and of their visual and spatial processing improved significantly.[10]

What if you don't have twenty minutes a day? I liked a study at the University of Wisconsin–Stout that asked its volunteers to try to meditate for twenty-five minutes a couple of times a week, but where the reality ended up being more like five to fifteen minutes for many people. Even those at the five-minute end of the scale were seen to have shifts in patterns of brain activation consistent with the positive results seen in longer-term studies.[11]

What if you don't have five minutes? What if it's more like a minute, or even less? Can that be mindfulness, too? I say yes. Kira, our communications director, says: "I learned this meditation technique for workaholic people like me. It's just twenty-eight breaths, and even I can do that. The counting helps keep you focused. I do it most days.

Sometimes I think, 'Well, that didn't work,' because I feel like I wasn't able to settle my mind. But then it gets to be 6:00 p.m. and, magically, I'm still feeling calm. And on the days I skip my twenty-eight breaths, I'm anything but calm at that point in the day."

You might remember that Anthony, our digital marketing expert from Part II, has a quick "mindful pause" routine to better handle his workload. He also occasionally uses one of the many mindfulness smartphone apps that now exist. "Even though the introductions can seem slightly cheesy, they work well. You can listen to them on your headphones wherever you are. You don't have to close your eyes, so you can use them while you're sitting at your desk, and nobody knows what you're doing." The suggestions that pop up on the app can be as discreet as reminding him to focus on the way his toes feel on the floor for a few seconds.

Ros, the healthcare manager, had a similar breakthrough with mindfulness when she realized "it can be as small as properly noticing what I'm doing now, really paying attention to the thoughts I'm having and the way I'm feeling—whether I'm in the middle of something at work or reading a bedtime story to my kids." As for me, I like focusing on the way each foot hits the ground when I'm going for my morning walks.

So it's worth experimenting until you find a pause-and-focus routine that fits your personality and lifestyle. And if that means you find yourself gazing intently at a glass of wine or an ice cream—well, you can tell everyone that meditation takes many forms.

## STAYING STRONG

Whenever you're facing a lot of ups and downs, work the mind-body loop:

➡ Sleep. Stay calmer and wiser by taking extra care to prioritize your sleep routine. If that's especially tough to achieve right now, consider whether there's a way you could take a nap now and then.

➡ Exercise. You can instantly clear your head and lift your mood with twenty minutes of moderate exercise. Split it into two or three chunks of fast walking if that helps you fit it into your day.

➡ Mindfulness. Try a few different pause-and-focus techniques, and then build your favorite one into your daily routine to reap some of the cognitive and emotional benefits of mindfulness.

# PART VII

# Energy

## Boosting Your Enthusiasm and Enjoyment

Energy enables a man to force his way through irksome drudgery and dry details, and carries him onward and upward in every station in life. It accomplishes more than genius, with not one-half the disappointment and peril.

—SAMUEL SMILES (1897)

At this point, you've got a full "good day" tool kit. You're focusing on the right things, and organizing your time to give those priorities your best attention. You're handling every interaction with sensitivity and aplomb, and feeling sharp. Everything you say and do is having great impact. You're breezing past setbacks with your mojo intact, and feel well set to handle even the most difficult of days.

This part of the book is intended as a bonus—a source of extra fuel for those moments when your tank is running a little low, or the times when you want to burn a little brighter. Perhaps you're going through a patch where you're feeling uninspired by your work. Or perhaps it's just a busy time and you could do with a boost to get through the longer hours of the day. Either way, the advice in the pages ahead will help you turbocharge your slow and weary days, and make your already good days great.

I'll first show you some practical tactics that will help you lift your mental, emotional, or physical energy, to give you a shot in the arm when you most need it. The final chapter will then lay out a strategy for creating a longer-lasting, deeper enthusiasm for your work—with easy first steps that will bear fruit immediately.

# TWENTY

# Topping Up the Tank

When we're out of juice at work, of course we can spur ourselves on with the promise of rest and recreation once we get home—or once we get to the weekend. (Or vacation. Failing that, retirement.) But with an understanding of the way our mind works, we can do considerably better than that. Drawing on what we know about the brain's reward system and the psychology of well-being, there are lots of ways to give ourselves a quick boost when we're feeling more stretched or drained than we would like. I've picked out seven tactics to share in this chapter, all of which work well in fast-paced professional life because they're so simple and instantaneously effective. After that, I'll also suggest two ways to make the most of these energy boosting tactics—first, by being analytical about the times when you need to deploy a boost; second, by making sure that you use one of them to end on a high note.

## 1. THREE GOOD THINGS

One of the easiest ways to lift your spirits is to think about things you're glad about. Psychologists often call this the "gratitude exercise"; I refer to it as the "three good things," since that's a good description of how it actually works. Which is simply this: take a moment to think about three positive things that have happened to you. And yes, you will feel better as a result, even if the good things aren't very big. In fact, several studies found that doing this each day for just one week left people saying they still felt happier months later.[1]

It's not hard to imagine why a little repetition makes the effects of the "three good things" exercise endure. Remember how in Chapter 3 we learned that each of our thoughts corresponds to a network of neurons connecting with each other, and that those neural connections get stronger the more often they're called on. So the more we focus on negative things, the more readily we spot the bad stuff in our days. Conversely, we each have a neural network responsible for the thought that begins "Well, the good thing about this is that . . . ," and if that network gets activated a lot, we strengthen the pathways in our brain that are associated with that perspective on life. And that makes it easier and easier to boot up the "glass half full" version of ourselves over time.

So whenever you need a burst of energy, think of three things that have gone well today, things you're grateful for, or simply moments that made you smile. (Some German researchers found that asking people to think of three *funny* things was as effective as thinking of three good things.)[2] On so-so days, I find my list can include tiny wins such as "remembering my umbrella." But it still works. And once you start thinking of good things, even if it feels hard initially, your associative brain will often trigger a cascade of other positive memories from the day—things that you might otherwise have all but forgotten about.

Here are some ideas to help you get the most out of this technique:

- ➡ Schedule a daily calendar reminder to prompt you to review your good things each day.

- ➡ Keep a notebook where you can write down your good things.

- ➡ Try it with your partner or your children as an upbeat way of ending the day, or when you're lying in bed and ready to fall asleep.

- ➡ Use a short version at the beginning of meetings, to help put everyone in a good mood (and create a discovery-mode thinking environment, as I said in Chapter 10).

### 2. RANDOM ACTS OF KINDNESS

It might seem counterintuitive to suggest that when we feel in need of a boost, we should give one to other people. But it's true. University of Pennsylvania professor Martin Seligman is one of the world's foremost experts on human flourishing and well-being, and as he says, "doing a kindness produces the single most reliable momentary increase in well-being of any exercise we have tested."[3] An international team of neuroscientists led by Jorge Moll, director of the D'Or Institute in Brazil, confirmed that when volunteers decided to give money to charity, their brain's reward system was engaged in the same way as when they received money themselves.[4] (In fact, Elizabeth Dunn and Michael Norton, from the University of British Columbia and Harvard, respectively, found that spending money on other people makes us *happier* than spending money on ourselves.)[5] The UN's *World Happiness Report* confirms that people seem to find their own generosity uplifting, whatever culture they've grown up in.[6]

Finally, just as visualizing our past successes can help us rekindle a confident state of mind by activating many of the same neural connections, *recalling* kindnesses is almost as good as *doing* them. A group of researchers in Japan found that people felt happier after merely counting the acts of kindness they'd done in the previous week; a North American team found the same.[7] So doing one favor can repay you many times when you think back on it in the future.

How to be generous and kind, even on a busy day:

➡ **Give someone an unsolicited compliment.** Say something like "You guys are always so friendly," or "I'm impressed at how organized you are," or "I like your music [or watch, or other random thing]."

➡ **Express appreciation.** Take a moment to tell someone you're grateful for something they've done, rather than racing on to the next thing in your schedule.

➡ **Be helpful.** If you see someone who's struggling, take a moment to ask if you can help. You can specify how long you've got: "I've got fifteen minutes before I have to head off. Do you need a hand?"

➡ **Do something unexpectedly delightful.** Give up your seat. Let a driver cut in front of you. Bring treats to share. Introduce someone especially warmly.

## 3. FIND *SOMETHING* INTERESTING

If you're bored, one way of quickly lifting your energy is to figure out ways to make your work more interesting. Easier said than done, you say? The whole reason you need a boost is because you're uninspired by what you're doing? I hear you. But let me remind you of the magic of "buzzword bingo." If you haven't played this game, the rules are something like this: Define some overused, jargon-heavy phrases that you suspect will be mentioned in the day's presentations, meetings, or conversations. Agree on the list of phrases with your fellow players. Then listen for them, checking off each hackneyed gem as you hear it. The winner is the first person to get bingo. Somewhere in the mid-1990s, I had teammates who sometimes used this technique to liven up dull meetings, and the result was a lot of laughter. But it's also undeniable that we paid more attention overall—not just to the silly jargon—and we felt less drained at the end of it all.

Why did it lift our spirits so much? Largely because we *decided* that there was something worth listening to, and directed our attention accordingly. Remember that our brains are always filtering out some of the information around us to avoid overloading our limited neural capacity. We focus on whatever confirms our expectations (among other things) and tend to filter out the rest. So if I've decided that what I'm about to hear is going to be boring, I'll tend to see and hear things that confirm I'm right to be bored. If I've decided it's going to be interesting, I have half a chance of finding it a little more so. We know the reality we perceive is highly subjective; we might as well seek out the more interesting aspects of reality if we want to feel more energized by everyday life.

So there's a lot to be said for this simple but effective strategy: get into the habit of deciding to find *something* interesting in what's going on around you. Home in on something worth learning or remembering, even if it's a bit subversive ("Today I'm going to learn how not to completely lose it when dealing with the office psychopath"). If you're in an interminable training course that's going way too slowly, decide to find something noteworthy about the way it's being taught, something that could improve the way you communicate your own ideas to others. If you're engaged in the most boring task on the planet, perhaps you can at least find the quickest or slickest way of doing it.

By any measure, Ruby is someone who's had a thrillingly varied career. Early on, she was a sought-after interpreter; many years later, she was head of a business school. These days, she devotes her time to filmmaking. But after graduating with a degree in international business, Ruby's first job was in the shipping industry in Taiwan—and there, she found herself calling on the "find *something* interesting" technique just about every day. She says, "Nothing was computerized back then, there was just a big book with lots of prices in it, which I had to use to price shipments. I spent the first week memorizing as much as I could, but after a month I was really bored. The work turned out to be really mechanical. I knew I needed to look for a different job, but in the meantime I decided to learn about other people's roles, by chatting to my colleagues and asking them about their work. I learned how the U.S. shipping line worked, then how the Europe and Middle East lines worked. I even learned how to run the switchboard in my spare time at lunch, which helped me understand more about how the company worked. And I learned about the CEO's job by getting to know the CEO's personal assistant. It made my day-to-day experience feel so much more bearable—worthwhile, even. And it gave me more to talk about when I was interviewing for my next job."

## 4. GIVE YOURSELF A QUICK WIN

We feel good when we achieve a goal we've set for ourselves. Each time we tick a box, our reward system glows with pleasure, which in turn boosts our motivation to carry on. It can be a great virtuous circle: work, achieve, glow, push on, work, achieve, glow, et cetera. That's why some of us will retrospectively add an achievement to our to-do list, just to experience the momentary joy that comes from ceremonially crossing it off. And we can use this insight to manufacture ourselves a quick buzz whenever our morale and focus are flagging, by choosing a small achievable goal that we can nail with satisfaction.

Some quick wins are better than others for lifting our spirits. We're all familiar with displacement activity, where we avoid something that's pretty important in favor of organizing our stationery. These activities give us a small amount of gratification. But the best small goals are those that help us take baby steps toward big goals that really mean something to us. That's clear from the findings of Harvard's Teresa Amabile and Stephen Kramer, who conducted a huge research project to explore the day-to-day experiences of more than two hundred professionals working at seven companies.[8] After diligently working through twelve thousand days' worth of data, they concluded: "Of all the things that can boost emotions, motivation, and perceptions during a workday, the single most important is making progress in meaningful work." So the trick is to:

➡ Pick something that really matters to you.

➡ Ask yourself: "What would be the smallest first step I could take toward that today?" Perhaps it's making a phone call, or sending an email.

➡ Then do it—right now—and cross it off the list with contentment.

### 5. MAKE TIME FOR HUMAN CONNECTION

Hundreds of studies have compared the levels and causes of well-being reported by people in different countries, and their findings are clear: money matters, but not that much. On average, the UN's *World Happiness Report* found that income explains just 2 percent of the differences in overall life satisfaction ratings between countries, and none of our day-to-day level of happiness.[9] What's far more important, researchers found, is the quality of people's relationships. In fact, using a huge cache of British data, London School of Economics professor Nattavudh Powdthavee found that meaningful personal interactions with others had as much impact on well-being as an extra $142,000 of income a year.[10]

And we don't always need to chat with our nearest and dearest friends, family, or co-workers to reap useful social benefits. Even the tiniest sense of connection with a fellow human being can boost us. Research by Gillian Sandstrom and Elizabeth Dunn (from the University of Cambridge and the University of British Columbia, respectively) suggests the importance of what's known as "weak ties" with people they refer to as the "minor characters in our daily lives." They found that both extroverts *and* introverts felt happier on days when they had more interactions, and that interactions with acquaintances—in their experiments, even something as minimal as a brief friendly exchange with a barista or a fellow commuter—were almost as powerful a mental boost as interactions with friends.[11]

What does that mean for us, practically? I'm not suggesting we should be chatting with strangers nonstop. But it does help to sustain our energy if we can make time for some moments of human connection during the day.

Catherine is the director of executive education for a top-flight university and a self-proclaimed "deep introvert," but she, too, swears by the importance of having a little social time in her day. "I came to realize that although I'm not an extrovert, it's still a reliable boost for me to have a conversation with someone," she says. "So I try to make time to sit with people at lunch. It would be easier to eat at my desk on my own, but I notice the difference in my energy on days when I make time for those random, pleasant interactions. I'm much less likely to have a 'sense of humor malfunction,' and the work feels easier."

To make sure you don't run short of social sources of energy, try this each day:

➡ Take time to connect with someone important to you, even if you do it remotely and briefly instead of face-to-face. If you're planning to meet a friend and you're considering canceling because of workload, think twice. Make it short, if you have to, but don't throw away the opportunity for a psychological boost that will ultimately make you more productive.

➡ Turn transactions into interactions when dealing with strangers. Instead of having your eyes glued to your phone as you wordlessly hand over your money at the register, pause for a second. Smile. Make eye contact. Initiate a brief exchange with a simple sympathetic comment such as "Looks like a busy afternoon for you" or "You in for a long day?"

➡ Seek out people who radiate good vibes. I've talked previously about how emotions are contagious. If you're hitting a low, consider deliberately seeking out the most optimistic, upbeat person you know, and standing next to that person for a while.

## 6. FIND THE PERSONAL PURPOSE

Earlier in the book, I talked about how we're more likely to achieve great things if we're chasing goals we've set for ourselves, rather than those imposed on us by others. I also pointed out research that suggests a sense of purpose is helpful in developing the psychological resilience to sail through the ups and downs of life. So it probably won't surprise you to know that injecting a touch of personal purpose can also be a useful pick-me-up when you're wading through a task that isn't delighting you. As in: Why do *you* (as opposed to your boss or colleagues) think this work is important? Or at least, why is the *way* you're going about it important to you? Even when you don't have a lot of space to choose what you're doing, the "why" is usually yours to define or interpret in your own way.

Catherine, our executive education director, used this approach when the division she managed was restructured as part of a larger reorganization of her company. The restructuring was resulting in many weeks of work that didn't feel necessary to her—changing people's reporting lines, in some cases moving staff to new locations, and facilitating the conversations needed between newly formed teams. "It felt like a big waste of time at first. But it helped me to find something behind it that I believed in." It wasn't easy at first, because she was so ticked off. "But there *was* something: I found I did believe in the idea of creating a more global organization, which was going to be one of the benefits of the changes we were making—I could see that it would become easier for us to share best practices between colleagues across the world. That would be a good thing, because I do ultimately believe that the work of my team makes the world a slightly better place. That was a big enough idea to fire me up when I started to feel worn down by it."

When you need to reconnect your work to the big picture, there are two ways to do it.

➡ Backward. Start from what's meaningful to you and work back to what you're doing, like this:
  • What do you really care about—values, causes, personal development goals?
  • How does what you're doing contribute to those values, causes, or goals?

➡ **Forward.** Start from what you're doing, and connect it to what's meaningful for you. Ask yourself:
  - What is possible as a result of the task you're doing?
  - And what's ultimately possible as a result of *that*, for society and/or for yourself?

Your first answers may be a bit sarcastic if you're having a bad day ("I'm enabling that jerk to get all the credit—*that's* what's 'ultimately possible'"). Push beyond that, until you get to something that makes you nod rather than scowl.

## 7. DON'T FORGET TO SMILE

Talking of scowling, let's talk about facial expressions. Start with a familiar causal link: when you're happy, you smile. Not everyone does it exactly the same way, but smiling is a universal human expression of pleasure. What's surprising is that the direction of causation appears to work in reverse, too: when you smile, you're happy—or, at least, happier. And that seems to be the case even when it's not a genuine smile. When we force ourselves to smile, our brain takes that cue to mean "Ah, I'm happy"—thus boosting our mood for real.

Researchers have been experimenting with the surprising mood-enhancing power of fake smiles for some years. Back in the 1970s, an enterprising psychologist named James D. Laird put electrodes on the faces of some willing volunteers, to cause small spasms in their muscles while they watched a cartoon.[12] In one group, the muscles being stimulated were those involved in smiling, so they were being involuntarily induced to smile. This group reported finding the cartoon funnier than those with electrodes placed elsewhere on their faces. (Pretty amazing that they were willing to find anything funny, I'd say, in the circumstances.) Other researchers have since tricked volunteers into fake smiling by less invasive means, such as asking them to try writing with a pen held between their teeth, and have found the same encouraging effects.[13] One research team found that smiling can help you weather unpleasant moments, too. Their fake smilers felt less aggravated when asked to shove their hands into unpleasantly cold water, plus their heart rates also returned more quickly to normal after the icy shock.[14]

The two-way street between smiling and positive mood is known as *facial feedback*. I find it an exceptionally useful mind-body loop to know about, because it's so quick and easy to build into whatever I'm doing. Just before giving speeches and running workshops, you'll see me put down my papers and start grinning at people. (They don't seem to mind.)

So, try it for yourself—when your mental or emotional energy is running low, crack a smile. The more realistic the better, but if in doubt, give your face a workout and your mood should follow.

## BRINGING IT ALL TOGETHER: KNOW THYSELF

One thing I've noticed about people who are able to sustain their energy in grueling jobs is that they know themselves really well. They understand what causes their typical peaks and troughs, and they know the quickest way to lift their spirits and their stamina when needed.

One of those people is Rakesh, who's been an emergency room doctor for fifteen years. Describing the job, he says: "You're constantly handling problems. You don't have much time, and you never stop moving. In one hour, you're making perhaps one hundred or two hundred decisions: which tests to order, where to send a patient, and what interventions are needed. You're on different shifts, sometimes morning, sometimes night. A twelve-hour shift can turn into fourteen hours if something bad happens with one of your patients." And Rakesh confirms that the job is emotionally draining as well as mentally and physically challenging. "It's very hard when you get an outcome you don't want or expect. Initially I used to say 'Nobody's going to die on my watch,' but that's not realistic."

So Rakesh takes a calculated approach to keeping on what he calls his "game face" throughout a long shift. For example, he uses music to shape and shift his mental state. "You know you're going to walk into a full waiting room, and as soon as you walk in you're going to need to spring into action. So I need to pump up my energy levels on the drive into work, and I pick music that I know will do that for me, like some Linkin Park. Once I arrive, I switch to reggae, and we have it playing in the background for everyone. It's sort of happy but also relaxed, which is how I need to feel to perform at my best under pressure."

Rakesh also knows when the highs and lows of the shift are going to happen, and plans accordingly. "You've got to be aware of your own biorhythms to get through something as tiring as ER work," he says. "For example, I always know that my highest energy levels are going to be in the first two to three hours of each shift. My brain's working fast, I feel alert. So I don't waste that time. I want to capitalize on that and see as many patients as I can in that time." Then, when he's flagging, Rakesh says: "I make sure to keep the conversations going with staff and with patients. I like asking patients to tell me about their lives, especially the older ones. The other day I found out that someone I was treating had been a B-52 tail gunner. You can have a meaningful conversation in just a few minutes, and it helps the patient as well as improving my alertness."

It doesn't take a lot to become as self-aware as Rakesh—it's just a matter of paying more attention to our personal patterns. If we know what's likely to feel especially draining, and we know the most reliable way to pick ourselves up again, we can be far more proactive in managing our mood and productivity throughout a long day. Here's what you can do to build that self-awareness:

➡ Draw a timeline from morning to night. Plot some of the peaks and troughs you've experienced in recent days (or weeks)—the moments when you're full of energy, and moments when you feel depleted.

➡ Notice the patterns in your highs and lows. What reliably lifts or depresses your energy level? Here are some categories to consider:
  • Mental: analysis, creative thinking, planning, reading
  • Physical: exercise, travel, manual labor
  • Social: specific individuals, types of people, being in a group vs. alone
  • Surroundings: music and sounds, workspace, natural environment
  • Time of day: circadian rhythms, family or personal routines
  • Themes from this chapter's list of seven energizers: gratitude, generosity, curiosity, achievement, connection, purpose, and humor (assuming that funny things make you smile).

➡ Then decide how to apply your most reliable energy boosts to smooth out the troughs. In particular:
  • On days that promise to be tiring, or at times of day when your energy regularly dips, manufacture a peak or two: for example, plan a conversation with a friend or tackle a task you always enjoy.
  • See if you can attack your more energy-sapping tasks while sur-

rounding yourself with things that boost you—perhaps an uplifting location, energizing people, or some upbeat music.

## THE PEAK-END EFFECT (OR: WHY YOU SHOULD ALWAYS END ON A HIGH NOTE)

If I ask how happy you are today, there are two types of happiness that you'll subconsciously evaluate. There's instantaneous happiness—the experience of how happy you are right now, as you answer the question. And then there's remembered happiness—your memory of what's happened in the day so far, and how it makes you feel as you look back on it. Of the two, research has found that remembered happiness has the bigger impact on our sense of well-being—after all, it's the story we tell ourselves about our day.[15] The edited sum of our memories becomes our view of whether life is good, or not. So what we remember matters.

But what we remember about the quality of our day isn't typically the sum of *everything* that's happened. Instead, we tend to rate experiences as an average of the most intense moment (the peak) and how it finishes (the end). That's what scientists call the *peak-end effect*. That's our brain's automatic system economizing on mental effort again, by creating a simple version of reality to file away in our memory banks—one that relies on just a couple of data points, rather than requiring us to recall and evaluate every single moment.[16]

Daniel Kahneman, the eminent Princeton psychologist whose work spawned the field of behavioral economics, demonstrated the peak-end effect by exposing volunteers to a variety of disagreeable experiences. In one experiment, he made them put their hands into uncomfortably cold water (14°C/57.2°F) for sixty seconds—something chilly enough to make the average person wince and squirm. Kahneman found that people rated this experience as less unpleasant if it was followed by *another* thirty seconds in just barely warmer water (15°C/59°F).[17] Since 15°C still feels pretty bad, the upshot was this: people preferred ninety seconds of discomfort to sixty seconds of discomfort, just because the last part wasn't quite as awful. And this is true in general. Research finds that people rate unpleasant experiences (such as colonoscopies and loud noise) as less unpleasant if a period of slightly milder discomfort is *added* to the end of the experience.[18] In other words, ending with something slightly less bad makes people feel better about the whole thing.

Endings have a disproportionate effect on positive experiences, too. In another study, people who had volunteered to do some fundraising for a nonprofit were offered a free DVD to thank them for their time. They were given their choice of movie from a list of highly rated films. For some, the offer stopped there, while others were subsequently offered a second movie, from a slightly less well-reviewed list of titles.[19] Sure enough, those who got just one stellar DVD were happier than those who got one stellar DVD and then one middling DVD.

So the peak-end effect provides us with some big pointers on how to boost our overall sense that we've had a good day. First, we should keep trying to engineer the kind of peaks described in the rest of this chapter. If we have one strikingly good flashbulb moment in a humdrum meeting, it will help us remember the whole thing more positively. But the bigger implication of the peak-end effect is that it's worth being more systematic about ending everything—each interaction, each task, each day—on a high note. Here are some ways to do that:

➡ An evening routine that includes the "three good things" exercise is an excellent way of changing the way that you remember the day.

➡ You can end most conversations by recapping their most upbeat moment—for example, say, "It was great to hear about your good news!" It brings the positive stuff back to the front of the mind—yours and theirs.

➡ In formal discussions, as you wrap up, you can also say: "So what worked well for us today that we should do again?" It gives people a chance to review what they found useful or interesting in the way a meeting was set up. If you don't have time to ask the question, you can simply comment on what you liked about the discussion—for example, "That was a great discussion. It was good to do some real problem solving together."

Sabine is a senior editor at a newspaper, and she has an interesting take on this "end on a high note" idea. Though she's very highly rated at her job, her current boss is not someone who gives a lot of praise. But Sabine found a way to finish every day with a burst of appreciation. "I searched online for a photo of a wise, friendly boss—just a stock photo, someone totally anonymous, someone who looked like the sort of person I'd enjoy working for—and then I stuck the photo on the back of my door. Every time I leave the office, I see the photo and imagine this perfect boss giving me feedback on the things I did well that day. Obviously it's funny, and the comic relief is good, but the process also gives me distance—it makes me step back and remember achievements I might have forgotten." And, like clockwork, it delivers a reliable peak for Sabine every evening.

## Topping Up the Tank

To become more adept at boosting your energy on tiring days, take the following steps:

➡ **Experiment with the seven energy boosters.** See which of these works best for you: three good things; random acts of kindness; finding *something* interesting; giving yourself a quick win; making time for social connection; finding a personal purpose; smiling widely (even if you're not quite feeling it).

➡ **Know thyself.** Identify where your typical energy highs and lows usually occur. Notice what tends to boost or drain you. (Look for patterns in the mental, physical, and social activities involved; surroundings and times of day; the themes of the seven boosters above—gratitude, generosity, curiosity, achievement, connection, purpose, and humor.) Decide on one or two reliable strategies you can use to preempt or reverse a slump when it happens.

➡ **End on a high note.** Plot how to end each day—and indeed every interaction or task—on a high note, to take advantage of the peak-end effect. Try the three good things as an evening routine.

➡ And to underpin all of this, do refer back to Chapter 5 on **downtime** and Chapter 19 on **staying strong** to remind yourself why and how to build enough energy-boosting breaks and bodily maintenance into your schedule.

# TWENTY-ONE

# Playing to Your Strengths

Most of us seek to better ourselves if we can; we don't want to stay in an entry-level job all our lives. That's not only because we might crave greater financial security or social standing. Decades of research by Carol Dweck, the eminent Stanford psychologist, suggests it's also important for our psychological well-being to know that our talents aren't fixed and that we have a chance to develop our abilities over time.[1] It helps us bounce back after mistakes and gives us a sense of possibility and novelty—things that our brain finds rewarding.

But if we're not content with standing still, it's likely that there will be times when our work stretches or exhausts us. We might have thrown ourselves in the deep end of a new professional project, and be struggling to remember how to swim. Perhaps we're in a tough or dull role that we're seeing as a stepping-stone to something better, or we're pushing ourselves hard in the hope of making the next career leap up the ladder. How can we navigate these kinds of professional challenges (and multiple metaphors) with energy and enthusiasm? In this chapter, I'm going to show you that the answer often lies in being more deliberate about playing to our strengths, to help us stay in discovery mode as we move through the more testing aspects of our work.

This approach stands in contrast to the way that many of us have thought about self-improvement in the past, where our focus has often been on fixing our weaknesses. There's a point to doing that, of course—if we're terrible at something that's important in life, like basic arithmetic or turning up on time, it's worth bringing those abilities up to an acceptable level. But it's problematic if this fix-it mentality comes to dominate our attitude to personal development at work, because focusing on our failings tends to undermine our sense of competence—and, as we know from Chapter 9, that can all too easily provoke a threat response in our brains. And when we're in defensive mode, it's harder for us to think clever thoughts—making us even less good at what we're doing. It can end up being a vicious circle.

What does the strength-based alternative look like? Broadly speaking: we figure out what our strengths are, then we find ways to play to them more fully—especially in the more difficult challenges that we're facing at work. (I'll explain more about how to do this in a moment.) As a result, work might still feel tough, but it's easier for us to keep our brain in high-performance discovery mode when we're not constantly beset by a feeling that we're incompetent.

There's lots of research describing the motivation and performance gains that are associated with this approach. For example, in a series of large-scale studies, Gallup has consistently found that people's job satisfaction improves when they're given feedback on their personal strengths and guidance on how to play to them more fully in the role they're in (e.g., "You're great at X—here's how you could use that skill more fully in challenges Y and Z"). They observed that profitability was 9 percent higher in companies with this strengths-based approach to performance feedback, versus comparable businesses with a more traditional "fix the weakness" approach to appraisals.[2] The Corporate Leadership Council found even sharper correlations. In a large study of nearly twenty thousand employees from thirty-four organizations, seven industries, and twenty-nine countries, performance was between 21 percent and 36 percent higher in companies where managers emphasized strengths.[3]

And whether or not you work for an organization that has seen the light, quite extensive research suggests that you can put this knowledge to good use for yourself. Psychologists Alex Wood and Alex Linley, at Stirling University and the Centre of Applied Positive Psychology, respectively, found that when volunteers were encouraged to find a new way to use their personal strengths each day over the course of a week, they went on to report higher levels of well-being, self-esteem, and something the researchers called "vitality" (what I'm calling energy in this part of the book). Meanwhile, the volunteers also reported lower stress. And, importantly, those gains were sustained when researchers checked in three and six months later.[4] That's a good return on investment for a few minutes of reflection.

## YOU KEEP USING THAT WORD

But what kind of "strengths" are we talking about here? We usually think about the word in terms of knowledge or skills: I know macroeconomic theory; I know how to play the piano. That sort of thing. But these types of knowledge-based strengths are often useful only in specific contexts. It's only rarely that it's going to be useful for me in my coaching work to be able to spout about monetary policy, or tickle the ivories.

So when researchers invite people to "play to their strengths" more fully, they mean more than just applying accumulated knowledge. They're asking us to make use of the qualities that define us when we're at our best as human beings, that stem from our personalities and values. They're asking not only what we're good at, but also what we most care about and are most inspired by.

To see what I mean, take a look at this list created by psychologists Martin Seligman and Christopher Peterson. They were the first to come up with a taxonomy of what they call "character strengths," and these are their categories:

➡ **Wisdom:** Strengths that involve the acquisition and use of knowledge, such as creativity, curiosity, judgment, love of learning, and perspective.

➡ **Courage:** Strengths requiring the exercise of will to accomplish goals in the face of opposition, like valor, perseverance, honesty, and zest.

➡ **Humanity:** Interpersonal strengths that involve understanding and supporting others, including love, kindness, and social intelligence.

➡ **Justice:** Strengths that underlie healthy civic and community life such as teamwork, fairness, and leadership.

➡ **Temperance:** Strengths that protect against excess and extreme behavior, including forgiveness, humility, prudence, and self-regulation.

➡ **Transcendence:** Strengths that help provide meaning and purpose to life, like appreciation (of excellence or beauty), gratitude, hope, humor, and a sense of spirituality.

So you might know that you're good at marshaling spreadsheets or designing logos, but you may not be as conscious of the way that you complement these technical skills with behavioral talents reflecting some themes in the list above. For example, perhaps you're great at rallying people around an idea (signs of "zest," "social intelligence," and "leadership"), or you have an unusual ability to stay calm and see the best in a bad situation ("perspective," "self-regulation," and "hope").

Of course, there are plenty of different ways to label these kinds of character strengths. Seligman and Peterson's themes might resonate with you, or you might prefer different words to describe similar ideas ("empathy" rather than "love," or "enthusiasm" rather than "zest," for example). There are now multiple strength taxonomies around, each with its own terminology. But whatever language we use, the key idea remains: when we get a chance to deploy our signature strengths, the research suggests that we will feel especially energized and absorbed by what we're doing (almost by definition). And because this puts us so firmly in discovery mode, it enables higher performance, too.

## HOW TO IDENTIFY YOUR STRENGTHS

So how do you identify your signature strengths—or remind yourself of what they are—so that you can more consciously draw on them in your day-to-day work? Based on what I've seen work well with my clients, here are three complementary ways I'd suggest you get a handle on your strengths:

➡ **Analyze some especially satisfying past successes of yours, whether big or small.** Focus on the kind of personal triumph where you caught yourself thinking, "I wish I felt like this every day," or "This is so enjoyable that it doesn't feel like work." You can also think about peaks you've experienced outside a professional setting. Maybe you were able to resolve a difficult family situation or you organized a successful community event. For each example, write down:
  • What exactly did you do, say, and think that helped you succeed?
  • What personal talents and qualities enabled you to do, say, or think those things? (These are your strengths.)

➡ **Ask a handful of trusted people—co-workers, friends, family—for their take.** Explain that you're trying to get a clearer picture of your personal strengths. Ask them to give you one or two specific examples of times you seemed particularly enthused or impressive, and ask them what they think that means your signature strengths are.

➡ **Complete a strengths survey.** There are now several strengths surveys available online.[5] They're not a replacement for examining your personal peaks and developing your own sense of your strengths, but taking one may help you surface patterns in your examples, or provide useful labels for talents you're struggling to name.

When you're defining your strengths, strive to get beyond the headlines typically seen in a corporate performance appraisal. For example, don't just say "I'm good at communication." Dig a little to uncover what's really distinctive about your strength as a communicator. Ask yourself: "What is it that makes me really good at this?" It might be empathy for your audience. It might be mastery of language, or an ability to think on your feet. You might be open and honest in a way that always wins people over.

Also remember that you're looking for the kind of personal qualities that truly energize you when you give them free rein. We've all learned to do plenty of things we don't totally love, in response to the challenges of our jobs and personal lives. But to put our brains in discovery mode, we want to stimulate the neurochemistry of interest and reward, not the neurochemistry of duty and obligation. So, as you think about your personal peaks, try to distinguish between those moments where you were doing the things you're *supposed* to enjoy, and the moments when you really were feeling fired up.

Ted is an engineer by background and a senior executive in a global electrical manufacturing company, and he puts it this way. "I'd always assumed that since I was good at analytical work, analysis was my biggest strength. But contrary to my beliefs about myself, where I got real energy from was teaching others. When I looked back, to my surprise, the real highs happened when I was helping to develop our young high-potentials. I remember running a brainstorming session with them, to encourage them to be more imaginative in their thinking, and it was more enjoyable than anything else I was doing." Following this revelation, Ted made more time in his days for coaching and mentoring junior colleagues—with the result that he felt more excited by his work than he had for the previous two decades.

## FIND NEW WAYS TO APPLY YOUR STRENGTHS

Now, how can you apply your strengths more deliberately to your workday? How would you approach your tasks differently if you were applying one of your personal strengths?

When I worked at McKinsey, I discovered that I had a particular appetite for inventing new services for our clients. (Perhaps no surprise, given that my top strength on Seligman and Peterson's character strengths survey turned out to be "love of learning.") McKinsey had an established way of launching these kinds of entrepreneurial initiatives, which entailed presenting your ideas to colleagues until you found someone who thought your ideas could help their clients. I started my first business-building effort that way, when I was establishing a service to improve the effectiveness of senior executive teams. It involved a lot of long nights, some delightful teammates, a lot of paper, and a long, slow accretion of small but spreading successes that left me feeling great in the long run. But along the way, I felt drained by the effort.

So the next time I started a new initiative, I tried something different. I decided to play to the interpersonal qualities that also figured strongly in my list of signature strengths, by using a more people-focused approach. My entrepreneurial goal this time around was to build a new business in helping healthcare organizations improve their performance. Instead of writing pages of material, this time I sent an enthusiastic email to hundreds of people, asking who might be interested in helping out. A few generous souls replied—more than enough to get started. Then I focused on creating and nurturing a community of colleagues who would build the new service together. Some people helped hospitals redesign patient care; others helped biotech companies speed up their drug development processes. I would convene meetings for them to share their experience and expertise with each other, while giving them all the support I could. This approach meant a rather different set of priorities for me as a leader. For one thing, I worried less about formal presentations. I spent much less time in front of a computer, and much more time in coaching conversations with my new community.

Both approaches ended up being successful, for me and for the firm. Neither was the "right" approach. But the energy I got from tapping into my extroverted personality meant I felt as if I was on a perpetual high the second time around. Of course, if a top strength of mine had instead been "making order out of chaos," I might still have gotten other people involved. But then I would have focused on coordinating the creation of a seamless standardized product, rather than encouraging my colleagues to let a hundred flowers bloom. And *that* would have been highly energizing for me. The point is, we can approach the same task in many different ways—and our chances of having fun and being brilliant are higher when we're using at least one of our strengths as a springboard.

So consider how you can use your talents and interests more fully in your work, especially in areas where you're uninspired or overwhelmed. For example, explore whether you could:

➡ Apply your strengths in the way you approach your existing work. Think about the tasks on your plate right now. What would it take to use your strengths more fully in the way you tackle them? For example, if you know you're good at finding clarity amid confusion, can you be more deliberate in using that talent to help yourself and others stay focused on what matters? If you have strong social intelligence, can you do more to engage a coalition of supporters around the work you're doing, or to address important interpersonal angles that colleagues might otherwise miss?

➡ Use your strengths to help you embrace new challenges. When we take on a new responsibility, we usually have plenty to learn—but we can still lean on what we know we're good at to keep ourselves in discovery mode as we wrestle with what's unfamiliar. For example, perhaps you're giving a presentation to your board for the first time. If you're great at digging insights out of complex data, you might choose to lead with a startling fact and build your presentation from that starting point. But if you enjoy meeting new people, you might decide to find out about each board member's interests, so you can speak directly to them in the meeting. Either way, you'll be more relaxed and impressive than if you completely ignored what you know you're good at.

These subtle tweaks can make the difference between you feeling exhausted and having energy left at the end of the day. And over time, being aware of your strengths puts you in a better position to create and seize opportunities that will add to your daily job satisfaction, by taking on tasks or projects that reflect your strengths more fully. This doesn't mean changing jobs or taking on more work, necessarily—it just means taking the initiative to redefine the focus of your job, within your existing job description. It's what management professors Amy Wrzesniewski (Yale) and Jane Dutton (University of Michigan) call "job crafting."[6]

Ben discovered the power of job crafting when he was working for an agency that provided civilian oversight of the New York Police Department. An average day might involve conducting community interviews and reviewing ballistics reports—but in the evenings, he'd shift gears completely by performing on the stand-up comedy circuit. Ben enjoyed his day job, he says, but he liked it even more when he found ways to apply his wider talents as a performer. He shares an example: "I worked with three other colleagues, and our team had a number of training commitments, such as giving lectures on how search-and-seizure laws work. Any one of us could have done it, but I volunteered to give them because I realized it was a chance for me to make use of my relative comfort with being onstage. I could be funny and entertaining, which held people's attention, making the sessions more impactful. I realized that humor could be an asset to me in any context, not just after work." Reflecting on this, Ben says: "You need to make a commitment to understanding yourself. Get an honest view of what's enjoyable to you, and then figure out how to do more of those things. That way, you can avoid being one of those guys whose only focus at work is keeping their heads above water."

## PUTTING YOUR PERSONAL INTERESTS TO WORK

Ben found a way to bring a private talent more fully into the workplace. But what if your personal interests seem nothing at all to do with your day job? What then? That's where Catherine (from the previous chapter) was, some time back. She'd been in her job as a senior operational manager for five years, and she found she was starting to get less energy out of her days than she was putting in. "On the surface, everything seemed great. I was still getting the work out the door. But my motivation was getting weaker. The days felt longer, and it seemed to take ages to get anything done."

Ever since childhood, Catherine had been into art, literature, and history, and she'd even had a spell working for a classical music recording company. But now her days were filled with budgeting and knocking heads together. One day, she had a chance conversation with someone about her past. "This guy commented on how mismatched my interests were with what I did for a living. He asked me, 'How do you stay sane?' and I realized he was right—something was missing." Her cultural interests felt completely separate from her day-to-day work.

Catherine decided to be more creative in finding a way to connect the things she loved to the things she did for a living. "I embarked on what I called a 'structured reinspiration program.' I'd watch a classic movie every week with my professional life in mind, and take something from it into my work. For example, one had the character of Thomas More in it, who was basically an administrator in King Henry VIII's court in sixteenth-century England, and I realized his job was not unlike mine." Identifying with More's courage in standing up to the king gave her a lift. Leaving aside the historical detail that More ended up being beheaded, "there was at least one day when thinking of Thomas More helped me to take a stand about something I cared about at work, in a way I felt good about."

Catherine started visiting art galleries with the same goal. She would pick a painting to look at, then think about how it related to issues she was wrestling with at work. "It always put a spring in my step," she says. "Sometimes I came away inspired with a new idea. Sometimes it just made me feel better about something bad happening at work. After all, there's so much tragedy in history that it helps you see that someone screwing up slightly is okay. Life will go on."

And that paid dividends in the way she felt about her job, she says. "My days quickly started to feel less bogged down. I felt like my horizons opened up again, and I was able to focus again on what was possible in my job, with more creativity in thinking of solutions." And now whenever she feels at a low ebb, Catherine says, "I tell myself, 'Time for a reinspiration intervention.' It always works."

To create your own "reinspiration program" based on your interests outside work, ask yourself:

➡ What topics or activities most interest you? What do you find genuinely intriguing to read or learn about, without being asked or expected to do so?

➡ How might you make a stronger connection between that interest and your everyday work?

- Could it yield an insight you can apply in a professional context?
- Is there a technique or tool you could borrow?
- Failing that, could you form an interest group with like-minded colleagues—a book group, a choir, a team—to bring more personal joy into the workplace?

In his book *Give and Take*, University of Pennsylvania psychologist Adam Grant describes an experiment where employees were given a chance to do exactly what Ben and Catherine did, crafting a "more ideal but still realistic vision of their jobs" by adapting their responsibilities to match their personal strengths, interests, and values. Some took on new projects. Some customized existing tasks to make them feel more enjoyable or meaningful. Many found ways to delegate tasks that simply weren't a great fit—perhaps using a version of the "positive no" technique I mentioned in Part II. Grant reports that "six weeks later, their managers and co-workers rated them as significantly happier *and* more effective."[7] And that's something we would surely all say yes to.

## Playing to Your Strengths

To sustain your professional energy and enthusiasm (and boost your performance) over time:

➡ Identify your signature strengths. Set aside time to reflect on your signature strengths—the personal qualities, values, and skills that are characteristic of you when you're at your best. Examine your peaks, ask others for input, and take a survey. Notice the themes that emerge.

➡ Apply your strengths more consciously. Every day for a week, find a way to play to one of your strengths more fully in the way you approach your work. When you take on new challenges, consider how to use your personal strengths to help you embrace the things you need to learn.

➡ Harness your personal interests for reinspiration. Be creative about ways you can relate your personal interests to your work. What insight or tool might you be able to bring into your professional life?

# Making It Stick

I'd like to leave you with some final words of encouragement as you try out the approaches in the book, because I know it can sometimes feel hard to break old habits and adopt glorious new ones. We might mean to set deliberate intentions for an important conversation, but then forget to do it until we're already halfway through the meeting. We might like the idea of using "brain-friendly feedback" techniques with our junior colleagues, but then find ourselves doing what we've always done: simply telling them what they should do differently. None of that is surprising given that our brains seek to save energy by running on autopilot where they can. Left to themselves, they'll tend to run the same old routines.

And yet, despite the stickiness of our habits, our brains are tremendously adaptable. Every single new thought or experience channels a fresh set of connections between our billions of neurons, with the result that our neural networks are always changing. That's why Professor Michael Merzenich of U.C. San Francisco, one of the world's experts on the brain's ability to reorganize itself, describes the brain as "soft-wired" rather than hard-wired: partly fixed, yes, but partly flexible.[1] This soft-wiring is what gives us scope to develop new skills and practices, *if* we know how to nurture our inherent capacity for change.

So what can we do to shift the balance from autopilot to adaptability? Three useful pointers emerge from the research: reward, remind, and repeat.

## REWARD

When you do score a success in trying a new approach at work, do you stop to congratulate yourself? Most people don't. As we saw in Chapter 10, we tend to bank successes without too much reflection, because our attention is naturally drawn to the things that *didn't* work so well. But neuroscientists, economists, and psychologists all agree that we're more likely to repeat a behavior if we find it rewarding, because the payoff motivates our brains to seek out more of that behavior. So if you want a new habit to stick, it's a good idea to find some way to reward yourself for any effort you make.

What kind of reward am I talking about? Well, most obviously, you could allow yourself a personal treat—a break, a snack, a chat. But rewards that involve reviewing our successes are even more useful, since reflection is a cognitive process that enhances our ability to learn from our experience (as we saw in Chapter 5).

For example, suppose you tried a brain-friendly feedback technique when talking to a colleague, and it resulted in a satisfyingly productive conversation. Like Peter in Chapter 10, you started by detailing all the things you liked about something they'd done, before saying what would make you like it even better. Your colleague was visibly energized rather than demotivated by your input, and came up with an excellent plan for improvement. Great! But it will be easy for you to forget about that triumph once the next challenge of the day rolls around. So you should take a moment to review what worked well—ideally, make a note of it, too—and let yourself feel good about it for a few seconds.

I know one professional who extends the reward further by keeping a tally of these kinds of successes on a whiteboard by the door in his office (using a code that only he understands); he says it gives him a boost each time he walks past it. You can also add a social dimension to the sense of reward, by telling others about the changes you're making and the interesting results you're seeing. Bigger triumphs can even be added to a running list of achievements to talk about during your next performance review, as Cristine showed in Chapter 16. All these actions help to feed your brain's reward system, as well as reinforcing what you've learned.

What if you do something new and it doesn't work exactly as you'd hoped? Draw on the fact that we find it rewarding to discover new information, by choosing to view the experience as an experiment. Ask yourself the "How fascinating! What can I learn from this?" question from Chapter 17. And salute whichever aspects of your "experiment" *did* work—even if it's merely that you remembered afterward what it was you were supposed to do.

## REMIND

If you want to change your behavior, it helps to make the shift as effortless as possible. One way of doing that is to decide on a very specific, achievable aim, and then to link that desired new behavior to something that's already part of your day. The trick is to identify a cue that you'll definitely encounter—perhaps an activity, a situation, or an object—and to associate that cue with the action you want to take. As I said in Chapter 2, research suggests that establishing these sorts of "when-then" reminders can triple your chances of achieving your goals. Which is pretty great.

For example, if you're trying to get better at building exercise into your day, it's going to take time for your brain to form all the new connections needed for you to develop a whole new gym habit. But you can make immediate progress if you use something you already do regularly (e.g., go to lunch) as a prompt for the action you want to take (more exercise). You might say to yourself, "*when* I go to lunch, *then* I will take the stairs rather than the elevator." You might go further and say "*whenever* I see a choice between stairs and elevator, *then* I'll take the stairs." Going back to the example of the brain-friendly feedback techniques, you might make a note of the steps on your phone, and decide: "*when* I feel a burning need to provide input to a colleague, *then* I will check my phone to decide which feedback technique to use."

For a more visual approach, you could take inspiration from several of my clients who use their screensavers as reminders of the approaches in this book. One of them has an image of an iceberg on her screen; when she looks at it, she remembers the "good person, bad circumstances" idea, because the submerged iceberg reminds her that everyone's behavior reflects hidden influences below the surface. I met another person who prefers tactile reminders; he keeps a pebble in his jacket pocket, because he says it helps him remember whatever new habit he's working on whenever he touches it. (It's not a bad idea: pebbles are cheap and have great battery life.)[2] Everyone's different. Choose whichever reminders make sense to you and are easiest to build into your daily routine.

### REPEAT, REPEAT, REPEAT

As kids, we worked hard at learning to ride a bike; when we fell off, we got back on again, until it became second nature to us. But when we try something novel in our adult lives we'll typically make just one attempt before judging whether it's worked. If we don't quite pull it off the first time, or if it feels a little awkward, we'll tell ourselves it wasn't a success rather than giving it another shot.

That's a shame, because repetition is central to the process of re-wiring our brains. Consider the idea that your brain has a network of neurons that will connect with each other whenever you remember to use a brain-friendly feedback technique. Those connections aren't very reliable at first, which may make your first efforts a little hit-and-miss. You might remember one of the steps involved, and not the others. But I mentioned in Chapter 3 that neuroscientists have a saying: "neurons that fire together, wire together." In other words, repetition of an action strengthens the connections between the neurons involved in that action. That means the more times you try using that new feedback technique, the more easily it will come to you when you need it.

So it's worth channeling some of your childhood perseverance when trying something new. Remind yourself that it's okay if your first attempts aren't perfect; each try is still worthwhile, because it helps to strengthen a useful new pattern of connections in your brain. And eventually, that "new" technique will be the first thing that naturally comes to mind when you need it.

◆ ◆ ◆

Finally, I'd encourage you to try everything in the book at least once until you find the techniques that most resonate with you. As Ros, the healthcare executive, puts it: "You can intellectually know that some-thing is a good idea, but the point at which you really learn is when you try it out for real. And understanding that it takes time for new approaches to get imprinted on your brain has freed me from worrying about getting it right the first time." Doug, our retailer, concludes: "It takes some trial and error to see what works best for you, so it helps to experiment. Then, if you keep the skills fresh by using them regularly, I've found you're in better and better shape to handle things well—whatever the day throws your way." And that seems a very fine note to end on.

# How to Be Good at Meetings

Meetings come in many guises—informal chats, routine check-ins, slow-paced calls, fancy presentations. Our days are often peppered with them. But that's not usually seen as a good thing. "Meeting" has somehow become a dirty word; when we hear someone say "I had a day full of meetings," we feel pity rather than envy. How have we let that happen? Meetings are a form of interaction, and we're social creatures. So why do we see them as so onerous?

The answer, I think, is that we often pay a lot of attention to *what* we're discussing—the document we're sharing, the decision we need to make, the message we want to get across—and very little attention to *how* we're having the conversation. Think about the last meeting you were in. How much time went into thinking about the setup of the conversation and the right way to encourage great contributions from everyone? Not much, I'd guess. I can't count the number of times I've seen smart people spend hard, long weeks putting together a presentation, followed by just a few bare minutes—often on the way to the meeting—on how to make the most of the interaction. It's a huge missed opportunity.

So this section is designed to help you apply the advice in *How to Have a Good Day* to each meeting you have. If you only try even one or two of these ideas, it should enable you to start recapturing the love—whether you're running the meeting or just attending it.

## PREPARING FOR THE MEETING

Some steps you can take to prepare yourself for a good meeting:

➡ Set intentions, by answering these kinds of questions before you walk in:
  - Aim: If you could achieve only one thing in the meeting, what would it be? So what really matters most?
  - Attitude: Acknowledge what's top of mind for you as you go into the meeting. Recognize that this will shape your experience.
  - Assumptions: Specifically, do you have any negative expectations about the meeting? Can you challenge them?
  - Attention: Given your actual aim, where do you want to focus your attention in the meeting? What do you want to notice?
  - (Think about the other attendees. What might be *their* answers to these intention-setting questions?)

➡ Actions: What specific actions will help you make those intentions a reality? Which "when-then" triggers will remind you to do these things?

➡ Mental contrasting: What's going to get in the way of things going as you hope? What can you plan to do, to keep things on track?

➡ Mind's-eye rehearsal: Visualize the way you'd like this upcoming meeting to go. What does success look like?

➡ Mind-body loops: If you're stressed about the meeting, use physical feedback loops to encourage your brain to come off high alert: smile broadly and breathe deeply; spread yourself out—shoulders back, head up, feet firmly planted. Try it in a restroom or when greeting people (as well as during the meeting).

If you have a hand in planning the meeting, also try these steps:

➡ Make the meeting slightly shorter than a full hour or half hour, to give people some mental recovery time afterward. (And don't let it run longer than ninety minutes without a proper break.)

➡ Try listing and introducing agenda items as questions, not statements. (For example, "How can we improve team communication?" rather than "Team communication.")

➡ Choose the location and set up the space to mirror what you want from the discussion. Want informality? Push formal tables to the side, or at least sit on adjoining sides of the table rather than opposite each other. Upbeat discussion? Make sure the room is brightly lit. And so on.

### STARTING ON A STRONG FOOTING

➡ Encourage some collaborative goal setting by asking, "Where do we want to be by the end of this meeting?" And then "What's the best way for us to achieve that?" (These are questions you can ask even if you're not formally chairing the meeting.)

➡ If you can, suggest a no-devices rule. Otherwise, people will use up some of their brain's precious working memory on monitoring their phones and tablets, making everyone just a little dumber than they would be if they were concentrating on the conversation. In long meetings, I've been known to set up a "smartphone daycare" box where people can voluntarily deposit their phones, with visiting rights during breaks. (If you can't do any of this, at least put your own devices away.)

➡ Start with something positive to put people into discovery mode. It doesn't have to be hokey—you can just ask people to share recent successes. Ask "What's going well so far?" or "What's the best thing that's happening on your part of the project?"

### MAKING YOUR MARK

➡ To make your contributions memorable, illustrate your points with an anecdote or real-life example that shows the effect on colleagues or customers.

➡ With longer comments, break your point into clear chunks to make it easier for people to process what you're saying. "There are three things that strike me about this. One . . . Two . . . Three . . ."

➡ If you need to disagree or raise a concern, help others stay in open-minded discovery mode as you share your views by using one of the brain-friendly feedback techniques. (a) Say what you like about the idea on the table. Be very specific. Then say, "What would make me like it more is . . ." (b) Say "yes, and . . ." rather than "yes, but . . ." (c) Ask "what would have to be true to make that work?"

➡ Provide cues that nudge people toward whatever you need from them. If you want three suggestions, write an indicative "1, 2, 3" on a flip chart. Ask "If you had three suggestions, what would they be?"

## IMPROVING THE DISCUSSION

### Avoiding Groupthink

It can feel great to reach quick agreement. But if you're talking about something important and there's no challenge in the room, you're probably missing part of the picture. Ask some of these questions to improve the group's thinking:

➡ "If we had to pick holes in this, where would they be?"

➡ "If Person X were here, criticizing our idea, what would they say—and what would we need to do to reassure them?"

➡ "Let's project forward and assume things have gone badly wrong. What did we miss?"

➡ "Who's going to be affected by our plans? What will they worry about?"

➡ "If we played devil's advocate, what would be the other side of the argument?"

### Reaching Closure

You may have the opposite problem, where there's nothing anyone agrees on. Reduce the temperature in the room by doing this:

➡ Clarify what you can all agree on. That promotes a sense of in-group and calms people's instinctive threat response.

➡ Ask if it's possible to agree to disagree on the rest. The answer might be yes, if it's clear that you already agree on the things that matter.

➡ If not: Do your best to summarize each position objectively, doing justice to each idea. Ask what would have to be true for each position to be the best one. Decide together on the process for getting evidence to test each position.

If the issue is less about disagreement and more about lack of focus, create a "parking lot" for off-topic ideas or issues that surface during the conversation. It helps everyone feel heard while focusing people's attention on the meeting's real priorities. Make a visible list on a flip chart, whiteboard, or notepad.

### HANDLING CHALLENGING BEHAVIOR

If people are being annoying, remember that they're probably feeling threatened by one of the common triggers: exclusion, unfairness, feeling unappreciated, a lack of autonomy, lack of competence, a threat to their values, or uncertainty. If they didn't get enough sleep or are physically exhausted, their sensitivity to all these sorts of "threats" will also be heightened. To improve the situation, ask yourself:

➡ What exactly are they doing or saying? (Just observe the facts.)

➡ What could be triggering those actions—what need of theirs might not be getting met?

➡ How can you reduce that "threat" by meeting that need more fully? For example, even if you're not in the chair, you can help them feel included by expressing interest in their views, and you can make them feel heard and respected by referring back to something they've said.

## WRAPPING UP

Always allow a moment to recap key decisions or reflect on the insights gained from the meeting, and agree on steps that each person will take. If you can, also do some kind of positive roundup. You can combine it with a "next steps" summary from each person, by asking everyone to say (a) one thing they were interested or inspired to hear in the meeting, and (b) what they're committed to doing, by when.

## LIGHTENING THE LOAD

One last point. Many people say they hate meetings because there are just too many in their schedule. Improving meetings helps, but they simply need fewer of them. If that rings true to you, consider taking inspiration from Nayan, the bank CFO we met in Chapter 12. After taking a hard look at his schedule, he discovered he was signed up for no fewer than forty-two regular, repeating meetings. To slash the number of meetings he was attending, we applied some of the concepts from Chapter 6, on managing overload.

First, Nayan thought about what mattered most to him professionally for the coming year—what his big-picture intentions were. It quickly became clear that many of his meetings were unconnected to those priorities; they were a legacy of past commitments. For those meetings, he began to send out a series of "positive nos," to extricate himself gracefully. Then, for the remaining meetings that truly did match his priorities, he asked himself whether attending passed the "comparative advantage" test: Was he truly the only person who could contribute? Or could someone more junior step in for him and do a reasonable job? By attending only those meetings where he had a unique role to play, he not only created opportunities for his younger colleagues to shine, but halved the number of meetings he regularly attended. And got his life back.

# How to Be Good at Email

Professional email traffic accounts for 110 billion messages a day, and that figure is growing steadily.[1] Email has great advantages: it's faster than a meeting, it's more flexible than a phone call, and it conveys more formality than instant messaging or SMS. But if you ask anyone what they think of email, you're likely to encounter at least one roll of the eyes. They'll talk about feeling overwhelmed by the sheer volume of it, for a start. Most of us have a backlog of unanswered messages, many of them unread. And yet: we get annoyed when others don't respond to *us*, or do so in what seems like an offhand manner. Meanwhile, we use email for sensitive purposes that it was never designed to handle. We spend ages drafting a tricky message even though we know we'd easily find the right words if speaking face-to-face. As a result of all this, surveys report, we're typically spending at least a quarter of every day sending and responding to messages, and we're not happy about it.[2]

So what does behavioral science tell us about ways to improve things? What's the best way to send messages that have the impact we want, and manage the inflow so we end up with a happy inbox?

## WRITE EMAILS THAT PEOPLE WANT TO READ

### Make your emails easy to understand and act on

Like it or not, because of the brain's preference for *processing fluency* people are more convinced by information that's easy to process. So:

➡ Keep most email to just a few lines if you can. Use simple language, short sentences, and snappy phrases. Save your rhetoric for your novel or your wedding speech.

➡ For unavoidably longer emails, break them up into short paragraphs and make them easy to navigate, maybe using bullets and headings.

➡ Highlight any action or decision that you're asking the recipient to take. Assume he or she only has time to read the first couple of lines. What would you lead with?

*Start with something positive*

Sometimes you have to flag challenging issues in emails—but emails that put people on the defensive within the first couple of lines often get misinterpreted, because the recipient's brain launches into defensive mode. So:

➡ Start with some appreciation. Instead of writing: "Thanks for the report. Can I give you some comments?" take an extra ten seconds to comment on at least one thing you liked: "Thanks for the report. I liked the way you included the customer perspective. Can I give you some comments?" Praising something specific is more effective than making general warm statements, as we saw in Chapter 10.

➡ Lead with solutions, not problems. Instead of saying: "Unfortunately, our original idea isn't going to work because . . . , so what we're going to do is . . . ," lead with your proposed solution: "What we think will work best is . . . That's different from our original plan because . . ." Same content, different sequence, different emotional impact.

➡ Engage the recipient on why it matters. Suppose somebody's done something wrong. What do you say? "This is a terrible mess. You absolutely have to fix it." You'll get action, but it might be based on defensive rather than smart thinking. Try this approach, which engages their reward system by inviting them to pursue the benefits of resolving the problem: "This is critically important for us to get right because of XYZ. What can you do to fix it?"

*Mirror their tone*

Try to match the other person's tone without losing your own voice. Remember that we're all psychologically drawn to people who look and behave like us, and much less likely to treat others as a potential threat if we think we're on the same team. The smallest things can enhance, or undermine, that in-group feeling.

➡ If the last email you received from them is warm in tone but you have a more formal style, add one warm comment—for example, by saying you're looking forward to seeing the person.

➡ If the other person's communication style is brisk, get to the point quickly in your reply. Brevity doesn't have to mean coldness; you can still be collegial in your tone.

➡ Echo their choice of vocabulary, just as you would naturally do in speech. Consider copying their greeting and sign-off style. Bonus tactic: try to mirror the number of exclamation marks they've used.

### MASTER THE VOLUME

How can you climb out from underneath the weight of your inbox and spend less time on it each day? Behavioral science has a lot to say about this.

*First, stop looking at your email all the time*

Processing our email throughout the day—while working on a task, during meetings, as we're walking—makes us feel busy and efficient. But it means we're taking longer over it than needed. As I explained in Chapter 4, multitasking forces our brains to switch attention from one task to another, wasting time and effort whenever we flit from task to email to task again. Instead, "batch" your emailing so that you process emails a few times every day, not a few times every minute.

*Second, filter your inbox*

Just as our brain wastes time switching from tasks to email and back to tasks again, it wastes some time by flipping between different *types* of emails requiring very different types of cognitive response. There are messages from important people who want a reply, mail you're merely cc'ed on, subscriptions, meeting invitations, and junk of various types. They all make different types of demands on your brain. So you can save yet more neural processing time if you fully exploit your email program's capacity to filter emails into different folders, allowing you to group together different types of email and deal with each in turn. Here are some filters and folders you might want to create:

➡ Email sent from individuals to you directly. If you can, separate out the emails where you're merely cc'ed. You can create a special folder or tab for especially important people.

➡ Calendar invitations should also be separated, if you get a lot of them.

➡ Things to read. It's easy to drown in "things someone thinks you'd find interesting," not to mention subscriptions that end up making you feel burdened rather than informed. I have a folder for potentially useful research material, and I review it once a week or even less frequently.

### Third, Only Handle It Once (OHIO)

When you do engage with the email in your inbox, only handle it once. If you revisit a message three times before replying, you're tripling the time you're giving it—and, as you know, your brain has very limited deliberate system capacity to go around. To paraphrase David Allen, the author of the marvelous book *Getting Things Done*, when you're reviewing your email, aim for one of the four D's:[3]

➡ Do: make the decision and respond.

➡ Delegate: if it's something that can reasonably be handled by someone else, forward it on.

➡ Defer: file for future action or reference. Send an "I'll get back to you" response if needed.

➡ Delete: if none of the above applies, delete.

Sometimes, despite your best intentions, you can still let an email sit in the inbox day after day. So I take a weekly look at any long-standing email lurking in the inbox and ask: "Is leaving this one more day going to allow me to improve my response?" If the answer is no, I tell myself to just do it, because a short response is better than a late one.

### ACKNOWLEDGE, ACKNOWLEDGE, ACKNOWLEDGE

### *Avoid radio silence*

If you value the sender, don't sit on his or her email. People's brains see social exclusion and uncertainty as a threat, and you pose that threat in a minor way every time you delay in responding to an email. The sender doesn't know if you've got it, read it, hated it, thought it foolish, ignored it, or deleted it. That's not good for your relationship. So, for people who matter to you:

➡ Send a short, positive email response within twenty-four hours if possible. The longer you leave it, the more you'll feel obliged to write at greater length. If you're not ready to respond to their request, send a one-line acknowledgment: "Thanks for your email. I look forward to getting into it in detail."

➡ If you don't even have time to send a one-liner, consider setting up an automated email response explaining that you're going through a busy period and conveying your likely response time. While I was working on this book, creating an auto-response that said "I'm busy but I'm not ignoring you" allowed me to process my email when I was properly able to engage with it.

➡ If you get an unmanageable amount of incoming mail from strangers or casual acquaintances, draft some polite, standard email responses that you (or an assistant) can quickly paste and send.

### *Deploying the positive no*

A typical reason we leave email unanswered is that we don't want to deal with the issue that it presents, which is usually the need to dodge or challenge what someone is proposing: "No, I'm afraid I won't be able to meet your deadline" or "No, I don't think we should be going with the high-cost option." Our heart sinks as we think about writing back, so we put it off for another day. Here, it's helpful to use the "positive no" technique I described in Chapter 6. A reminder of how this works:

➡ Start with warmth. Say something appreciative, or at least thank the sender for the email.

➡ Your "yes." Tell the other person about something that you're positively committed to—a goal, a priority, an appointment.

➡ Your "no." *Then* explain that this positive commitment means you need to decline the person's request or suggestion.

➡ End with warmth, by wishing the other person well with his or her endeavors.

We're so used to starting with "I'm sorry" that the positive no often requires a rewrite of your email before you send. If you catch yourself typing those words at the beginning of an email, pause and consider whether there's an opportunity for a more positive opening.

### PUT THE FLAMES OUT

Try not to send email when you're freshly irritated or upset about something. You're probably in defensive mode, so the smarter part of your brain will be taking a backseat. As a result, however carefully phrased you think your killer email is, you won't be using your most sophisticated mental resources as you draft it. Pause and revisit when you're calmer—perhaps after a night's sleep.

If you find it cathartic to type out an angry note, using the *affect labeling* technique from Chapter 17, then type away—but first delete all the names from your "To" field so that you can't inadvertently broadcast your anger to the world. Save it to the drafts folder when done, so you can revisit it and think, "Thank goodness I didn't send that."

If the source of the irritation is an annoying email you received, don't immediately assume bad intent on the part of the sender. Remember that we tend to make the *fundamental attribution error,* assuming that negative behavior is driven by negative motivations rather than circumstances. It means we often assume that a curt email comes from a rude rather than rushed sender. And if we're reading in an irritable frame of mind, we can also suffer from *inattentional blindness* and completely miss more conciliatory nuances. How many times have you gone back to reread an ostensibly outrageous email, only to realize that it wasn't as bad as it first seemed?

Taken together, those two pieces of advice add up to a third: don't handle sensitive interactions over email if you can avoid it. Call the person or suggest an in-person meeting, especially if you've already exchanged one or two slightly strained messages. Our social brains are fairly good at reading others' feelings, but less so when we're not face-to-face. Researchers found that when people used sarcastic humor in an email, it was correctly understood as sarcasm only 56 percent of the time.[4] People were slightly better at recognizing sarcasm in voice-mail messages, but face-to-face was where people scored most highly on tests of their emotional radar.

### CREATE LESS TRAFFIC

A single email can quickly spawn three, five, or ten more, especially if it's sent to multiple recipients. A study in the *Harvard Business Review* showed how this "contagion ratio" worked in a real office with eighty employees and five executives.[5] When each executive sent ten fewer emails in a day, the number received by everyone else shrank more than three times as much. With those emails taking an average of one and a half minutes to process, that small step freed up four working hours each day. So it's smart business to generate less email traffic, if you can. Here are some steps that help:

➡ **Reduce ambiguity.** Be clear on what you want people to do as a result of reading your email, and be explicit when your messages don't need emailed replies.

➡ **Don't force people to chase you for responses.** Delaying a reply often generates a fresh round of emails. Send a quick holding response if you're underwater.

➡ **Make concrete suggestions on times, locations, and deadlines.** It limits the back-and-forth that happens when making arrangements over email and thanks to *default bias*, your suggestions are quite likely to be accepted.

Follow these suggestions, and your inbox should be less cluttered and less of a source of stress—and your colleagues will thank you for it.

# How to Reinvigorate Your Routine

Very few of us look at our schedules and say, "Wow—that looks like a recipe for joy, please bring it on." But it doesn't take much effort to more proactively include activities that will make the day more delightful. Here is a different way of seeing your daily routine, one that draws on all the science in this book. Use this checklist to design a day that will leave you feeling good.

| | | |
|---|---|---|
| **BEFORE WORK** | Set your intentions | Think about the day ahead—maybe in the shower, maybe on the way to work. Ask yourself: "What matters most today? What does that mean for my attitude, attention, and actions? What specific goals should I set for the day?" |
| | Visualize the ideal | Take a moment to imagine the most important thing you're doing today. Picture yourself doing it and being at your best. Notice what you're doing and saying. |
| | Plan a peak | Decide what you're most looking forward to today, however small. Small becomes bigger when you think about it. |
| **AS YOU GET STARTED** | Batch your tasks | Plan a block of uninterrupted thinking time to work on your most complex task. Create another slot (or two) for reading and responding to all your messages. Batch other similar tasks together—you'll get them done more quickly. |
| | Prime yourself | Decide what mental attributes you most need in your thinking today, and create whatever cues might help prompt that—an image, a song, a change in your workspace setup. |

| DURING THE DAY | Set the tone | Decide what behavior you want from other people and how you can project that tone yourself. They will mirror it back at you, whether either of you realizes it or not. |
| --- | --- | --- |
| | Express random appreciation | Do a random act of kindness. Compliment someone for something, ideally unprompted. Be unexpectedly helpful or generous in some way. Notice the effect on both of you. |
| | Protect your thinking time | In your block of focused thinking time, divert/switch off your devices and notifications. If needed, set expectations for colleagues/clients, e.g., through an automatic email response promising a reply later in the day. |
| | Assume good person, bad circumstances | If you encounter bad behavior, try assuming you're dealing with a decent person whose sense of self-worth or social standing has been threatened. To quickly reduce tension, say something appreciative. |
| | Borrow a good mood | Give yourself a boost using facial feedback: smile. Even a fake smile will start the ball rolling. |
| | Label any frustrations | When you feel irritated or upset, write down what the facts are (free from interpretation) and how they make you feel. If you have time—it can be later—read back what you've written and decide what your "best self" (or wisest friend) would say or do. |
| | Keep your eyes on the prize | At less wonderful moments of the day, ask yourself, "What really matters most today?" Write it on a sticky note or whiteboard—whatever helps to keep it front and center in your mind. |
| | Refresh and reboot | Take a break every ninety minutes, even if it's just getting up and stretching your legs. It's especially important if you're involved in some tough, complex work, where allowing some subconscious processing might help you reach insight. |

| LUNCH | Connect with someone | Make space to have at least one short interaction with someone you like. It doesn't have to be much. If you can't make it happen in person, take a moment to get in touch with a friend or have a warmer-than-usual exchange with a stranger. |
| --- | --- | --- |
| | Do some exercise | Exercise doesn't have to be flashy to boost our mood and focus. Take a brisk walk. Climb the stairs. Do some jumping jacks. It all helps. |
| FOR EACH TASK | Maximize your motivation | Ask yourself: "What's most interesting about this task?" "What's the bigger reason for getting this done?" "If I could apply my personal strengths in the way I do this work, how would I go about it?" "When has this been done well before (by me or others), and what can I learn from that?" |
| | Start on a strong footing | Start with a positive question (e.g., "What's going well so far?" or "What's the ideal outcome?"). Do this before you get into the challenging stuff. |
| | Get unstuck | If something has been on your to-do list for a while, be honest about what's getting in the way—ask a few "whys" until you get to the real blockage. To resolve it, what would you have to do? And what would be the very smallest first step? Replace your to-do with *that*. |
| AT THE END OF THE DAY | End on a high note | Think about the three best things that happened today. Write them in a small bedside notebook, tell your partner as you're unwinding from the day, or use them as a meditative reflection when you're lying in bed. They might be tiny things—that's okay. |
| | Sleep the good sleep | Avoid looking at any lit screens right before bedtime; it will make it harder to sleep. That means not bringing your phone into the bedroom. If you don't have an alarm clock and have to use the phone to wake up, put the phone by the door, facedown. (And then, tomorrow, buy a real alarm clock.) |

# SUGGESTED FURTHER READING

There are many great books for the general reader interested in psychology, behavioral economics, and neuroscience. These are some of my favorites if you want to read more deeply on any of the topics in this book.

First, two wide-ranging books on how neuroscience relates to the working world, touching on many topics in *How to Have a Good Day*:

David Rock, *Your Brain at Work*. How an understanding of neuroscience can improve performance and interactions in the workplace.

Tara Swart, Kitty Chisholm, Paul Brown, *Neuroscience for Leadership*. How to use neuroscience to sharpen your leadership skills.

Then, for each section of the book:

## THE SCIENCE ESSENTIALS

### TWO-SYSTEM BRAIN

Jonathan Haidt, *The Happiness Hypothesis*. Discusses wide-ranging psychological implications of the interplay of the two systems for well-being, and relates these new insights to ancient wisdom on how to live a good life.

Daniel Kahneman, *Thinking Fast and Slow*. Masterwork from one of the most influential thinkers in behavioral science.

### DISCOVER-DEFEND AXIS

Matt Lieberman, *Social*. The importance of social threats and rewards, and the implications of our highly social nature.

Dan Pink, *Drive*. The importance of intrinsic rewards for motivation: autonomy, competence, purpose.

## MIND-BODY LOOP

Arianna Huffington, *The Sleep Revolution*. Engaging overview of the issues in modern society's view of sleep, and how to get more of the kind of rest you need.

Gretchen Reynolds, *The First 20 Minutes*. Accessible review of research on the powerful effects of even small amounts of exercise.

Jon Kabat-Zinn, *Wherever You Go, There You Are*. Classic book showing how to apply mindfulness techniques in modern life. There are many books on secular mindfulness but this is the one they all refer back to.

## PART I: PRIORITIES

Chris Chabris and Daniel Simons, *The Invisible Gorilla*. Entertaining review of the overwhelming evidence on selective attention.

Heidi Grant Halvorson, *Succeed*. The book to read if you want to go deeper into how to set goals you'll actually meet.

David Allen, *Getting Things Done*. Classic book which spans Part I and Part II in its advice on the right way to set clear intentions, create to-do lists, and manage your time accordingly.

## PART II: PRODUCTIVITY

Edward Hallowell, *Driven to Distraction at Work*. A practical program for retraining you to focus your attention more effectively.

Paul Hammerness and Margaret Moore. *Organize Your Mind, Organize Your Life*. Weaves neuroscience around stories of people who've changed their routine to allow them to think more clearly and get more done.

Tim Ferriss, *4-Hour Workweek*. Wide-ranging practical advice on ways to think creatively about where you spend your time.

## PART III: RELATIONSHIPS

Douglas Stone, Bruce Patton, Sheila Heen, *Difficult Conversations*. Step-by-step guidance on navigating tough conversations.

Max Landsberg, *The Tao of Coaching*. Great (short) book for those keen to adopt the GROW coaching model.

Nancy Kline, *Time to Think*. Describes a system for improving any interaction through more effective listening.

## PART IV: THINKING

Tom Kelley and David Kelley, *Creative Confidence*. Shows how creative thinking can be encouraged even in non-creative types of work.

Dan Ariely, *Predictably Irrational*. Enjoyable illustration of how our choices are subject to cognitive shortcuts, by one of the giants of behavioral economics.

Edward Russo and Paul Schoemaker, *Winning Decisions*. Practical advice on how to make great business decisions, including case studies and worksheets.

### PART V: INFLUENCE

Chip and Dan Heath, *Made to Stick*. Expands on the topic of making sure all your messages have real impact.

Richard Thaler and Cass Sunstein, *Nudge*. Famous behavioral economics book describing how policy makers can nudge people toward making good choices.

Adam Grant, *Give and Take*. Compelling explanation of the importance of reciprocity, and the benefits of giving as well as taking.

### PART VI: RESILIENCE

Carol Dweck, *Mindset*. Optimism-inspiring review of the evidence showing that seeing scope for change and learning boosts both performance and well-being in the face of failure.

Victor Frankl, *Man's Search for Meaning*. Prisoner-of-war memoir that beautifully illustrates the power of reappraisal and mental contrasting.

Bill George, *True North*. How to get clearer on the psychological pillars that can support you through ups and downs. Framed in the context of leadership, but the core of the book is relevant to anyone.

### PART VII: ENERGY

Jim Loehr and Tony Schwartz, *The Power of Full Engagement: Managing Energy, Not Time, Is the Key to High Performance and Personal Renewal*. Practical advice on boosting multiple types of energy.

Sonja Lyubomirsky, *The How of Happiness*. Guidance on ways to build the energy-boosting activities in Part VII into your life, as well as boosting your resilience (Part VI) when things go wrong.

Marcus Buckingham, *Go Put Your Strengths to Work*. Shows how to adapt your work to allow you to play to your strengths more fully.

### POSTSCRIPT

Norman Doidge, *The Brain That Changes Itself*. Readable yet in-depth review of the way the brain adapts to the demands placed on it.

Charles Duhigg, *The Power of Habit*. Further explanation of the mechanism of habit formation, and its application to personal (and organizational) change.

# GLOSSARY

**AMYGDALA (OR AMYGDALAE, PL.):** Two almond-shaped brain areas that play a central role in processing ambiguous, uncertain, or novel emotional experiences, including potentially threatening situations. Part of the brain's *survival circuits*.

**ANCHORING:** If we're exposed to a piece of information (an "anchor"), even if it's irrelevant to the question at hand, we'll subliminally use it as a starting point for our thinking—and we won't drift too far from it.

**ATTRIBUTION ERROR:** Making a mistake in our assumptions about the motivations behind other people's behavior. See also *Fundamental Attribution Error*.

**AUTOMATIC SYSTEM:** Also known as reflexive (or "X") system, system 1, fast system, or the unconscious. Wide range of brain areas that together control the majority of the brain's activity, acting below the level of our consciousness.

**CERTAINTY EFFECT:** We generally prefer the "sure thing" to taking risk and prefer to avoid ambiguity where we can.

**COMPARATIVE ADVANTAGE:** The task where the gap between your capabilities and someone else's is biggest. (Contrast with "absolute advantage," which simply says you're better than someone else at doing something.)

**CONFIRMATION BIAS:** We tend to seek out information that confirms our expectations and assumptions, and tend to ignore anything contradictory. Example of *selective attention*.

**CURSE OF KNOWLEDGE:** Where knowing something leads you to overestimate the chances that someone else knows that same thing, making you inadvertently unclear in your communication.

**DECISION FATIGUE:** The intense cognitive load created by taking many decisions in succession, as a result of decision making being tiring for the brain's *deliberate system*. Results in a decline in performance of the deliberate system.

**DEFAULT BIAS:** If someone makes a clear suggestion that's halfway reasonable and requires no active decisions from us, we'll generally accept it.

**DEFENSIVE MODE:** The state where the brain diverts significant mental energy toward an automatic defensive (*fight, flight, or freeze*) response to a perceived physical, social, or personal *threat*, whether real or imagined. Reduces the resources available to the brain's *deliberate system*. See also *discovery mode*.

**DELIBERATE SYSTEM:** Also known as the controlled (or "C") system, system 2, slow system, executive function, or the conscious part of the brain. Responsible for sophisticated cognitive functions including: reasoning, self-control (including emotional regulation and the ability to focus our attention), and planning (including weighing the future vs. the present). Capacity for all these functions is limited by the size of our *working memory*.

**DISCOUNTING:** We prefer options that deliver real benefits here and now, versus options that aren't going to pay off right away. They're more taxing to wrap our heads around, so we value them less.

**DISCOVERY MODE:** A state where we're focused on the rewarding aspects of an experience rather than on the potential threats it poses to us, allowing us to stay out of *defensive mode* and therefore maximize the mental resources available to the brain's *deliberate system*.

**EINSTELLUNG EFFECT:** The cognitive impairment experienced when we have a task that's unfinished in the back of our minds, as a result of a small amount of mental energy being devoted to mulling that incomplete task.

**EMOTIONAL REGULATION:** The ability to keep our emotions fairly stable in the face of ups and downs, rather than spiraling into despair when things go wrong.

**ENDOWMENT EFFECT:** We place disproportionate value on things we already have, versus things we don't have that are of equal value. Applies even when there is no sentimental attachment involved.

**FIGHT-FLIGHT-FREEZE:** Three common alternative forms of protective reaction launched by the brain in *defensive mode*. "Fight or flight" is the typical phrasing in everyday speech, but "freeze" is another common threat response which typically results when there's uncertainty about the nature of the potential threat.

**FUNDAMENTAL ATTRIBUTION ERROR:** A common *attribution error*, where we assume bad behavior in others results from bad character, rather than from difficult circumstances that are causing a good person to behave badly.

**GROUPTHINK:** If everyone around us thinks something, we're likely to agree. Not only does it save our brain some energy in working out what to think, but it gives us an evolutionarily important sense of belonging.

**IMPLEMENTATION INTENTION:** The technical name for a "when-then" goal, where we articulate a clear situational trigger to remind us to take the action we intend to take. (Also known as an "if-then.")

**INATTENTIONAL BLINDNESS:** Our *automatic system* tends to direct our conscious attention to anything that we believe to be important, while filtering out other information so that we're not aware of it. Example of *selective attention*.

**IN-GROUP:** People who seem like us in some way, who are therefore less likely to be treated by our brain as a potential threat.

**LOSS AVERSION:** Losses loom larger in our minds than gains of the same size; we get more upset at the prospect of losing $10 than we get excited at the prospect of winning $10.

**MENTAL CONTRASTING:** An approach to goal-setting that contrasts the ideal outcome with the reality of the obstacles we're currently facing, resulting in a more robust and successful plan of action.

**OMISSION BIAS:** We tend to assess the pros and cons of doing something, but not to assess the pros and cons of *not* doing that thing.

**PEAK-END EFFECT:** The value we place on an experience is disproportionately affected by its peak and the way it ends. It saves us thinking about all the data in between those points.

**PLANNING FALLACY:** We tend to estimate the time it will take to complete a task based on the best experience we've ever had, rather than the average time it's taken in the past.

**PREFRONTAL CORTEX:** Evolutionarily newer part of the brain where much of the *deliberate system*'s activity occurs.

**PRESENT BIAS:** It takes a lot of mental energy to conceive of the abstract future, so we tend to give much more weight to whatever's present and known to us.

**PRIMING:** How being exposed to a cue (word, image, object) may help prompt an action or emotion in us, thanks to the *spreading activation mechanism* and an underlying association in our past between that cue and our reaction.

**PROCESSING FLUENCY:** We naturally gravitate toward ideas that are easy to understand. (Also known as "cognitive fluency.")

**PROJECTION BIAS:** We tend to assume that everyone else is more or less like us, so that we don't have to puzzle out why they're behaving the way they're behaving.

**RECENCY BIAS:** Whatever has happened recently tends to dominate our view of what's likely and true about the world.

**REWARD:** Benefits that the brain's *reward system* judges to be worth pursuing. As well as things that meet basic physical needs, includes rewards that boost our sense of self-worth and social standing, and informational gains.

**REWARD SYSTEM:** Complex array of brain areas involved in motivating us to seek out and pursue potentially rewarding experiences. See *reward*.

**SELECTIVE ATTENTION:** The subjectivity of our conscious perceptions of the world, resulting from our *automatic system* filtering the data and options we consciously perceive.

**SOCIAL PROOF:** If we hear that other people like us are in favor of something, we're also likely to get on board.

**SPREADING ACTIVATION MECHANISM:** Being reminded of one part of a memory can automatically prompt the recall of other related parts of that memory, including associated states of mind.

**STATUS QUO BIAS:** It's mentally taxing to conceive of unknown futures. So we tend to prefer to keep things as they are, all other things being equal.

**SUNK COST FALLACY:** When deciding whether to continue investing in a project, we tend to be distracted by what we've already invested rather than focusing on what's actually at stake: the pros and cons of future investment.

**SURVIVAL CIRCUITS:** Networks in the brain that are engaged in noticing and identifying potential threats, and in launching us into *defensive mode* by triggering a *fight-flight-freeze* response.

**THREAT:** Anything perceived by the brain as potentially undermining our physical security, sense of self-worth, or social standing.

**WORKING MEMORY:** The brain's storage space for temporarily holding and processing information. Limited in capacity but crucial for the functions of the *deliberate system*. (You're using it now to understand this sentence.)

# ACKNOWLEDGMENTS

Writing this broad, personal book has drawn together many threads of my life—with the result that I feel like thanking every person who's ever given me ten minutes of their time. But let me pick out some of the marvelous people who were directly involved in making this project a possibility.

I'll start with the three groups of people at the heart of this book. First, the people who shared their stories—and not just those who ended up being named in the book, but all those whose reflections helped to shape the book. You inspired me greatly with your wisdom, and I'm confident that everyone who reads this book will feel the same. Then, there are the many clients I've worked with over the years, ever willing to try these ways of working and thinking, and ever tolerant of my terrible brain drawings. Through them, I learned how to teach the things that matter most. And to the hundreds of scientists whose work I have merrily plundered for this book, I can't show enough gratitude and awe.

Thank you to Todd Shuster, Jane von Mehren, Esmond Harmsworth—the world-class team at Zachary Shuster Harmsworth who helped me take the germ of an idea and grow it into something far bigger than I could have imagined possible. Thank you to everyone at Crown, for their unstinting excitement about the project and for backing me with such magical skills throughout: especially Roger Scholl, Tina Constable, Cindy Berman, Sally Franklin, Ayelet Gruenspecht, Carisa Hays, Megan Perritt, and Campbell Wharton. Enormous thanks, too, to the team at Pan Macmillan, especially Cindy Chan, Robin Harvie, and Laura Langlois, for making me feel like a rock star on home turf.

There's an extended Sevenshift team that created the space and support I needed to get the book written—I couldn't have done it without them: Hannah Bullmore, Alex Hardy, Susan Moore, Shireen Peermohamed, Tom Warner. Thank you for taking such good care of me. Special thanks to Audree Fletcher, my COO in the first days of the project, for helping me get the whole beast off the ground and being a wise sounding board for all my early ideas.

I owe an unfathomable amount to the colleagues at McKinsey who have supported me over the years. My early mentors in the Organization Practice guided and encouraged my behavioral work, even as it took me far from the crowd: Colin Price was there through it all, showing me the power of high aspirations; Keith Leslie taught me how to design transformative learning experiences; Jonathan Day convinced me that it was desirable to read one nonfiction book every week; Mary Meaney showed me how to build and tell my story. And each of the following people deserves a paragraph of their own to describe the guidance and encouragement they provided at important points in my career: Zafer Achi, Gassan Al-Kibsi, Maria-Eugenia Arias, Nora Aufreiter, Steve Bear, Nina Bhatia, David Birch, Felix Brück, Ian Davis, Derek Dean, Carolyn Dewar, John Dowdy, John Drew, Pierre Gurdjian, Nico Henke, Suzanne Heywood, Nathalie Hourihan, Tsun-yan Hsieh, Vivian Hunt, Neil Janin, Conor Kehoe, Scott Keller, Michiel Kruyt, Kevin Lane, Emily Lawson, Mark Loch, Nick Lovegrove, Judy Malan, Martin Markus, Tore Myrholt, Jeremy Oppenheim, Michael Rennie, Tim Roberts, Peter Slagt, Karen Tanner, Catherine Tilley, David Turnbull, Magnus Tyreman, Laura Watkins, Quentin Woodley.

I want to call out a particularly special group of practitioners for the profound impact they've had on this book. Kirstan Marnane, my treasured thought partner, whose creativity and wisdom have made so many fascinating things possible in my professional life. Joanna Barsh, the remarkable leader of a remarkable revolutionary movement. The extraordinary Centered Leadership gang, in particular: Natacha Catalino, Elizabeth Schwarz Hioe, Johanne Lavoie, Renate Osterchrist, Svea Steinweg, Gauthier van Eetvelde. The brilliant behavioral science skunkworks group: Matthias Birk, Claudia Braun, Nils Cornelissen. At Mobius, Amy Fox and Erica Fox, who've been treasured collaborators, sages, and friends throughout. The ideas and the spirit of all of these people lie between the lines of this book.

Several colleagues have gone out of their way to help me take the book out into the world. In particular, Rik Kirkland has been a source of generous support and enthusiasm from the very earliest stages of the book. Sean Brown and Allen Webb have helped me engage the kind of networks that authors dream of.

And then there are the countless other McKinsey colleagues who made everything possible: the practice and office leaders of every place I touched down in the firm; the partners and teams I worked with (especially in the Organization and Healthcare practices); the world-class researchers and administrators; and the facilities teams who let me do strange things to meeting rooms around the world. Thank you, all.

I've been fortunate to be able to lean on several pillars of the coaching community over the years, people who helped me develop as a practitioner and, at various points, made sure I took my own medicine: Myles Downey, Judith Firman, Carol Kauffman, Jane Meyler, Anne Scoular, David Webster.

I owe thanks to several economists who helped me see beyond the conventional boundaries of the discipline: Andi Kumalo who started it all; Bill Allen, who fostered my interest in the human side of economic development; Paul Fisher, who convinced me that I really was an economist, even if I didn't fit the mold; DeAnne Julius, who showed me that it was possible to roam between the private and public sectors; John Vickers, who encouraged my move to McKinsey; Mervyn King, who taught me never to write a word that I couldn't back up with evidence and good syntax.

Alongside my wonderful editors, Roger Scholl and Cindy Chan, there were some kind and hardy people who reviewed the book in depth, providing invaluable feedback on both stylistic and technical issues: Dan Bilefsky, Molly Crockett, Brian Dumaine, Audree Fletcher, Cabe Franklin, Alex Hardy, Paul Schoemaker, Peter Slagt, Tara Swart, Nik Webb. Their challenges and comments made the book immeasurably better. An additional thanks to my neurobuddies, Molly Crockett and Tara Swart, for many-faceted support that made me both smarter and braver as the months passed. Elizabeth Feldman Barrett and Jessica Payne also gave me more help than I dared to hope for, on affective and cognitive neuroscience respectively. Any weaknesses remaining are mine, all mine.

Many more people generously provided suggestions, help, or encouragement on the book at key points over the four years of the project. They include: David Allen, Guy Barnes, Eric Beinhocker, Vaughan Bell, Lauren Bern, Geoff Bird, Charles Duhigg, Lynda Gratton, Henry Hitchings, Valerie Keller, Max Landsberg, Antony Mayfield, Deborah Mattinson, Margaret Moore, Gus O'Donnell, David Rock, Paul Schoemaker, Owain Service, Laurence Shorter, Greg Simon, Hitendra Wadhwa, and Laurie Young. Thank you to Janet Bedol for teaching me EndNote and saving me from my references. Thanks also to my wonderful family and friends for therapeutic tapas, midterm martinis, and superwomen summits. You cheered me on when I needed it, and didn't mind when I disappeared into the bunker.

Nicole Webb planted all the seeds of this book early in my life: an appetite for intellectual exploration, a love of writing, and an understanding of the transformational power of teaching. Thank you for the weekly pep talks, and for always being willing to talk through whatever was most on my mind (whether it involved dopamine or dinner).

And finally, I'm beyond gratitude to Cabe Franklin, the great thinker and teammate by my side at every step of this adventure. I've been dazzled by your many acts of extreme intellectual and emotional support along the way. No doubt about it—being married to you is the biggest piece of luck there is.

# NOTES

## INTRODUCTION

1. For example, Gallup found that only 29 percent of employees in the US feel engaged by their work, and that "engagement rates trend downward slightly with employees' higher levels of educational attainment." Worldwide, they found only 13 percent felt engaged: Gallup (2013) *State of the American Workplace*. (Free download available from http://www.gallup.com/services/176735/state-global -workplace.aspx.) The Conference Board said "for the eighth straight year, less than half of US workers are satisfied with their jobs," in: Cheng, B., Kan, M., Levanon, G., & Ray, R.L. (2014). *Job Satisfaction Survey*: The Conference Board.

## THE SCIENCE ESSENTIALS

1. Milgram, S. (1963). Behavioral study of obedience. *Journal of Abnormal and Social Psychology, 67*(4), 371–378.

2. Kahneman, D., & Tversky, A. (1979). Prospect theory: An analysis of decision under risk. *Econometrica, 47*(2), 263–291.

3. Keith Stanovich and Richard West, in particular, wrote an influential paper defining the two systems as System 1 and System 2, terminology that Daniel Kahneman also uses. Stanovich, K.E., & West, R.F. (2000). Individual difference in reasoning: Implications for the rationality debate? *Behavioral and Brain Sciences, 23*, 645–726.

4. A version of Daniel Kahneman's Nobel Prize acceptance speech on December 8, 2002, was published as: Kahneman, D. (2003). A perspective on judgment and choice: Mapping bounded rationality. *American Psychologist, 58*(9), 697–720.

5. Kahneman, D. (2011). *Thinking Fast and Slow*. New York: Farrar, Straus and Giroux.

6. When a string of data—for example, a group of digits—is sufficiently closely connected in our memories that recalling one part of it draws forth the rest, it can count as one "chunk." So the reason that we might remember a seven-digit phone number is because we've turned it into two chunks of three and four digits, respectively—or even, with repetition, one single chunk. See: Cowan, N. (2008). What are the differences between long-term, short-term, and working memory? *Progress in*

*Brain Research 169,* 323–338. See also: Cowan, N. (2001). The magical number 4 in short-term memory: A reconsideration of mental storage capacity. *Behavioral and Brain Sciences, 24,* 87–185.

7.   Dux, P.E., Ivanoff, J., Asplund, C.L., & Marois, R. (2006). Isolation of a central bottleneck of information processing with time-resolved FMRI. *Neuron, 52*(6), 1109–1120. (See Chapter 4 for other multitasking references.)

8.   Baumeister, R., & Tierney, J. (2011). *Willpower: Rediscovering the Greatest Human Strength.* New York: Penguin.

9.   Shiv, B., & Fedorikhin, A. (1999). Heart and mind in conflict: The interplay of affect and cognition in consumer decision making. *Journal of Consumer Research, 26,* 278–292.

10. Treisman, A., & Geffen, G. (1967). Selective attention: Perception or response? *Quarterly Journal of Experimental Psychology, 19*(1), 1–17.

11. Simons and Chabris write entertainingly about this and other selective attention research in their book: Chabris, C.F., & Simons, D.J. (2010). *The Invisible Gorilla: And Other Ways Our Intuitions Deceive Us.* New York: Crown. The original academic article is: Simons, D.J., & Chabris, C.F. (1999). Gorillas in our midst: Sustained inattentional blindness for dynamic events. *Perception, 28*(9), 1059–1074. You'll see that those counting black shirts were more likely to see the gorilla, presumably because the gorilla was also black—so their brains treated the gorilla as slightly more "relevant" than those counting white shirts.

12. If you haven't seen the video, I've now blown the surprise. Sorry about that. But if you're still keen to watch it, here it is: https://www.youtube.com/watch?v=vJG698U2Mvo. You can also try watching this excellent video made by psychologist Richard Wiseman, which I use with my clients now that the gorilla (sorry, I mean basketball) video is so widely known: https://www.youtube.com/watch?v=v3iPrBrGSJM.

13. LeDoux, J. (2012). Rethinking the emotional brain. *Neuron, 73*(4), 653–676.

14. Adrenaline is sometimes known as epinephrine, and noradrenaline is sometimes called norepinephrine.

15. The amygdala plays a complex role in directing the brain's attention toward anything that's emotionally ambiguous, whether positive or negative. Research has focused especially on the central role of the amygdala in our response to potential threats. For example, this study found that people's amygdalas respond when exposed to a frightened face for only thirty milliseconds, too short a period to consciously notice: Whalen, P.J., et al. (1998). Masked presentations of emotional facial expressions modulate amygdala activity without explicit knowledge. *Journal of Neuroscience, 18*(1), 411–418. This article found that people's amygdalas subconsciously responded to angry expressions in photos even when they were being asked to focus on buildings in the same photos: Anderson, A.K., Christoff, K., Panitz, D., De Rosa, E., & Gabrieli, J.D. (2003). Neural correlates of the automatic processing of threat facial signals. *Journal of Neuroscience, 23*(13), 5627–5633. In this study, researchers found that damage to the amygdala meant that people weren't able to recognize fearful expressions on others' faces: Adolphs, R., et al. (1995). Fear and the human amygdala. *Journal of Neuroscience, 15*(9), 5879–5891.

16. Arnsten, A. (2009). Stress signalling pathways that impair prefrontal cortex structure and function. *Nature Reviews Neuroscience, 10*(6), 410–422. For a less

academic overview of the basic principle, this is a good read: Arnsten, A. (1998). The biology of being frazzled. *Science, 280* (5370), 1711–1712.

17. Andreas Eder and colleagues review "discover and defend" behavioral patterns in the modern world, in: Eder, A.B., Elliot, A.J., & Harmon-Jones, E. (2013). Approach and avoidance motivation: Issues and advances. *Emotion Review, 5,* 227–229.

18. For example, the work that Mark Beeman has done with colleagues at Northwestern, referenced in: Subramaniam, K., et al. (2009). A brain mechanism for facilitation of insight by positive affect. *Journal of Cognitive Neuroscience, 21*(3), 415–432. See also Alice Isen's comprehensive review: Isen, A. (2000). Positive affect and decision-making. In M. Lewis & J. Haviland-Jones (Eds.), *The Handbook of Emotions,* 2nd ed. New York: Guilford Press.

19. Deci, E.L., Koestner, R., & Ryan, R.M. (1999). A meta-analytic review of experiments examining the effects of extrinsic rewards on intrinsic motivation. *Psychological Bulletin, 125*(6), 627–668.

20. Dunbar, R.I.M. (2003). The social brain: Mind, language, and society in evolutionary perspective. *Annual Review of Anthropology, 32*(1), 163–181.

21. See Matt Lieberman's excellent book on our social brains for an overview of this research: Lieberman, M. (2013). *Social.* New York: Crown.

22. Ryan, R.M., & Deci, E.L. (2000). Self-determination theory and the facilitation of intrinsic motivation, social development, and well-being. *American Psychologist, 55*(1), 68–78.

23. Loewenstein, G. (1994). The psychology of curiosity: A review and reinterpretation. *Psychological Bulletin, 116*(1): 75–98. More recent work can be found in Kang, M.J., et al. (2009). The wick in the candle of learning: Epistemic curiosity activates reward circuitry and enhances memory. *Psychological Science, 20*(8), 963–973.

24. Payne, J.D. (2010). Memory consolidation, the diurnal rhythm of cortisol, and the nature of dreams: A new hypothesis. In A. Clow & P. McNamara (Eds.), *International Review of Neurobiology,* vol. 92. Waltham, MA: Academic Press.

25. It's true that there's a tiny proportion of people who need less sleep, but researchers have only ever found a few people who are truly "short sleepers." Daniel Buysse, professor of psychiatry and clinical and translational science at the University of Pittsburgh Medical Center, says, "Out of every 100 people who believe they only need five or six hours of sleep a night, only about five people really do." Quoted in Melinda Beck, "The sleepless elite," *Wall Street Journal,* April 5, 2011.

26. Czeisler, C., & Fryer, B. (2006). A conversation with Harvard Medical School professor Charles A. Czeisler. *Harvard Business Review,* October.

27. For a great review of the evidence on the benefits of exercise, including many references to studies that are themselves meta-analyses, see Ratey, J.J., & Loehr, J.E. (2011). The positive impact of physical activity on cognition during adulthood: A review of underlying mechanisms, evidence and recommendations. *Reviews in the Neurosciences, 22*(2), 171–185. For a meta-analysis of 150 studies showing beneficial workplace effects, see also Conn, V.S., et al. (2009). Meta-analysis of workplace physical interventions. *American Journal of Preventative Medicine, 37*(4), 330–339.

28. For a full list of references, see Ratey, J.J., & Loehr, J.E. (2011). The positive impact of physical activity on cognition during adulthood: A review of underlying mechanisms, evidence and recommendations. *Reviews in the Neurosciences, 22*(2), 171–185.

29. Coulson, J.C., et al. (2008). Exercising at work and self-reported work performance. *International Journal of Workplace Health Management, 1*(3), 176–197.

30. From the website for Ratey's book: Ratey, J.J. (2008). *Spark: The Revolutionary New Science of Exercise and the Brain.* New York: Little, Brown. http://sparkinglife .org/page/why-exercise-works.

31. U.S. Department of Health and Human Services (2008). *Physical Activity Guidelines, Advisory Committee Report.* The guidelines suggest 500 MET minutes each week, equivalent to 150 minutes of moderate aerobic activity. For a narrative description of the implications of this report, see: Reynolds, G. (2012). *The First 20 Minutes: Surprising Science Reveals How We Can Exercise Better, Train Smarter, Live Longer.* New York: Hudson Street Press.

32. For example, on emotional regulation: Farb, N.A., et al. (2010). Minding one's emotions: Mindfulness training alters the neural expression of sadness. *Emotion, 10*(1), 25–33. On working memory and concentration: Mrazek, M.D., et al. (2013). Mindfulness training improves working memory capacity and GRE performance while reducing mind wandering. *Psychological Science, 24*(5), 776–781. With military personnel: Jha, A.P., et al. (2010). Examining the protective effects of mindfulness training on working memory capacity and affective experience. *Emotion, 10*(1), 54–64.

33. Hasenkamp, W., & Barsalou, L.W. (2012). Effects of meditation experience on functional connectivity of distributed brain networks. *Frontiers in Human Neuroscience, 6,* 38; Farb, N.A., et al. (2010). Minding one's emotions: Mindfulness training alters the neural expression of sadness. *Emotion, 10*(1), 25–33; Holzel, B.K., et al. (2010). Stress reduction correlates with structural changes in the amygdala. *Social Cognitive and Affective Neuroscience, 5*(1), 11–17; Brewer, J.A., et al. (2011). Meditation experience is associated with differences in default mode network activity and connectivity. *Proceedings of the National Academy of Sciences USA, 108*(50), 20254–20259.

34. Moyer, C.A., et al. (2011). Frontal electroencephalographic asymmetry associated with positive emotion is produced by very brief meditation training. *Psychological Science, 22*(10), 1277–1279. Other studies showing positive benefits of mindfulness from modest amounts of practice include this study which saw lasting changes in cognitive performance after just four days of practice: Zeidan, F., et al. (2010). Mindfulness meditation improves cognition: Evidence of brief mental training. *Consciousness and Cognition, 19*(2), 597–605.

35. This philosophy runs through Langer's book: Langer, E. (1989). *Mindfulness.* Reading, MA: Addison Wesley.

## CHAPTER 1: CHOOSING YOUR FILTERS

1.   Chabris, C., & Simons, D. (2010). *The Invisible Gorilla: And Other Ways Our Intuitions Deceive Us.* New York: Crown.

2.   Drew, T., Võ, M.L.H., & Wolfe, J.M. (2013). The invisible gorilla strikes again: Sustained inattentional blindness in expert observers. *Psychological Science, 24*(9), 1848–1853.

3.   Radel, R., & Clement-Guillotin, C. (2012). Evidence of motivational influences in early visual perception: Hunger modulates conscious access. *Psychological Science, 23*(3), 232–234.

4.   Forgas, J.P., & Bower, G.H. (1987). Mood effects on person-perception judgments. *Journal of Personality and Social Psychology, 53*(1), 53–60.

5.   Riener, C.R., Stefanucci, J.K., Proffitt, D.R., & Clore, G. (2011). An effect of mood on the perception of geographical slant. *Cognition & Emotion, 25*(1), 174–182.

6.   Hansen, T., Olkkonen, M., Walter, S., & Gegenfurtner, K.R. (2006). Memory modulates color appearance. *Nature Neuroscience, 9*(11), 1367–1368.

7.   The phrase is central to his short story "The Claustrophile," which can be found in: Sturgeon, T. (2013). *And Now the News . . . Volume IX: The Complete Stories of Theodore Sturgeon.* London: Hachette UK.


## CHAPTER 2: SETTING GREAT GOALS

1.   Locke, E.A., & Latham, G.P. (2002). Building a practically useful theory of goal setting and task motivation: A 35-year odyssey. *American Psychologist, 57*(9), 705–717.

2.   Elliot, A.J., & Church, M.A. (1997). A hierarchical model of approach and avoidance achievement motivation. *Journal of Personality and Social Psychology, 72*(1), 218–232.

3.   Deci, E.L., & Ryan, R.M. (2000). The "what" and "why" of goal pursuits: Human needs and the self-determination of behavior. *Psychological Inquiry, 11*(4), 227–268.

4.   Externally generated goals are processed in the lateral prefrontal cortex; internal ones in the medial prefrontal cortex. Berkman, E., & Lieberman, M.D. (2009). The neuroscience of goal pursuit: Bridging gaps between theory and data. In G. Moskowitz & H. Grant (Eds.), *The Psychology of Goals* (pp. 98–126). New York: Guilford Press.

5.   Peter Gollwitzer has led much of the research on implementation intentions, as "when-then" statements are known. A key reference is Gollwitzer, P.M., & Brandstätter, V. (1997). Implementation intentions and effective goal pursuit. *Journal of Personality and Social Psychology, 73*(1), 186–199. Also: Vallacher, R.R., & Wegner, D.M. (1987). What do people think they're doing? Action identification and human behavior. *Psychological Review, 94*(1), 3–15; Trope, Y., & Liberman, N. (2003). Temporal construal. *Psychological Review, 110*(3), 403–421.

6.  Grant Halvorson, H. (2014). Get your team to do what it says it's going to do. *Harvard Business Review*, May.

## CHAPTER 3: REINFORCING YOUR INTENTIONS

1.  Quote from Collins, J. (2001). *Good to Great: Why Some Companies Make the Leap—and Others Don't*. New York: HarperBusiness.

2.  Oettingen, G. (2014). *Rethinking Positive Thinking: Inside the New Science of Motivation*. New York: Penguin Random House.

3.  Collins, A., & Loftus, E. (1975). A spreading-activation theory of semantic processing. *Psychological Review, 82*(6), 407–428.

4.  This is known as Hebb's Rule. For the original reference, see: Hebb, D.O. (1949). *The Organization of Behavior*. New York: Wiley & Sons.

5.  Kay, A.C., Wheeler, S.C., Bargh, J.A., & Ross, L. (2004). Material priming: The influence of mundane physical objects on situational construal and competitive behavioral choice. *Organizational Behavior and Human Decision Processes, 95*(1), 83–96.

6.  Aarts, H., & Dijksterhuis, A. (2003). The silence of the library: Environment, situational norm, and social behavior. *Journal of Personality and Social Psychology, 84*(1), 18–28.

7.  Adam, H., & Galinsky, A.D. (2012). Enclothed cognition. *Journal of Experimental Social Psychology, 48*(4), 918–925.

8.  Taking a short walk in open or green space seems mentally refreshing for many of us. Berman, M.G., Jonides, J., & Kaplan, S. (2008). The cognitive benefits of interacting with nature. *Psychological Science, 19*(12), 1207–1212. Oppezzo, M., & Schwartz, D. L. (2014). Give your ideas some legs: The positive effect of walking on creative thinking. *Journal of Experimental Psychology: Learning, Memory, and Cognition, 40*(4), 1142–1152.

9.  Kosslyn, S.M. (2005). Mental images and the brain. *Cognitive Neuropsychology, 22*(3–4), 333–347.

10. Pascual-Leone, A., Nguyet, D., Cohen, L.G., Brasil-Neto, J.P., Cammarota, A., & Hallett, M. (1995). Modulation of muscle responses evoked by transcranial magnetic stimulation during the acquisition of new fine motor skills. *Journal of Neurophysiology, 74*(3), 1037–1045.

## PART II: PRODUCTIVITY

1.  Schor, J. (2003). The (even more) overworked American. In J. De Graaf (Ed.), *Take Back Your Time: Fighting Overwork and Time Poverty in America* (p. 7). San Francisco: Berrett-Koehler.

2.  For example, the large-sample Whitehall study found a robust relationship between longer working hours (beyond forty hours a week) and lower scores on verbal and reasoning tests: Virtanen, M., et al. (2009). Long working hours and cognitive function: The Whitehall II Study. *American Journal of Epidemiology*,

*169*(5), 596–605. The OECD also published data showing a negative relationship between average national levels of productivity and working hours between 1990 and 2012. Accessible at http://stats.oecd.org/Index.aspx?DatasetCode=LEVEL#.

### CHAPTER 4: SINGLETASKING

1.  Dux, P.E., Ivanoff, J., Asplund, C.L., & Marois, R. (2006). Isolation of a central bottleneck of information processing with time-resolved fMRI. *Neuron, 52*(6), 1109–1120. In fact, other researchers found that longer interruptions increased the error rate further—while a two-second break in concentration doubled the error rate, a four-second distraction tripled it: Altmann, E.M., Trafton, J.G., & Hambrick, D.Z. (2014). Momentary interruptions can derail the train of thought. *Journal of Experimental Psychology: General, 143*(1), 215–226.

2.  Speier, C., Valacich, J.S., & Vessey, I. (1999). The influence of task interruption on individual decision making: An information overload perspective. *Decision Sciences, 30*(2), 337–360.

3.  Iqbal, S.T., & Horvitz, E. (2007). Disruption and recovery of computing tasks: Field study, analysis, and directions. Paper presented at the Proceedings of the SIGCHI Conference on Human Factors in Computing Systems, San Jose, California.

4.  Tombu, M.N., Asplund, C.L., Dux, P.E., Godwin, D., Martin, J.W., & Marois, R. (2011). A unified attentional bottleneck in the human brain. *Proceedings of the National Academy of Sciences, 108*(33), 13426–13431.

5.  Bailey, B.P., & Konstan, J.A. (2006). On the need for attention-aware systems: Measuring effects of interruption on task performance, error rate, and affective state. *Computers in Human Behavior, 22*(4), 685–708.

6.  I'm defining "serious" crashes as those where someone was injured; 18 percent of these involved a distracted driver. *Traffic Safety Facts—Research Note (Summary of Statistical Findings)* (2014). DOT HS 812 012. Washington, DC: U.S. Department of Transportation. Retrieved from http://www-nrd.nhtsa.dot.gov/Pubs/812012.pdf.

7.  Ophir, E., Nass, C., & Wagner, A.D. (2009). Cognitive control in media multitaskers. *Proceedings of the National Academy of Sciences, 106*(37), 15583–15587.

8.  Sanbonmatsu, D.M., Strayer, D.L., Medeiros-Ward, N., & Watson, J.M. (2013). Who multi-tasks and why? Multi-tasking ability, perceived multi-tasking ability, impulsivity, and sensation seeking. *PLoS ONE, 8*(1), e54402.

9.  For an example of the way that typical "time of day" advice fails to apply equally to larks and owls, see: Gunia, B.C., Barnes, C.M., & Sah, S. (2014). The morality of larks and owls: Unethical behavior depends on chronotype as well as time of day. *Psychological Science, 25*(12), 2272–2274. They were responding to widely reported findings that people are more moral in the mornings. That turns out to be true for morning people; for nighttime folks, it's the opposite.

## CHAPTER 5: PLANNING DELIBERATE DOWNTIME

1.  Danziger, S., Levav, J., & Avnaim-Pesso, L. (2011). Extraneous factors in judicial decisions. *Proceedings of the National Academy of Sciences, 108*(17), 6889–6892.

2.  Baumeister, R., & Tierney, J. (2011). *Willpower: Rediscovering the Greatest Human Strength*. New York: Penguin.

3.  Dai, H., Milkman, K.L., Hofmann, D.A., & Staats, B.R. (2014). The impact of time at work and time off from work on rule compliance: The case of hand hygiene in health care. *Journal of Applied Psychology*.

4.  Food plays an important part in refreshing our capacity to embrace the next wave of work. There's some disagreement on exactly why, though. Most argue it's because the brain needs blood sugar; see Baumeister, R., & Tierney, J. (2011). *Willpower: Rediscovering the Greatest Human Strength*. New York: Penguin. Others say it's because hunger is a drain on the brain's deliberate system, because it causes an unpleasant distraction that has to be managed with self-control: Kohn, D. (2014). Sugar on the brain. *New Yorker,* May 6. The upshot is the same, though. You need to feed your brain and you'll get tetchy and distracted if you don't.

5.  Raichle, M.E. (2010). The brain's dark energy. *Scientific American, 302,* 28–33. A more academic article covering similar ground is: Raichle, M.E. (2010). Two views of brain function. *Trends in Cognitive Sciences, 14*(4), 180–190.

6.  Sami, S., Robertson, E.M., & Miall, R.C. (2014). The time course of task-specific memory consolidation effects in resting state networks. *Journal of Neuroscience, 34*(11), 3982–3992.

7.  Di Stefano, G., Gino, F., Pisano, G., & Staats, B. (2014). Learning by thinking: How reflection aids performance. Harvard Business School Working Paper, No. 14-093, March 2014.

8.  Telephone interview with Jessica Payne, March 5, 2015.

9.  Ericsson, K.A., et al. (1993). The role of deliberate practice in the acquisition of expert performance. *Psychological Review, 100*(3), 363–406.

10. Tuominen, S., & Pohjakallio, P. (2013). *The Workbook: Redesigning Nine to Five.* Available from http://www.925design.fi.

11. Read Robyn's eloquent blog on the topic at: https://medium.com/@robynscott/the-30-second-habit-with-a-lifelong-impact–2c3f948ead98.

## CHAPTER 6: OVERCOMING OVERLOAD

1.  Kahneman, D., & Tversky, A. (1979). Intuitive prediction: Biases and corrective procedures. *TIMS Studies in Management Science, 12,* 313–327.

2.  Masicampo, E.J., & Baumeister, R.F. (2011). Consider it done! Plan making can eliminate the cognitive effects of unfulfilled goals. *Journal of Personality and Social Psychology, 101*(4), 667–683.

3.  http://lifehacker.com/5458741/productivity-in-11-words; the original Twitter account is dormant.

4.  It's quite common (even in reputable publications) to see people referring to "comparative advantage" as meaning "the thing you're best at," or "a thing where

you're the best." That's incorrect—they're simply referring to "absolute advantage," which doesn't tell us much about prioritization if you happen to be excellent at a lot of things. You have a *comparative* advantage in the thing where the capability gap between you and another person is biggest. You can find this written up properly in any basic economics textbook, but the original reference is here: Ricardo, D. (1817). *On the Principles of Political Economy and Taxation.* London: John Murray.

5.  Lewis, M. (2012). Obama's way. *Vanity Fair.*

### CHAPTER 7: BEATING PROCRASTINATION

1.  Akerlof, G.A. (1991). Procrastination and obedience. *American Economic Review, 81*(2), 1–19.

2.  Ersner-Hershfield, H., Garton, M.T., Ballard, K., Samanez-Larkin, G.R., & Knutson, B. (2009). Don't stop thinking about tomorrow: Individual differences in future self-continuity account for saving. *Judgment and Decision Making, 4*(4), 280–286.

3.  Crockett, M.J., Braams, B.R., Clark, L., Tobler, P.N., Robbins, T.W., & Kalenscher, T. (2013). Restricting temptations: Neural mechanisms of precommitment. *Neuron, 79*(2), 391–401. The "temptations" deployed by the researchers were actually erotic pictures, rather than the slightly more sedate thrill of procrastination, but the mechanism is the same.

### PART III: RELATIONSHIPS

1.  See, for example, Helliwell, J.F., Layard, R., & Sachs, J. (2013). *World Happiness Report 2013.* New York: UN Sustainable Development Solutions Network. The report summarizes studies showing the effects of "having someone to count on."

2.  See Matt Lieberman's book for an excellent in-depth explanation of the social nature of our brains: Lieberman, M. (2013). *Social: Why Our Brains Are Wired to Connect.* New York: Crown Archetype.

### CHAPTER 8: BUILDING REAL RAPPORT

1.  Tamir, D.I., & Mitchell, J.P. (2012). Disclosing information about the self is intrinsically rewarding. *Proceedings of the National Academy of Sciences USA, 109*(21), 8038–8043.

2.  An interesting essay on this powerful follow-up question: "Tell me more: The art of listening," in Ueland, B. (1992). *Strength to Your Sword Arm: Collected Writings of Brenda Ueland.* Duluth, MN: Holy Cow! Press.

3.  For an overview of how empathy plays out toward in-group and out-group members, see: Cikara, M., Bruneau, E., Van Bavel, J.J., & Saxe, R. (2014). Their pain gives us pleasure: How intergroup dynamics shape empathic failures and counterempathic responses. *Journal of Experimental Social Psychology, 55,* 110–125.

4.  Mitchell, J.P., Macrae, C.N., & Banaji, M.R. (2006). Dissociable medial prefrontal contributions to judgments of similar and dissimilar others. *Neuron, 50*(4), 655–663.

5.   Rivera, L.A. (2012). Hiring as cultural matching: The case of elite professional service firms. *American Sociological Review, 77*(6), 999–1022.

6.   Ratner, K.G., & Amodio, D.M. (2013). Seeing "us vs. them": Minimal group effects on the neural encoding of faces. *Journal of Experimental Social Psychology, 49*(2), 298–301.

7.   Valdesolo, P., & DeSteno, D. (2011). Synchrony and the social tuning of compassion. *Emotion, 11*(2), 262–266.

8.   Martin, L.J., et al. (2015). Reducing social stress elicits emotional contagion of pain in mouse and human strangers. *Current Biology, 25*(3), 326–332.

9.   van Baaren, R.B., Holland, R.W., Steenaert, B., & van Knippenberg, A. (2003). Mimicry for money: Behavioral consequences of imitation. *Journal of Experimental Social Psychology, 39*(4), 393–398.

10. Axelrod, R., & Hamilton, W. (1981). The evolution of cooperation. *Science, 211*(4489), 1390–1396.

11. The brains of people playing the Prisoner's Dilemma were examined in: Rilling, J.K., Sanfey, A.G., Aronson, J.A., Nystrom, L.E., & Cohen, J.D. (2004). Opposing BOLD responses to reciprocated and unreciprocated altruism in putative reward pathways. *Neuroreport, 15*(16), 2539–2543. Other games requiring cooperation or competition were examined by Decety, J., et al. (2004). The neural bases of cooperation and competition: An fMRI investigation. *Neuroimage, 23*(2), 744–751.

12. Aron, A., Melinat, E., Aron, E.N., Vallone, R.D., & Bator, R.J. (1997). The experimental generation of interpersonal closeness: A procedure and some preliminary findings. *Personality and Social Psychology Bulletin, 23*(4), 363–377.

13. Przybylski, A.K., & Weinstein, N. (2013). Can you connect with me now? How the presence of mobile communication technology influences face-to-face conversation quality. *Journal of Social and Personal Relationships, 30*(3), 3237–3246.

**CHAPTER 9: RESOLVING TENSIONS**

1.   Rapoport, A. (1960). *Fights, Games, and Debates*. Ann Arbor: University of Michigan Press.

2.   Precisely how our biology allows this contagion is one of the hottest unresolved debates in neuroscience—some believe "mirror neurons" are responsible; others point out that mirror neurons haven't yet been directly observed in human brains. But the effects aren't in dispute. We all know that when one person walks into a room in a foul mood, the gloom can spread without a word being spoken.

3.   Friedman, R., et al. (2010). Motivational synchronicity: Priming motivational orientations with observations of others' behaviors. *Motivation and Emotion, 34*(1), 34–38.

4.   Buchanan, T.W., White, C.N., Kralemann, M., & Preston, S.D. (2012). The contagion of physiological stress: Causes and consequences. *European Journal of Psychotraumatology, 3*.

5.   Wild, B., et al. (2001). Are emotions contagious? Evoked emotions while viewing emotionally expressive faces: Quality, quantity, time course and gender differences. *Psychiatry Research, 102*(2), 109–24.

6.  Ross, L.D., Amabile, T.M., & Steinmetz, J.L. (1977). Social roles, social control, and biases in social-perception processes. *Journal of Personality and Social Psychology, 35*(7), 485–494. See also: Gilbert, D.T., & Malone, P.S. (1995). The correspondence bias. *Psychological Bulletin, 117*(1), 21–38.

7.  Gilbert, D.T., Pelham, B.W., & Krull, D.S. (1988). On cognitive busyness: When person perceivers meet persons perceived. *Journal of Personality and Social Psychology, 54*(5), 733–740.

8.  Ross, L.D., Amabile, T.M., & Steinmetz, J.L. (1977). Social roles, social control, and biases in social-perception processes. *Journal of Personality and Social Psychology, 35*(7), 485–494.

9.  Izuma, K., Saito, D.N., & Sadato, N. (2008). Processing of social and monetary rewards in the human striatum. *Neuron, 58*(2), 284–294.

10. Goldin, P.R., McRae, K., Ramel, W., & Gross, J.J. (2008). The neural bases of emotion regulation: Reappraisal and suppression of negative emotion. *Biological Psychiatry, 63*(6), 577–586.

## CHAPTER 10: BRINGING THE BEST OUT OF OTHERS

1.  See Nancy Kline's book for more on ways to create an effective thinking environment for another person: Kline, N. (1999). *Time to Think: Listening to Ignite the Human Mind*. London: Octopus.

2.  Deci, E.L., & Ryan, R.M. (2000). The "what" and "why" of goal pursuits: Human needs and the self-determination of behavior. *Psychological Inquiry, 11*(4), 227–268.

3.  Williams, G.C., Gagne, M., Ryan, R.M., & Deci, E.L. (2002). Facilitating autonomous motivation for smoking cessation. *Health Psychology, 21*(1), 40–50.

4.  Baumeister, R.F., Bratslavsky, E., Finkenauer, C., & Vohs, K.D. (2001). Bad is stronger than good. *Review of General Psychology, 5*(4), 323–370.

5.  Camerer, C.F., & Thaler, R.H. (1995). Anomalies: Ultimatums, dictators and manners. *Journal of Economic Perspectives, 9*(2), 209–219.

6.  Tabibnia, G., et al. (2008). The sunny side of fairness: Preference for fairness activates reward circuitry (and disregarding unfairness activates self-control circuitry). *Psychological Science, 19*(4), 339–347. For a more general discussion of the way that fairness is treated by the brain, see Rilling, J.K., & A.G. Sanfey (2011). The neuroscience of social decision-making. *Annual Review of Psychology, 62*, 23–48.

## CHAPTER 11: REACHING INSIGHT

1.  This is a long-standing finding in cognitive psychology. The seminal paper that coined the term is: Luchins, A.S. (1942). Mechanization in problem solving: The effect of Einstellung. *Psychological Monographs, 54*(6).

2.  Senay, I., Albarracin, D., & Noguchi, K. (2010). Motivating goal-directed behavior through introspective self-talk: The role of the interrogative form of simple future tense. *Psychological Science, 21*(4), 499–504.

3.  For example: Burnkrant, R.E., & Howard, D.J. (1984). Effects of the use of introductory rhetorical questions versus statements on information processing. *Journal of Personality and Social Psychology, 47*(6), 1218–1230.

4.  Creswell, J.D., et al. (2012). Mindfulness-based stress reduction training reduces loneliness and pro-inflammatory gene expression in older adults: A small randomized controlled trial. *Brain, Behavior, and Immunity, 26*(7), 1095–1101.

5.  Bos, M.W., Dijksterhuis, A., & van Baaren, R.B. (2008). On the goal-dependency of unconscious thought. *Journal of Experimental Social Psychology, 44*(4), 1114–1120; Zhong, C.B., Dijksterhuis, A., & Galinsky, A.D. (2008). The merits of unconscious thought in creativity. *Psychological Science, 19*(9), 912–918.

6.  Abadie, M., Waroquier, L., & Terrier, P. (2013). Gist memory in the unconscious-thought effect. *Psychological Science, 24*(7), 1253–1259.

7.  Mueller, P.A., & Oppenheimer, D.M. (2014). The pen is mightier than the keyboard: Advantages of longhand over laptop note taking. *Psychological Science, 25*(6), 1159–1168.

## CHAPTER 12: MAKING WISE DECISIONS

1.  Kahan, D.M., Braman, D., Cohen, G.L., Gastil, J., & Slovic, P. (2010). Who fears the HPV vaccine, who doesn't, and why? An experimental study of the mechanisms of cultural cognition. *Law and Human Behavior, 34*(6), 501–516. For similar results: Nyhan, B., & Reifler, J. (2010). When corrections fail: The persistence of political misperceptions. *Political Behavior, 32*(2), 303–330.

2.  Buffett, W., & Loomis, C. (2001). Warren Buffett on the stock market. *Fortune,* December 10. See also: Zweig, J. (2013). Lesson from Buffett: Doubt yourself. *Wall Street Journal,* May 5.

3.  Jacowitz, K.E., & Kahneman, D. (1995). Measures of anchoring in estimation tasks. *Personality and Social Psychology Bulletin, 21*(11), 1161–1166.

4.  Ariely, D., Loewenstein, G., & Prelec, D. (2003). "Coherent arbitrariness": Stable demand curves without stable preferences. *Quarterly Journal of Economics, 118*(1), 73–106.

5.  Busse, M.R., Pope, D.G., Pope, J.C., & Silva-Risso, J. (2012). Projection bias in the car and housing markets. NBER Working Paper no. 18212.

6.  Song, H., & Schwarz, N. (2008). Fluency and the detection of misleading questions: Low processing fluency attenuates the Moses illusion. *Social Cognition, 26*(6), 791–799.

7.  Asch, S.E. (1951). *Effects of Group Pressure on the Modification and Distortion of Judgements in Groups, Leadership and Men.* Pittsburgh: Carnegie Press.

8.  Dweck, C.S. (2006). *Mindset: The New Psychology of Success.* New York: Random House.

9.  Kahneman, D., Knetsch, J.L., & Thaler, R.H. (1990). Experimental tests of the endowment effect and the Coase theorem. *Journal of Political Economy, 98*(6), 1325–1348.

10. Tversky, A., & Kahneman, D. (1991). Loss aversion in riskless choice: A reference-dependent model. *Quarterly Journal of Economics, 106*(4), 1039–1061.

11. Hoever, I.J., van Knippenberg, D., van Ginkel, W.P., & Barkema, H.G. (2012). Fostering team creativity: Perspective taking as key to unlocking diversity's potential. *Journal of Applied Psychology, 97*(5), 982–996.

12. Interview of Eric Schmidt: Manyika, J. (2008). Google's view on the future of business: An interview with CEO Eric Schmidt. *McKinsey Quarterly*, November.

13. Klein, G. (2007). Performing a project premortem. *Harvard Business Review, Project Management*, September.

14. Zhang, T., Gino, F., & Bazerman, M.H. (2014). Morality rebooted: Exploring simple fixes to our moral bugs. Harvard Business School NOM Unit Working Paper No. 14-105.

## CHAPTER 13: BOOSTING YOUR BRAINPOWER

1.  Friedman, R.S., & Forster, J. (2001). The effects of promotion and prevention cues on creativity. *Journal of Personality and Social Psychology, 81*(6), 1001–1013.

2.  Hamilton, D.L., Katz, L.B., & Leirer, V.O. (1980). Cognitive representation of personality impressions: Organizational processes in first impression formation. *Journal of Personality and Social Psychology, 39*(6), 1050–1063. Mitchell, J.P., Macrae, C.N., & Banaji, M.R. (2004). Encoding-specific effects of social cognition on the neural correlates of subsequent memory. *Journal of Neuroscience, 24*(21), 4912–4917.

3.  Wason, P.C., & Johnson-Laird, P.N. (1972). *Psychology of Reasoning: Structure and Content.* Cambridge, MA: Harvard University Press.

4.  Cosmides, L., & Tooby, J. (1992). *Cognitive Adaptations for Social Exchange in the Adapted Mind: Evolutionary Psychology and the Generation of Culture.* New York: Oxford University Press. Psychologists have debated exactly why the second test is so much easier for us to think through. Perhaps we're adept at spotting naughty cheating behavior. Perhaps we're simply better able to work out what information is relevant when it's set in a socially familiar context. Either way, it stems from our advanced social intelligence.

5.  Amabile, T.M., Mueller, J.S., Simpson, W.B., Hadley, C.N., Kramer, S.J., & Fleming, L. (2002). Time pressure and creativity in organizations: A longitudinal field study. Harvard Business School Working Paper No. 02-073.

6.  Kounios, J., Frymiare, J.L., Bowden, E.M., Fleck, J.I., Subramaniam, K., Parrish, T.B., & Jung-Beeman, M. (2006). The prepared mind: Neural activity prior to problem presentation predicts subsequent solution by sudden insight. *Psychological Science, 17*(10), 882–890.

7.  Ellenbogen, J.M., Hu, P.T., Payne, J.D., Titone, D., & Walker, M.P. (2007). Human relational memory requires time and sleep. *Proceedings of the National Academy of Sciences USA, 104*(18), 7723–7728.

8.  Walker, M.P., Liston, C., Hobson, J.A., & Stickgold, R. (2002). Cognitive flexibility across the sleep-wake cycle: REM-sleep enhancement of anagram problem solving. *Brain Research: Cognitive Brain Research, 14*(3), 317–324.

9. Harrison, Y., & Horne, J.A. (1999). One night of sleep loss impairs innovative thinking and flexible decision making. *Organizational Behavior and Human Decision Processes, 78*(2), 128–145.

10. Stickgold, R. (2009). How do I remember? Let me count the ways. *Sleep Medicine Reviews, 13*(5), 305–308.

11. Gooley, J.J., et al. (2011). Exposure to room light before bedtime suppresses melatonin onset and shortens melatonin duration in humans. *Journal of Clinical Endocrinology and Metabolism, 96*(3), E463–472.

12. Rosekind, M.R., et al. (1995). Alertness management: Strategic naps in operational settings. *Journal of Sleep Research, 4*(S2), 62–66.

13. Mednick, S., Nakayama, K., & Stickgold, R. (2003). Sleep-dependent learning: A nap is as good as a night. *Nature Neuroscience, 6*(7), 697–698.

14. National Sleep Foundation (2013). International Bedroom Poll. Available from: http://sleepfoundation.org/sites/default/files/RPT495a.pdf.

15. Personal email exchange with David Allen, June 18, 2015.

16. Ratey, J.J., & Loehr, J.E. (2011). The positive impact of physical activity on cognition during adulthood: A review of underlying mechanisms, evidence and recommendations. *Reviews in the Neurosciences, 22*(2), 171–185

17. Powell, K.E., Paluch, A.E., & Blair, S.N. (2011). Physical activity for health: What kind? How much? How intense? On top of what? *Annual Review of Public Health, 32*(1), 349–365.

## CHAPTER 14: GETTING THROUGH THEIR FILTERS

1. Falk, E.B., Morelli, S.A., Welborn, B.L., Dambacher, K., & Lieberman, M.D. (2013). Creating buzz: The neural correlates of effective message propagation. *Psychological Science, 24*(7), 1234–1242.

2. Unpublished study by Zakary Tormala. For more information: http://www.cmo.com/articles/2014/9/3/whiteboard_beats_pow.html.

3. Kensinger, E.A., & Schachter, D.L. (2008). Memory and emotion. In M. Lewis, J.M. Haviland-Jones, & L. Feldman Barrett (Eds.), *Handbook of Emotions*, 3rd ed. New York: Guilford Press.

4. McNeil, B.J., Pauker, S.G., Sox, H.C., Jr., & Tversky, A. (1982). On the elicitation of preferences for alternative therapies. *New England Journal of Medicine, 306*(21), 1259–1262.

5. Kensinger, E.A. (2009). Remembering the details: Effects of emotion. *Emotion Review, 1*(2), 99–113.

6. Berger, J., & Milkman, K.L. (2012). What makes online content viral? *Journal of Marketing Research, 49*(2), 192–205.

7. Mitchell, J.P., Macrae, C. N., & Banaji, M.R. (2004). Encoding-specific effects of social cognition on the neural correlates of subsequent memory. *Journal of Neuroscience, 24*(21), 4912–4917.

8. Small, D.A., Loewenstein, G., & Slovic, P. (2007). Sympathy and callousness: The impact of deliberative thought on donations to identifiable and statistical victims. *Organizational Behavior and Human Decision Processes, 102*(2), 143–153.

9.   McKinsey & Company Internal Communications Team (2014) McKinsey News Update. Internal report, May.

10. This is a great academic overview of various types of processing fluency: Alter, A.L., & Oppenheimer, D.M. (2009). Uniting the tribes of fluency to form a meta-cognitive nation. *Personality and Social Psychology Review, 13*(3), 219–235.

11. Alter, A.L., & Oppenheimer, D.M. (2006). Predicting short-term stock fluctuations by using processing fluency. *Proceedings of the National Academy of Sciences USA, 103*(24), 9369–9372.

12. McGlone, M.S., & Tofighbakhsh, J. (2000). Birds of a feather flock conjointly (?): Rhyme as reason in aphorisms. *Psychological Science, 11*(5), 424–428.

13. Begg, I.M., Anas, A., & Farinacci, S. (1992). Dissociation of processes in belief: Source recollection, statement familiarity, and the illusion of truth. *Journal of Experimental Psychology: General, 121*, 446–458.

14. For effects of easier visual layout: Reber, R., Winkielman, P., & Schwarz, N. (1998). Effects of perceptual fluency on affective judgments. *Psychological Science, 9*(1), 45–48. For effects of simpler language: Oppenheimer, D.M. (2006). Consequences of erudite vernacular utilized irrespective of necessity: Problems with using long words needlessly. *Applied Cognitive Psychology, 20*(2), 139–156.

15. Binder, J.R., Westbury, C.F., McKiernan, K.A., Possing, E.T., & Medler, D.A. (2005). Distinct brain systems for processing concrete and abstract concepts. *Journal of Cognitive Neuroscience, 17*(6), 905–917.

16. Behavioural Insights Team (2011). *Annual Update 2010–11.* Retrieved from https://www.gov.uk/government/uploads/system/uploads/attachment_data/file/60537/Behaviour-Change-Insight-Team-Annual-Update_acc.pdf.

17. Camerer, C., Loewenstein, G., & Weber, M. (1989). The curse of knowledge in economic settings: An experimental analysis. *Journal of Political Economy, 97*(5), 1232–1254.

18. Keysar, B., & Henly, A.S. (2002). Speakers' overestimation of their effectiveness. *Psychological Science, 13*(3), 207–212.

## CHAPTER 15: MAKING THINGS HAPPEN

1.   Langer, E.J., Blank, A., & Chanowitz, B. (1978). The mindlessness of ostensibly thoughtful action: The role of "placebic" information in interpersonal interaction. *Journal of Personality and Social Psychology, 36*(6), 635–642.

2.   Thaler, R.H., & Sunstein, C.R. (2009). *Nudge: Improving Decisions About Health, Wealth, and Happiness,* 2nd ed. New York: Penguin.

3.   Johnson, E.J., & Goldstein, D. (2003). Do defaults save lives? *Science, 302*(5649), 1338–1339.

4.   Rozin, P., Scott, S., Dingley, M., Urbanek, J.K., Jiang, H., & Kaltenbach, M. (2011). Nudge to nobesity I: Minor changes in accessibility decrease food intake. *Judgment and Decision Making, 6*(4), 323–332.

5.   Strack, F., & Mussweiler, T. (1997). Explaining the enigmatic anchoring effect: Mechanisms of selective accessibility. *Journal of Personality and Social Psychology, 73*(3), 437–446.

6.  Ames, D.R., & Mason, M.F. (2015). Tandem anchoring: Informational and politeness effects of range offers in social exchange. *Journal of Personality and Social Psychology, 108*(2), 254–274.

7.  Your request needs to feel reasonable. When volunteers were asked to come up with twelve examples of themselves being assertive, this left them rating themselves as *less* assertive than people who'd been asked to come up with only six examples, because it felt hard to come up with so many: Schwarz, N., Bless, H., Strack, F., Klumpp, G., Rittenauer-Schatka, H., & Simons, A. (1991). Ease of retrieval as information: Another look at the availability heuristic. *Journal of Personality and Social Psychology, 61*(2), 195–202.

8.  Platow, M.J., et al. (2005). "It's not funny if they're laughing": Self-categorization, social influence, and responses to canned laughter. *Journal of Experimental Social Psychology, 41*(5), 542–550.

9.  Kahan, D.M., Braman, D., Cohen, G.L., Gastil, J., & Slovic, P. (2010). Who fears the HPV vaccine, who doesn't, and why? An experimental study of the mechanisms of cultural cognition. *Law and Human Behavior, 34*(6), 501–516.

10. Langer, E.J. (1975). The illusion of control. *Journal of Personality and Social Psychology, 32*(2), 311–328.

11. Asking patients booking over the phone to repeat back their appointment details reduced no-shows by another 3.5 percent. And when those measures were combined with some social proof—posters saying things like "Last month, 99 percent of your fellow patients turned up for their appointments"—the number of missed appointments fell by a third. Martin, S.J., Bassi, S., & Dunbar-Rees, R. (2012). Commitments, norms and custard creams: A social influence approach to reducing did not attends (DNAs). *Journal of the Royal Society of Medicine, 105*(3), 101–104.

12. Adam Grant cites research by Katie Liljenquist, suggesting that people can sense if the request for advice is fake, in: Grant, A.M. (2013). *Give and Take: Why Helping Others Drives Our Success.* New York: Viking Penguin.

### CHAPTER 16: CONVEYING CONFIDENCE

1.  For example, on confidence in groups: Zarnoth, P., & Sniezek, J.A. (1997). The social influence of confidence in group decision making. *Journal of Experimental Social Psychology, 33*(4), 345–366. On confidence in eyewitness testimony: Sporer, S.L., Penrod, S., Read, D., & Cutler, B. (1995). Choosing, confidence, and accuracy: A meta-analysis of the confidence-accuracy relation in eyewitness identification studies. *Psychological Bulletin, 118*(3), 315–327. On confidence and assessments of probability: Price, P.C., & Stone, E.R. (2004). Intuitive evaluation of likelihood judgment producers: Evidence for a confidence heuristic. *Journal of Behavioral Decision Making, 17*(1), 39–57.

2.  Kilduff, G.J., & Galinsky, A.D. (2013). From the ephemeral to the enduring: How approach-oriented mindsets lead to greater status. *Journal of Personality and Social Psychology, 105*(5), 816–831.

3.  Fragale, A.R. (2006). The power of powerless speech: The effects of speech style and task interdependence on status conferral. *Organizational Behavior and Human Decision Processes, 101*(2), 243–261.

4. Jamieson, J.P., Mendes, W.B., & Nock, M.K. (2013). Improving acute stress responses: The power of reappraisal. *Current Directions in Psychological Science, 22*(1), 51–56.

5. Creswell, J.D., Welch, W.T., Taylor, S.E., Lucas, D.K., Gruenewald, T.L., & Mann, T. (2005). Affirmation of personal values buffers neuroendocrine and psychological stress responses. *Psychological Science, 16*(11), 846–851.

6. Kilduff, G.J., & Galinsky, A.D. (2013). From the ephemeral to the enduring: How approach-oriented mindsets lead to greater status. *Journal of Personality and Social Psychology, 105*(5), 816–831.

7. It's unclear whether the benefit comes simply from rebooting the associations that our brain has between "feeling confident" and "standing confidently," or whether a bolder stance also boosts hormones associated with risk-taking. This study found hormones were part of the mix: Carney, D.R., Cuddy, A.J., & Yap, A.J. (2010). Power posing: Brief nonverbal displays affect neuroendocrine levels and risk tolerance. *Psychological Science, 21*(10), 1363–1368. This larger later study replicated the effects on confidence (though not the effects on testosterone and cortisol): Ranehill, E., Dreber, A., Johannesson, M., Leiberg, S., Sul, S., & Weber, R.A. (2015). Assessing the robustness of power posing: No effect on hormones and risk tolerance in a large sample of men and women. *Psychological Science, 26*(5), 653–656.

8. Carney, D.R., Cuddy, A.J., & Yap, A.J. (2010). Power posing: Brief nonverbal displays affect neuroendocrine levels and risk tolerance. *Psychological Science, 21*(10), 1363–1368.

## PART VI: RESILIENCE

1. Wilson, T.D., & Gilbert, D.T. (2005). Affective forecasting: Knowing what to want. *Current Directions in Psychological Science, 14*(3), 131–134. See also Gilbert's highly accessible book: Gilbert, D.T. (2007). *Stumbling on Happiness*, 6th ed. New York: Vintage Books.

## CHAPTER 17: KEEPING A COOL HEAD

1. Wilson, T. (2004). *Strangers to Ourselves: Discovering the Adaptive Unconscious.* Cambridge, MA: Belknap Press.

2. Kircanski, K., Lieberman, M.D., & Craske, M.G. (2012). Feelings into words: Contributions of language to exposure therapy. *Psychological Science, 23*(10), 1086–1091.

3. Lieberman, M.D., Eisenberger, N.I., Crockett, M.J., Tom, S.M., Pfeifer, J.H., & Way, B.M. (2007). Putting feelings into words: Affect labeling disrupts amygdala activity in response to affective stimuli. *Psychological Science, 18*(5), 421–428.

4. For general references on the weaknesses of suppression as a coping strategy: Kross, E., & Ayduk, O. (2011). Making meaning out of negative experiences by self-distancing. *Current Directions in Psychological Science, 20*(3), 187–191. Other studies showing how suppression underperforms reappraisal as a technique: Goldin, P.R., McRae, K., Ramel, W., & Gross, J.J. (2008). The neural bases of emotion reg-

ulation: Reappraisal and suppression of negative emotion. *Biological Psychiatry,* *63*(6), 577–586; Gross, J.J., & John, O.P. (2003). Individual differences in two emotion regulation processes: Implications for affect, relationships, and well-being. *Journal of Personality and Social Psychology, 85*(2), 348–362. For a study that shows how suppression can backfire and affect others around us, see Butler, E.A., Egloff, B., Wilhelm, F.H., Smith, N.C., Erickson, E.A., & Gross, J.J. (2003). The social consequences of expressive suppression. *Emotion, 3*(1), 48–67.

5. Kross, E., et al. (2014). Self-talk as a regulatory mechanism: How you do it matters. *Journal of Personality and Social Psychology, 106*(2), 304–324.

6. Kross, E., & Ayduk, O. (2011). Making meaning out of negative experiences by self-distancing. *Current Directions in Psychological Science, 20*(3), 187–191.

7. Rutten, B.P., et al. (2013). Resilience in mental health: Linking psychological and neurobiological perspectives. *Acta Psychiatrica Scandinavia, 128*(1), 3–20. The following study also found that the ability to generate in-the-moment positive emotion boosted resilience: Cohn, M.A., & Fredrickson, B.L. (2010). In search of durable positive psychology interventions: Predictors and consequences of long-term positive behavior change. *Journal of Positive Psychology, 5*(5), 355–366.

8. Zander, R.S., & Zander, B. (2000). *The Art of Possibility.* Boston: Harvard Business School Press.

9. George, B., & Sims, P. (2007). *True North: Discover Your Authentic Leadership.* San Francisco: Jossey-Bass.

10. Rutten, B.P., et al. (2013). Resilience in mental health: Linking psychological and neurobiological perspectives. *Acta Psychiatrica Scandinavica, 128*(1), 3–20.

11. There's a good list of references cited in: Brown, R.P., Gerbarg, P.L., & Muench, F. (2013). Breathing practices for treatment of psychiatric and stress-related medical conditions. *Psychiatric Clinics of North America, 36*(1), 121–140.

12. Kahneman, D., & Tversky, A. (1986). Rational choice and the framing of decisions. *The Journal of Business, 59*(4), S251–S278.

13. Yoshida, W., Seymour, B., Koltzenburg, M., & Dolan, R.J. (2013). Uncertainty increases pain: Evidence for a novel mechanism of pain modulation involving the periaqueductal gray. *Journal of Neuroscience, 33*(13), 5638–5646.

14. Fernald, A., & O'Neill, D.K. (1993). Peekaboo across cultures: How mothers and infants play with voices, faces, and expectations. In *Parent-Child Play: Descriptions and Implications* (pp. 259–285). Albany: State University of New York Press.

15. Parrott, W.G., & Gleitman, H. (1989). Infants' expectations in play: The joy of peek-a-boo. *Cognition and Emotion, 3*(4), 291–311.

16. Arnsten, A.F. (1998). The biology of being frazzled. *Science, 280*(5370), 1711–1712.

### CHAPTER 18: MOVING ON

1. Macnamara, A., Ochsner, K.N., & Hajcak, G. (2011). Previously reappraised: The lasting effect of description type on picture-elicited electrocortical activity. *Social Cognitive and Affective Neuroscience, 6*(3), 348–358.

2.  Gross, J.J., & John, O.P. (2003). Individual differences in two emotion regulation processes: Implications for affect, relationships, and well-being. *Journal of Personality and Social Psychology, 85*(2), 348–362.

3.  McRae, K., Jacobs, S.E., Ray, R.D., John, O.P., & Gross, J.J. (2012). Individual differences in reappraisal ability: Links to reappraisal frequency, well-being, and cognitive control. *Journal of Research in Personality, 46*(1), 2–7.

4.  Ochsner, K.N., Ray, R.D., Cooper, J.C., Robertson, E.R., Chopra, S., Gabrieli, J.D.E., & Gross, J.J. (2004). Thinking makes it so: A social cognitive neuroscience approach to emotion regulation. In R.F. Baumeister & K.D. Vohs (Eds.), *Handbook of Self-Regulation: Research, Theory, and Applications.* New York: Guilford Press.

5.  Shiota, M.N., & Levenson, R.W. (2012). Turn down the volume or change the channel? Emotional effects of detached versus positive reappraisal. *Journal of Personality and Social Psychology, 103*(3), 416–429.

6.  Ochsner, K.N., & Gross, J.J. (2005). The cognitive control of emotion. *Trends in Cognitive Sciences, 9*(5), 242–249. Also: Macnamara, A., Ochsner, K.N., & Hajcak, G. (2011). Previously reappraised: The lasting effect of description type on picture-elicited electrocortical activity. *Social Cognitive and Affective Neuroscience, 6*(3), 348–358.

7.  Arkes, H.R., & Blumer, C. (1985). The psychology of sunk cost. *Organizational Behavior and Human Decision Processes, 35*(1), 124–140.

8.  Molden, D.C., & Hui, C.M. (2011). Promoting de-escalation of commitment: A regulatory-focus perspective on sunk costs. *Psychological Science, 22*(1), 8–12.

### CHAPTER 19: STAYING STRONG

1.  Walker, M.P., & van der Helm, E. (2009). Overnight therapy? The role of sleep in emotional brain processing. *Psychological Bulletin, 135*(5), 731–748. See also: van der Helm, E., & Walker, M.P. (2012). Sleep and affective brain regulation. *Social and Personality Psychology Compass, 6*(11), 773–791.

2.  Yoo, S.S., Gujar, N., Hu, P., Jolesz, F.A., & Walker, M.P. (2007). The human emotional brain without sleep—a prefrontal amygdala disconnect. *Current Biology, 17*(20), R877–R878.

3.  Mah, C.D., Mah, K.E., Kezirian, E.J., & Dement, W.C. (2011). The effects of sleep extension on the athletic performance of collegiate basketball players. *Sleep, 34*(7), 943–950.

4.  Cunningham, T.J., Crowell, C.R., Alger, S.E., Kensinger, E.A., Villano, M.A., Mattingly, S.M., & Payne, J.D. (2014). Psychophysiological arousal at encoding leads to reduced reactivity but enhanced emotional memory following sleep. *Neurobiology of Learning and Memory, 114*, 155–164.

5.  Pace-Schott, E.F., Shepherd, E., Spencer, R.M.C., Marcello, M., Tucker, M., Propper, R.E., & Stickgold, R. (2011). Napping promotes inter-session habituation to emotional stimuli. *Neurobiology of Learning and Memory, 95*(1), 24–36.

6.  Rethorst, C.D., Wipfli, B.M., & Landers, D.M. (2009). The antidepressive effects of exercise: A meta-analysis of randomized trials. *Sports Medicine, 39*(6), 491–511.

7. For example, Kramer, A.F., et al. (1999). Ageing, fitness and neurocognitive function. *Nature, 400*(6743), 418–419. Cited in: Ratey, J.J., & Loehr, J.E. (2011). The positive impact of physical activity on cognition during adulthood: A review of underlying mechanisms, evidence and recommendations. *Reviews in the Neurosciences, 22*(2), 171–185.

8. Brewer, J.A., Worhunsky, P.D., Gray, J.R., Tang, Y.Y., Weber, J., & Kober, H. (2011). Meditation experience is associated with differences in default mode network activity and connectivity. *Proceedings of the National Academy of Sciences USA, 108*(50), 20254–20259.

9. Levy, D.M., Wobbrock, J.O., Kaszniak, A.W., & Ostergren, M. (2012). The effects of mindfulness meditation training on multitasking in a high-stress information environment. Paper presented at the Proceedings of Graphics Interface 2012, Toronto, Ontario, Canada.

10. Zeidan, F., Johnson, S.K., Diamond, B.J., David, Z., & Goolkasian, P. (2010). Mindfulness meditation improves cognition: Evidence of brief mental training. *Consciousness & Cognition, 19*(2), 597–605.

11. Moyer, C.A., et al. (2011). Frontal electroencephalographic asymmetry associated with positive emotion is produced by very brief meditation training. *Psychological Science, 22*(10), 1277–1279.

## CHAPTER 20: TOPPING UP THE TANK

1. Key articles include: Seligman, M.E.P., Steen, T.A., Park, N., & Peterson, C. (2005). Positive psychology progress: Empirical validation of interventions. *American Psychologist, 60*(5), 410–421; Mongrain, M., & Anselmo-Matthews, T. (2012). Do positive psychology exercises work? A replication of Seligman et al. (2005). *Journal of Clinical Psychology, 68*(4), 382–389.

2. Gander, F., Proyer, R., Ruch, W., & Wyss, T. (2013). Strength-based positive interventions: Further evidence for their potential in enhancing well-being and alleviating depression. *Journal of Happiness Studies, 14*(4), 1241–1259.

3. Seligman, M.E.P. (2011). *Flourish: A Visionary New Understanding of Happiness and Well-being*. New York: Free Press.

4. Moll, J., Krueger, F., Zahn, R., Pardini, M., de Oliveira-Souza, R., & Grafman, J. (2006). Human fronto-meso limbic networks guide decisions about charitable donation. *Proceedings of the National Academy of Sciences USA, 103*(42), 15623–15628.

5. There is lots of evidence on this in the book by Dunn, E., & Norton, M. (2013). *Happy Money: The Science of Happier Spending*. New York: Simon & Schuster. This study also showed that people go on to be more generous after recalling their generosity, so it starts a virtuous circle: Aknin, L., Dunn, E., & Norton, M. (2012). Happiness runs in a circular motion: Evidence for a positive feedback loop between prosocial spending and happiness. *Journal of Happiness Studies, 13*(2), 347–355.

6. Another finding from the World Happiness Report's agglomeration of happiness surveys. Helliwell, J., Layard, R., & Sachs, J. (2013). *World Happiness Report 2013*. New York: UN Sustainable Development Solutions Network.

7. Otake, K., Shimai, S., Tanaka-Matsumi, J., Otsui, K., & Fredrickson, B.L. (2006). Happy people become happier through kindness: A counting kindness intervention. *Journal of Happiness Studies, 7*(3), 361–375; Aknin, L., Dunn, E., & Norton, M. (2012). Happiness runs in a circular motion: Evidence for a positive feedback loop between prosocial spending and happiness. *Journal of Happiness Studies, 13*(2), 347–355.

8. Amabile, T.M., & Kramer, S.J. (2011). *The Progress Principle: Using Small Wins to Ignite Joy, Engagement, and Creativity at Work.* Watertown, MA: Harvard Business Review Press.

9. Helliwell, J., Layard, R., & Sachs, J. (2013). *World Happiness Report 2013.* New York: UN Sustainable Development Solutions Network.

10. Powdthavee, N. (2008). Putting a price tag on friends, relatives, and neighbours: Using surveys of life satisfaction to value social relationships. *Journal of Socio-Economics, 37*(4), 1459–1480.

11. Sandstrom, G.M., & Dunn, E.W. (2014). Social Interactions and Well-Being: The Surprising Power of Weak Ties. *Personality and Social Psychological Bulletin, 40*(7), 910–922.

12. Laird, J.D. (1974). Self-attribution of emotion: The effects of expressive behavior on the quality of emotional experience. *Journal of Personality and Social Psychology, 29*(4), 475–486.

13. Strack, F., Martin, L.L., & Stepper, S. (1988). Inhibiting and facilitating conditions of the human smile: A nonobtrusive test of the facial feedback hypothesis. *Journal of Personality and Social Psychology, 54*(5), 768–777.

14. Kraft, T.L., & Pressman, S.D. (2012). Grin and bear it: The influence of manipulated facial expression on the stress response. *Psychological Science, 23*(11), 1372–1378.

15. Kahneman, D. (1999). Objective Happiness. In D. Kahneman, E. Diener, & N. Schwartz (Eds.), *Well-Being: Foundations of Hedonic Psychology.* New York: Russell Sage Foundation. Daniel Kahneman's TED talk also covers the topic: Kahneman, D. (2010). The riddle of experience vs. memory.

16. Fredrickson, B.L. (2000). Extracting meaning from past affective experiences: The importance of peaks, ends, and specific emotions. *Cognition and Emotion 14*(4), 577–606.

17. Kahneman, D., Fredrickson, B.L., Schreiber, C.A., & Redelmeier, D.A. (1993). When more pain is preferred to less: Adding a better end. *Psychological Science, 4*(6), 401–405.

18. Colonoscopies: Redelmeier, D.A., & Kahneman, D. (1996). Patients' memories of painful medical treatments: Real-time and retrospective evaluations of two minimally invasive procedures. *Pain, 66*(1), 3–8. Loud noises: Schreiber, C.A., & Kahneman, D. (2000). Determinants of the remembered utility of aversive sounds. *Journal of Experimental Psychology: General, 129*(1), 27–42. Overview of peak-end findings: Fredrickson, B.L. (2000). Extracting meaning from past affective experiences: The importance of peaks, ends, and specific emotions. *Cognition and Emotion, 14*(4), 577–606.

19. Do, A.M., Rupert, A.V., & Wolford, G. (2008). Evaluations of pleasurable experiences: The peak-end rule. *Psychonomic Bulletin & Review, 15*(1), 96–98.

## CHAPTER 21: PLAYING TO YOUR STRENGTHS

1.  Summarized in: Dweck, C.S. (2006). *Mindset: The New Psychology of Success.* New York: Random House.

2.  In researching *Strengths-Based Leadership*, the report from which these figures are drawn, Gallup researchers studied more than one million work teams, conducted more than 20,000 in-depth interviews with leaders, and interviewed more than 10,000 followers. These specific numbers come from a study of 65,672 employees, 530 "work units" (i.e., teams), and 469 business units ranging from retail stores to factories.

3.  Corporate Leadership Council (2002). *Building the High-Performance Workforce: A Quantitative Analysis of the Effectiveness of Performance Management Strategies.* Washington, DC.

4.  The original study showing these results was: Seligman, M.E.P., Steen, T.A., Park, N., & Peterson, C. (2005). Positive psychology progress: Empirical validation of interventions. *American Psychologist, 60,* 410–421. Alex Linley's work has been particularly useful in showing the stickiness of long-term effects, e.g., in: Govindji, R., & Linley, A.P. (2007). Strengths use, self-concordance and well-being: Implications for strengths coaching and coaching psychologists. *International Coaching Psychology Review, 2*(2), 143–153; and Wood, A.M., Linley, P.A., Maltby, J., Kashdan, T.B., & Hurling, R. (2011). Using personal and psychological strengths leads to increases in well-being over time: A longitudinal study and the development of the strengths use questionnaire. *Personality and Individual Differences, 50*(1), 15–19.

5.  The original strengths survey that formed part of Seligman and Peterson's research can be found at http://www.viacharacter.org. Gallup also maintains a suite of strength-based tools that you can access for a fee at https://www.gallupstrengths center.com. The Centre for Applied Positive Psychology offers a survey that distinguishes between learned vs. innate strengths, and realized vs. unrealized strengths, at https://assessment.r2profiler.com.

6.  Wrzesniewski, A., & Dutton, J.E. (2001). Crafting a job: Revisioning employees as active crafters of their work. *Academy of Management Review, 26*(2), 179–201. You can take the "job crafting" survey they designed by going to http://jobcrafting .org.

7.  Grant, A.M. (2013). *Give and take: Why helping others drives our success.* New York: Penguin.

## POSTSCRIPT

1.  Merzenich, M. (2013). *Soft-wired: How the new science of brain plasticity can change your life.* San Francisco: Parnassus.

2.  There's even research to suggest he's right about the power of the pebble. In a study that tested the effectiveness of various interventions in prompting people to save more, Dan Ariely and colleagues found that a "tangible track-keeping device" (in this case, a large shiny coin kept close to hand) did better than anything else. Akbas, M., Ariely, D., Robalino, D.A., Weber, M. (2015) *How to Help the Poor to Save a Bit: Evidence from a Field Experiment in Kenya.* Duke University Working Paper, January.

## APPENDIX B: HOW TO BE GOOD AT EMAIL

1.   Radicati Group (2015). *Email Statistics Report, 2015–2019.* Palo Alto, CA.

2.   Chui, M., Manyika, J., & Bughin, J. (2012). *The Social Economy: Unlocking Value and Productivity Through Social Technologies.* McKinsey Global Institute.

3.   Allen, D. (2001). *Getting Things Done: The Art of Stress-Free Productivity.* New York: Viking Penguin.

4.   Kruger, J., Epley, N., Parker, J., & Ng, Z.W. (2005). Egocentrism over e-mail: Can we communicate as well as we think? *Journal of Personality and Social Psychology, 89*(6), 925–936.

5.   Brown, C., Killick, A., & Renaud, K. (2013). To reduce e-mail, start at the top. *Harvard Business Review*, September.

# INDEX